NATIONAL GEOGRAPHIC KiDS

Ultimate Globetrotting World Atlas

By Sally Isaacs

NATIONAL GEOGRAPHIC

SCHOLASTIC INC.

TABLE OF CONTENTS

This atlas takes you on a journey around the globe. In its colorful maps, amazing pictures, and tons of fun information, you will discover cool things about each of the world's countries. If you plan to visit any of these places, you should always check for alerts published by your government concerning travel to specific countries or locations.

NORTH AMERICA

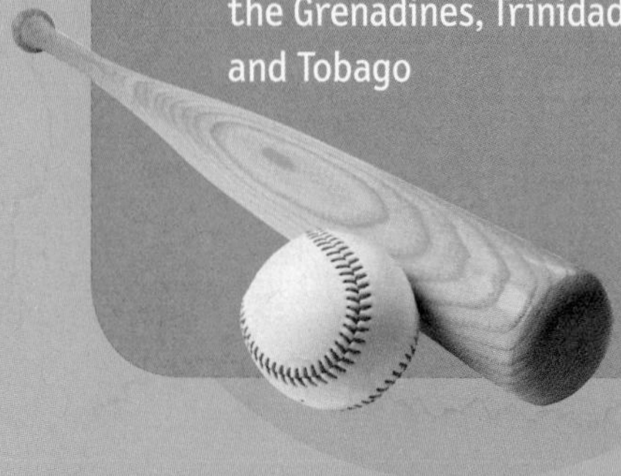

SOUTH AMERICA

EUROPE

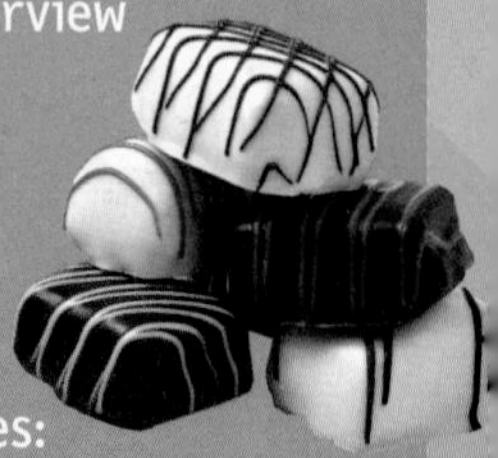

ASIA

AFRICA

AUSTRALIA AND OCEANIA

ANTARCTICA

AROUND THE WORLD FUN

HOW TO USE THIS ATLAS

There are almost 200 countries in the world. Our globetrotter trip starts in Canada, but you can start your adventure in any country you wish. This spread will guide you through the features on each page before you start your own journey. When you're done, buckle up ... and follow Aunt Bertha's tips to experience a trip of a lifetime!

COUNTRY IMAGE
Iconic images conjure up a real flavor of the country or region.

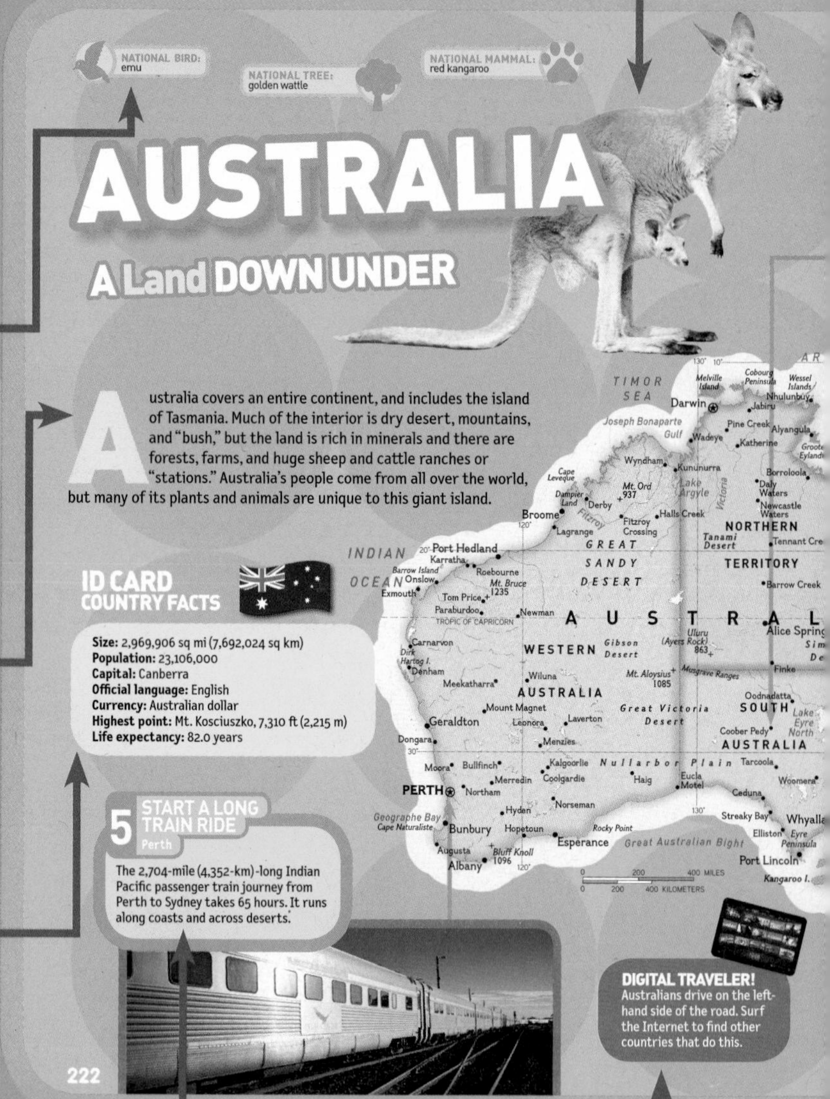
NATIONAL BIRD: emu
NATIONAL TREE: golden wattle
NATIONAL MAMMAL: red kangaroo

AUSTRALIA

A Land DOWN UNDER

Australia covers an entire continent, and includes the island of Tasmania. Much of the interior is dry desert, mountains, and "bush," but the land is rich in minerals and there are forests, farms, and huge sheep and cattle ranches or "stations." Australia's people come from all over the world, but many of its plants and animals are unique to this giant island.

ID CARD COUNTRY FACTS

Size: 2,969,906 sq mi (7,692,024 sq km)
Population: 23,106,000
Capital: Canberra
Official language: English
Currency: Australian dollar
Highest point: Mt. Kosciuszko, 7,310 ft (2,215 m)
Life expectancy: 82.0 years

5 START A LONG TRAIN RIDE
Perth

The 2,704-mile (4,352-km)-long Indian Pacific passenger train journey from Perth to Sydney takes 65 hours. It runs along coasts and across deserts.

DIGITAL TRAVELER!
Australians drive on the left-hand side of the road. Surf the Internet to find other countries that do this.

222

COUNTRY FACTS
For the names of the country's mammal, flower, tree, or bird, look above the country name. The species listed are either official choices or those widely recognized as being iconic or representative of the country.

INTRODUCTION
This brief introduction offers an overview of the country's location, landscape, features, and its people.

ID CARD
Look for the national flag and key facts, figures, and statistics on easy-to-use ID cards. For spreads with more than one country, turn to page 246 to find their ID cards.

MEASUREMENTS
In the text, measurements are given first in U.S. units and then in metric units. Often, these abbreviations are used: ft = feet; mi = miles; m = meters; km = kilometers; F = Fahrenheit; C = Celsius; mph/kph = miles/kilometers per hour.

DIGITAL TRAVELER!
You can discover even more about a country by doing your own investigations and explorations using a digital device and by taking photographs wherever you are.

5 COOL THINGS TO DO

These are five places to visit or things to do in the country or region. They will give you a true globetrotter's insight into the location. Follow the pointer from each picture or story to the map to find out exactly where these cool things are. Then plan your journey, save up for your ticket, and get packing!

GLOBETROTTER ATTRACTIONS

Three main landscape features or city highlights are listed and described here.

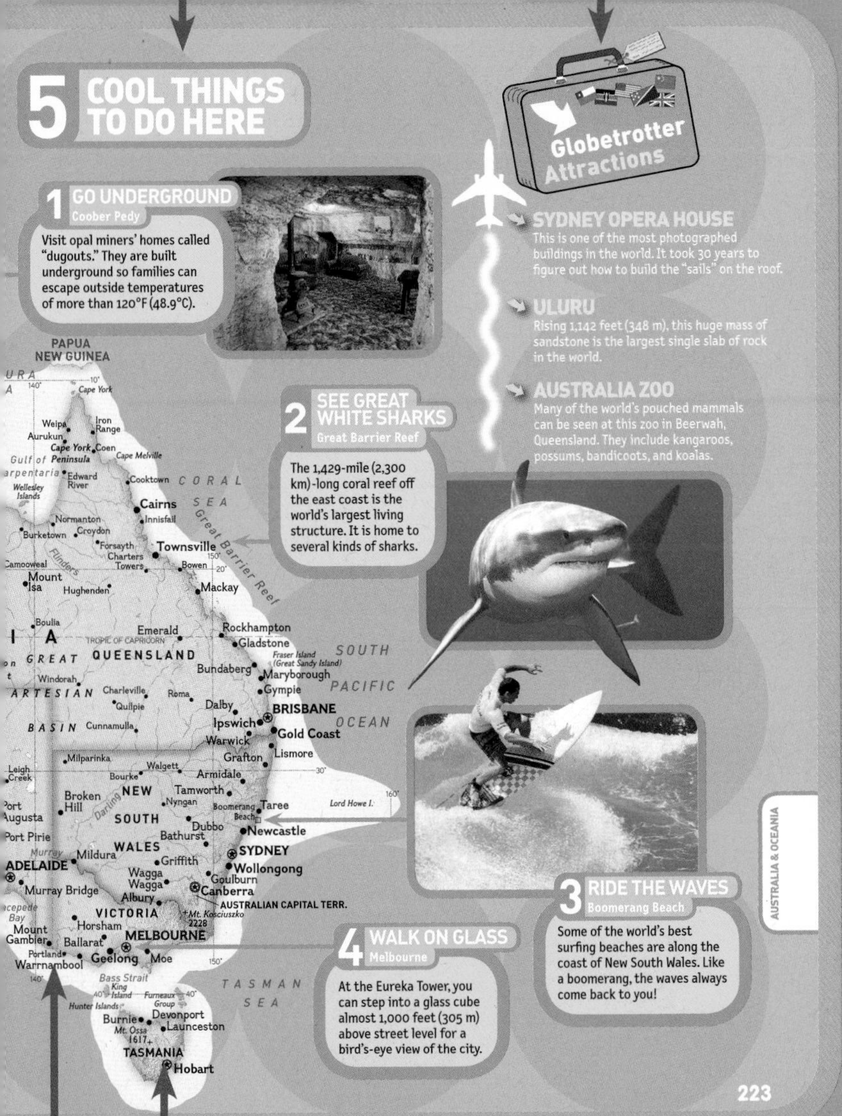
5 COOL THINGS TO DO HERE
1 GO UNDERGROUND
Coober Pedy
Visit opal miners' homes called "dugouts." They are built underground so families can escape outside temperatures of more than 120°F (48.9°C).
2 SEE GREAT WHITE SHARKS
Great Barrier Reef
The 1,429-mile (2,300 km)-long coral reef off the east coast is the world's largest living structure. It is home to several kinds of sharks.
3 RIDE THE WAVES
Boomerang Beach
Some of the world's best surfing beaches are along the coast of New South Wales. Like a boomerang, the waves always come back to you!
4 WALK ON GLASS
Melbourne
At the Eureka Tower, you can step into a glass cube almost 1,000 feet (305 m) above street level for a bird's-eye view of the city.
Globetrotter Attractions
SYDNEY OPERA HOUSE
This is one of the most photographed buildings in the world. It took 30 years to figure out how to build the "sails" on the roof.
ULURU
Rising 1,142 feet (348 m), this huge mass of sandstone is the largest single slab of rock in the world.
AUSTRALIA ZOO
Many of the world's pouched mammals can be seen at this zoo in Beerwah, Queensland. They include kangaroos, possums, bandicoots, and koalas.
PAPUA NEW GUINEA
QUEENSLAND
NEW SOUTH WALES
VICTORIA
TASMANIA
CORAL SEA
SOUTH PACIFIC OCEAN
TASMAN SEA
BRISBANE
SYDNEY
Canberra
MELBOURNE
ADELAIDE
Hobart
AUSTRALIA & OCEANIA
223

MAP KEY

CITIES

- Country capital
- Other capitals
- Towns
- Small country or possession
- Point of interest
- Ruin

WATER FEATURES

- Drainage
- Intermittent drainage
- Canal
- Intermittent lake
- Dry salt lake
- Swamp
- Falls or rapids
- Dam

BOUNDARIES

- Defined
- Undefined
- Disputed
- Offshore line of separation
- Disputed area

PHYSICAL FEATURES

- 3,348 Elevation in meters
- Pass
- Lava and volcanic debris
- Sand
- Below sea level
- Glacier

MAP

To find locations mentioned on the pages, check out the map! Then look for regions, major cities and towns, rivers, mountain ranges, lakes, and islands.

MAP SYMBOLS

Geographical features are shown on the map using a variety of shapes and colors. Use the map key to interpret these symbols. For more information about maps see pages 6 and 7.

HOW TO USE MAPS

Maps tell visual stories about the world, but you have to learn how to read them to understand what they are illustrating. The maps in this book show the shape, size, landscape, and position of continents, regions, and countries. They also show some of the places and features humans have made on Earth—for example cities, canals, and national parks. All maps in this book are shown with North at the top.

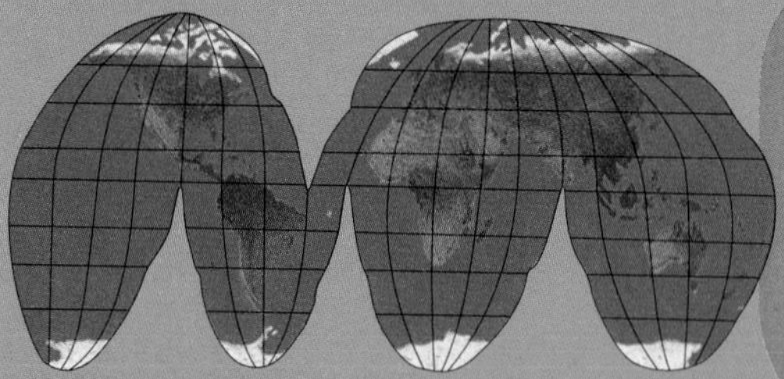

PROJECTIONS

To make flat maps, a round image of Earth is cut into sections and spread out. These sections—and the gaps that exist between them—can be different shapes and sizes. The exact way sections are cut and laid flat is known as the map "projection." Projections are usually very close to the actual shape of countries or regions but are not 100 percent accurate.

CONTINENTS

Earth's land area is mainly made up of seven giant landmasses known as continents. People have divided the continents into smaller political units called countries. Australia is a continent and also a single country. Antarctica is a continent with no countries. The five other continents include almost 200 independent countries.

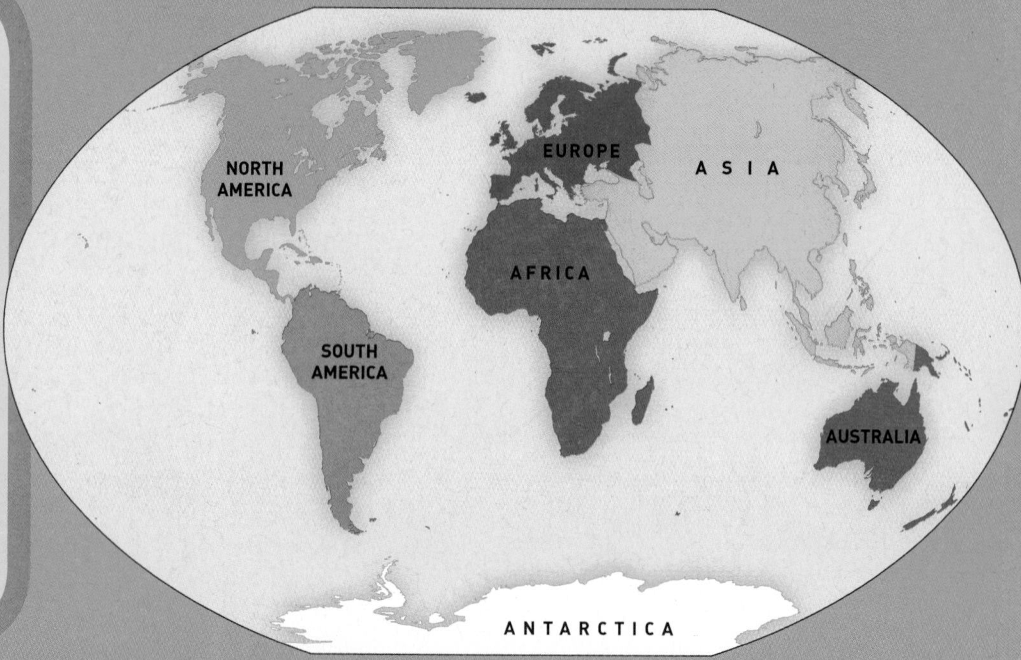

SCALE AND DIRECTION

The scale on a map may be shown as a fraction or comparison in words. A bar scale is a line or bar with measurements that compare distances on the map with those in the real world. Maps may include an arrow or compass rose to indicate North. If North is to the top, then East is to the right, West to the left, and South is to the bottom.

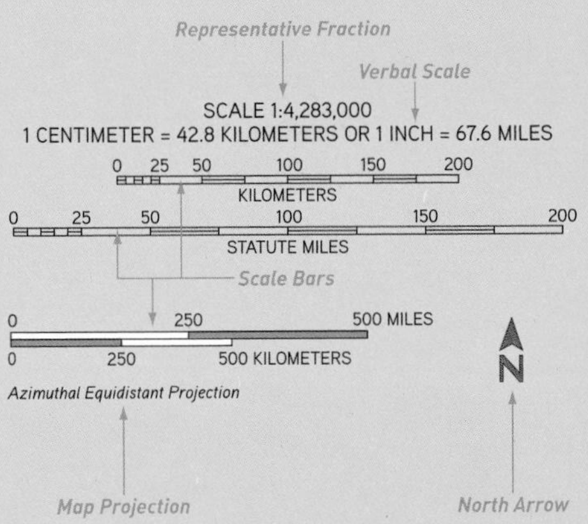

GRID LINES AND SYMBOLS

The grid lines you see on maps are imaginary. They are lines of longitude and latitude that help locate places. Other lines are used to show boundaries, roads, or rivers and can vary in thickness and color. Points or circles represent the location of places or things. Area symbols use patterns or color to show regions.

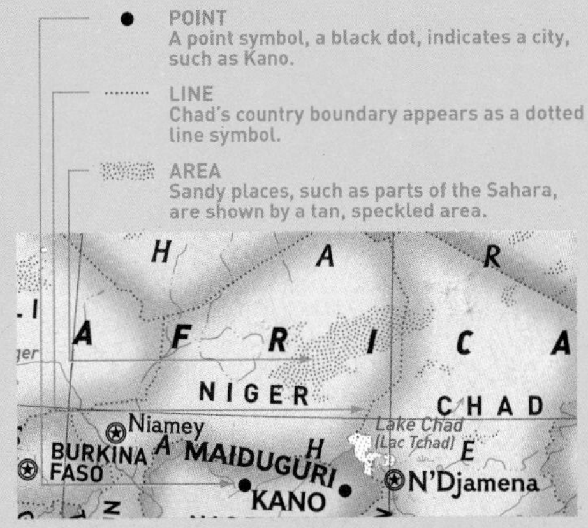

LATITUDE AND LONGITUDE

The Equator marks the middle of the world. Lines of latitude indicate distances north or south of the Equator. Lines of longitude indicate distances east or west. They start at the Prime Meridian, which is 0° longitude.

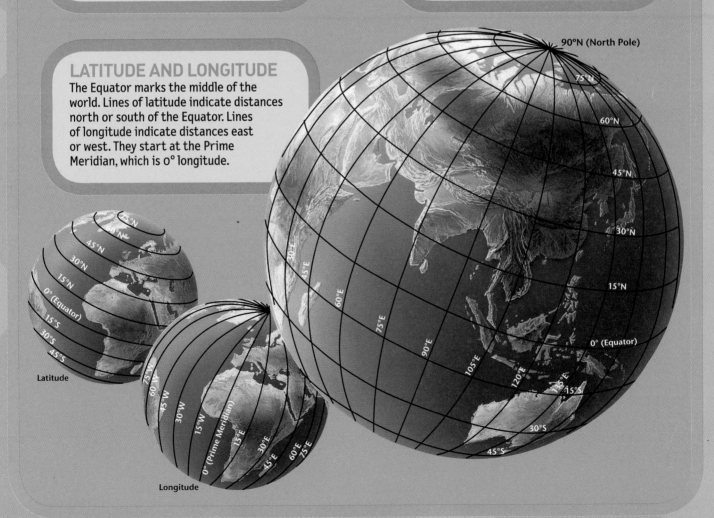

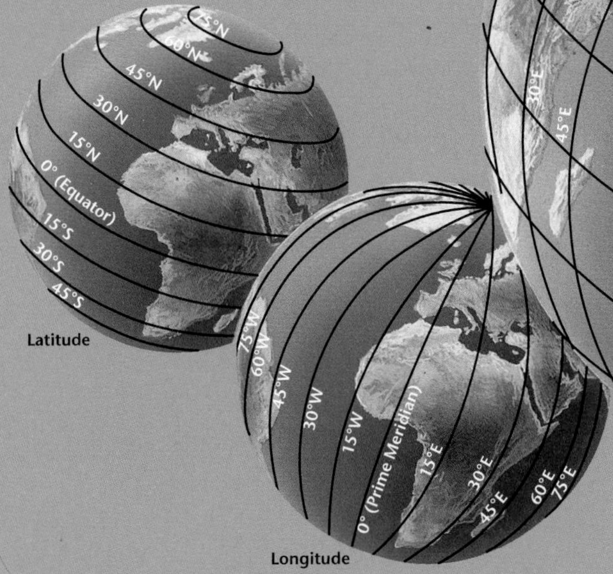

WORLD MAP

ARCTIC
GREENLAND (KALAALLIT NUNAAT) Denmark
RUSSIA
ALASKA United States
ARCTIC CIRCLE
Nuuk (Godthåb)
ICELAND
Reykjavík
Juneau
CANADA
NORTH AMERICA
UNITED KINGDOM
LONDON
DUBLIN
IRELAND
NORTH
NORTH
Ottawa
For detail of Europe, see pages 64–111
ATLANTIC
MADRID
PORTUGAL
Lisbon
SPAIN
UNITED STATES
Washington
Azores Portugal
PACIFIC
Bermuda Islands United Kingdom
OCEAN
Madeira Islands Portugal
RABAT
MOROCCO
HAWAI'I United States
Honolulu
TROPIC OF CANCER
MEXICO
Nassau
BAHAMAS
Canary Islands Spain
Laayoune
WESTERN SAHARA Morocco
HAVANA
CUBA
PORT-AU-PRINCE
DOMINICAN REP.
SANTO DOMINGO
San Juan
Kingston
BELIZE
JAMAICA
HAITI
PUERTO RICO United States
MEXICO CITY
Belmopan
San Juan
Nouakchott
MAURITANIA
OCEAN
GUATEMALA
HONDURAS
ARUBA Neth.
For detail of the Lesser Antilles, see pages 36–37
CAPE VERDE
Praia
SENEGAL
DAKAR
GUATEMALA CITY
TEGUCIGALPA
CURAÇAO Neth.
BONAIRE Neth.
Banjul
GAMBIA
Bissau
San Salvador
EL SALVADOR
NICARAGUA
GUINEA-BISSAU
GUINEA
Managua
San José
CARACAS
CONAKRY
COSTA RICA
PANAMA
Panama City
VENEZUELA
Georgetown
Paramaribo
Cayenne
Freetown
SIERRA LEONE
MONROVIA
LIBERIA
CÔTE D'IVOIRE
Yamoussoukro
ABIDJAN
ACCRA
POLYNESIA
LINE ISLANDS
BOGOTÁ
COLOMBIA
GUYANA
SURINAME
FRENCH GUIANA France
EQUATOR
QUITO
ECUADOR
GALÁPAGOS ISLANDS (Archipiélago de Colón) Ecuador
KIRIBATI
SOUTH AMERICA
PERU
BRAZIL
MARQUESAS ISLANDS France
LIMA
BRASÍLIA
AMERICAN SAMOA U.S.
SAMOA
Apia
Pago Pago
COOK ISLANDS New Zealand
TUAMOTU ARCHIPELAGO
FRENCH POLYNESIA France
BOLIVIA
La Paz
Sucre
TONGA IS.
TONGA
Nuku'alofa
SOCIETY ISLANDS
SOUTH
PARAGUAY
SOUTH
TROPIC OF CAPRICORN
Isla San Félix Chile
Isla San Ambrosio
Asunción
AUSTRAL ISLANDS
Easter Island (Isla de Pascua) Chile
Isla Sala y Gómez Chile
CHILE
ARGENTINA
SANTIAGO
URUGUAY
MONTEVIDEO
PACIFIC
Juan Fernández Islands Chile
BUENOS AIRES
ATLANTIC
OCEAN
FALKLAND ISLANDS (ISLAS MALVINAS) U.K.
Stanley
OCEAN
ANTARCTIC CIRCLE
ANTAR
120° 90° 60° 30° 60° 30° 0° 30° 60° 180° 90° 150° 120° 90° 60° 30°

COUNTRIES OF THE WORLD

This is a "political" map of the world. It shows country boundaries, country names, and major cities. It also shows the world's oceans.

O C E A N
SVALBARD
Norway
ARCTIC CIRCLE
NORWAY
SWEDEN
FINLAND
Helsinki
Tallinn
ESTONIA
STOCKHOLM
Oslo
COPENHAGEN
Riga
LATVIA
LITHUANIA
Vilnius
BELARUS
DENMARK
BERLIN
POLAND
MINSK
MOSCOW
GERMANY
WARSAW
KIEV
UKRAINE
PARIS
FRANCE
ITALY
Corsica
France
ROME
E U R O P E
R U S S I A
A S I A
Astana
KAZAKHSTAN
Ulaanbaatar
MONGOLIA
TASHKENT
Bishkek
KYRGYZSTAN
UZBEKISTAN
Dushanbe
TAJIKISTAN
TURKMENISTAN
Ashgabat
TBILISI
GEORGIA
AZERBAIJAN
ARMENIA
BAKU
YEREVAN
ANKARA
GREECE
Athens
TURKEY
CYPRUS
SYRIA
DAMASCUS
LEBANON
AMMAN
ISRAEL
JORDAN
BAGHDAD
IRAQ
TEHRAN
IRAN
KABUL
AFGHANISTAN
Islamabad
PAKISTAN
New Delhi
INDIA
NEPAL
Kathmandu
Thimphu
BHUTAN
BANGLADESH
DHAKA
C H I N A
BEIJING
Pyongyang
NORTH KOREA
SEOUL
SOUTH KOREA
JAPAN
TOKYO
NORTH
PACIFIC
OCEAN
60°
30°
TAIPEI
TAIWAN
TROPIC OF CANCER
Tunis
TUNISIA
ALGIERS
TRIPOLI
LIBYA
ALGERIA
CAIRO
EGYPT
KUWAIT
BAHRAIN
QATAR
SAUDI ARABIA
RIYADH
Abu Dhabi
UNITED ARAB EMIRATES
Muscat
OMAN
KHARTOUM
Asmara
ERITREA
Sanaa
YEMEN
NIGER
AFRICA
Niamey
CHAD
N'Djamena
SUDAN
NIGERIA
ABUJA
BENIN
LOMÉ
YAOUNDÉ
CAMEROON
CENTRAL AFRICAN REPUBLIC
Bangui
SOUTH SUDAN
Juba
ADDIS ABABA
ETHIOPIA
DJIBOUTI
SOMALIA
MOGADISHU
Malabo
EQUATOR. GUINEA
Libreville
GABON
São Tomé
SAO TOME & PRINCIPE
CONGO
BRAZZAVILLE
KINSHASA
DEMOCRATIC REPUBLIC OF THE CONGO
RWANDA
KIGALI
UGANDA
KAMPALA
KENYA
NAIROBI
BURUNDI
Bujumbura
Dodoma
DAR ES SALAAM
TANZANIA
SEYCHELLES
Victoria
LUANDA
ANGOLA
ZAMBIA
LUSAKA
MALAWI
Lilongwe
COMOROS
Moroni
HARARE
ZIMBABWE
MOZAMBIQUE
NAMIBIA
Windhoek
BOTSWANA
Gaborone
Mbabane
MAPUTO
SWAZILAND
Lobamba
Johannesburg
SOUTH AFRICA
Bloemfontein
LESOTHO
Maseru
CAPE TOWN
MADAGASCAR
Antananarivo
MAURITIUS
MYANMAR (BURMA)
Nay Pyi Taw
YANGON (RANGOON)
LAOS
Vientiane
HANOI
VIETNAM
THAILAND
BANGKOK
CAMBODIA
PHNOM PENH
Colombo
SRI LANKA
Sri Jayewardenepura Kotte
Male
MALDIVES
MANILA
PHILIPPINES
BRUNEI
Bandar Seri Begawan
MALAYSIA
KUALA LUMPUR
SINGAPORE
INDONESIA
JAKARTA
Dili
TIMOR-LESTE (EAST TIMOR)
PAPUA NEW GUINEA
Port Moresby
NORTHERN MARIANA ISLANDS
Saipan
United States
U.S. Guam
MICRONESIA
PALAU
Melekeok
FEDERATED STATES OF MICRONESIA
Palikir
CAROLINE ISLANDS
MARSHALL ISLANDS
Majuro
KIRIBATI
Tarawa (Bairiki)
EQUATOR
0°
NAURU
Yaren
MELANESIA
POLYNESIA
SOLOMON ISLANDS
Honiara
TUVALU
Funafuti
VANUATU
Port Vila
FIJI
Suva
NEW CALEDONIA
France
Nouméa
I N D I A N
O C E A N
TROPIC OF CAPRICORN
AUSTRALIA
SOUTH PACIFIC OCEAN
Canberra
NEW ZEALAND
Wellington
MILES
0
1500
3000
KILOMETERS
ANTARCTIC CIRCLE
ANTARCTICA
30°
60°
90°
120°
150°
180°

NORTH AMERICA

Wild and WONDROUS

From icy glaciers, lakes, and mountains to deserts, forests, and swamps, North America is a rugged, scenic continent. It is also home to tourist destination cities such as Vancouver, San Francisco, New York, Mexico City, and Acapulco.

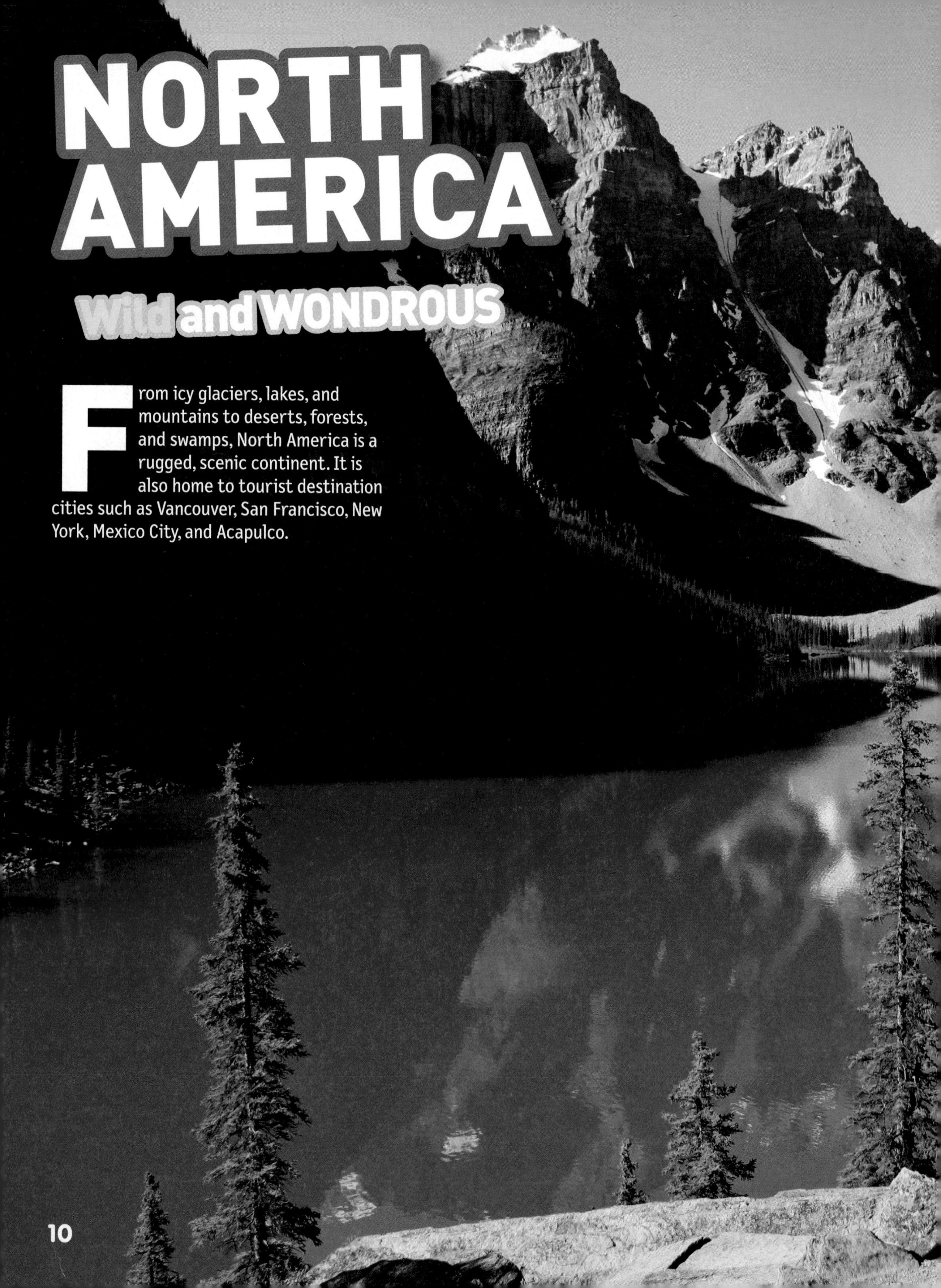

Moraine Lake in Banff National Park, Alberta, Canada. The lake is surrounded by boulders and rock debris dumped by glaciers as they move down mountainsides. The lake water is melted ice and snow.

NORTH AMERICA

A Mix of Cultures and Customs in the NEW WORLD

North America has a rich mix of cultures—from the traditions of Native Americans to the customs of immigrants from Europe, Asia, and Africa. It is still sometimes called the "New World" to contrast it with the Old World of Europe, Africa, and Asia. This is because North America was first explored by Europeans as recently as the 1500s.

TIKAL PYRAMIDS
Guatemala

The Maya people built this giant pyramid 1,000 to 2,500 years ago.

BRONCO RIDING
United States

A cowboy rides a bronco, an untrained horse, in a contest called a rodeo. Horses were first brought to North America from Spain in the 1500s.

AUNT BERTHA'S TRAVEL TIPS

CHOOSE YOUR LANGUAGE
The main languages of North America are European in origin—English, Spanish, and French. Bring your dictionaries!

WATCH YOUR STEP
Traveling east to west you will go back in time, crossing at least 5 of the world's 24 time zones. Be sure to set your watch.

TIME FLIES
Be prepared for a long trip. To fly east to west can take more than 7 hours. Flight time from north to south can be up to 10.5 hours.

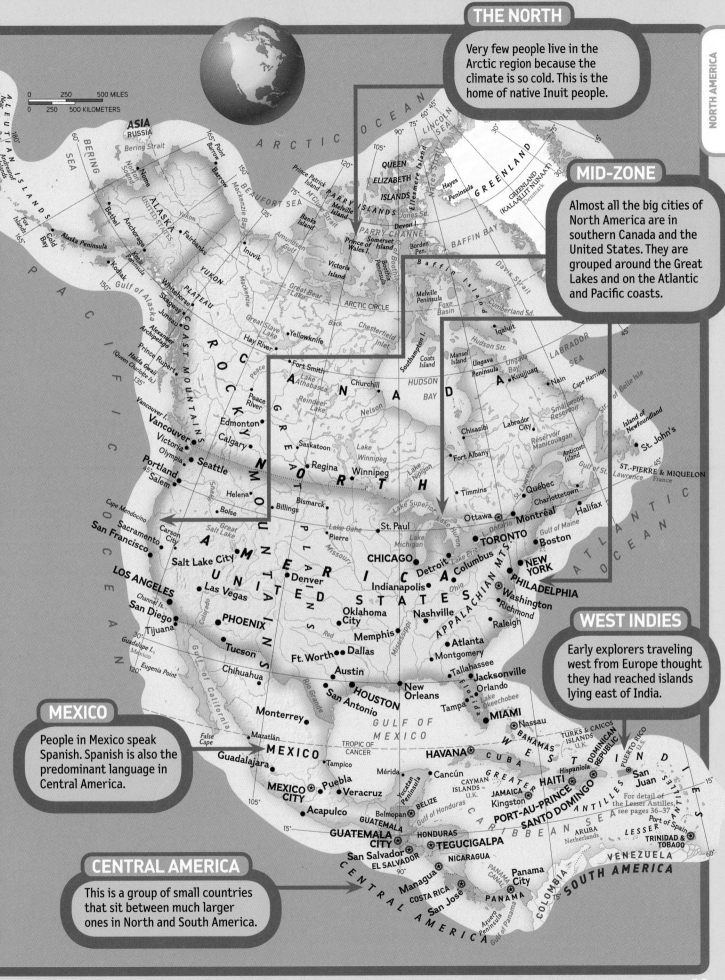

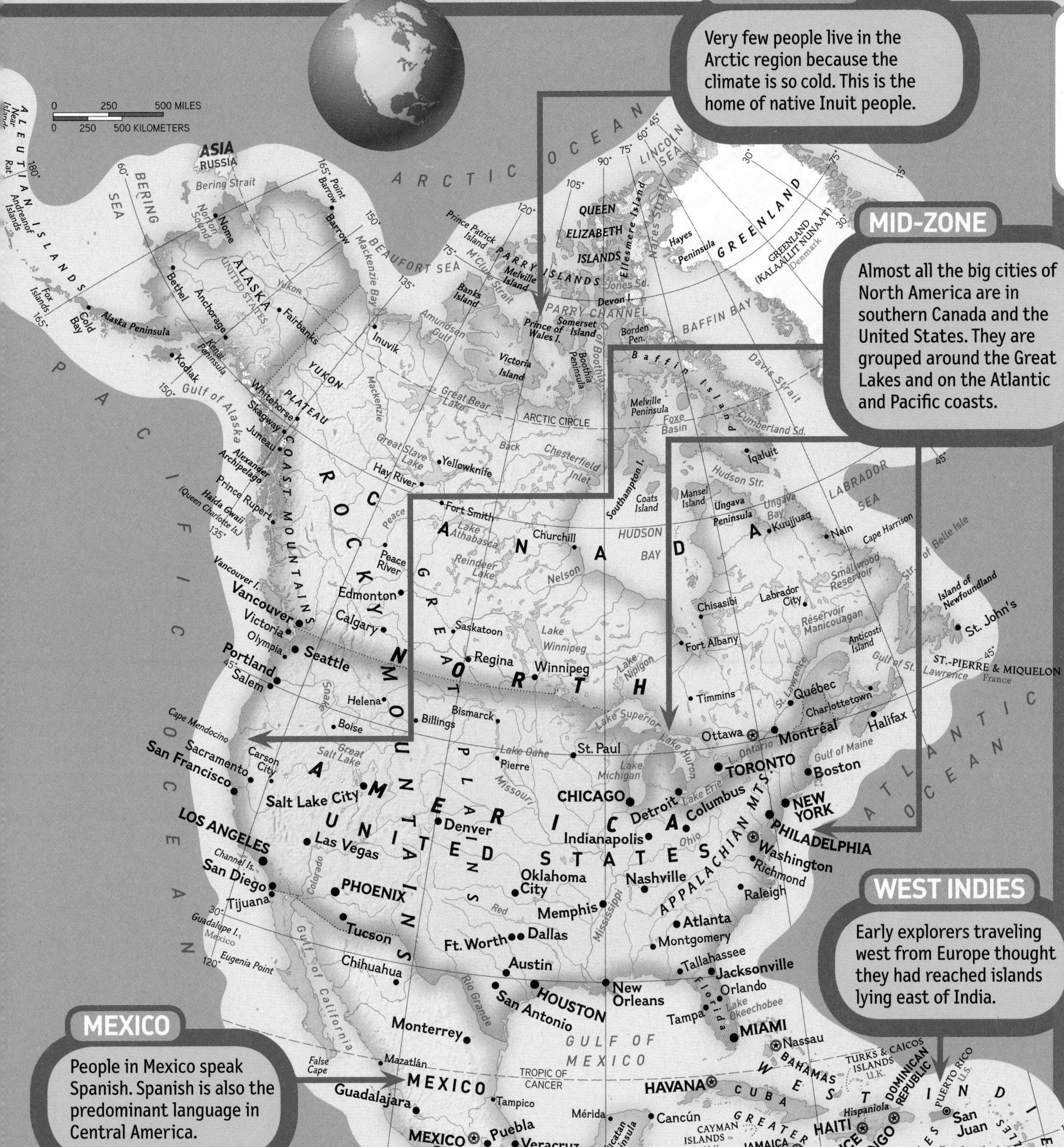

THE NORTH

Very few people live in the Arctic region because the climate is so cold. This is the home of native Inuit people.

MID-ZONE

Almost all the big cities of North America are in southern Canada and the United States. They are grouped around the Great Lakes and on the Atlantic and Pacific coasts.

WEST INDIES

Early explorers traveling west from Europe thought they had reached islands lying east of India.

MEXICO

People in Mexico speak Spanish. Spanish is also the predominant language in Central America.

CENTRAL AMERICA

This is a group of small countries that sit between much larger ones in North and South America.

5 COOL THINGS TO DO HERE

1 CHEER FOR MUSHERS
Yellowknife

Drivers, called mushers, guide sleds that are powered by 12 dogs each. Visit the Yellowknife Dog Derby, which happens every March, and see who wins.

2 RIDE THE ROCKIES
Kamloops

Take a four-day railroad journey from east to west and view the forests and Rocky Mountains from a railroad observation car.

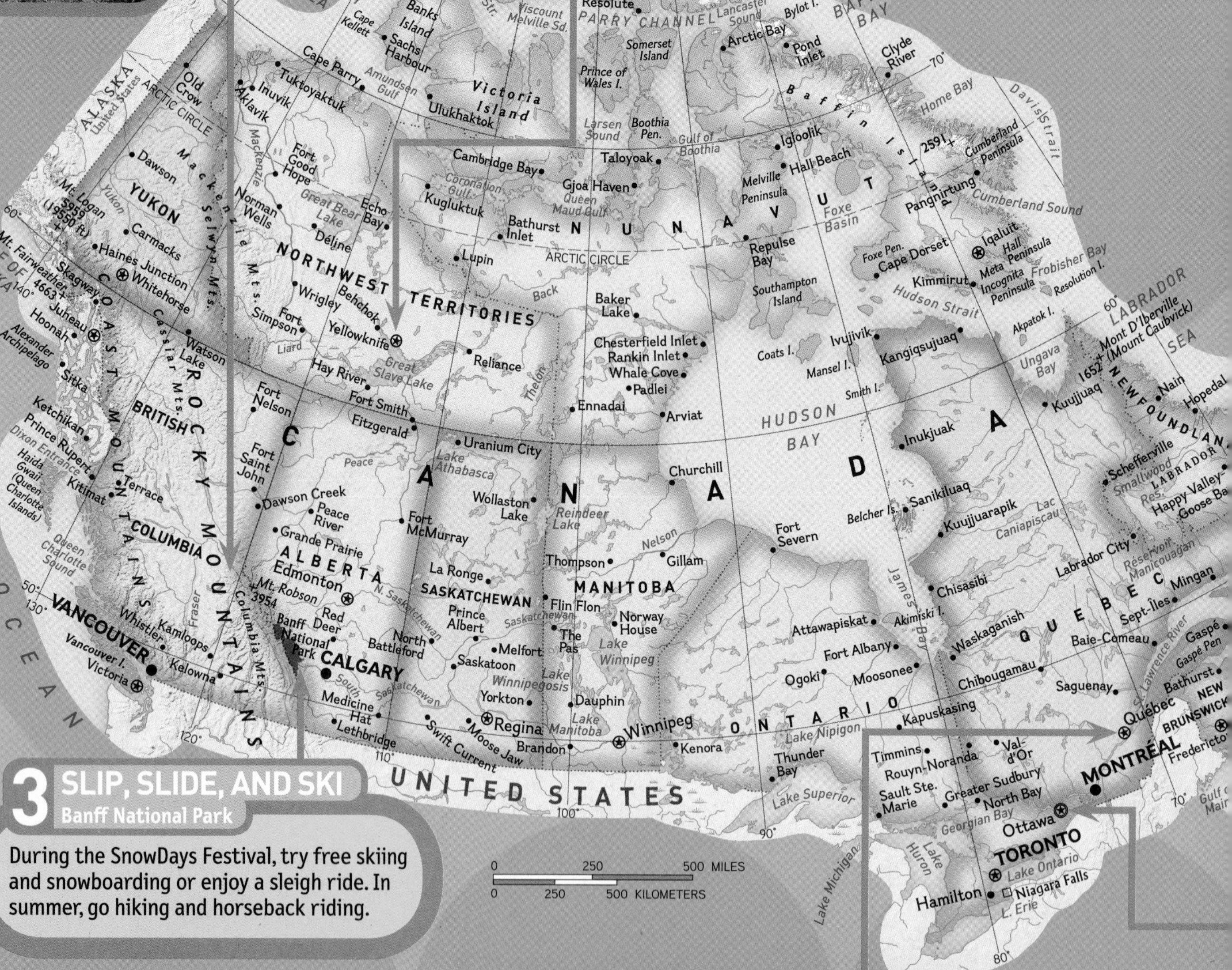

3 SLIP, SLIDE, AND SKI
Banff National Park

During the SnowDays Festival, try free skiing and snowboarding or enjoy a sleigh ride. In summer, go hiking and horseback riding.

4 EXPLORE "NEW FRANCE"
Québec

With its castle-like hotel, Chateau Frontenac, this is the capital of French-speaking Canada. Be sure to explore the Ramparts, the only remains of a protective city wall in North America.

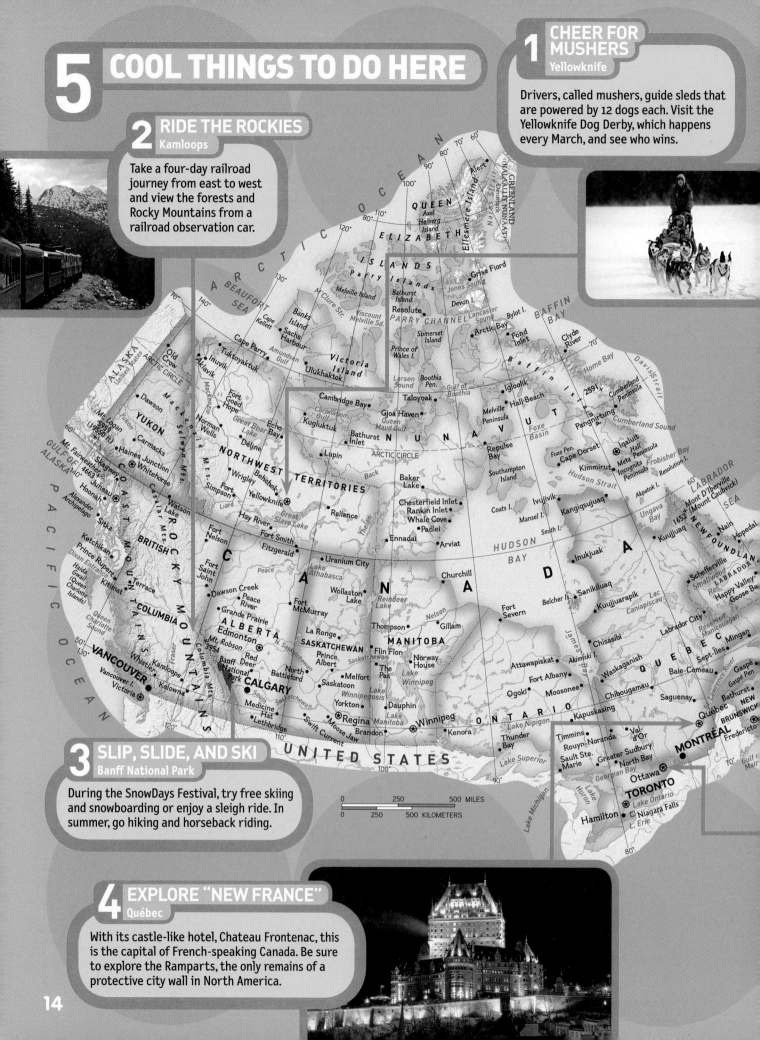

NATIONAL BIRD: Canada goose

NATIONAL TREE: maple

NATIONAL MAMMAL: beaver

CANADA

The Land of Snow and ICE

Canada is the second-largest country in area in the world, after Russia. At 5,525 miles (8,892 km) from west to east, it stretches nearly a quarter of the way around the globe. This huge country contains some of the world's most spectacular and wildest scenery. In the far north are giant frozen islands of the Arctic Ocean. To the south are the Great Lakes, the largest group of freshwater lakes in the world.

ID CARD COUNTRY FACTS

Size: 3,855,102 sq mi (9,984,670 sq km)
Population: 35,250,000
Capital: Ottawa
Official languages: English and French
Currency: Canadian dollar
Highest point: Mount Logan, 19,551 ft (5,959 m)
Life expectancy: 81.6 years

NIAGARA FALLS

About 3,160 tons (2,867 mt) of water flow over Niagara Falls every second. The falls have the capacity to produce electricity for 1 million homes in Canada and the United States.

CN TOWER

Toronto's 1,815-foot (553-m)-high telecommunications and viewing tower is the tallest structure in North America.

WHISTLER AND BLACKCOMB

These stunning mountains hosted the 2010 Winter Olympics. They are often snowcapped all year long.

5 MEET A MOUNTIE

Ottawa

At the Musical Ride event, the Royal Canadian Mounted Police—the Mounties—show their horseriding skills. Before the event, you can visit the stables.

DIGITAL TRAVELER!
In eastern Canada, road signs use French and English. On your computer make a two-column chart of English and French travel words for your trip.

NATIONAL BIRD: bald eagle

NATIONAL FLOWER: rose

NATIONAL TREE: oak

UNITED STATES

Stretching from the Atlantic to the PACIFIC

The United States stretches across North America and includes Alaska and the Hawaiian islands. The U.S. is the third largest country in the world in population and fourth largest in land area. A drive across the country will take you through small farm towns, bustling cities, and everything in-between. You can find any kind of outdoor fun you want—from sailing off the coast of Maine to hiking in the Rocky Mountains.

1 DRIVE THROUGH A TREE
Leggett

Redwoods are among the world's biggest trees. A tunnel was carved into this one to allow cars to drive through.

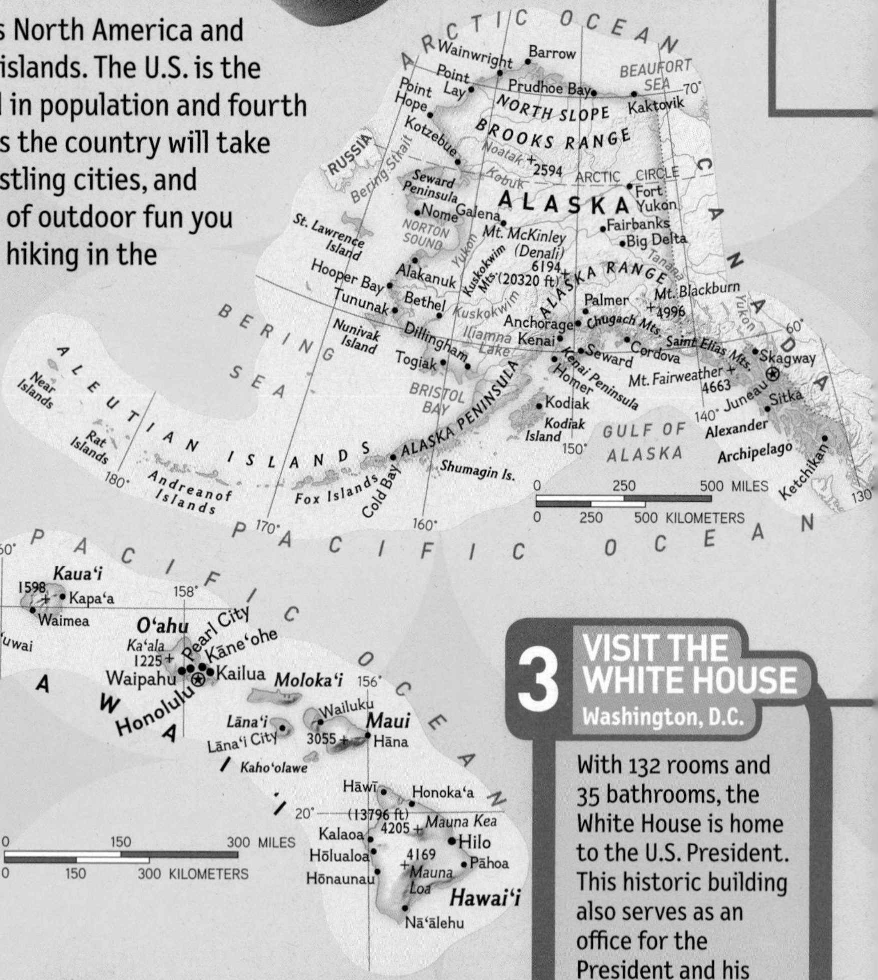

NEW YORK CITY
From the bright lights of Broadway's theater district to the glorious Statue of Liberty in the harbor, this city of skyscrapers never sleeps.

THE GRAND CANYON
Gaze down from the rim of this one-mile (1,610-m)-deep canyon, ride down on a mule, or raft along the Colorado River.

KENNEDY SPACE CENTER
On the coast of Florida, this space center has been launching astronauts and unmanned rockets into space since 1968.

3 VISIT THE WHITE HOUSE
Washington, D.C.

With 132 rooms and 35 bathrooms, the White House is home to the U.S. President. This historic building also serves as an office for the President and his staff.

ID CARD
COUNTRY FACTS

Size: 3,794,100 sq mi (9,826,675 sq km)
Population: 316,158,000
Capital: Washington, D.C.
Official language: English
Currency: U.S. dollar
Highest point: Mount McKinley (Denali), 20,320 ft (6,194 m)
Life expectancy: 78.6 years

5 COOL THINGS TO DO HERE

2 FIND THE PRESIDENTS
Mount Rushmore

Four presidents' faces are carved into the Black Hills. Try to identify these historic U.S. leaders.

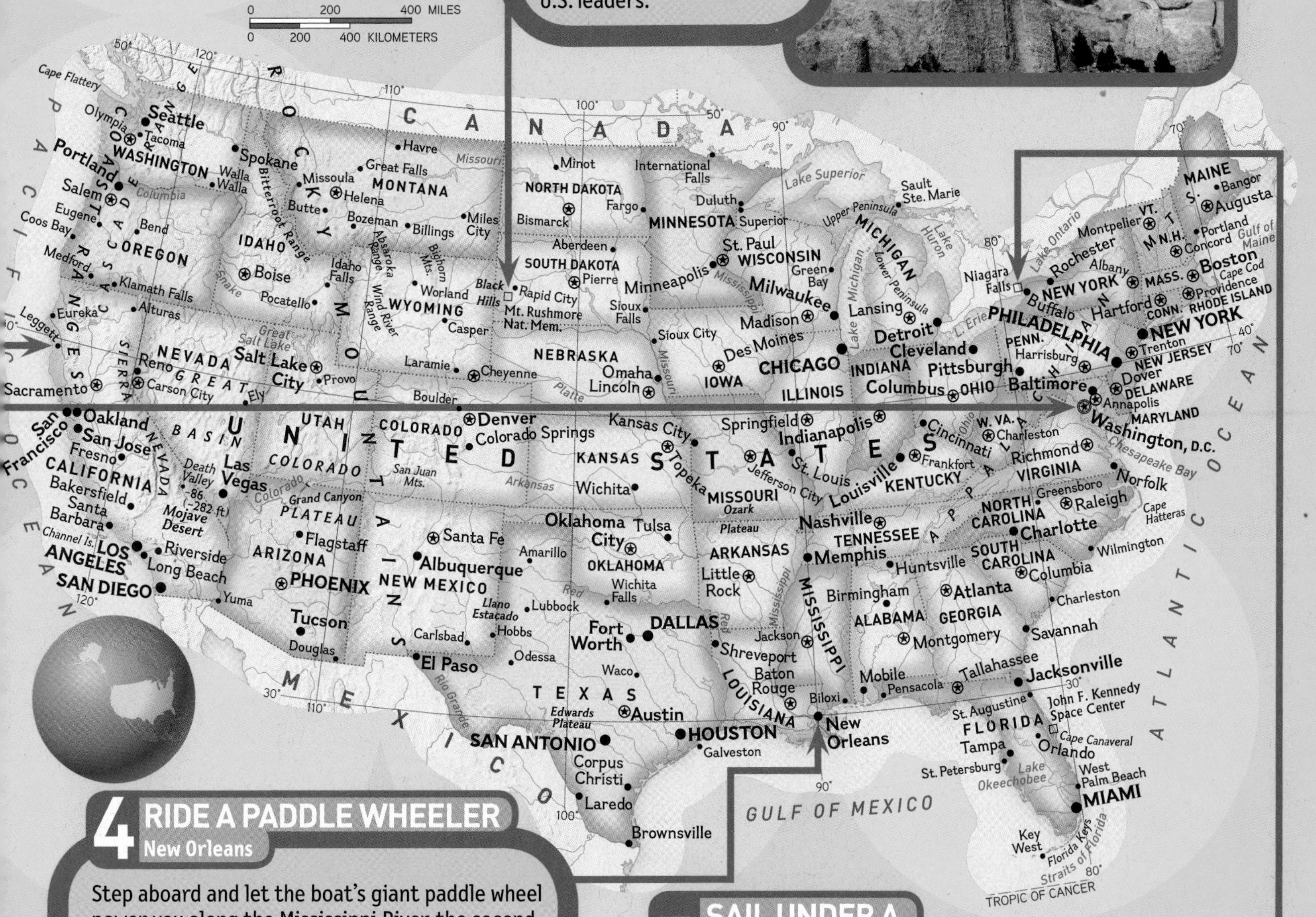

4 RIDE A PADDLE WHEELER
New Orleans

Step aboard and let the boat's giant paddle wheel power you along the Mississippi River, the second longest river in the country.

5 SAIL UNDER A WATERFALL
Niagara Falls

Put on a raincoat and get ready to be misted, and possibly soaked, as the *Maid of the Mist* takes you up close to the continent's most famous waterfalls. These boats have been giving tours of the falls since 1846.

DIGITAL TRAVELER!
Baseball is called "America's National Pastime." Find a list on the Internet of all the teams in Major League Baseball. Which states have more than one team?

NATIONAL BIRD: crested caracara

NATIONAL MAMMAL: jaguar

NATIONAL FLOWER: dahlia

MEXICO

From Maya Ruins to Mariachi PARADES

Mexico is a large country just south of the United States. Its capital, Mexico City, is one of the world's largest cities in population. You can see signs of Mexico's long history in the ruins of cities left by Maya and Aztec civilizations. Today Mexico's population is a mix of native Indian peoples and the Spanish people who set up a colony there in the 1500s. The beaches on the Pacific Ocean and the Gulf of Mexico are popular vacation destinations.

ID CARD COUNTRY FACTS

Size: 758,449 sq mi (1,964,375 sq km)
Population: 117,574,000
Capital: Mexico City
Official language: Spanish
Currency: Mexican peso
Highest point: Volcan Pico de Orizaba, 18,406 ft (5,610 m)
Life expectancy: 76.9 years

DIGITAL TRAVELER!
Chihuahua dogs came from Chihuahua, Mexico. Search online for photos of these dogs. Look for a variety of sizes, colors, and other features. Which do you think is cutest?

5 COOL THINGS TO DO HERE

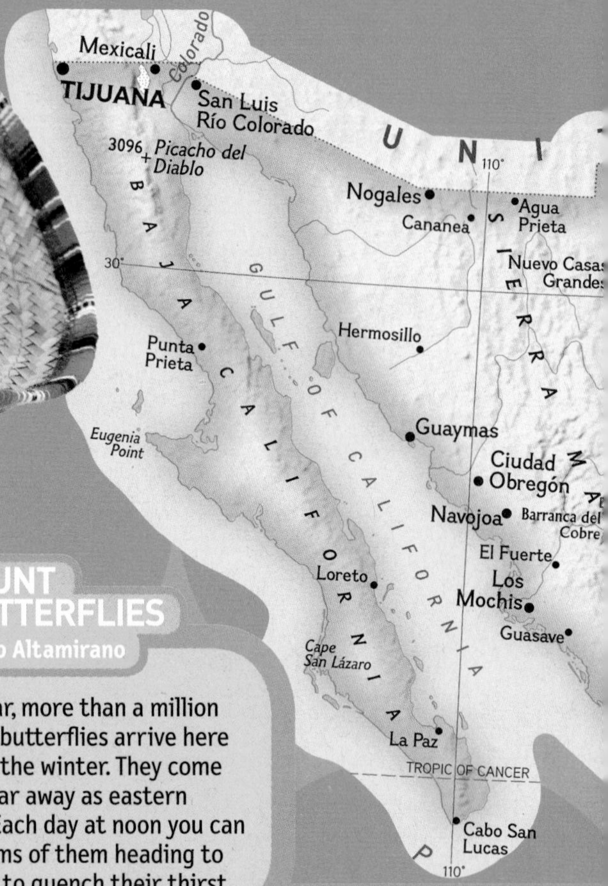

2 COUNT BUTTERFLIES
Cerro Altamirano

Every year, more than a million Monarch butterflies arrive here to spend the winter. They come from as far away as eastern Canada. Each day at noon you can see swarms of them heading to the river to quench their thirst.

3 CLAP FOR CLIFF DIVERS
Acapulco

Hold your breath as you watch these trained divers plunge 136 feet (41 m) into the Pacific Ocean. They must watch the waves and dive when the water is deepest.

1 SING WITH COWBOYS
Guadalajara

Stop in a restaurant and listen to mariachis singing their favorite tunes. They dress like *charros* (cowboys) but with fancier clothes.

PARQUE NATURAL BARRANCA DEL COBRA (COPPER CANYON)
This group of canyons is larger than the Grand Canyon in the U.S.A., and parts of it are deeper. You can hike, drive, or ride a horse through the scenery. Or you can ride a train. The Copper Canyon Railroad travels through cliff walls and over 36 bridges.

CHICHÉN ITZÁ
This was one of the most important Maya cities, built from A.D. 900 to 1200. The ruins of walls, pyramids, and ball courts can be seen today.

THE ARCH
At the tip of the Baja California Peninsula, the Pacific Ocean meets the Sea of Cortez. Here a stunning natural rock formation serves as a window to the blue waters of the ocean.

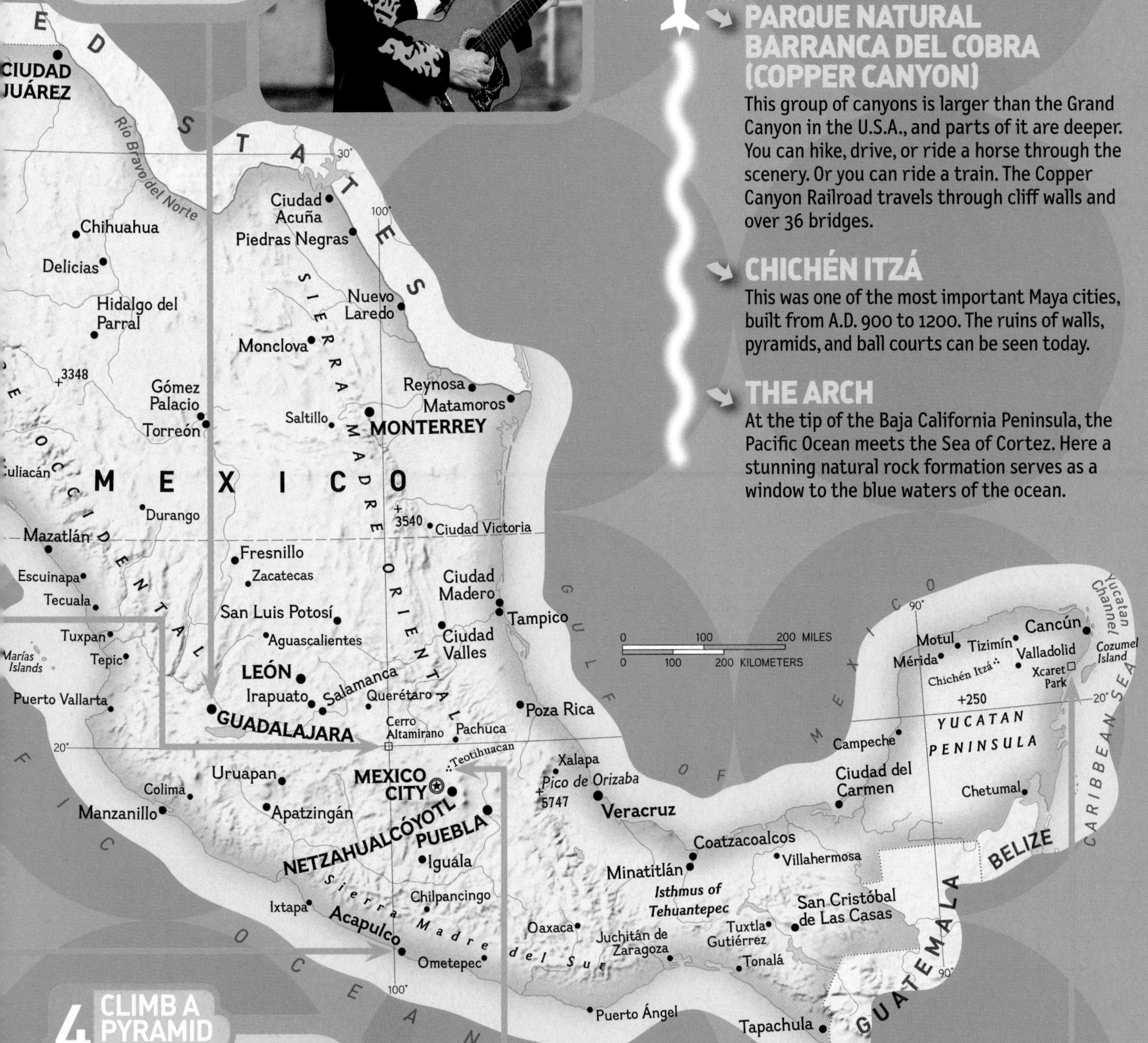

4 CLIMB A PYRAMID
Teotihuacan

Take lots of photos of this ancient city built between the first and seventh centuries. Teotihuacan was a holy city with pyramids all along the Avenue of the Dead.

5 FLOAT DOWN AN UNDERGROUND RIVER
Xcaret

Put on a life jacket and snorkel through cool caves in this ecological theme park.

	NATIONAL BIRD:	NATIONAL FLOWER:	NATIONAL MAMMAL:
BELIZE	keel-billed toucan	black orchid	Baird's tapir
GUATEMALA	quetzal	monja blanca	Maya mouse

BELIZE AND GUATEMALA

Land of Caves, Colors, and COCOA

Belize is a small country with a flat, swampy, coastal plain and low mountains. It was once home to the ancient Maya people. Guatemala is a larger, more mountainous country. About half its people are descended from the ancient Maya. Many of them also speak native Indian languages.

3 TASTE JUICY FRUIT
Chichicastenango

At the main market, breathe in the smell of flowers and spices, and taste colorful melons and mangoes. Then watch shoppers buy all kinds of goods.

DIGITAL TRAVELER!
From September to January, sea turtles lay their eggs on Guatemala's beaches. Use the Internet to learn what happens when the turtle eggs hatch.

4 RIDE A ROLLER COASTER
Retalhuleu

Choose a roller coaster that's right for you at Xetulul amusement park. Ride the Avalancha, with eight inversions that turn you upside down. If you prefer a calmer coaster, the Choconoy might be a better choice.

5 LEARN TO MAKE CHOCOLATE
Antigua

Tour the cacao plantation, where they pick cacao beans for chocolate. Then step inside the "Chocolate Museum" and learn how to make your own candy.

5 COOL THINGS TO DO HERE

1 GO WILD AT A ZOO
Belmopan

See more than 45 different kinds of animals in the Belize Zoo. They include the jaguar, monkeys, and macaws, which also live in the wild in Belize.

2 MIMIC HOWLER MONKEYS
Bermudian Landing

Take a nature walk at the Community Baboon Sanctuary. You'll probably see lots of howler monkeys, called baboons in Belize. You may need to cover your ears! They scream loudly at dusk and dawn.

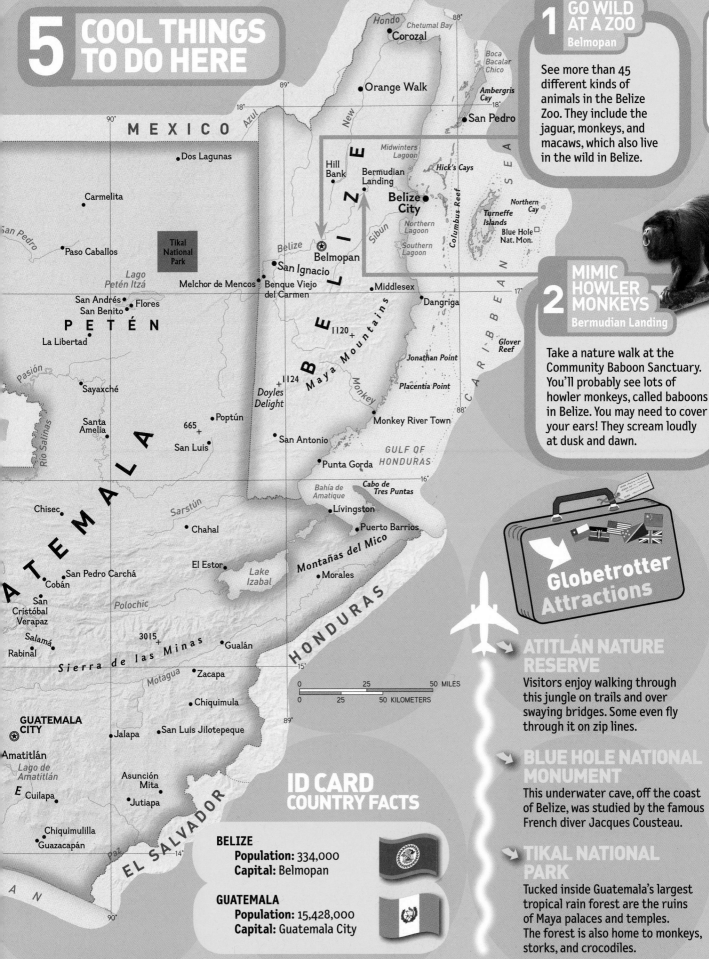

ATITLÁN NATURE RESERVE
Visitors enjoy walking through this jungle on trails and over swaying bridges. Some even fly through it on zip lines.

BLUE HOLE NATIONAL MONUMENT
This underwater cave, off the coast of Belize, was studied by the famous French diver Jacques Cousteau.

TIKAL NATIONAL PARK
Tucked inside Guatemala's largest tropical rain forest are the ruins of Maya palaces and temples. The forest is also home to monkeys, storks, and crocodiles.

ID CARD COUNTRY FACTS

BELIZE
Population: 334,000
Capital: Belmopan

GUATEMALA
Population: 15,428,000
Capital: Guatemala City

5 COOL THINGS TO DO HERE

1 WATCH A SOCCER GAME
San Salvador

Estadio Cuscatlan is the largest stadium in Central America. The El Salvador national soccer team plays here. Soccer is a very popular sport in both El Salvador and Honduras.

2 REEL IN A FISH
Lago de Yojoa

The largest lake in Honduras is a popular spot for fishing. The lake was formed from volcanic craters and lava flow.

3 RIDE A FERRY BOAT
La Ceiba

Board a ferry boat and motor across the blue Caribbean Sea to one of the Bay Islands. When you get there, stretch out on the white sandy beach and relax.

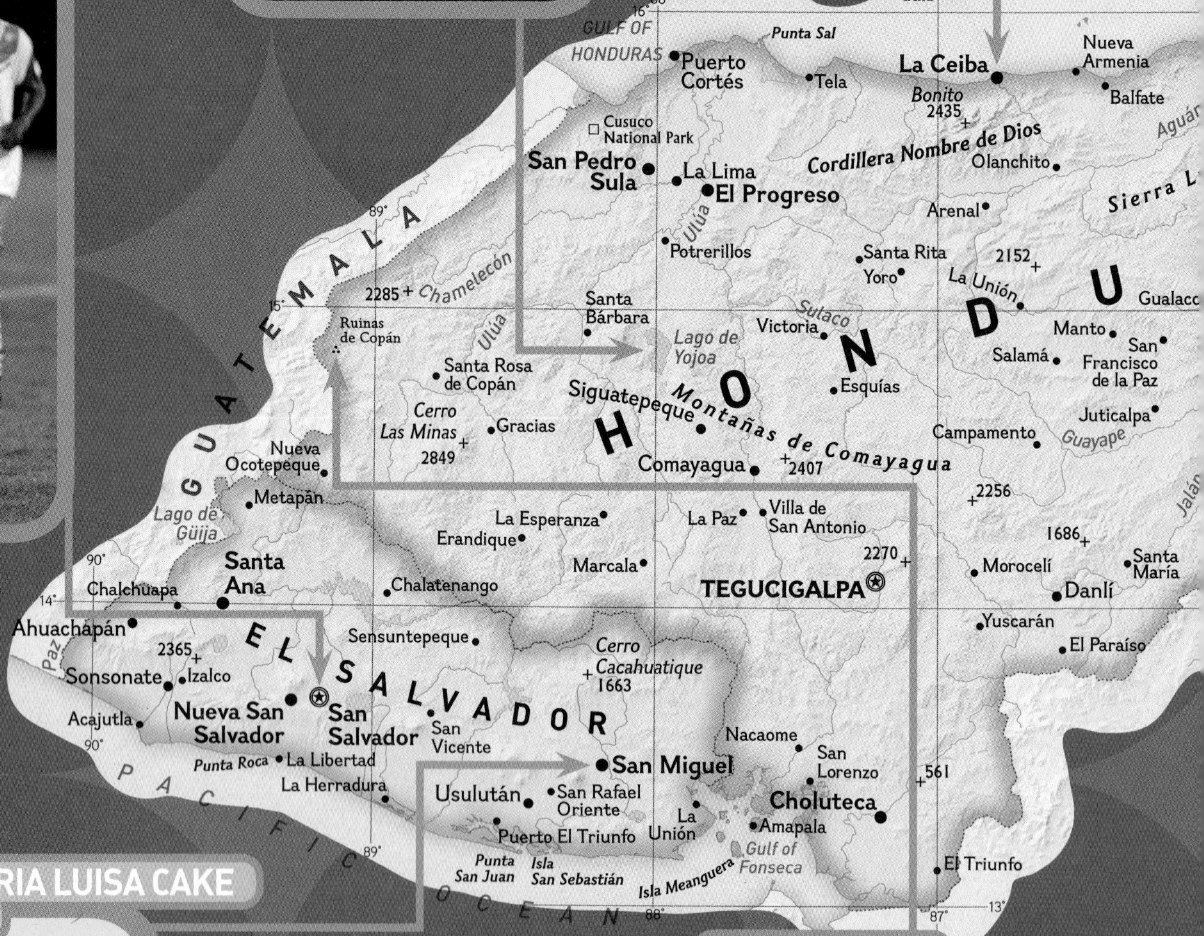

4 EAT MARIA LUISA CAKE
San Miguel

Search the bakeries to find the best Maria Luisa cake. It is a layer cake soaked in orange marmalade and topped with powdered sugar.

5 CHAT WITH MACAWS
Ruinas de Copán

Stand next to a parrot and try to have a conversation— it can repeat words. Macaw Mountain Bird Park and Nature Reserve takes care of rescued tropical birds.

	NATIONAL BIRD:	NATIONAL FLOWER:	NATIONAL MAMMAL:
EL SALVADOR	torogoz	flor de Izote	jaguarundi
HONDURAS	scarlet macaw	orchid	white-tailed deer

EL SALVADOR AND HONDURAS

The Heart of CENTRAL AMERICA

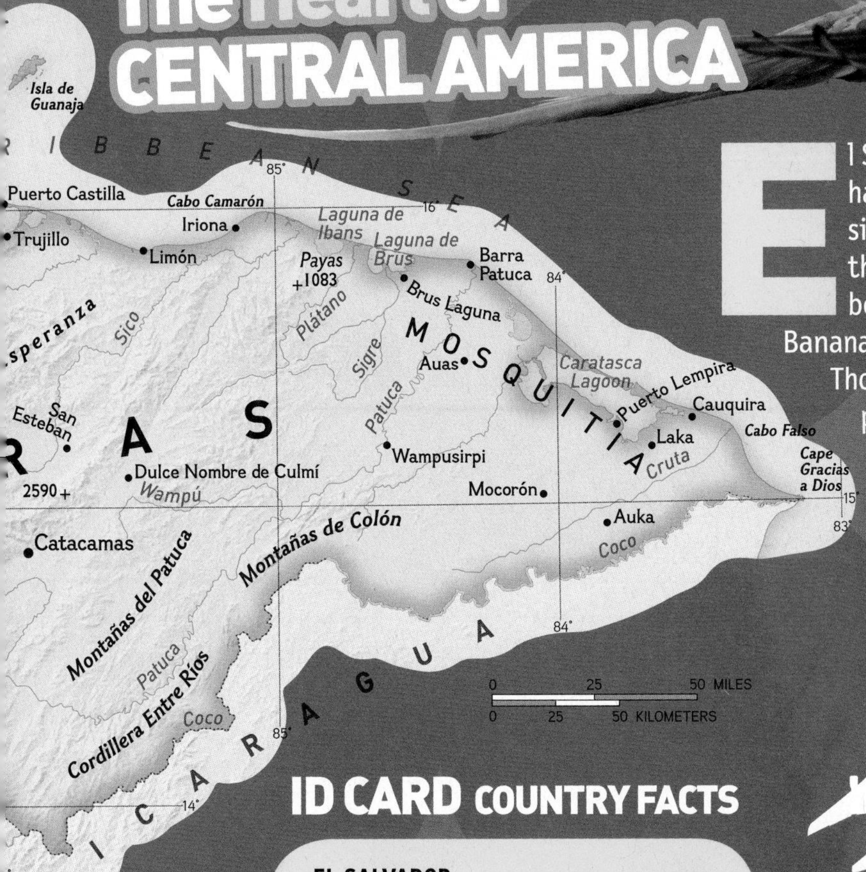

El Salvador and Honduras are neighbors that have some geographical and cultural similarities. Both countries share Spanish as their official language, and have mountains, beautiful beaches, and coffee plantations. Bananas are another important crop in Honduras. Though El Salvador is smaller in area, it has more people per square mile than Honduras and most other countries on the continent do.

ID CARD COUNTRY FACTS

EL SALVADOR
Population: 6,307,000
Capital: San Salvador

HONDURAS
Population: 8,555,000
Capital: Tegucigalpa

CUSUCO NATIONAL PARK
This huge park in Honduras is divided into four different kinds of forests, including "cloud forests" on the mountain slopes and "dwarf forests" with trees no more than 10 feet (3 m) high.

MAYA RUINS AT COPÁN
These ruins in Honduras include a 328-foot (100-m)-wide staircase with more than 1,800 Maya pictures. It is one of the longest known Maya inscriptions. Another stairway has sculptures of jaguars.

PUNTA ROCA
This is one of the most popular beaches in El Salvador. Surfers from all over the world say it is one of the best surfing beaches in the world.

DIGITAL TRAVELER!
What kind of music do they play in Honduras? Search for the answer online. Then download something you like.

NATIONAL BIRD: turquoise-browed motmot

NATIONAL MAMMAL: puma

NATIONAL FLOWER: sacuanjoche

NICARAGUA

Land Between Sea and OCEAN

ID CARD COUNTRY FACTS

Size: 50,336 sq mi (130,370 sq km)
Population: 6,043,000
Capital: Managua
Official language: Spanish
Currency: Gold cordoba
Highest point: Mogoton, 6,913 ft (2,107 m)
Life expectancy: 74.0 years

Nicaragua is a large country with fewer people per square mile than most others in Central America. Most people live by the Pacific Ocean, where Managua, the capital city, is located. The Caribbean Sea region is so swampy that it is called the "Mosquito Coast," but the name originally came from Miskito people who have been living in the region for more than 350 years. Rain forests cover most of this land.

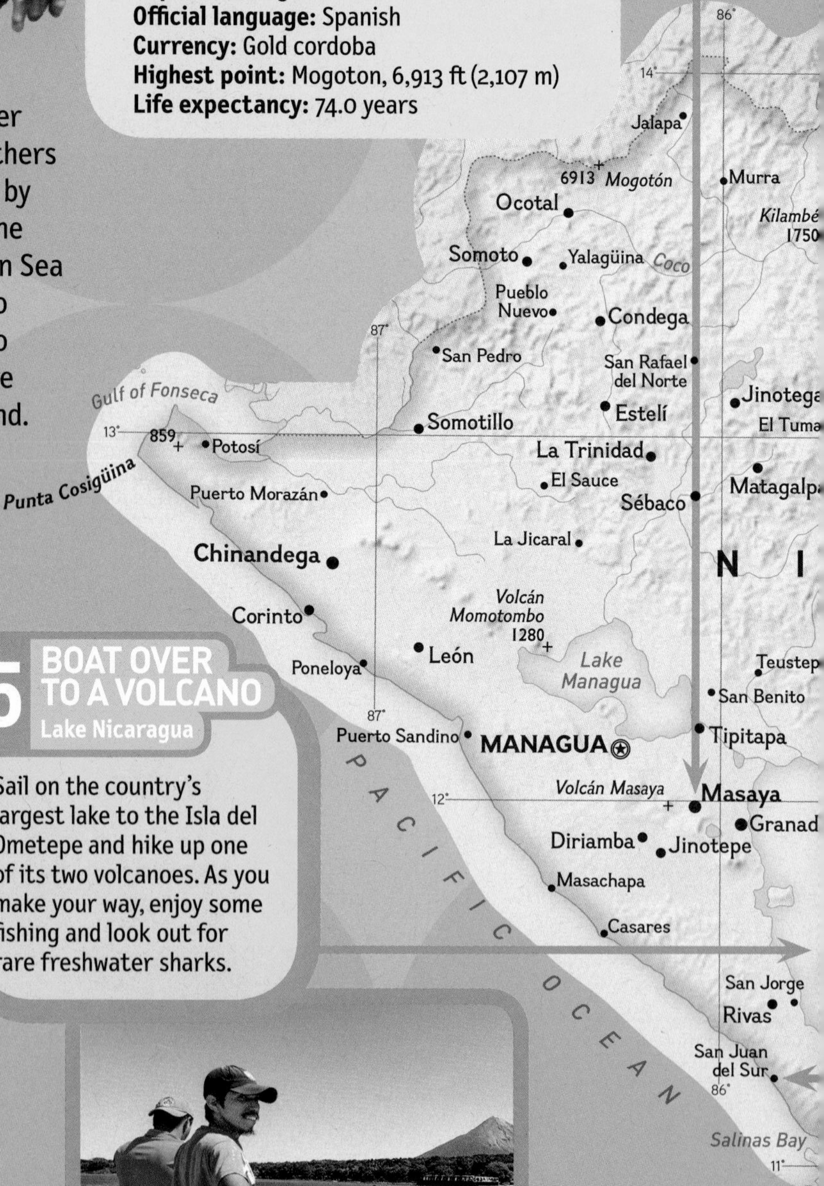

CATEDRAL DE LEÓN

The largest cathedral in Central America took more than 100 years to build. It holds the tombs of several famous poets.

BOSAWÁS BIOSPHERE RESERVE

This is one of the largest rain forests in the world with more than 150,000 kinds of insects and at least 100 kinds of birds.

MASAYA VOLCANO

Nicaragua's most active volcano spews gas almost all the time.

5 BOAT OVER TO A VOLCANO

Lake Nicaragua

Sail on the country's largest lake to the Isla del Ometepe and hike up one of its two volcanoes. As you make your way, enjoy some fishing and look out for rare freshwater sharks.

5 COOL THINGS TO DO HERE

1 SHOP AROUND
Masaya

Watch how a craftsperson weaves a rope rug. Many artists sell hammocks, pottery, blankets, and soap. Nicaraguans also go to the main, city-center market to buy meat, vegetables, and live chickens.

2 STROLL ON A BEACH
Bilwi

Walk on the beach at Puerto Cabezas and look at the long wooden dock where ships from the U.S. and elsewhere deliver products and machinery. Nicaragua grows and exports coffee, beef, and sugar.

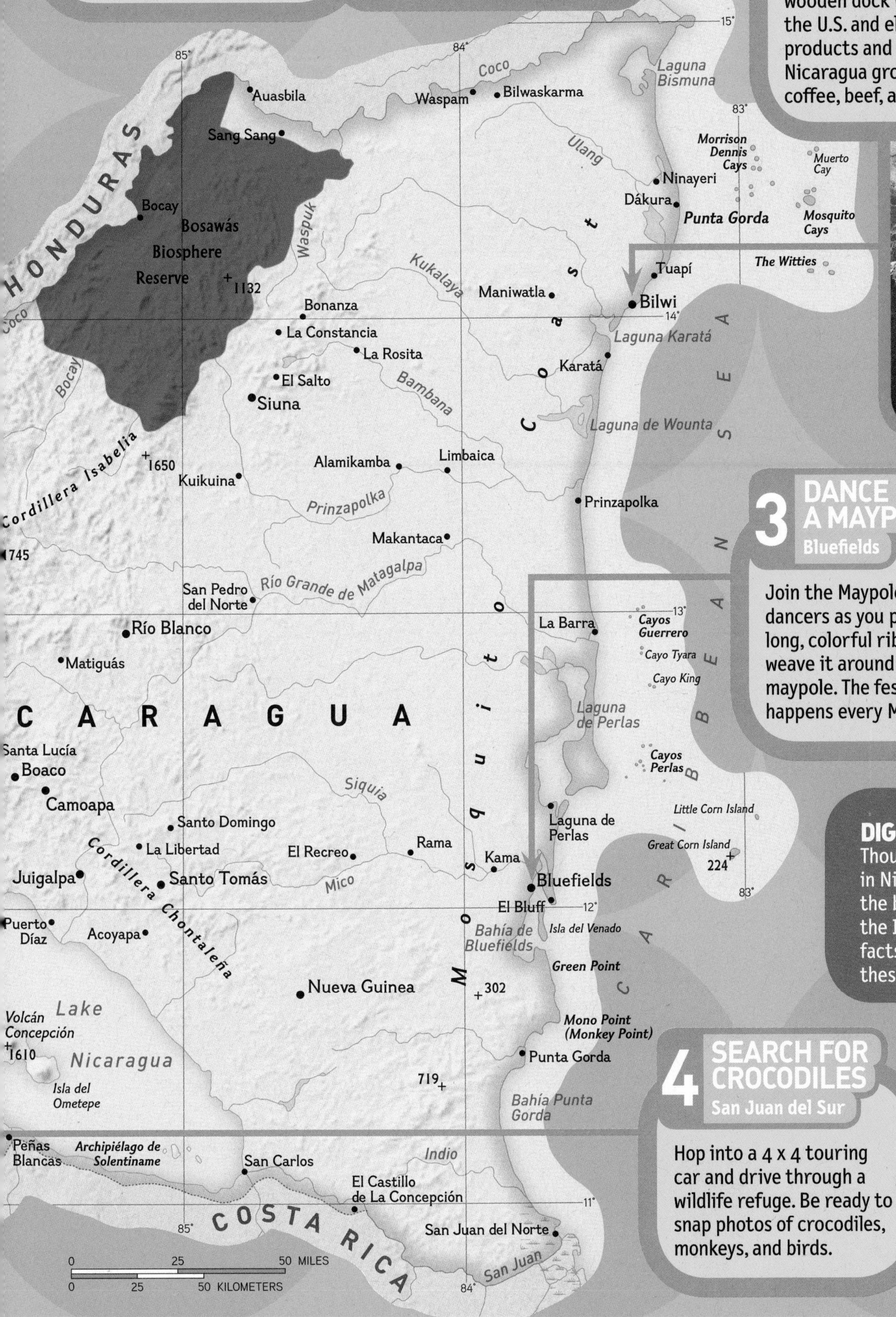

3 DANCE ROUND A MAYPOLE
Bluefields

Join the Maypole Festival dancers as you pick up a long, colorful ribbon and weave it around the maypole. The festival happens every May.

DIGITAL TRAVELER!
Thousands of vampire bats live in Nicaragua. They survive on the blood of other animals. Surf the Internet to find more fun facts about and pictures of these cool creatures.

4 SEARCH FOR CROCODILES
San Juan del Sur

Hop into a 4 x 4 touring car and drive through a wildlife refuge. Be ready to snap photos of crocodiles, monkeys, and birds.

5 COOL THINGS TO DO HERE

1 GET WET AND WARM UP
Fortuna

Relax in the warm water of Tabacon Hot Springs. The water flows in from the Tabacon River, which begins in the Arenal Volcano. The volcano heats the water to 101°F (38°C).

5 WALK IN THE CLOUDS
Monteverde Forest Reserve

Follow hiking trails through the sky-high cloud forests. This reserve was set aside to protect the wildlife, which includes 420 kinds of orchids and 100 kinds of animals including jaguars and ocelots. Be sure to pick a trail that crosses one of the five suspension bridges.

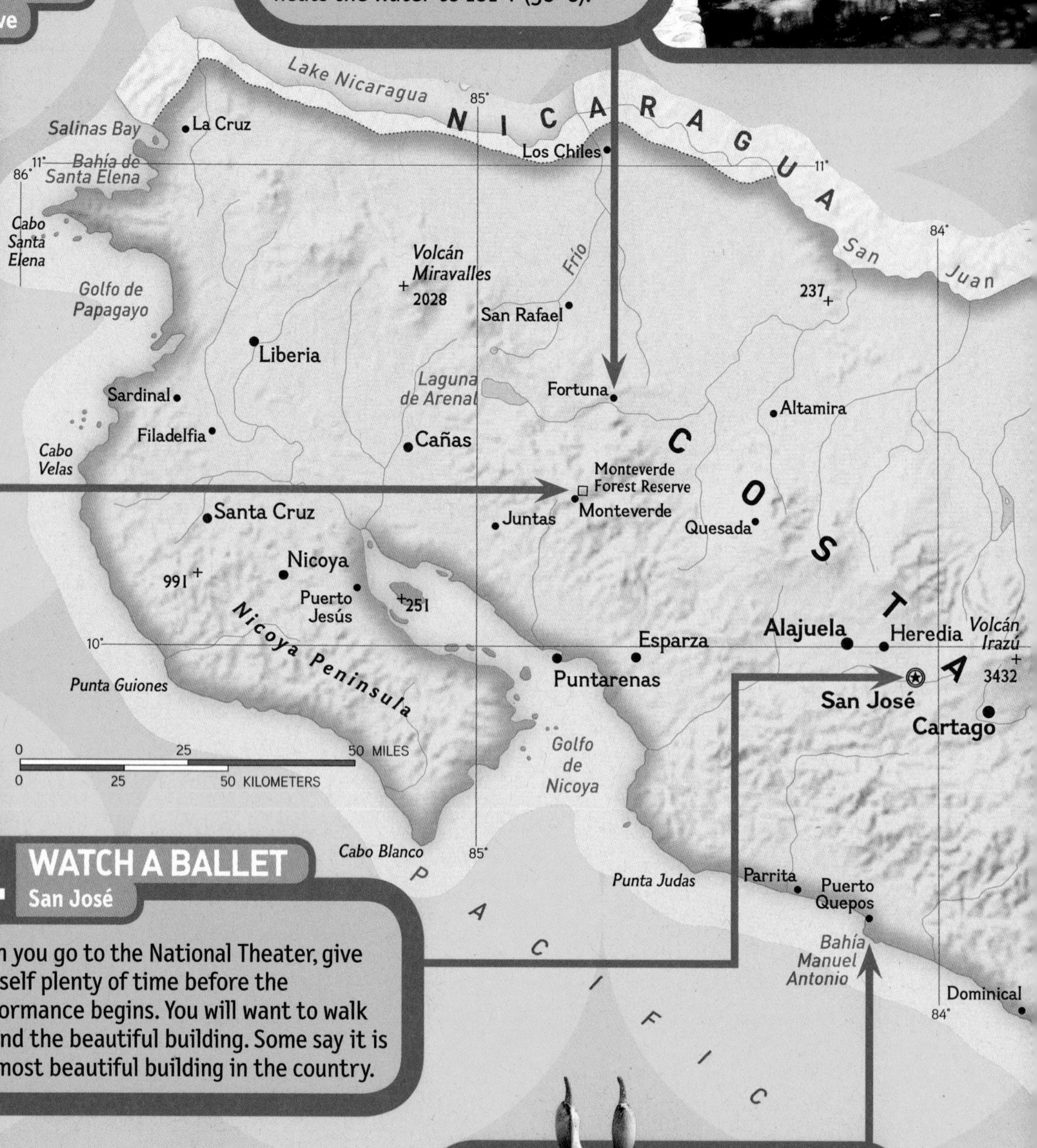

4 WATCH A BALLET
San José

When you go to the National Theater, give yourself plenty of time before the performance begins. You will want to walk around the beautiful building. Some say it is the most beautiful building in the country.

3 FOLLOW A GHOST CRAB
Manuel Antonio

Try to catch a glimpse of these small but super-fast crabs as they scurry across the beach. They spend most of their time burrowed in the sand waiting for a wave to bring their next meal.

ID CARD COUNTRY FACTS

Size: 19,729 sq mi (51,100 sq km)
Population: 4,713,000
Capital: San José
Official language: Spanish
Currency: Costa Rican colon
Highest point: Cerro Chirripó, 12,530 ft (3,819 m)
Life expectancy: 79.0 years

DIGITAL TRAVELER!
Gallo pinto is a favorite breakfast in Costa Rica. Find a recipe and ask a grown-up to help you make it.

NATIONAL BIRD: clay-colored thrush

NATIONAL FLOWER: guaria morada

NATIONAL MAMMAL: white-tailed deer

COSTA RICA

A Jungle PARADISE

The people of Costa Rica call themselves Ticos. When Ticos greet one another, they say, "*Pura vida.*" In Spanish, this means "pure life." The people enjoy their beautiful mountains, forests, and beaches and all the animals and plants that make Costa Rica home. There are many nature reserves and parks to protect the wildlife. Many Ticos work on coffee plantations and cattle ranches, but about one quarter of the people in the country live in and around the busy capital city of San José.

2 SEE SLOTHS
Penshurst

Visit the Sloth Sanctuary where people study, protect, and teach others about Costa Rica's two kinds of sloths: two-toed and three-toed sloths.

MOUNT CHIRRIPÓ
At 12,530 feet (3,819 m), Mount (Cerro) Chirripó is Costa Rica's highest mountain. Hikers who reach the mountaintop can see the Pacific Ocean and the Caribbean Sea.

ARENAL VOLCANO
One day in 1968, there were ten hours of earthquakes followed by the eruption of Arenal Volcano. Now, quite frequently, the volcano explodes with a fiery glow and flowing lava.

TORTUGUERO NATIONAL PARK
This large park is on Costa Rica's Caribbean coast. Its name *Tortuguero*, Spanish for "turtle catcher," is very fitting since hawksbill sea turtles and green sea turtles build their nests in the park's black sand.

NATIONAL BIRD: harpy eagle

NATIONAL FLOWER: holy ghost orchid

NATIONAL MAMMAL: ocelot

PANAMA

Linking Two CONTINENTS

Panama is often called the "Crossroads of the World." It connects North and South America. The Atlantic Ocean is on one side of the country, and the Pacific is on the other. Every year, thousands of ships sail through the Panama Canal. There is busy city activity around the canal. The rest of the country has quieter towns.

ID CARD COUNTRY FACTS

Size: 29,119 sq mi (75,420 sq km)
Population: 3,850,000
Capital: Panama City
Official language: Spanish
Currency: balboa
Highest point: Volcán Barú, 11,400 ft (3,475 m)
Life expectancy: 77.0 years

5 LOOK FOR LEATHERBACKS
Bastimentos

These huge turtles swim in the Caribbean Sea. The females lay hundreds of eggs on the beach every two or three years. Do not disturb the nests and babies.

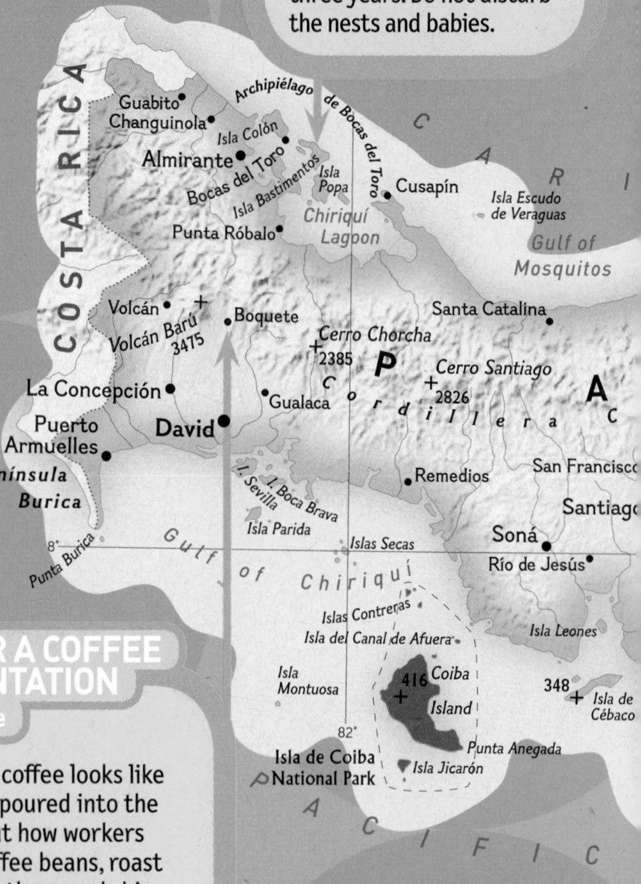

4 TOUR A COFFEE PLANTATION
Boquete

Learn what coffee looks like before it is poured into the cup. Find out how workers pick the coffee beans, roast them, grind them, and ship the coffee all over the world.

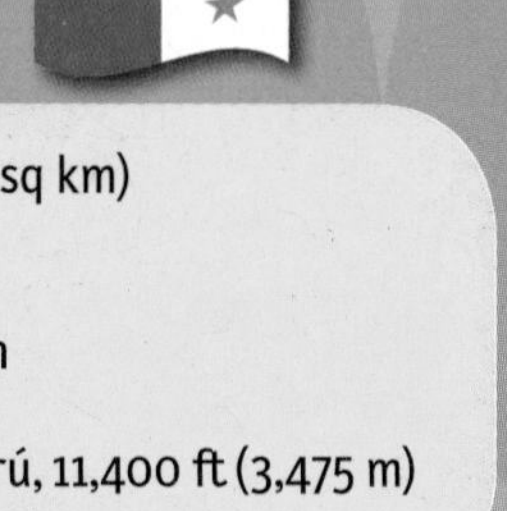

DIGITAL TRAVELER!
How did people travel from Europe to California and other places in the western hemisphere before the Panama Canal provided a shortcut? Find a map of the world online and map the journey to find out.

5 COOL THINGS TO DO HERE

1 CRUISE THROUGH THE CANAL
Panama Canal

Board a cruise ship and travel on the famous waterway that links two oceans. Learn how ships go through a series of gates that lift them to a higher water level. Before the canal was completed in 1914, ships had to travel about 7,800 miles (12,552 km) more than they do today to go from ocean to ocean.

Globetrotter Attractions

AMADOR CAUSEWAY
This road starts at the Panama Canal (Panama City) and leads to four islands. There is a beautiful path for walking, jogging, and watching ships coming into the canal. The causeway is made from rock that was dug up when the canal was built.

METROPOLITAN PARK
The only Central American protected area located within a major city (Panama City) is home to many species of plants and animals.

COIBA NATIONAL PARK
The park has 38 islands and is known for its jungle wildlife. It is also famous for a prison that held dangerous criminals until 2004.

2 WATCH WHALES
Archipiélago de las Perlas

Look for humpback whales that migrate to this region each year to give birth.

3 JOIN A CARNIVAL
Panama City

During the four days of Carnival, enjoy nonstop dancing in the streets. Take some photos of the beautiful costumes. Stay up late for the fireworks!

	NATIONAL BIRD:	NATIONAL FLOWER:	NATIONAL MAMMAL:
CUBA	tocororo	white mariposa	Cuban yellow bat
JAMAICA	doctor-bird	lignum vitae	Jamaican coney

CUBA AND JAMAICA

Islands of EXCITEMENT

Cuba and Jamaica are island countries that both have a mix of Caribbean and African cultures. Cuba also has Spanish roots, and almost all Cubans speak Spanish. In Havana, Cuba's capital, classic cars like the one above serve as taxis to take tourists to see the city's beautiful old buildings. Jamaica was once a British colony and English is the main language there.

Globetrotter Attractions

5 EXPLORE A FORT
Havana

Walk around the Castillo de la Real Fuerza, Havana's oldest fort. The castle was built to protect against pirates, though it was too far inside the bay to see much action.

DUNN'S RIVER FALLS

This 600-foot (183-m)-high waterfall attracts many tourists. Swim below the falls or hold hands with friends and let a guide lead you down the rocks to the pool area.

BELLAMAR CAVES

A tour of this network of caves goes by underground fountains, rivers, and ancient cave drawings. Calcite crystals make rock sculptures glitter in the dark. The network of caves lies 1.2 miles (1.9 km) underground.

THE MALECON

This is a pedestrian walkway that runs along Havana's waterfront. It is a popular spot for festivals and parades.

DIGITAL TRAVELER!

Since 1948 Jamaican athletes have won more than 65 medals at the Olympic Games. Search the Internet for the names and sports of five of these medal-winning athletes.

5 COOL THINGS TO DO HERE

ID CARD COUNTRY FACTS

CUBA
Population: 11,258,000
Capital: Havana

JAMAICA
Population: 2,712,000
Capital: Kingston

1 RIDE A STEAM TRAIN
Valle de los Ingenios

Spend a day riding a train through the Valley of the Sugar Mills. Visit a mansion on a former sugar plantation. Trains once carried sugarcane to ports for shipping to other countries.

2 TOUR WITH A GOAT
Bayamo

Jump into a carriage to tour Bayamo. The city decided to use horse-drawn carriages to save gas, keep the air clean, and reduce traffic. Small children take goat-drawn carriage rides for fun.

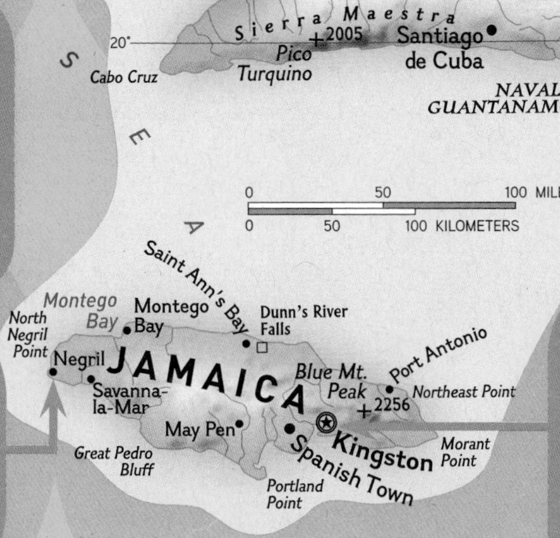

4 RELAX AT THE BEACH
Negril

Build a sand castle, chase a wave, play beach volleyball, or take a walk along the seven miles (11 km) of beautiful beach.

3 DANCE TO REGGAE MUSIC
Kingston

Snap your fingers, smile, and sway your body to the beat of Jamaican music. Reggae singers play guitars, bongos, shakers, cowbells, and other instruments.

5 COOL THINGS TO DO HERE

1 TAKE SNAPSHOTS OF TAP TAPS
Cap-Haïtien

See how many of these brightly painted buses you can photograph. Local people ride these *tap taps* when going on long trips or just traveling around town.

2 FLY A KITEBOARDER
Cabarete Beach

Stand on the sand and watch kiteboarders skim above the waves. Their feet are strapped to boards as they hold the handlebars of their kites.

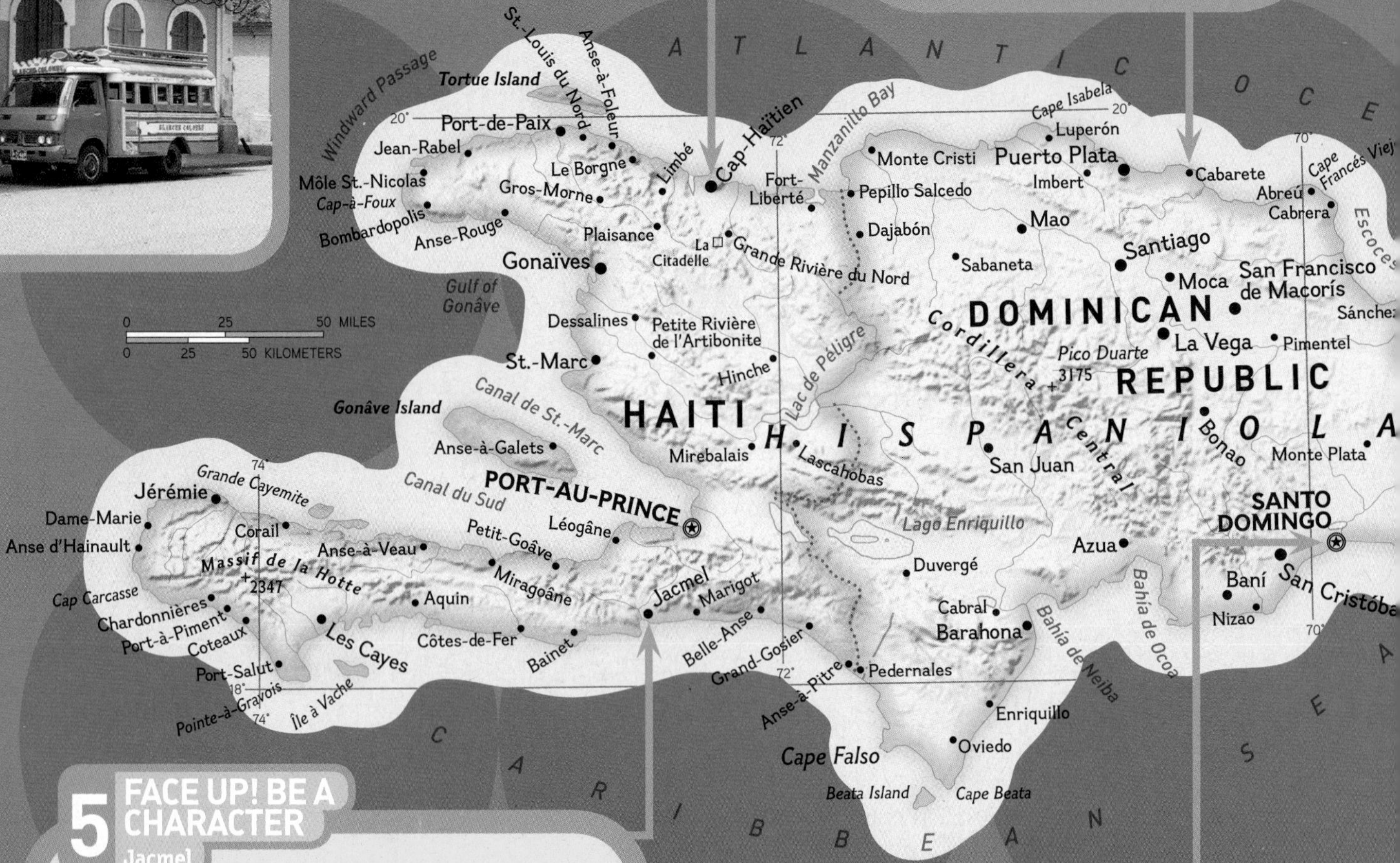

5 FACE UP! BE A CHARACTER
Jacmel

Choose a colorful mask at the market. Artists make masks with papier-mâché, a mix of paper, flour, and water. They dry the masks in the sun, then paint them.

4 CHEER FOR A BASEBALL TEAM
Santo Domingo

Sit in the stands of Quisqueya Stadium and cheer for one of the D.R.'s six teams. Many baseball players in the U.S. Major Leagues started playing in this stadium.

	NATIONAL BIRD:	NATIONAL FLOWER:	NATIONAL MAMMAL:
DOMINICAN REP.	palmchat	rose of Bayahibe	West Indian manatee
HAITI	Hispaniolan trogon	haitia	Caribbean monk seal

DOMINICAN REPUBLIC AND HAITI

Mountains, Marine Life, and Merengue MUSIC

The Dominican Republic (D.R.) and Haiti share the island of Hispaniola. The D.R. makes up more than half the island. Christopher Columbus landed on Hispaniola in 1492 and some historians say he is buried in the Dominican city of Santo Domingo. Both countries were at times colonies of Spain and France. Many Haitians are descendants of African slaves and follow African customs. French is Haiti's official language. In the D.R. most people speak Spanish.

3 SNORKEL IN AN AQUARIUM
Punta Cana

Swim in a real aquarium with nurse sharks and stingrays. The Marinarium will lend you snorkeling gear and guide you through their sea kingdom. If you'd rather stand outside and watch, that is okay, too.

ID CARD COUNTRY FACTS

DOMINICAN REPUBLIC
Population: 10,260,000
Capital: Santo Domingo

HAITI
Population: 10,421,000
Capital: Port-au-Prince

DIGITAL TRAVELER!

The lively merengue dance comes from the Dominican Republic. Go online and find a clip of merengue dancers. See if you can do the steps, too.

Globetrotter Attractions

CUEVA DE LAS MARAVILLAS

The name means "Cave of Wonders." The Taino Indians drew more than 250 pictures when they lived in this cave in the D.R. long ago. Bats live in the cave now, but they hide during the daytime when people are visiting.

THE CITADELLE

It took 20,000 workers to build this fortress on a mountaintop above Cap-Haïtien, Haiti. In the 1800s, the royal family lived here with 5,000 soldiers. Today the Citadelle still houses 100 cannons and 5,000 cannonballs.

MASSIF DE LA HOTTE

Thirteen endangered frog species live with many other animals in this remote mountain area of Haiti. People are working to preserve this region's plants and animals.

NATIONAL BIRD: Caribbean flamingo

NATIONAL FLOWER: yellow elder

NATIONAL MAMMAL: hutia

BAHAMAS

Fun in the SUN

5 DANCE THE LIMBO

Grand Bahama

Set up some island music and form a line of dancers. Two people will move the limbo pole lower and lower. Bend back and dance under it. See how low you can go!

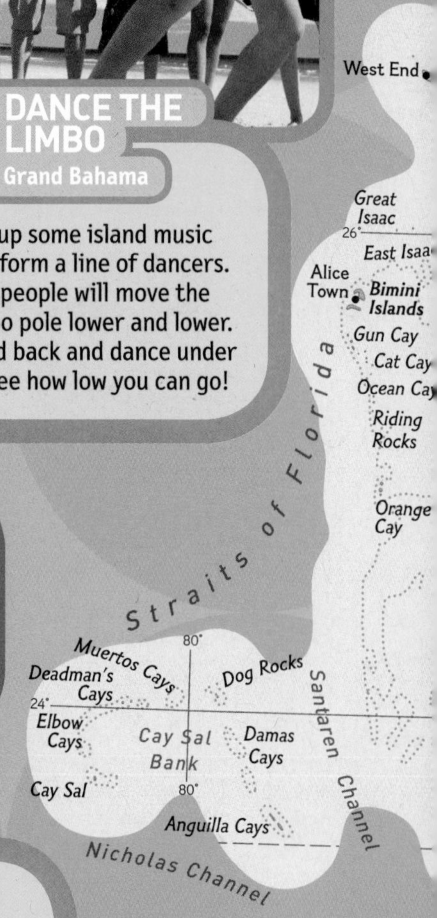

There are more than 700 islands in the Bahamas. People live on only 30 of them. Many of the people have West African roots and customs: Their ancestors were enslaved and brought here to work on cotton plantations. The country was once a British colony. Nassau, the capital, has many beautiful vacation resorts.

DIGITAL TRAVELER!
Many beaches in the Bahama islands are scattered with seashells of all shapes and sizes. Take photographs of shells, make them into postcards, and send them to your friends.

4 GO ON AN AQUAVENTURE

Paradise Island

Explore a huge waterscape park alongside the Atlantis Paradise Hotel. There are swimming pools, high-speed waterslides, and a river ride with rolling rapids and wave surges within a lush, tropical man-made environment.

ANDROS ISLAND
Made up mainly of three large islands, this area is rich in mangrove, tidal swamp, and cave wildlife.

LAKE WINDSOR (LAKE ROSA)
This lake is a protected reserve for flamingos, the national bird. They build their nests in the spring and adult females may each lay one egg a year.

LUCAYAN NATIONAL PARK
This park includes mangrove swamps, tropical beaches, and an underground cave system that is more than 300 miles (480 km) long.

5 COOL THINGS TO DO HERE

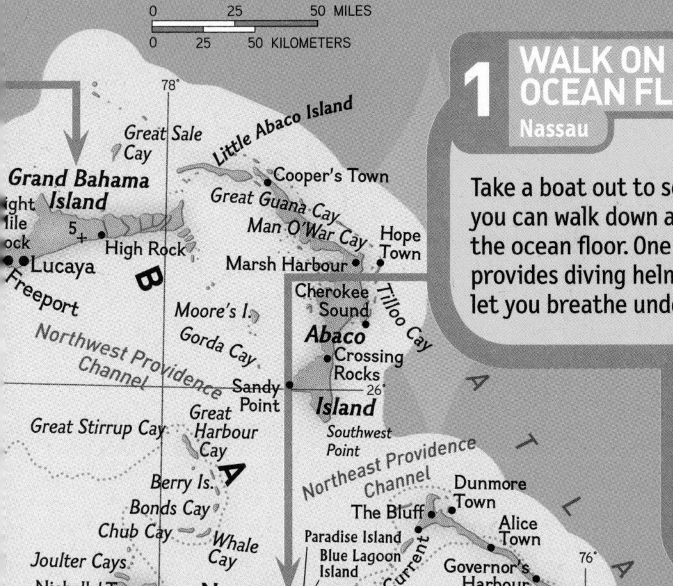

1 WALK ON THE OCEAN FLOOR

Nassau

Take a boat out to sea where you can walk down a ladder to the ocean floor. One tour provides diving helmets that let you breathe underwater.

ID CARD COUNTRY FACTS

Size: 5,359 sq mi (13,880 sq km)
Population: 350,000
Capital: Nassau
Official language: English
Currency: Bahamian dollar
Highest point: Mount Alvernia, 207 ft (63 m)
Life expectancy: 75.0 years

2 SWIM WITH STINGRAYS

Blue Lagoon Island

Jump into Stingray City and swim with stingrays, moray eels, and crawfish. If you arrive at mealtime, you can feed the marine animals, too.

3 STAND WHERE OCEAN MEETS SEA

Eleuthera Island

Visit the northern end of Eleuthera Island and stand on the beach. Look into the water and try to see where the churning, dark Atlantic Ocean bumps up to the calm, turquoise Caribbean Sea.

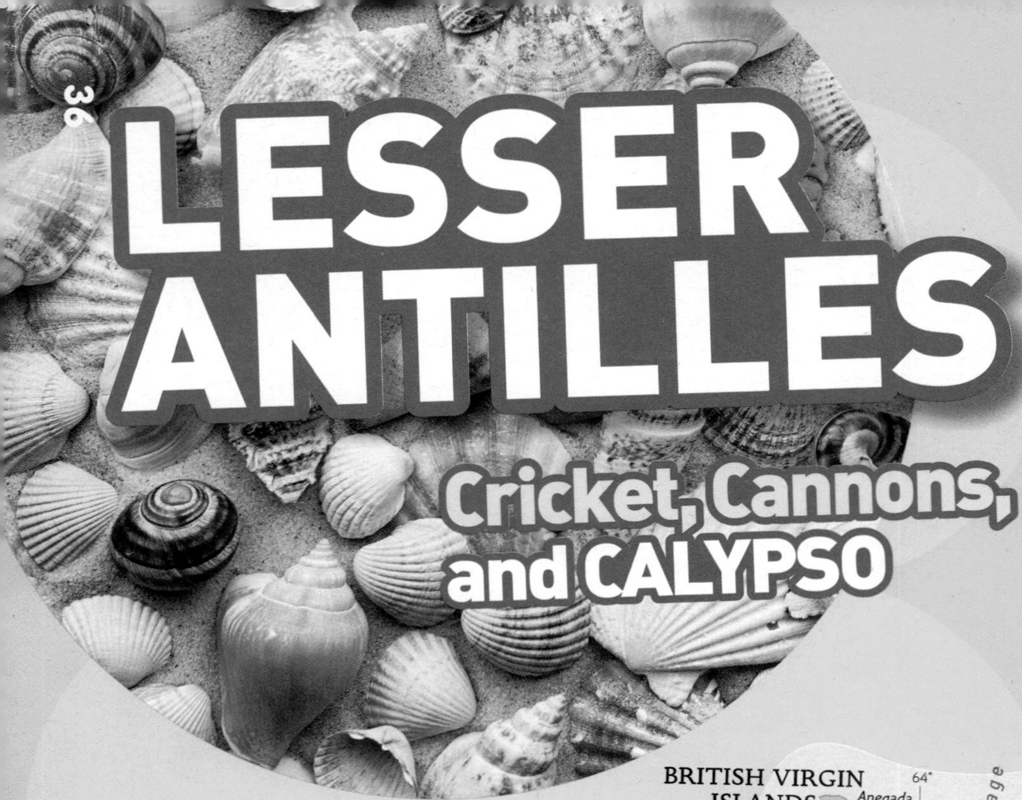

LESSER ANTILLES

Cricket, Cannons, and CALYPSO

On a map, this long string of islands looks like the boundary line between the Atlantic Ocean and the Caribbean Sea. Before 1496, the original islanders were the Arawaks, the Caribs, and the Ciboney. By the middle of the 1600s, people from Spain, England, France, and the Netherlands had settled there. They set up trading centers, which also led to pirate raids. Many of the islands are mountainous with beautiful beaches and warm weather.

5 COOL THINGS TO DO HERE

1 HIKE TO A BOILING LAKE
Dominica

Hike through the volcanic debris in Morne Trois Pitons National Park. See steam rise from the world's second-largest actively boiling lake. Scientists say the water is heated by molten lava below the lake. You can see bubbles belching from the center.

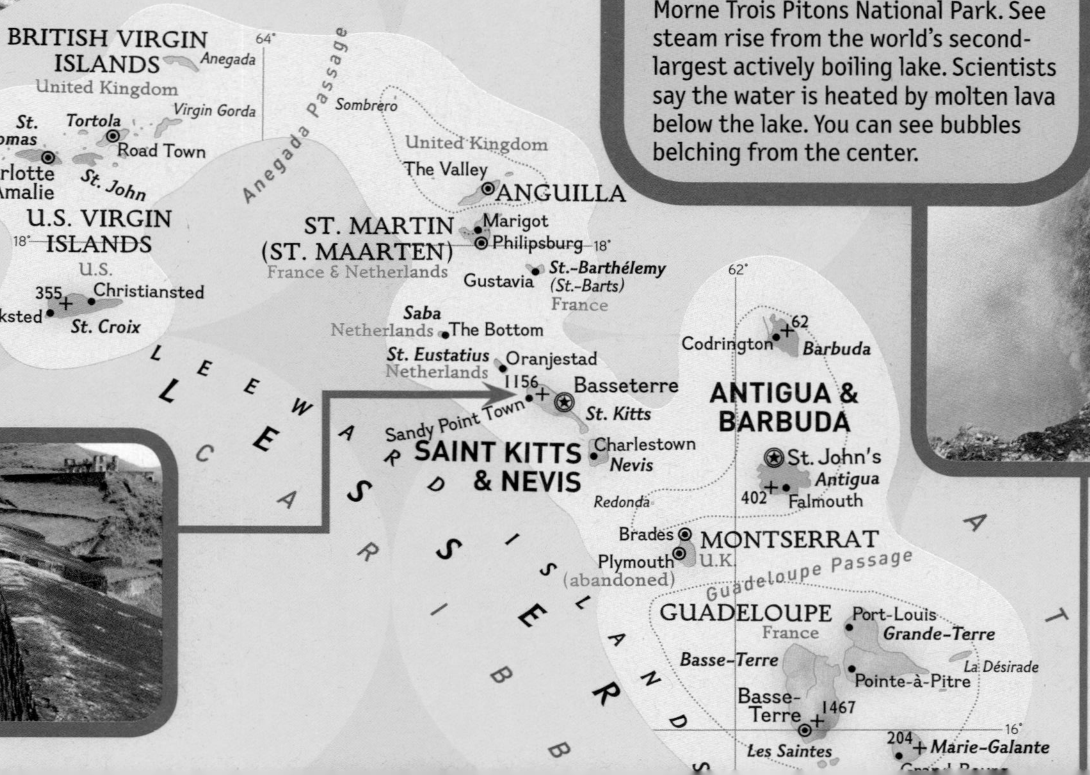

2 COUNT CANNONS
Sandy Point Town

Count more than 20 cannons as you walk around Brimstone Hill Fortress National Park. In the 1700s and 1800s, this huge British fort protected present-day St. Kitts and Nevis from invaders. British engineers designed the fort and African slaves built it on the side of a volcanic mountain.

3 JOIN THE CRICKET CROWD

Bridgetown

Watch the score change as the bowlers and batters play an exciting game. A game can last from one to five days.

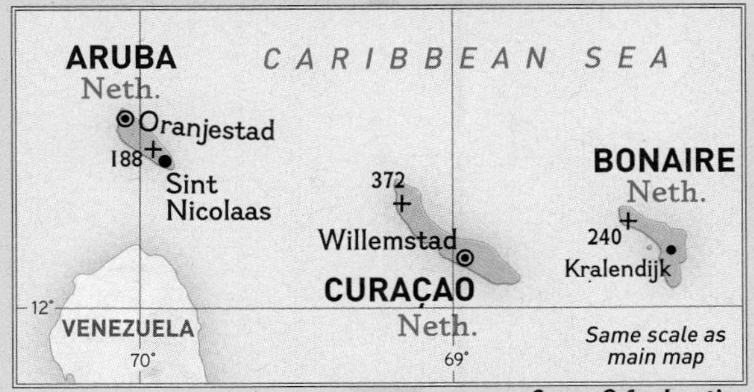

See p. 8 for location

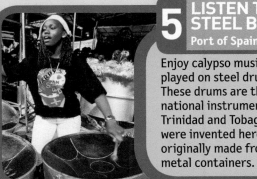

ID CARD COUNTRY FACTS

BARBADOS
Population: 253,000
Capital: Bridgetown

DOMINICA
Population: 155,000
Capital: Roseau

GRENADA
Population: 112,000
Capital: Saint George's

ST. KITTS & NEVIS
Population: 55,000
Capital: Basseterre

ST. LUCIA
Population: 170,000
Capital: Castries

ST. VINCENT & THE GRENADINES
Population: 108,000
Capital: Kingstown

TRINIDAD & TOBAGO
Population: 1,341,000
Capital: Port of Spain

4 VISIT PIRATE SCENES

Bequia Island

Visit sites where parts of *Pirates of the Caribbean: The Curse of the Black Pearl* were filmed. Then take a refreshing dip in the nearby Falls of Baleine.

5 LISTEN TO A STEEL BAND

Port of Spain

Enjoy calypso music played on steel drums. These drums are the national instrument of Trinidad and Tobago. They were invented here and originally made from metal containers.

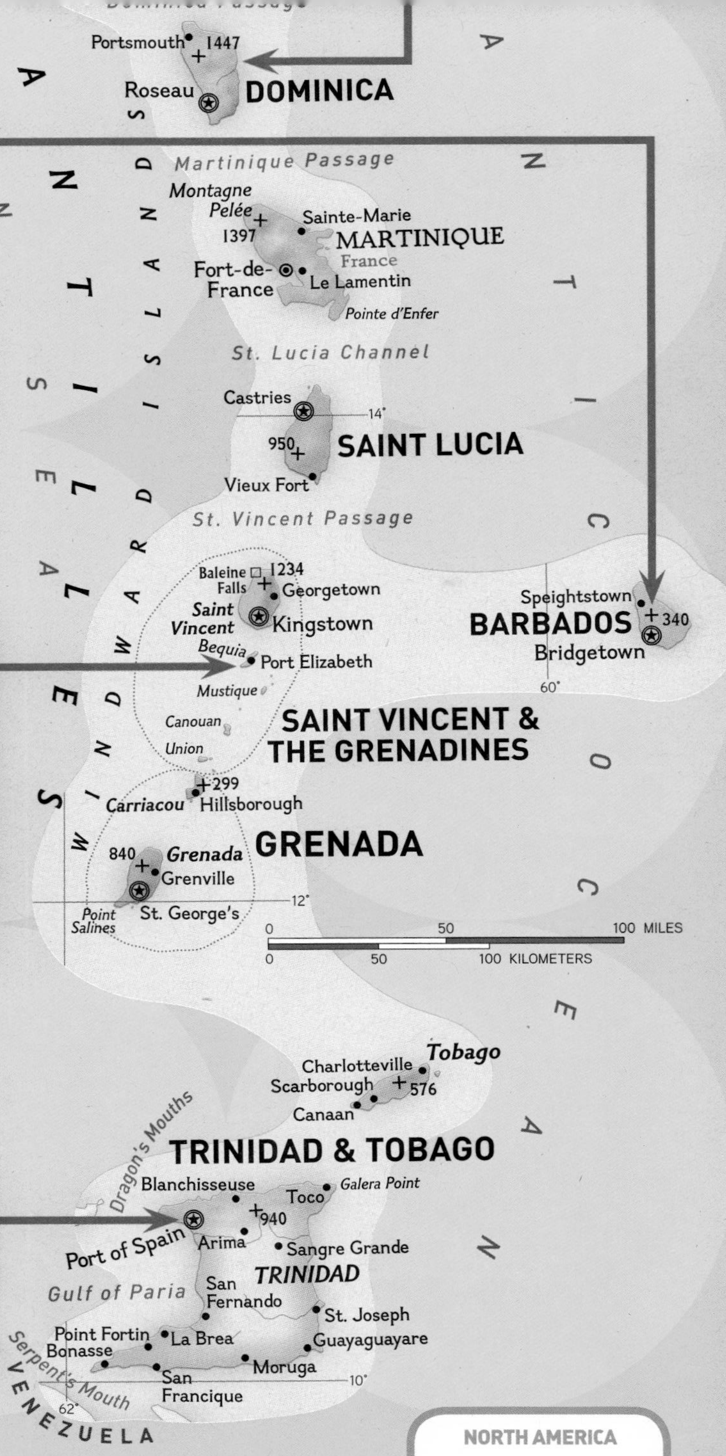

SOUTH AMERICA

Geographical WONDERS

South America is covered with tropical rain forests, mighty rivers, high waterfalls, massive mountains, hot deserts, glaciers, and island chains. It also has big, bustling cities, rural areas, and hilltop villages.

San Rafael Waterfall, Ecuador Park, Ecuador. South America gets more rainfall than any other continent, creating some of the world's longest rivers and highest waterfalls.

SOUTH AMERICA

From Tropical North to Icy Cold SOUTH

The original people of this continent are known as Amerindians. Following the European discovery of the Americas by Christopher Columbus in 1492, Spanish and Portuguese explorers and settlers spread throughout the land. They introduced their languages, cultures, and traditions, which remain to this day.

SOCCER
Brazil

Soccer is a major sport across South America. Brazil, Argentina, and Uruguay have all won the World Cup.

FESTIVAL OF THE SUN
Peru

Amerindians celebrate ancient traditions such as Inti Raymi, the Festival of the Sun, which honors the Incan sun god Inti.

AUNT BERTHA'S TRAVEL TIPS

LEARN LATIN

Spanish and Portuguese—the two main languages of South America—have origins in Latin, the language of the ancient Romans.

WRAP UP WARM

Parts of South America can be very cold, falling to −14.3°F (−25.7°C) in southern Argentina. The coldest temperatures are in July and August, which are winter months in the Southern Hemisphere.

TAKE A BUS

In South America, most people travel long distances across countries by bus or car rather than by train. A bus trip from Rio de Janeiro, Brazil, to Buenos Aires, Argentina, takes about 40 hours.

NORTHWEST

This region is rich in wildlife and natural resources such as gemstones and oil. Many of the people are poor.

NORTHEAST

Brazil takes up most of the region. Countries to the north were once British, French, and Dutch colonies. The vast Amazon Rain Forest is threatened by farming, logging, and mining, which is destroying the plants and wildlife found there.

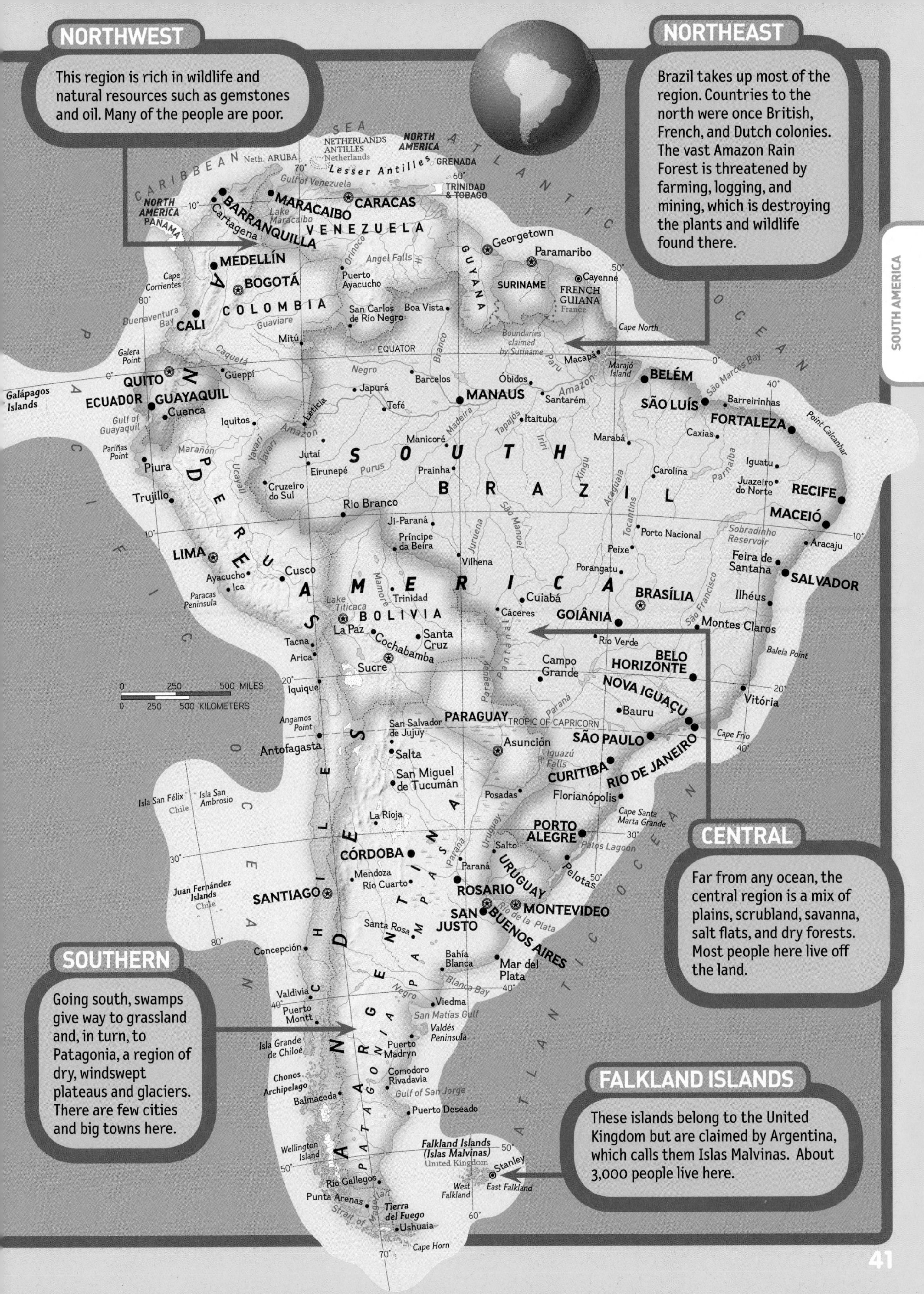

CENTRAL

Far from any ocean, the central region is a mix of plains, scrubland, savanna, salt flats, and dry forests. Most people here live off the land.

SOUTHERN

Going south, swamps give way to grassland and, in turn, to Patagonia, a region of dry, windswept plateaus and glaciers. There are few cities and big towns here.

FALKLAND ISLANDS

These islands belong to the United Kingdom but are claimed by Argentina, which calls them Islas Malvinas. About 3,000 people live here.

	NATIONAL BIRD:	NATIONAL FLOWER:	NATIONAL MAMMAL:
COLOMBIA	Andean condor	Columbian orchid	Andean squirrel
ECUADOR	Andean condor	rose	Galápagos fur seal

COLOMBIA AND ECUADOR

Ancient Ruins and Unique ANIMALS

It's hot in lowland Ecuador, for you are on the Equator. To cool off, head inland to the Andes Mountains, or take a boat to the Galápagos Islands, where you may meet the blue-footed booby. Ecuador and Colombia, once a single country, split in 1830. Most Colombians live in the valleys of the Andes Mountains, and Colombia is famous for growing coffee. The capital cities of both countries—Quito (Ecuador) and Bogotá (Colombia)—are more than 8,000 feet (2,438 m) above sea level.

ID CARD COUNTRY FACTS

COLOMBIA
Population: 48,028,000
Capital: Bogotá

ECUADOR
Population: 15,789,000
Capital: Quito

MEDELLÍN

This Colombian city has beautiful museums, breathtaking cable-car rides to nearby mountaintops, and the biggest flower parade in the world.

NAPO RIVER

Riverboat cruises take tourists through the Amazon Rain Forest of Ecuador. Everyone hopes to take a picture of a river dolphin, piranha, or giant frog.

INCA RUINS OF INGAPIRCA

The ancient Canari and Inca peoples showed amazing building skills with rocks and mortar. These ruins include the Temple of the Sun where, at the right time of year and day, sunlight beams through the exact center of a doorway.

5 PHOTOGRAPH GIANT TORTOISES

Galápagos Islands

Take this rare opportunity to see the world's largest tortoise. The biggest one ever recorded was five feet (1.5 m) long and weighed 550 pounds (249 kg). They can live more than 100 years.

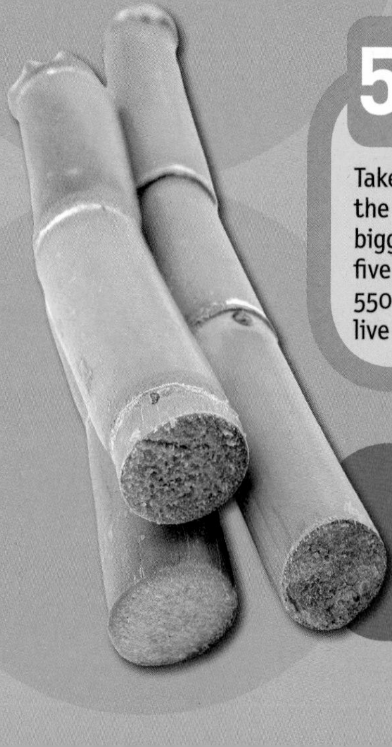

DIGITAL TRAVELER!
Sugarcane grows in Colombia. Go online and find out how sugarcane becomes the sugar we put into the sweets we eat.

5 COOL THINGS TO DO HERE

1 JUMP INTO A MUD POOL
Santa Catalina

Climb stairs that lead to the top of Tortumo Volcano and then jump in. It's okay, you'll land in a shallow pool of mud. Relax!

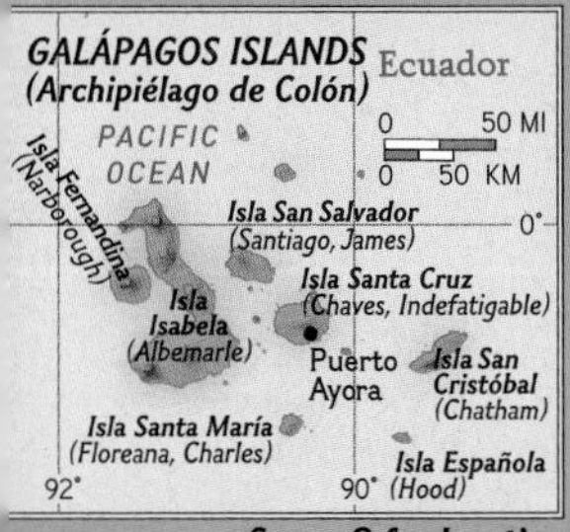

See p. 8 for location

2 BLINK AT THE BLING
Bogotá

Walk through the Gold Museum and see shiny objects made by native artists who lived here before the Europeans arrived.

SOUTH AMERICA

3 STAND ON THE EQUATOR
San Antonio

Straddle the yellow line at the Middle of the World Monument. This line represents the Equator, the imaginary line that separates the northern and southern hemispheres. Modern GPS devices show that the real equator is about 800 feet (244 m) north of the monument.

4 TOUR A BANANA PLANTATION
Guayaquil

Learn how bananas grow from tiny reddish flowers into the fruit we eat. Ecuador exports more bananas than any other country.

5 COOL THINGS TO DO HERE

1 SHOUT AT A BULLFIGHT
Valencia

See the matador face the bull in Valencia's bullring. It is the second largest in Latin America.

2 VISIT A PALACE
Caracas

See Miraflores Palace where the President of Venezuela works. Inside is the Sun Room, decorated with gold donated by Peru.

5 VIEW WILDLFE
Hato el Cedral

Take a tour of this wildlife area where you'll see capybaras, the largest living rodents on Earth. They can be more than 4 feet (122 cm) long and weigh more than 100 pounds (45 kg).

4 RIDE A CABLE CAR
El Ávila National Park

Get a bird's-eye view of Caracas as the cable car climbs the mountain. When you get to the top, you can go skating or play at the playground.

NATIONAL BIRD: Venezuelan troupial

NATIONAL FLOWER: flor de mayo orchid

NATIONAL TREE: araguaney

VENEZUELA

From the Andes to the AMAZON

Venezuela is on the north coast of South America. Columbus landed here in 1498. You'll find broad grasslands called llanos, and mountains as tall as 16,000 feet (4,877 m) high. South America's largest lake, Lake Maracaibo, is really a lagoon open to the ocean. Oil and gas make Venezuela one of South America's richest countries, with busy expressways linking the capital Caracas to other cities. Like many South Americans, Venezuelans are mostly Spanish-speaking.

ID CARD COUNTRY FACTS

Size: 352,144 sq mi (912,050 sq km)
Population: 29,679,000
Capital: Caracas
Official language: Spanish
Currency: bolivar
Highest point: Pico Bolivar, 16,427 ft (5,007 m)
Life expectancy: 75.0 years

Globetrotter Attractions

ANGEL FALLS

This is the world's tallest waterfall and is 20 times higher than Niagara Falls. It drops 3,212 feet (979 m) over the edge of Auyantepui Mountain in Canaima National Park.

MOCHIMA NATIONAL PARK

Pods of dolphins frequently swim by the 36 islands that make up this national park. Visitors enjoy swimming and snorkeling in the coral reefs.

PARQUE DEL ESTE

This popular park in the capital, Caracas, has a snake house and an awesome planetarium.

3 BEWARE THE DUNGEON!

La Asunción

Walk around Santa Rosa castle, a fort that protected the city 330 years ago. Inside there is a dungeon where prisoners were kept during the Venezuelan War of Independence from Spain of 1811 to 1823.

DIGITAL TRAVELER!
There is a place in Venezuela called The Serpent's Mouth. Search the Internet to find its location and the best way to travel there.

	NATIONAL BIRD:	NATIONAL FLOWER:	NATIONAL MAMMAL:
GUYANA	hoatzin	*Victoria Regia* lily	jaguar
SURINAME	great kiskadee	*Sloanea gracilis*	water opposum

GUYANA AND SURINAME

From Colonial Houses to JUNGLE CATS

Neighbors on the northeast coast of South America, Guyana and Suriname are separated by the Corantijn River. Tropical forest covers much of the land, which rises to grassy highlands and mountains more than 9,000 feet (2,743 m) high in Guyana. Most people live along the low-lying coast. Natural resources include forest lumber, and minerals such as bauxite ore, from which aluminum is made. Expect to hear English and Dutch, because Guyana was once British-ruled, while Suriname was Dutch.

5 COOL THINGS TO DO HERE

1 HAVE A FUN DAY
Georgetown

Celebrate the Hindu holiday of Phagwah, also known as Holi. Watch a parade and join the colorful activities. Many Guyanese are descendants of people brought from India in the 1800s to work on sugar plantations.

2 BE A SUGAR SCHOLAR!
Mariënburg

Take a tour of an old sugar plantation. In the late 1800s, there were sugar fields and a sugar factory here plus Suriname's first railroad, which was used for sending sugar to markets.

3 DO SOMETHING DUTCH
Paramaribo

Take pictures of Dutch houses in Paramaribo. It became a Dutch colonial town in the 1600s. The Dutch West India Company built their trading business here.

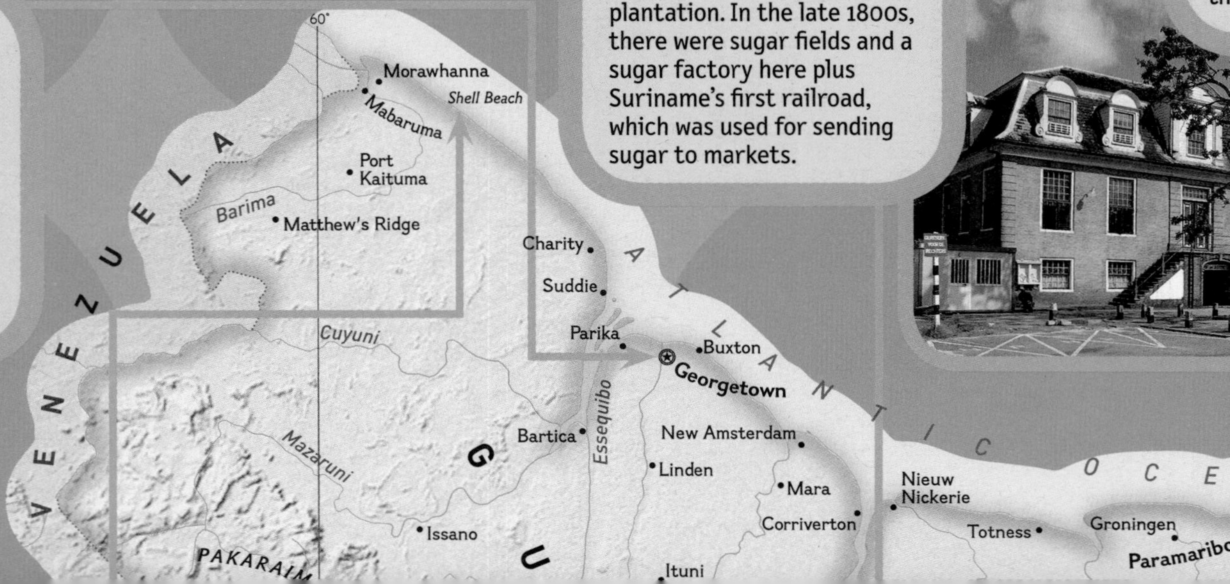

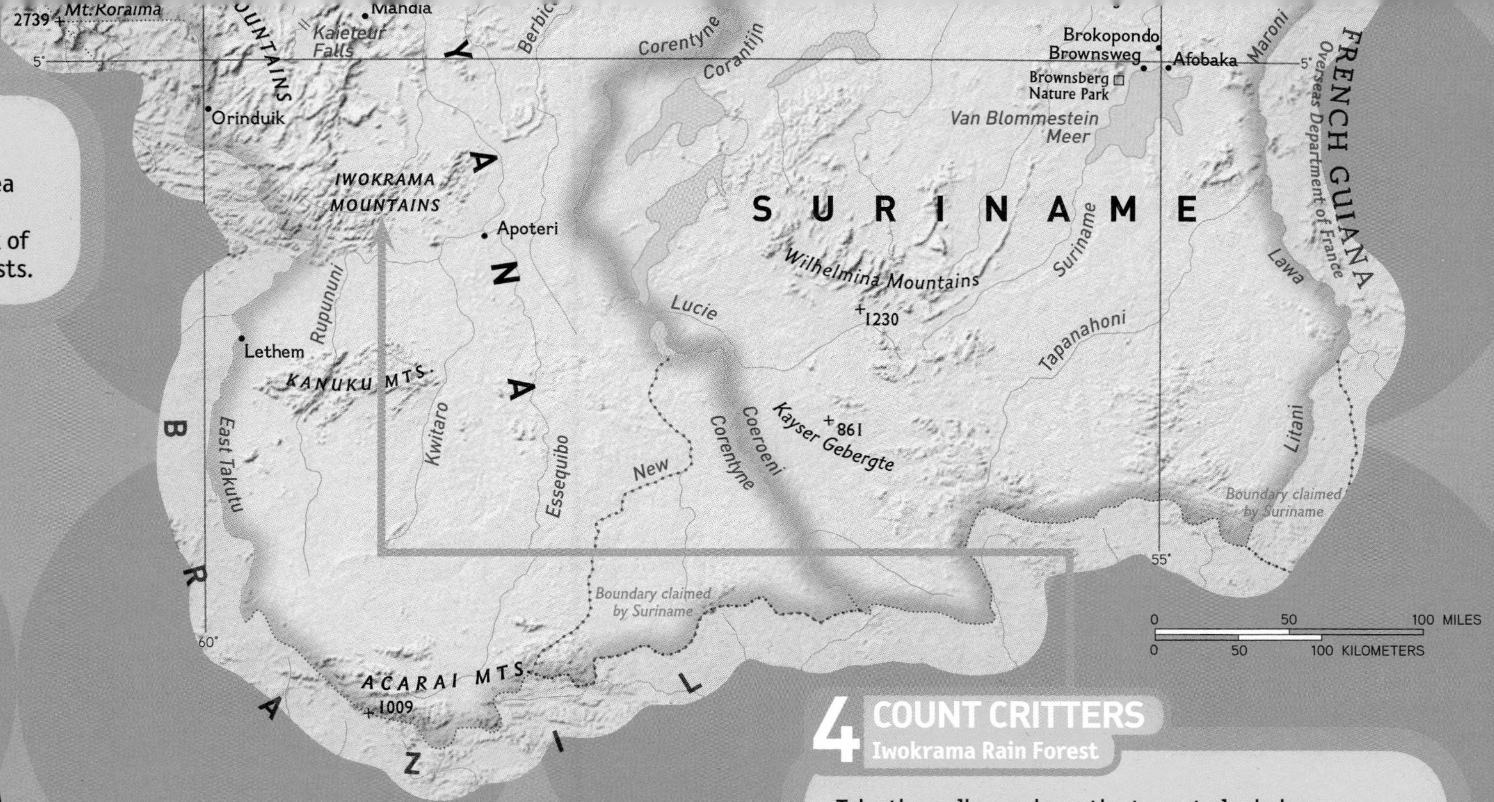

5 LEARN ABOUT TURTLES
Shell Beach

Ride a boat by Shell Beach, where sea turtles make their nests. Special teams tag the turtles to keep track of them. Be sure not to disturb the nests.

Globetrotter Attractions

KAIETEUR FALLS
One of the world's most powerful waterfalls lies in Guyana's rain forest. It is powerful because of its height—741 feet (226 m)—and the amount of water rushing over it.

BROWNSBERG NATURE PARK
Guests who stay in hotels in this Suriname park get to watch howler monkeys swinging through the trees.

CENTRAL MARKET
The large marketplace at Paramaribo's waterfront has its special sights, sounds, and smells. See pyramids of fresh fruit, rows of fish, and blankets loaded with trinkets.

4 COUNT CRITTERS
Iwokrama Rain Forest

Take the walkway above the trees to look down on anteaters, otters, and jaguars—the continent's largest cats. There are many insects and more recorded species of fish and bats here than anywhere on Earth.

ID CARD COUNTRY FACTS

GUYANA
Population: 800,000
Capital: Georgetown

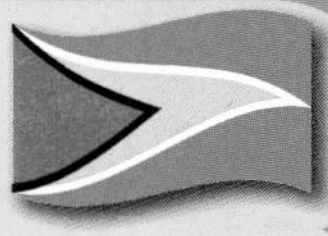

SURINAME
Population: 558,000
Capital: Paramaribo

DIGITAL TRAVELER!
People in Suriname celebrate Keti Koti on July 1 each year. Go online to find out what they are celebrating.

NATIONAL BIRD: macaw

NATIONAL TREE: golden trumpet tree

NATIONAL MAMMAL: jaguar

BRAZIL

The Center of SOUTH AMERICA

South America's biggest country has more people than the rest of the continent combined. Brazil is so big it takes 25 hours to drive from Rio Grande on the coast to the capital Brasília. To explore the Amazon Rain Forest, take a plane and see it from above, or sail up the Amazon River. Visit the coastal cities to see where most Brazilians live, and enjoy Rio de Janeiro's colorful Carnival. Learn some Portuguese, too—it's the main language of Brazil.

5 COOL THINGS TO DO HERE

1 BOUNCE THROUGH A RUBBER MUSEUM
Manaus

Walk through a jungle and learn how workers tapped rubber trees to remove the latex sap. Tour the estate owner's home and learn how rubber made many people rich in the late 1800s. Then take a boat ride to the area where ships picked up rubber to deliver it worldwide.

2 IMAGINE THE FUTURE
Brasília

Stroll past this futuristic cathedral in Brazil's capital. Before 1956, this area looked like a desert. The president invited architects and builders to create a modern city.

3 PLAY BEACH VOLLEYBALL
Recife

Join a friendly game of volleyball next to the Atlantic Ocean. Recife has many miles of beaches. After a few games, buy a refreshing coconut drink and take a stroll on the boardwalk.

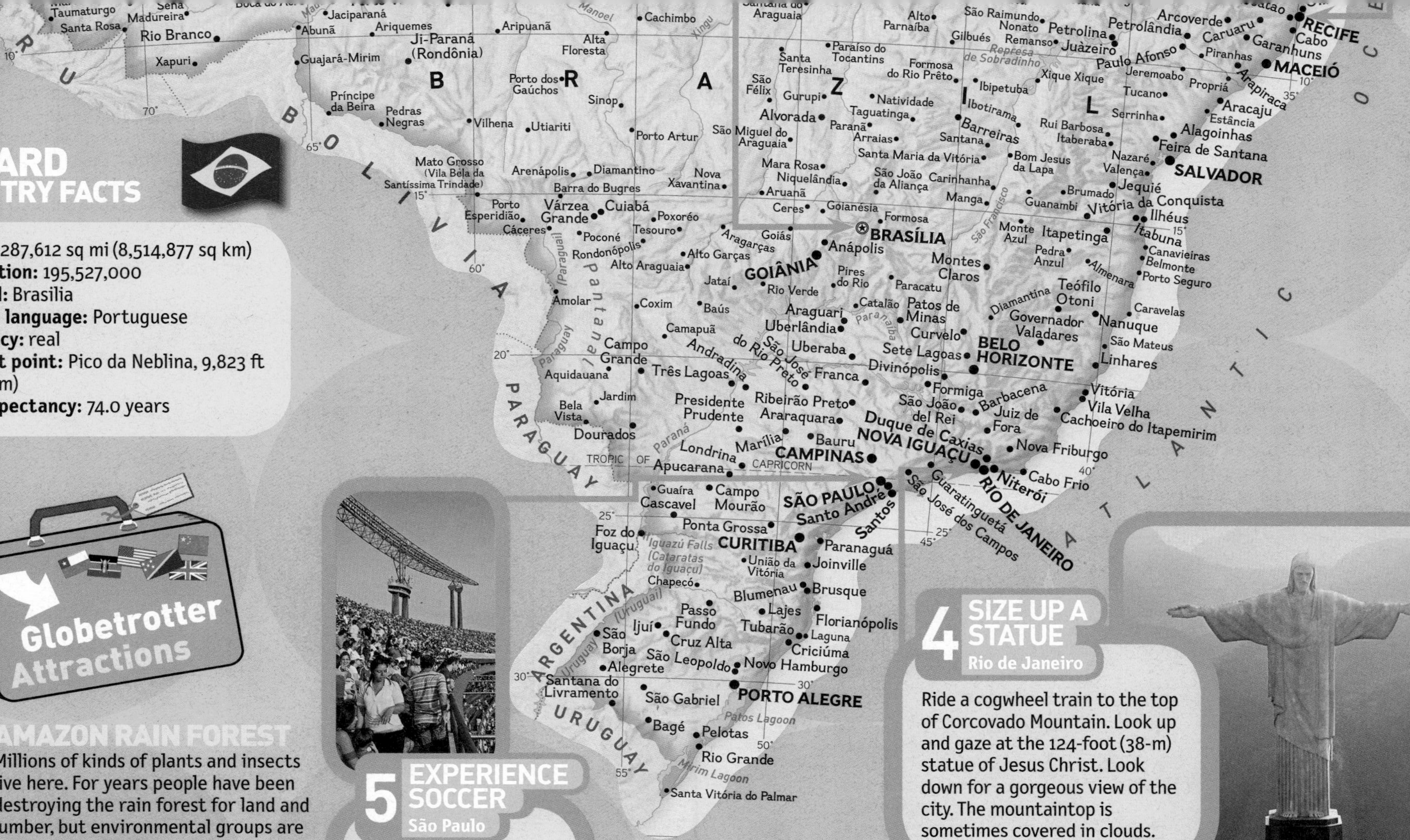

ID CARD
COUNTRY FACTS

Size: 3,287,612 sq mi (8,514,877 sq km)
Population: 195,527,000
Capital: Brasilia
Official language: Portuguese
Currency: real
Highest point: Pico da Neblina, 9,823 ft (2,994 m)
Life expectancy: 74.0 years

Globetrotter Attractions

AMAZON RAIN FOREST
Millions of kinds of plants and insects live here. For years people have been destroying the rain forest for land and lumber, but environmental groups are working to protect it.

PANTANAL
Many rare and endangered animals live in this floodplain, including giant anteaters and giant otters.

SUGARLOAF MOUNTAIN
This mountain in Rio de Janeiro looks like a large granite rocket. A cable car zips tourists up to the top.

5 EXPERIENCE SOCCER
São Paulo

Cheer for one of the São Paolo soccer teams. The city has several teams and stadiums. Morumbi Stadium is the largest, with 84,000 seats. The famous soccer player, Pele, played for a São Paolo team.

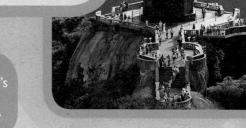

4 SIZE UP A STATUE
Rio de Janeiro

Ride a cogwheel train to the top of Corcovado Mountain. Look up and gaze at the 124-foot (38-m) statue of Jesus Christ. Look down for a gorgeous view of the city. The mountaintop is sometimes covered in clouds.

DIGITAL TRAVELER!
Carnival in Rio de Janeiro is one of the world's greatest celebrations, with music, dance, costumes, and parades. Learn about, look at, and listen to Carnival on the Internet.

NATIONAL BIRD: Andean cock-of-the-rock

NATIONAL TREE: cinchona

NATIONAL MAMMAL: vicuna

PERU

A Diverse LANDSCAPE

In Peru, look forward to tasty fish dinners because Pacific Ocean fishing is a major industry here. Yet along the coast is a desert drier than the Sahara. Inland to the east rise the Andes Mountains, and farther inland, beyond the Andes, are tropical rain forests and rivers. Lake Titicaca, which Peru shares with Bolivia, is the highest lake in the world that is navigable by ships.

Globetrotter Attractions

NASCA LINES
About 2,000 years ago, the Nasca people etched drawings in the desert floor. From airplanes, we can see these pictures of whales, monkeys, and other figures.

VOLCÁN MISTI
This cone-shaped peak sits in the Andes Mountains near Arequipa, Peru's second largest city. It last erupted in 1600.

LAKE TITICACA
Five major river systems and many streams flow into this lake. There is a single main outlet, to the south.

5 COOL THINGS TO DO HERE

1 SHOP NONSTOP
Piura

Check out Piura's shops and try to find the city's most famous things. Look for artists making straw hats, pottery, wooden bowls, silver objects, and colorful clothing. Piura was the first city in Peru that was settled by people from Spain.

2 FLUTTER BY BUTTERFLIES
Iquitos

See how many kinds and colors of butterflies you can find at Pilpintuwasi Butterfly Farm. This blue morpho butterfly looks like a delicate work of art. You may also see an owl butterfly. Its wings have dark circles that resemble the eyes of an owl.

5 DISCOVER TREASURE
Lima

Be amazed by hundreds of objects in the Gold Museum. Long ago, Peru was rich with gold. The people artistically turned the gold into statues, bracelets, rings, and face masks.

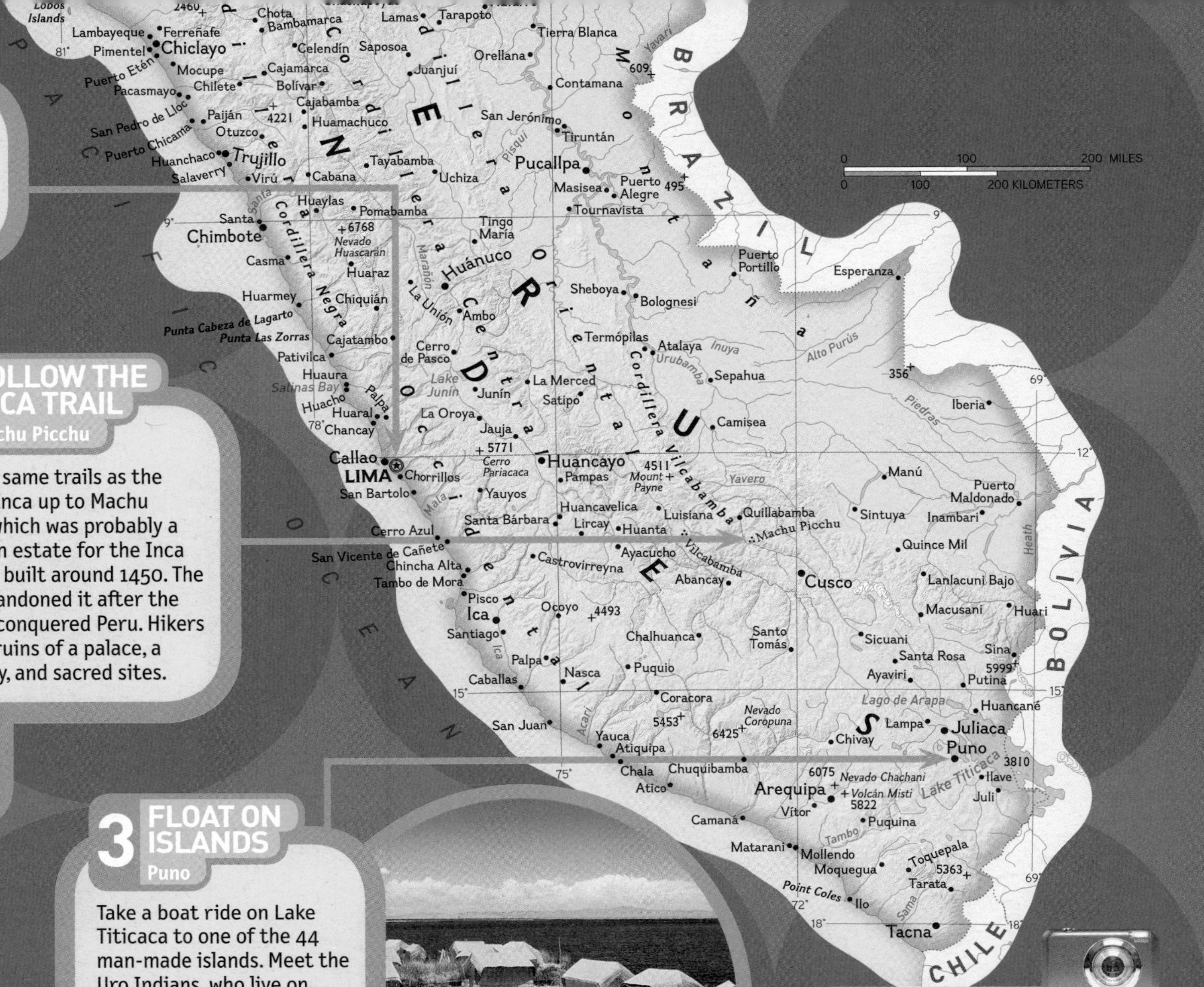

4 FOLLOW THE INCA TRAIL
Machu Picchu

Walk the same trails as the ancient Inca up to Machu Picchu, which was probably a mountain estate for the Inca emperor built around 1450. The Incas abandoned it after the Spanish conquered Peru. Hikers can see ruins of a palace, a cemetery, and sacred sites.

3 FLOAT ON ISLANDS
Puno

Take a boat ride on Lake Titicaca to one of the 44 man-made islands. Meet the Uro Indians, who live on islands made of floating reeds. They live in reed huts and eat fish from the lake.

ID CARD COUNTRY FACTS

Size: 496,224 sq mi (1,285,216 sq km)
Population: 30,475,000
Capital: Lima
Official languages: Spanish and Quechua
Currency: nuevo sol
Highest point: Nevado Huascarán, 22,205 ft (6,768 m)
Life expectancy: 74.0 years

DIGITAL TRAVELER!
Look for llamas, alpacas, guanacos, and vicunas. Photograph them or go online to see what they look like. Compare them to animals you see near home.

ID CARD
COUNTRY FACTS

Size: 424,164 sq mi (1,098,581 sq km)
Population: 11,020,000
Capital: La Paz
Official languages: Spanish, Quechua, and Aymara
Currency: boliviano
Highest point: Nevado Sajama, 21,463 ft (6,542 m)
Life expectancy: 67.0 years

5 COOL THINGS TO DO HERE

1 HAVE SALTENAS FOR BREAKFAST
La Paz

Buy these tasty pastries from a La Paz street vendor. By noon, many vendors are sold out of the baked dough packets filled with a sweet or spicy chicken or meat mixture. Enjoy them for your breakfast or a snack.

5 SAIL TO A LAKE ISLAND
Isla del Sol

Take a boat to Isla del Sol, an island in Lake Titicaca, where no motorized vehicles are allowed. Hike between villages and wander around the pre-Columbian Inca ruins, such as the Temple of the Sun.

4 THINK INCA
Tiwanacu

Examine the ruins of a pyramid built before the Inca Empire. Walk up to the Gate of the Sun, a doorway cut from a huge stone. Find the half-human, half-bird figures carved into it. The pyramid was probably an observatory and used for special ceremonies.

3 DON'T FORGET YOUR CAMERA
Cochabamba

Take a picture of the huge statue of Jesus Christ that stands on San Pedro Hill. Ride the cable car to the top of the hill for a better look at the statue, which is more than 108 feet (33 m) high. Admire the city of Cochabamba spread below.

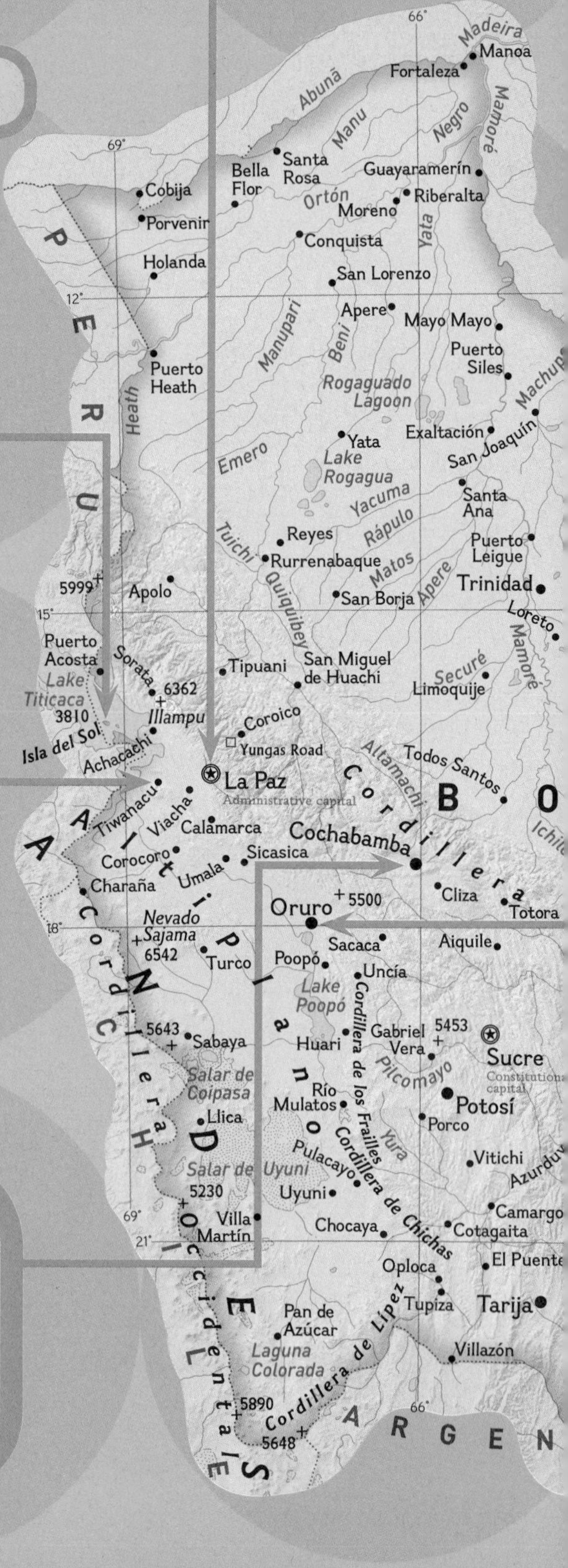

2 DANCE AT A CARNIVAL

Oruro

Watch up to 28,000 dancers in elaborate costumes and masks as they perform many types of dances. Listen to the 10,000 musicians who play music for the dancers. The Carnaval de Oruro always begins with the devil dance. Other performances reflect the traditions of groups that now make Bolivia their home: Amerindians, Africans, and Spanish.

NATIONAL BIRD: Andean condor

NATIONAL MAMMAL: alpaca

NATIONAL FLOWER: kantuta

BOLIVIA

Summits, Salt and SUN

Landlocked Bolivia is named for Simon Bolivar, a man who helped liberate much of the continent from Spanish rule in the early 1800s. The high Andes Mountains and the windswept Altiplano plateau are in the west, and in the east is the Oriente, a lowland region of grassland, forests, and rivers. Travel by road is difficult, so horses and llamas often get places cars cannot reach. Farmers in the Valles region, with its fertile valleys, produce much of Bolivia's food, including potatoes, corn, and a local grain called quinoa.

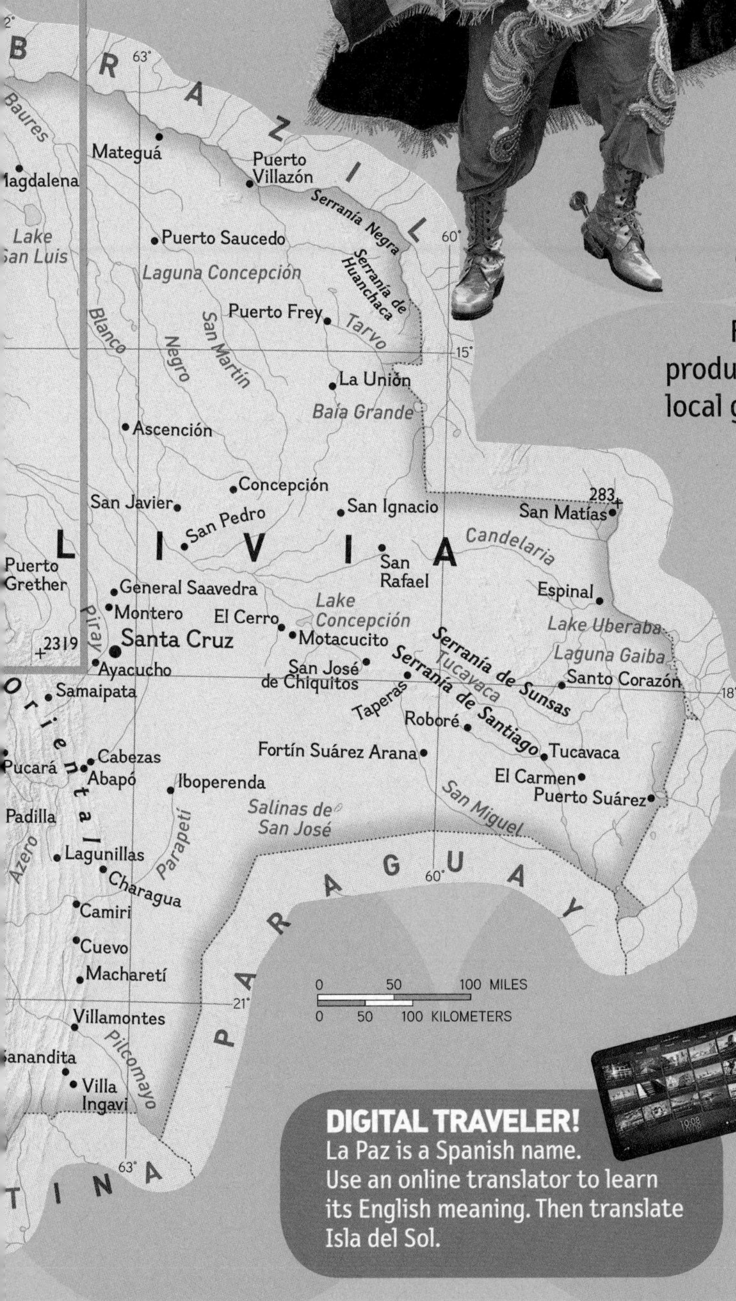

LA PAZ

High in the Andes is La Paz, the world's highest capital. The city's center is in a deep canyon but newer buildings are being built up the canyon walls. Lake Titicaca is nearby.

BIOCENTRO GUEMBE

Near the city of Santa Cruz is a natural paradise, with a giant butterfly park, orchid garden, and nature trails. It is surrounded by lush forest.

SALAR DE UYUNI

Uyuni Salt Flat is the world's largest inland area of salt. On the dry and very flat land, salt is gathered into big piles before trucks take it to nearby processing plants.

DIGITAL TRAVELER!

La Paz is a Spanish name. Use an online translator to learn its English meaning. Then translate Isla del Sol.

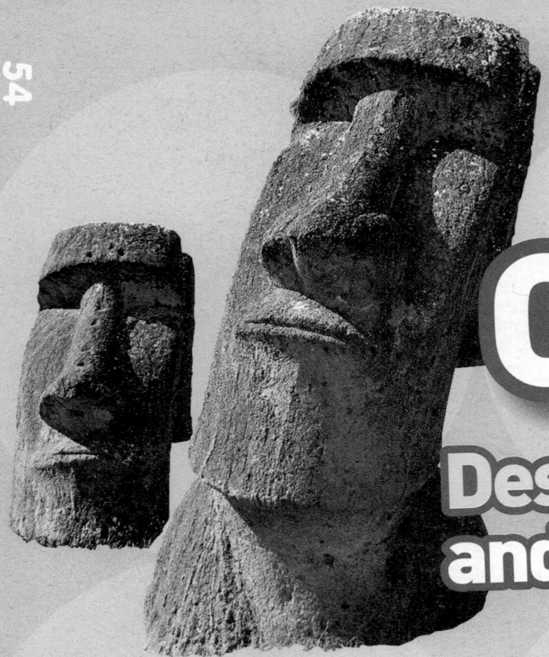

NATIONAL TREE: monkey-puzzle

NATIONAL FLOWER: copihue

NATIONAL MAMMAL: huemul

CHILE

Deserts, Glaciers, and MOUNTAINS

No other land is so long, yet so thin, as Chile. It stretches along the west side of South America for about 2,650 miles (4,265 km), but is only about 265 miles (426 km) wide. Chile has some of South America's most magnificent scenery: mountains, volcanoes, glaciers, forests, rocky islands, and rainless desert. Right at the southern tip is Tierra del Fuego, the "land of fire"—a group of islands shared between Chile and Argentina.

ID CARD
COUNTRY FACTS

Size: 291,932 sq mi (756,102 sq km)
Population: 17,557,000
Capital: Santiago
Official language: Spanish
Currency: Chilean peso
Highest point: Nevado Ojos del Salado, 22,615 ft (6,893 m)
Life expectancy: 79.0 years

5 COOL THINGS TO DO HERE

1 STARGAZE
Atacama Desert

Look up at the stars in the driest place on Earth. The cloudless skies allow a clear view of the heavens. NASA uses this desert to test instruments because its soil is similar to the soil on Mars.

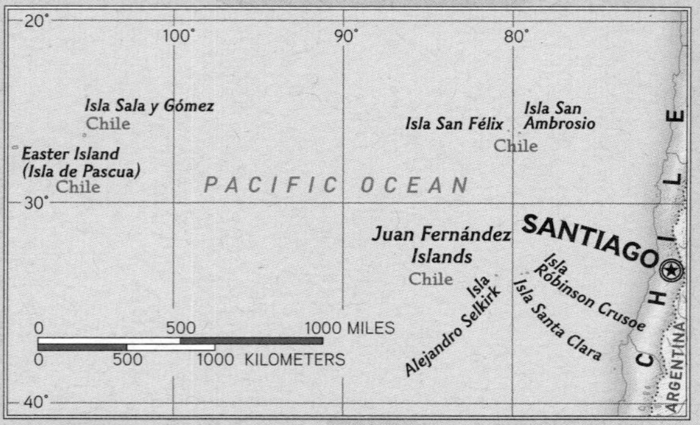

See p. 8 for location

EASTER ISLAND
This island, some 2,300 miles (3,680 km) west of South America, is home to 900 huge statues called *moai*. The moai are only heads and bodies and were carved from volcanic stone but no one is sure when or how.

PATAGONIA
The coast of this southern region of Chile has many fjords—long narrow inlets with steep sides that were carved by the local glaciers.

TORRES DEL PAINE NATIONAL PARK
This beautiful park in the Chilean Andes has mountains, lakes, glaciers, and rivers that you can explore.

DIGITAL TRAVELER!
There is an island off the coast of Chile called Robinson Crusoe Island. Search the Internet to learn how the island got its name.

5 TELL TIME WITH FLOWERS
Viña del Mar

Viña del Mar is known as "The Garden City." Check the time on this floral clock in one of its gardens. Then ride to its beautiful beaches in a traditional horse-drawn carriage.

4 SNOWBOARD IN JULY
Malalcahuello-Nalcas National Reserve

Swoop down a snow-covered slope in the Andes in July. Winter here is from June to September.

3 KAYAK TO A GLACIER
Puerto Natales

Glaciers, made of moving ice, change the landscape. Watch out for floating ice as you paddle in a glacial lake.

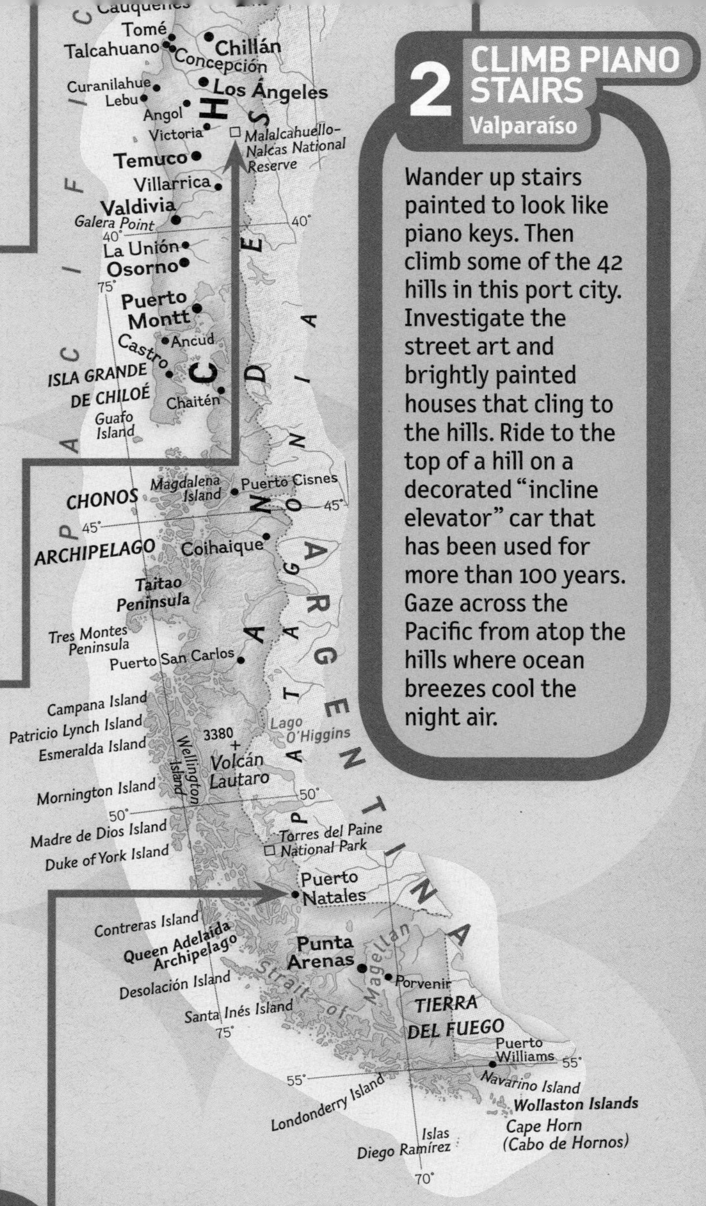

2 CLIMB PIANO STAIRS
Valparaíso

Wander up stairs painted to look like piano keys. Then climb some of the 42 hills in this port city. Investigate the street art and brightly painted houses that cling to the hills. Ride to the top of a hill on a decorated "incline elevator" car that has been used for more than 100 years. Gaze across the Pacific from atop the hills where ocean breezes cool the night air.

NATIONAL BIRD: rufous hornero

NATIONAL FLOWER: ceibo

NATIONAL MAMMAL: guanaco

ARGENTINA

Land of Beef and COWBOYS

Argentina is the second largest country in South America. The dramatic landscape includes the Andes Mountains in the west, and the windswept plateaus of Patagonia to the south. You will see Inca ruins, volcanoes, and South America's highest mountain, Aconcagua. Argentina's name comes from *argentum*, Latin for silver, which the Spanish sought during the 1500s but did not find. Instead, the Pampas plains are great for crops and cattle: Argentinians eat more beef than anyone else.

ID CARD COUNTRY FACTS

Size: 1,073,518 sq mi (2,780,400 sq km)
Population: 41,267,000
Capital: Buenos Aires
Official language: Spanish
Currency: Argentine peso
Highest point: Cerro Aconcagua, 22,831 ft (6,959 m)
Life expectancy: 76.0 years

5 COOL THINGS TO DO HERE

1 SMELL BARBECUE
The Pampas

Visit a working ranch and watch the gauchos, or cowboys, at work. They'll show off their skills in horseback riding and roping cattle. Then enjoy a gaucho barbecue, called *asado*.

5 LIKE THE BIKE!
Mendoza

Cheer the bike riders as they race through grape vineyards, up foothills, and into the mountains. Cyclists come from all over the world every February to compete in the La Vuelta Ciclista de Mendoza.

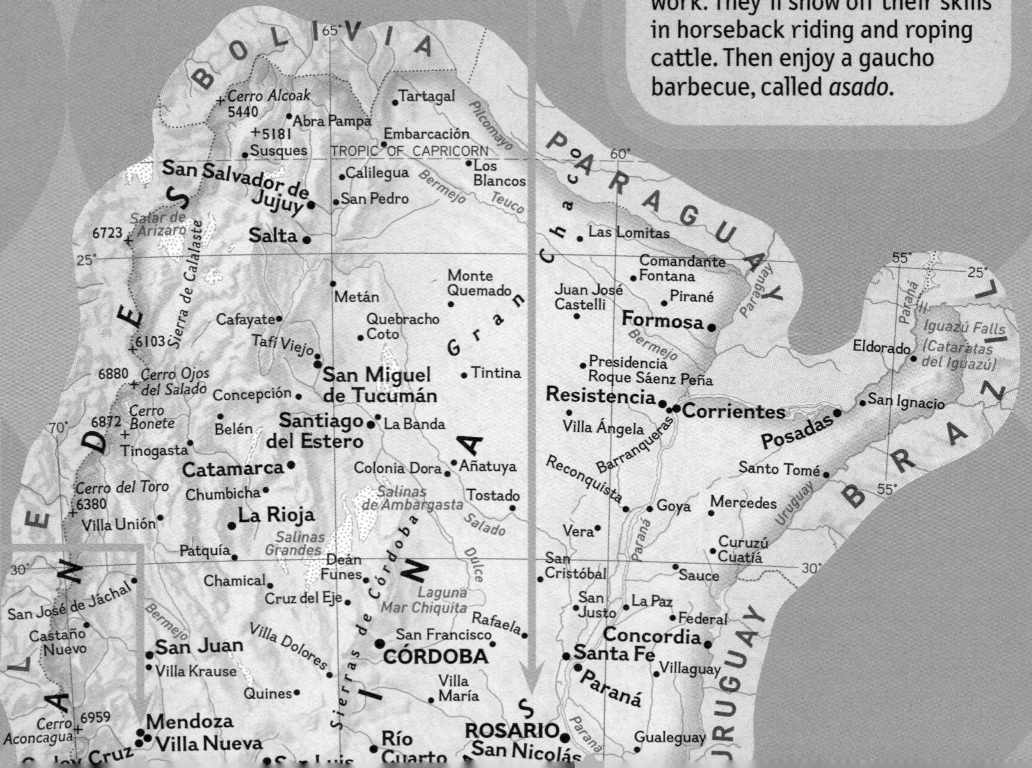

4 SAMPLE CHOCOLATE
San Carlos de Bariloche

Shop for chocolate in this city's candy stores. Famous for its chocolate, it hosts a Festival of Chocolate every Easter. Drool over the huge Easter egg or the giant chocolate bar that is almost 400 feet (122 m) long.

3 TAKE A TANGO LESSON
Buenos Aires

Dance the tango! This dance began in Buenos Aires more than 100 years ago, then spread to the rest of the world. It has changed over the years and today there are many different tango styles. Sometimes partners do very involved steps to very dramatic music.

2 GET A WHIFF OF SEALS
Mar del Plata

Hold your nose when you visit the colonies of seals or sea lions near this beach resort. The smell is strong, but the animals are fun to watch.

Globetrotter Attractions

IGUAZÚ FALLS
The horseshoe-shaped waterfall is really 275 separate ones. They are from 200 to 269 feet (61 to 82 m) high.

LOS GLACIARES NATIONAL PARK
In this park, huge masses of moving ice called glaciers drop icebergs into lakes.

TIERRA DEL FUEGO
This archipelago, or group of islands, is at the extreme southern end of South America. Here, summer days have 17 hours of sunlight.

DIGITAL TRAVELER!
When you meet the gauchos, learn why they use lassos. Take a photo of a gaucho with a lasso or go online to see pictures of gauchos.

5 COOL THINGS TO DO HERE

1 LISTEN FOR GROWLS
Defensores del Chaco National Park

Ride through this national park with a guide. Stay inside the vehicle for safety's sake because jaguars and pumas roam the thorn forest. Look out for tapirs and colorful birds.

2 MILK A COW
Filadelfia

Visit a Mennonite dairy farm. Since they arrived in 1927, a group of Christians called Mennonites have kept their European culture, language, and religion. Their successful dairy farms provide more than half of Paraguay's dairy products.

3 TREK ON THE TRAIN TRACKS
Asunción

Pretend you are riding on the oldest railroad in South America as you visit the Railroad Museum. Wander through restored railroad cars once used for sitting, eating, and sleeping. Check out photos of the trains and railroad tools.

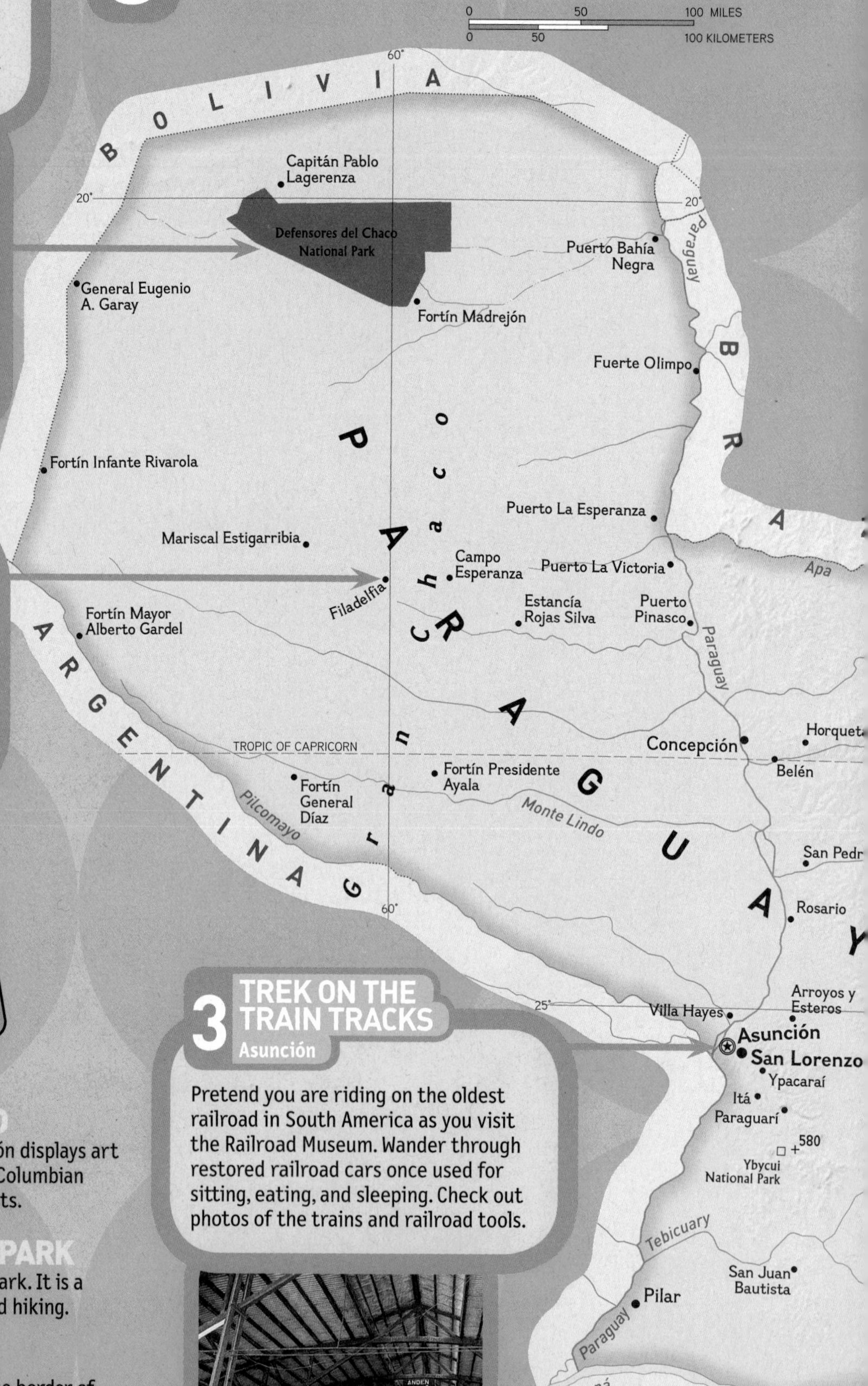

MUSEO DEL BARRO
The Museum of Clay in Asunción displays art made of clay and mud by pre-Columbian people and modern local artists.

YBYCUI NATIONAL PARK
This rain forest is a national park. It is a favorite place for camping and hiking.

ITAIPÚ DAM
This hydroelectric dam is on the border of Paraguay and Brazil and provides power to both countries. It took engineers almost 20 years to plan and build it, then move a river. Today, it is called a Wonder of the Modern World.

NATIONAL BIRD: bare-throated bellbird

NATIONAL FLOWER: mburucuya

NATIONAL MAMMAL: Pampas fox

PARAGUAY

A Country of CONTRAST

5 TRY AN ANIMAL MASK
Hernandarias

Discover Paraguay's cultural heritage at the Guaraní Museum. Examine the animal masks worn by the Guaraní people. Learn about their land, life, and language.

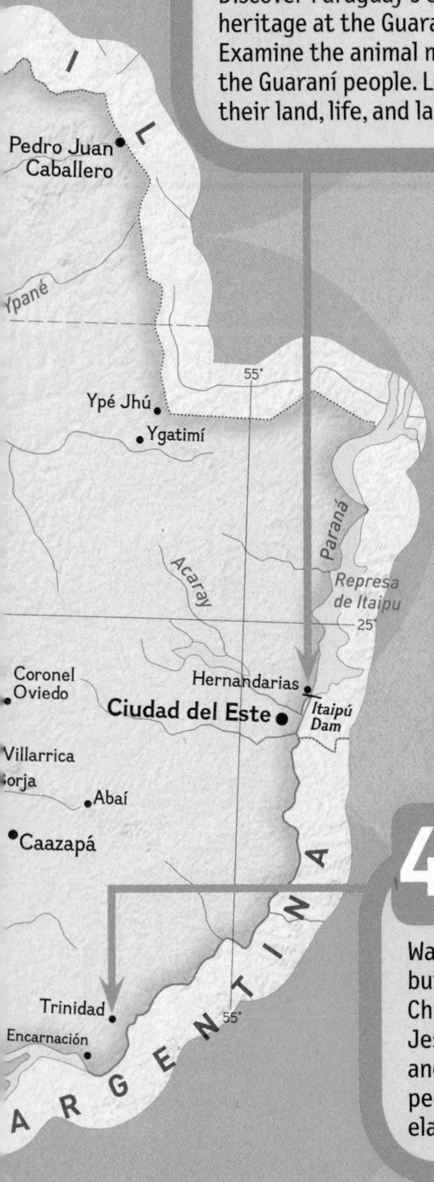

Paraguay is near the center of South America, with no sea-coast. Yet ships can travel on the Paraguay River right to the nation's capital, Asunción. The river splits Paraguay into two regions. To the east are ranchland, farms, and forest. To the west lies the hot, barren Chaco lowlands, with scrub and salt marshes. Don't miss the Itaipú Dam on the Paraná River, one of the world's biggest hydroelectric power plants.

4 ROCK ON AT RUINS
Trinidad

Wander in the ruins of these buildings that were part of a Christian religious community. Jesuits built them in the 1600s and 1700s to educate the local people. Made of stone, some are elaborately decorated.

ID CARD COUNTRY FACTS

Size: 157,047 sq mi (406,752 sq km)
Population: 6,798,000
Capital: Asunción
Official languages: Spanish and Guaraní
Currency: guarani
Highest point: Cerro Pero, 2,762 ft (842 m)
Life expectancy: 72.0 years

DIGITAL TRAVELER!

Yerba mate is the national drink of Paraguay. Search the Internet to find out what yerba mate is and how the Paraguayans prepare it.

NATIONAL BIRD: southern lapwing

NATIONAL MAMMAL: armadillo

NATIONAL TREE: arbol de Artigas

URUGUAY

Fun to EXPLORE

By South American standards, Uruguay is small and flat—the highest point is only 1,644 feet (513 m). It has a mild climate, and most of the country is grassland, good for ranching and farming. Along the Atlantic Ocean coast are superb beaches, popular with vacationers. Most Uruguayans live along the coastal plain, about a third of them (more than 1 million) in the nation's capital city Montevideo.

Globetrotter Attractions

MONTEVIDEO PORT
The old buildings in Montevideo's Cuidad Vieja are near an important deep-water port. Shoppers explore its nearby traditional marketplace.

S.O.S. RESCATE DE FAUNA
At this animal rescue center in Piriápolis, volunteers help schoolchildren feed rescued penguins, turtles, and dolphins.

PUNTA DEL ESTE
Visitors flock to the beaches of this city during summer. One side of the peninsula has quiet river beaches, while on the other side the Atlantic Ocean beaches are windier and better for surfing.

5 COOL THINGS TO DO HERE

1 POWER UP
Salto

Take a tour of Salto Grande Dam and see the water-driven turbines that produce 65 percent of Uruguay's electricity.

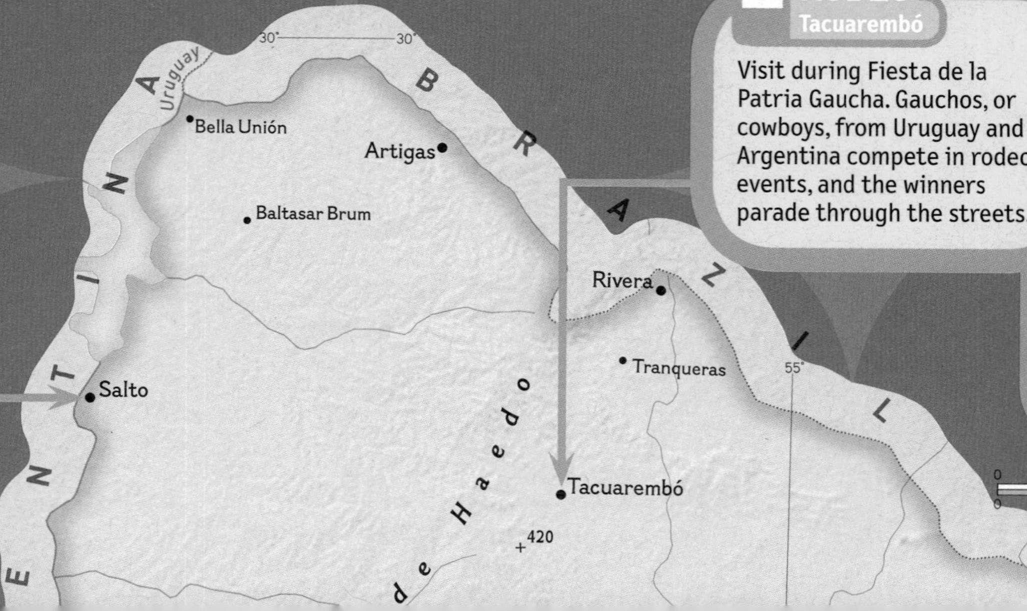

2 RUN OFF TO A RODEO
Tacuarembó

Visit during Fiesta de la Patria Gaucha. Gauchos, or cowboys, from Uruguay and Argentina compete in rodeo events, and the winners parade through the streets.

ID CARD
COUNTRY FACTS

Size: 68,037 sq mi (176,215 sq km)
Population: 3,392,000
Capital: Montevideo
Official language: Spanish
Currency: Uruguayan peso
Highest point: Cerro Catedral, 1,686 ft (514 m)
Life expectancy: 76.0 years

5 WALK ON COBBLESTONES
Colonia del Sacramento

Explore Colonia's historic 17th-century buildings and cobblestone streets. The Portuguese built the oldest buildings, and the Spanish and Uruguayans built the newer ones.

4 HAVE A (SOCCER) BALL
Montevideo

Attend a soccer game at Estadio Centenario. This stadium was built in 1930 for soccer's first World Cup. Uruguay's national soccer team has rarely lost in this stadium.

3 CLIMB ON FINGERS
Playa Brava

Have your picture taken while standing on the giant hand that rises from the sands of Playa Brava. Examine the graffiti that covers it.

DIGITAL TRAVELER!
What kind of food will you eat in Uruguay? Do some online research and pick out some meals you'd like to try.

EUROPE

Mixed and Sweeping LANDSCAPES

Europe's 47 countries range in size from the largest in the world, Russia, to the smallest, Vatican City. This continent is linked to Asia, lies close to Africa, and has a central landmass that is bordered by islands. Europe's Alps Mountains are famous for hiking and winter sports. Its mighty rivers have created important transportation routes, and its sweeping plains provide fertile farmland.

Neuschwanstein Castle in Germany is one of the most popular of the many castles in Europe. Throughout history, European kings, queens, knights, and lords built strongholds or grand houses to secure their territories and house their large families and servants.

EUROPE

Bustling Cities and Serene COUNTRYSIDE

Europe is home to the 0° meridian—a line on maps from which all time zones are measured. To the left of Greenwich, England—the compass direction west—clocks are set back, to the right (that is east) clocks are set forward. Europe's history includes the Ancient Greek and Roman empires, the Medieval Age of knights, castles, kings, and queens, the Industrial Revolution, and world empires.

THE NORTH

This area includes Scandinavia (Norway, Sweden, Finland, and Denmark) and the Baltic countries (Estonia, Latvia, and Lithuania).

AUNT BERTHA'S TRAVEL TIPS

IT'S ALL FOREIGN

Every country in Europe has its own language. Changing from one language to another may get your tongue in a twist!

GETTING AROUND

Public transportation is BIG in Europe. Experience European life by traveling on its buses, trains, subways, canal boats, ferries, and cable cars.

TASTY MEALS

Almost every European country has a favorite dish. Find out in which country you should try fish and chips, paella, croque-monsieur, pizza, bratwurst, smorgasbord, kebabs, borscht, strudel, and Chicken Kiev.

BIG ISLANDS

Iceland, Ireland, and Britain are islands in northwest Europe.

WESTERN EUROPE

The Iberian Peninsula (mainly Portugal and Spain), France, the Alps Mountain countries, and the lowlands of the north make up Western Europe.

EUROPEAN RUSSIA

The Ural Mountains split Russia between two continents, Europe and Asia. This European section has Europe's longest river, highest mountain, and biggest city.

EASTERN EUROPE

Once part of the Soviet Union, this region stretches from the Baltic Sea southeast to the Black Sea. All but Hungary and Moldova share Slavic languages, customs, and traditions.

SOUTHEAST EUROPE

The countries of this region are centered on the Balkan Mountains and lie between the Adriatic, Aegean, and Black seas.

CITYSCAPE
Paris

Major cities in Europe, such as Paris, France, are big, modern, traffic-filled, and bustling with people from all over the world speaking many different languages.

LEISURE TIME
Spain

People from across Europe spend their vacations on the coast of the Mediterranean Sea at resorts such as Salou.

NATIONAL BIRD: gyrfalcon

NATIONAL FLOWER: mountain avens

NATIONAL MAMMAL: Arctic fox

ICELAND

Land of Ice and FIRE

Hike across Iceland to see snowfields, geysers, glaciers, and waterfalls. Smoking volcanoes sometimes erupt! People bathe in pools heated by hot springs, but it's freezing in winter, and there is little farming because of the poor soil and harsh weather. Most Icelanders work in industry, commerce, tourism, and fishing. Fleets from Iceland fish in the Atlantic Ocean. The capital Reykjavík is a modern city, with links to Iceland's Viking history.

5 COOL THINGS TO DO HERE

1 GAZE AT A GEYSER

Selfoss

Watch the beautiful Skrokkur geyser erupt every four to eight minutes. A bubble of hot, often boiling, water is forced up from underground. When it becomes steam, stand back as the steam and boiling water can shoot 131 feet (40 m) into the air.

EYJAFJALLAJÖKULL VOLCANO

Its eruption in 2010 stopped European air traffic. It is one of 11 active volcanoes in Iceland that have erupted since 1900.

BLUE LAGOON

People visit this spa because the mud and water from a nearby geothermal power plant are warm and rejuvenating.

GOLDEN FALLS

Gullfoss's water looks golden as it makes a steep drop over stone steps and then disappears into a crevice.

ID CARD COUNTRY FACTS

Size: 39,768 sq mi (103,000 sq km)
Population: 323,000
Capital: Reykjavík
Official language: Icelandic
Currency: Icelandic krona
Highest point: Hvannadalshnúkur, 6,923 ft (2,110 m)
Life expectancy: 82.0 years

DIGITAL TRAVELER!
Iceland is a wonderland of geysers and glaciers. Start a travel journal. Look up the definitions of "geyser" and "glacier" and put them in your journal. Take or find photographs of geysers and glaciers, and use them as illustrations.

2 WATCH WHALES
Húsavík

Climb aboard a ship to go whale watching. More than 23 different types of whales live near Iceland. The best time to see them is from May to September.

3 SAIL BY PUFFINS
Lundey Island

Speed over to Lundey, or Puffin, Island. Spot large colonies of puffins living on the cliffs. Catch a glimpse of their colorful beaks as they fly or swim by.

4 CLIMB A WATERFALL TRAIL
Skogafoss

Hike this trail from the base to the top of Skogafoss waterfall, one of the highest in Iceland. Once there, you may see a rainbow! Locate even more waterfalls farther along the river.

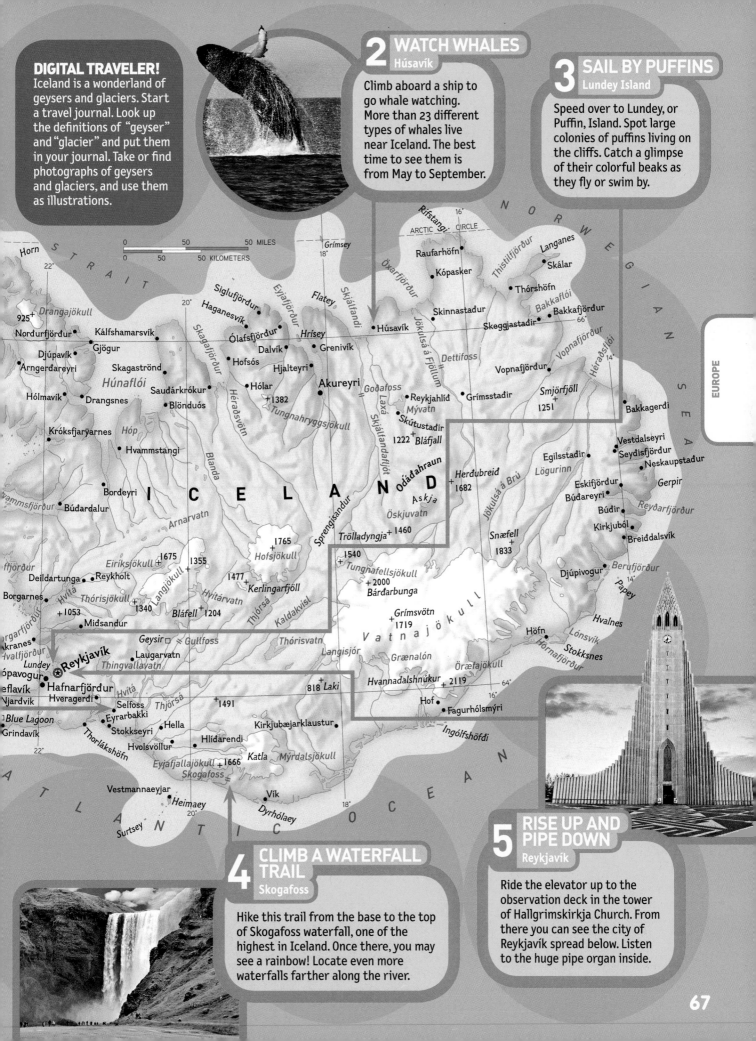

5 RISE UP AND PIPE DOWN
Reykjavík

Ride the elevator up to the observation deck in the tower of Hallgrimskirkja Church. From there you can see the city of Reykjavík spread below. Listen to the huge pipe organ inside.

5 COOL THINGS TO DO HERE

1 STEP INTO LEGOLAND®
Billund

Explore buildings made of 60 million Lego® bricks. Ride a dragon roller coaster and Lego boats. Swim in Pirate Lagoon or go on an African safari. Watch an exciting 4-D movie with lights, smoke, wind, and even rain.

2 SKIP ACROSS SHIFTING SAND
Skagen

Place one foot in the North Sea and the other in the Baltic Sea. Stay out of the way of the wandering sand dunes for these hills of sand cover anything in their path. Every year they move about 49 feet (15 m).

3 WAKE UP ZOO ANIMALS
Odense

Feed the giraffe before the Odense Zoo opens. Then visit the manatees, zebras, and lions. At the end of the day, help clean the cages before the animals say good night.

4 MARCH BEHIND GUARDS
Copenhagen

Follow the Danish Royal Guard marching through Copenhagen's streets. They're protecting the royal family's winter home, Amalienborg Palace.

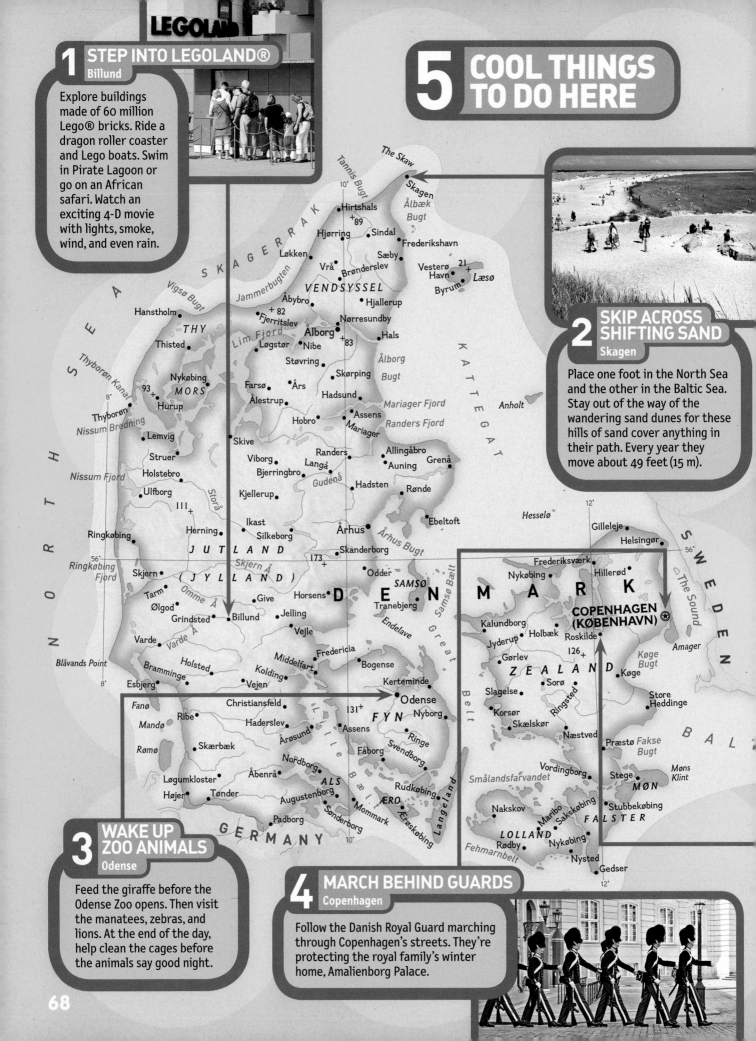

NATIONAL BIRD: mute swan

NATIONAL FLOWER: daisy

NATIONAL MAMMAL: lion

DENMARK

Land of FAIRY TALES

Denmark has more than 400 islands, some close together, others way out in the Atlantic Ocean. Even farther west is the vast Arctic island of Greenland, a part of Denmark but self-governing. The largest area of mainland Denmark is Jutland, a peninsula jutting out from Germany. Denmark is famed for farming, fishing, and fairy tales. In Copenhagen, see a mermaid based on a fairy tale by a famous storyteller.

EUROPE

ID CARD COUNTRY FACTS

Size: 16,638 sq mi (43,094 sq km)
Population: 5,613,000
Capital: Copenhagen
Official language: Danish
Currency: Danish krone
Highest point: Mollehoj/Ejer Bavnehoj, 561 ft (171 m)
Life expectancy: 80.0 years

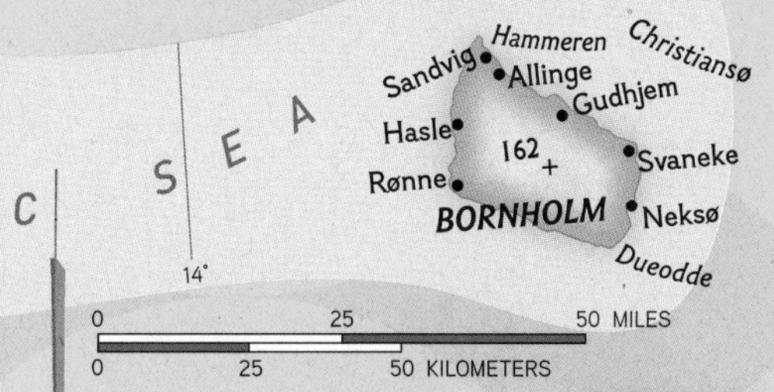

5 BE A VIKING FOR A DAY
Roskilde

Visit the 1,000-year-old Viking ships found in Roskilde Fjord. Learn about the Vikings, their culture, and how they made these ships. Dress in Viking costumes and climb onto the modern copies of a Viking cargo ship and a Viking warship.

ROSENBORG CASTLE
Once a royal summer house, this castle in Copenhagen now houses Denmark's crown jewels.

TIVOLI GARDENS
Copenhagen's historic amusement park has something for everyone: exciting rides, music and dance concerts, plays and musicals, and fireworks at night.

FAROE ISLANDS
Halfway between Norway and Iceland, these Danish islands are remote and beautiful. People living there depend on fishing, sheep, and tourists for their livelihoods.

DIGITAL TRAVELER!
A Little Mermaid statue in Denmark celebrates Hans Christian Andersen, the Danish author of the story and other fairy tales. Go online to find out what other stories he wrote.

NATIONAL TREE: Norway spruce

NATIONAL FLOWER: saxifrage

NATIONAL MAMMAL: lemming

NORWAY

Land of the MIDNIGHT SUN

Boats are the best way to explore Norway's long, rugged coast, with its fjords, cliffs, and waterfalls. This land of mountains and forests boasts Europe's largest glacier, but the climate is surprisingly mild until you head north inside the Arctic Circle, where the midsummer sun shines at midnight. You may even see polar bears there! Offshore oil and gas are major sources of income. In Oslo, the capital, Norway's maritime history is honored by statues, monuments, and ship museums.

Globetrotter Attractions

JOSTEDALSBREEN
This glacier is the largest in Europe. The moving mass of ice is about the size of Cape Cod. Hike on the surface of the glacier or raft in its melted waters.

PULPIT ROCK
The top of this rock has a view of Lysefjord and the cruise ships that sail in it.

GEIRANGERFJORD
Cruises and kayaks are a good way to see the waterfalls, mountains, farms, and villages in this protected area.

ID CARD COUNTRY FACTS

Size: 125,020 sq mi (323,802 sq km)
Population: 5,084,000
Capital: Oslo
Official language: Norwegian
Currency: Norwegian krone
Highest point: Galdhøpiggen, 8,100 ft (2,469 m)
Life expectancy: 81.0 years

5 COOL THINGS TO DO HERE

1 LIGHT UP THE NIGHT SKY
Tromsø

Dress warm in this city known as the "Gateway to the Arctic." Try to catch a view of the northern lights—bands of color that dance across the sky. Video the show if you can.

DIGITAL TRAVELER!
The midnight sun occurs here at the start of the Arctic summer. The sky never gets completely dark at night at this time of year. Use the Internet to find photographs of the midnight sun.

2 GO ISLAND HOPPING
Geiranger

Take a journey on one of the ferry boats that regularly sail far north along the coast. The boats stop at islands and small ports deep within fjords.

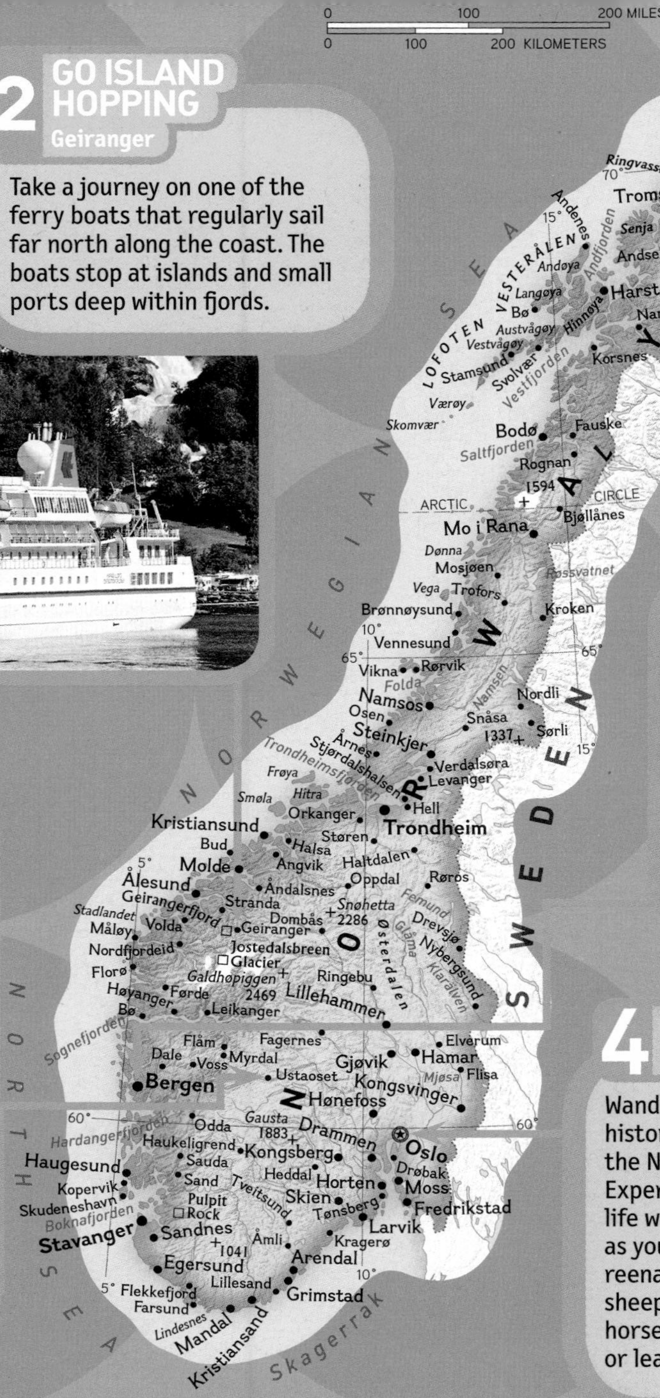

3 RIDE A TRAIN
Bergen

Enjoy the scenery of the high plateau between Oslo and Bergen. Take a side trip on the steep Flåm Railway. Watch for tunnels, deep ravines, and beautiful waterfalls along the way.

5 SHOUT MUSH!
Ustaoset

Sit in a dogsled behind a team of hardy dogs. When you call "Mush!" the dogs will pull the sled through thick snow.

4 TIME TRAVEL
Oslo

Wander through the historic buildings of the Norse Folk Museum. Experience what farm life was like in the past as you watch people reenact shearing sheep. Then ride in a horse-drawn carriage, or learn folk dancing.

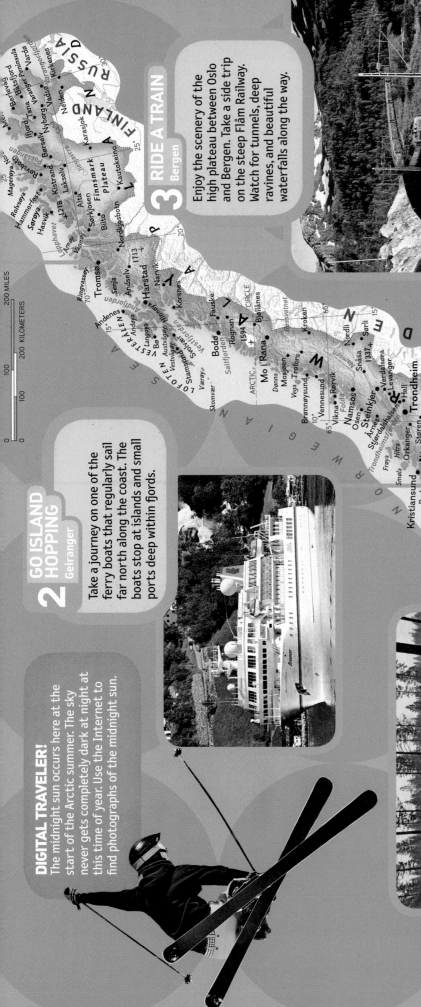

NATIONAL BIRD: blackbird

NATIONAL TREE: birch

NATIONAL MAMMAL: elk

SWEDEN

A Natural WONDERLAND

Similar to its Scandinavian neighbors Norway and Finland, Sweden has forests, lakes, mountains, and more islands than you can see in one trip. Lake Vänern is Europe's third largest lake, and in the far north is Lapland, a winter wonderland where nomads herd reindeer. Sweden's biggest cities, including Malmö and the capital Stockholm, are toward the south of this Scandinavian country that extends north–south more than 950 miles (1,529 km).

ID CARD COUNTRY FACTS

Size: 173,859 sq mi (450,295 sq km)
Population: 9,592,000
Capital: Stockholm
Official language: Swedish
Currency: Swedish krona
Highest point: Kebnekaise, 6,909 ft (2,106 m)
Life expectancy: 82.0 years

DIGITAL TRAVELER!
In delis, cafés, and restaurants, look out for smorgasbord—a table of open-faced sandwiches topped with smoked fish, cheese, or sliced meat. Make a mouth-watering photo collection of all the varieties you see.

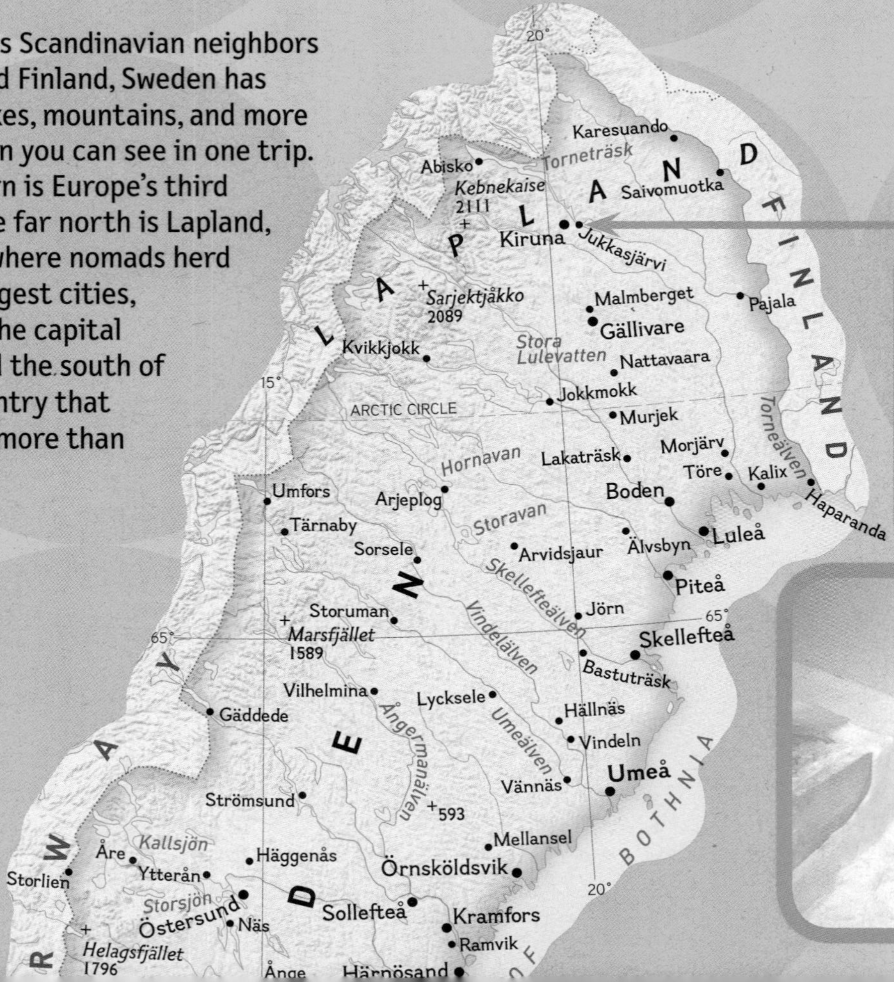

1 STAY IN AN ICE HOTEL
Jukkasjärvi

Sleep in a room and on a bed both built of ice. Every winter, artists use river water to create beautiful rooms, amazing statues, and even furniture. Then it all melts away when the temperatures rise in spring.

5 COOL THINGS TO DO HERE

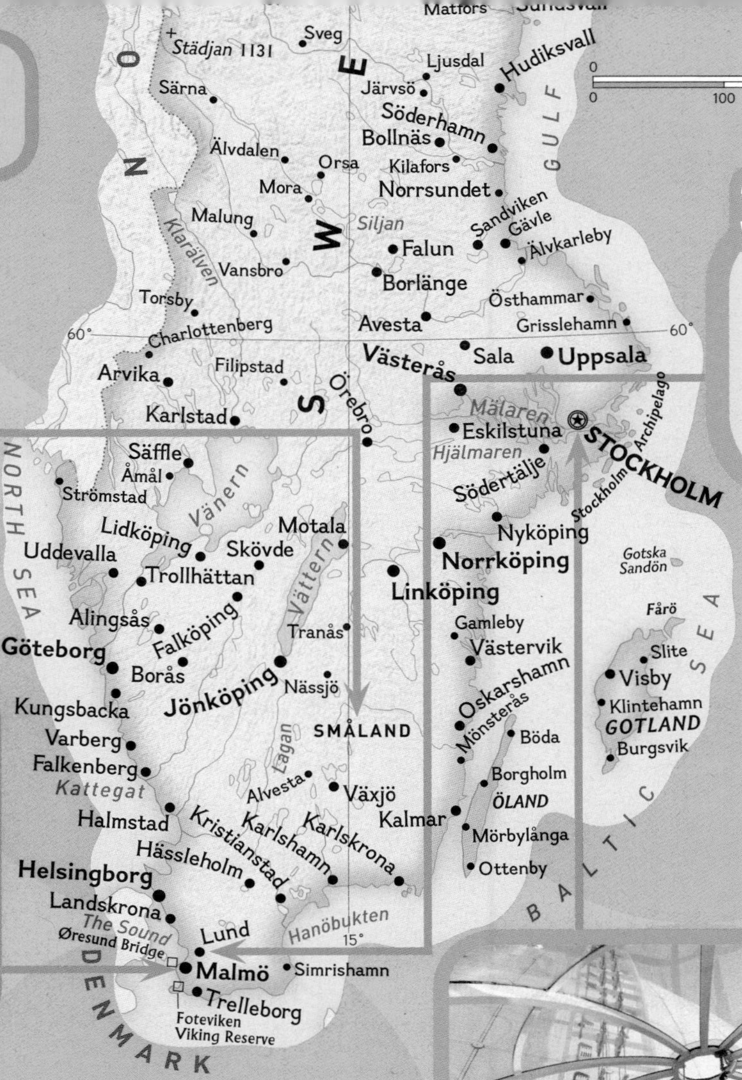

2 DON'T BREAK IT!
Småland

This region is called the Kingdom of Crystal because handblown glass has been made here since 1742. When you're visiting, watch the hot liquid sand as it's blown into a glass bowl. Then check out local crystalware.

3 TELL TIME, BIG TIME
Lund

Hear the organ music as it rolls from Lund's cathedral clock that was made in 1424. Twice a day, watch the six wooden figures move together with the music. This unique clock spent almost 90 years in storage before it was restored.

4 CYCLE CITY STREETS
Malmö

Cycle along special paths made so cyclists can travel safely and quickly. This city has worked hard to increase cycle traffic and decrease car travel. Malmö specializes in modern city planning for a better environment.

5 HAVE A (GLASS) BALL
Stockholm

Ride SkyView's glass spheres to the top of this Stockholm arena called the Ericsson Globe. Then view the city from above. Watch a sports event or hear a concert in this, the world's largest spherical building.

FOTEVIKEN VIKING RESERVE

Medieval Viking reenactors show visitors how they do their daily chores at this living museum. They even built a medieval cog ship.

ØRESUND BRIDGE

This almost 10-mile (16-km) ride goes between Sweden and Denmark. It is part bridge, part tunnel, and carries both a road and railroad.

STOCKHOLM ARCHIPELAGO

Ferries regularly go from island to island. See as many of the 30,000 islands as you can!

5 COOL THINGS TO DO HERE

1 ESCAPE TO A LAKESIDE CABIN
Suonenjoki

Sleep peacefully in a lakeside cabin, but have fun at the town's Strawberry Carnival. Find a lake district town that has a sauna. Enjoy the heat in a steamy, smoky room with friends. When it gets too hot, jump into the lake or roll in the snow.

2 RIDE A REINDEER SLEIGH
Lapland

Ride in a sleigh pulled by a reindeer and glide through the quiet, snowy forest. Watch for more reindeer out in the wild or feeding by the road.

3 GLOW IN THE DARK
Kokkola

Stare up at Tankar Lighthouse. This classic lighthouse, built in 1889, still guides ships along the Kokkola coast. Walk along the island's nature trail and visit its wooden church.

4 STEP INTO A STORYBOOK
Naantali

Admire Finnish children's storybook characters as they come to life. Wander around with them and join in the park's activities. Watch a play, do a craft activity, or walk through the witch's labyrinth.

5 SPEND A DAY WITH A KNIGHT
Savonlinna

Explore Olavinlinna Castle, a fortress built in the late 1500s. Hear the legend about the black ram that saved the castle by scaring away the enemy.

NATIONAL BIRD: whooper swan

NATIONAL FLOWER: lily of the valley

NATIONAL MAMMAL: reindeer

FINLAND

Land of Thousands of LAKES

In this country of many lakes, forests cover 70 percent of the land, and lumber is a major product. The larger lakes, and Finland's main cities, are in the south. In the far north is Lapland, a region shared with Sweden and Norway where, in summer, daylight lasts almost 24 hours. Winters are cold and dark, yet the spring thaw sees the return of migrant birds and forest floors covered in flowers such as lily of the valley.

ID CARD
COUNTRY FACTS

Size: 130,558 sq mi (338,145 sq km)
Population: 5,440,000
Capital: Helsinki
Official language: Finnish
Currency: euro
Highest point: Haltiatunturi, 4,357 ft (1,328 m)
Life expectancy: 81.0 years

DIGITAL TRAVELER!
The cloudberry is called Finland's Favorite Fruit. Search the Internet and find three facts about the cloudberry. For example, where does it grow? When does it grow? What can you do with it?

OULANKA NATIONAL PARK
This park is close to the Arctic Circle and borders a Russian national park. Plants and animals not usually found this far north live here because of the park's fertile soil and mild climate.

FORTRESS OF SUOMENLINNA
This Helsinki historic fort covers three islands. People live behind its thick, strong walls, as they have for hundreds of years.

ÅLAND ISLANDS
People live on 60 of the 6,500 or more islands in this area. Many are just small rocky spots. Here, people have their own government and speak Swedish, not Finnish.

NATIONAL BIRD: golden eagle

NATIONAL FLOWER: cornflower

NATIONAL TREE: oak

GERMANY

Peaks, Rivers, and FORESTS

Much is modern in Germany, the powerhouse of Western Europe's industry and economy. Germany was divided after World War II, when fighting devastated historic cities such as Berlin, Munich, and Hamburg. East and West Germany were reunited in 1990. Remains of the old Germany can still be seen today, with fairy-tale castles beside the Rhine River, and handsome churches and palaces. Nature is unspoiled in the beautiful Black Forest and in the Bavarian Alps.

3 EAT A FRANKFURTER

Frankfurt am Main

Chomp down on a hot dog in the city where they were first made. Buy one with sauerkraut or potato salad, as many are served on a plate, without a bun.

4 WAKE UP TO SLEEPING BEAUTY

Füssen

Tour the magnificent Neuschwanstein Castle. King Ludwig II planned it as an escape from his stressful duties. It is located in a beautiful mountain setting.

ID CARD COUNTRY FACTS

Size: 137,846 sq mi (357,022 sq km)
Population: 80,572,000
Capital: Berlin
Official language: German
Currency: euro
Highest point: Zugspitze, 9,721 ft (2,963 m)
Life expectancy: 80.0 years

5 COOL THINGS TO DO HERE

1 ENTER A LILLIPUTIAN WORLD
Hamburg

Wander through Miniatur Wunderland, the world's largest model train exhibit. See planes land at the model airport and visit many miniature countries.

DIGITAL TRAVELER!
The long, low dog called a dachshund was first bred in Germany in the 1600s. Its name translates in English to "badger dog." Go online to see pictures and find fun facts about these interesting dogs.

2 DRIVE ON AN AUTOBAHN
Würzburg

Ride along these superhighways. The Autobahns form the oldest and fourth longest network of highways in the world. They were started in the 1930s.

5 STRING ALONG WITH ACTORS
Munich

Applaud the marionettes that perform in this historic theater. Watch a fairy tale, opera, or new play. For almost 100 years, these handcarved wooden puppets have been used to act out stories.

BAVARIAN ALPS
This section of the Central Alps is along the German–Austrian border. Zugspitze, in Germany, is its highest peak.

BLACK FOREST
Mountain peaks, rivers, and forests fill this region. Tourists walk trails, ski, bike, or enjoy the region's natural spas.

BRANDENBURG GATE
After World War II, this gate in Berlin was a symbol of a divided Germany. It was reopened in 1989 before East Germany and West Germany reunited.

NATIONAL BIRD: black eagle

NATIONAL FLOWER: gentian

NATIONAL MAMMAL: brown bear

AUSTRIA

Mountains and MUSIC

Austria, the heart of an empire from the 1400s to 1900s, is a land of mountains and music. It borders seven countries, including Germany, with whom Austrians share a language. Most of Austria is mountainous, with high pastures, valleys, rivers, and several lakes. Winter sports attract many visitors, while others come to enjoy Salzburg's Mozart festival, and to admire palaces and gardens in Austria's capital city, Vienna.

1 GET A TASTE OF SALT

Hallstatt

Ride a train up a nearby mountain to the world's oldest salt mine. Enter the mountain and see the underground lake. Learn about the "white gold" first mined here 5,000 years ago.

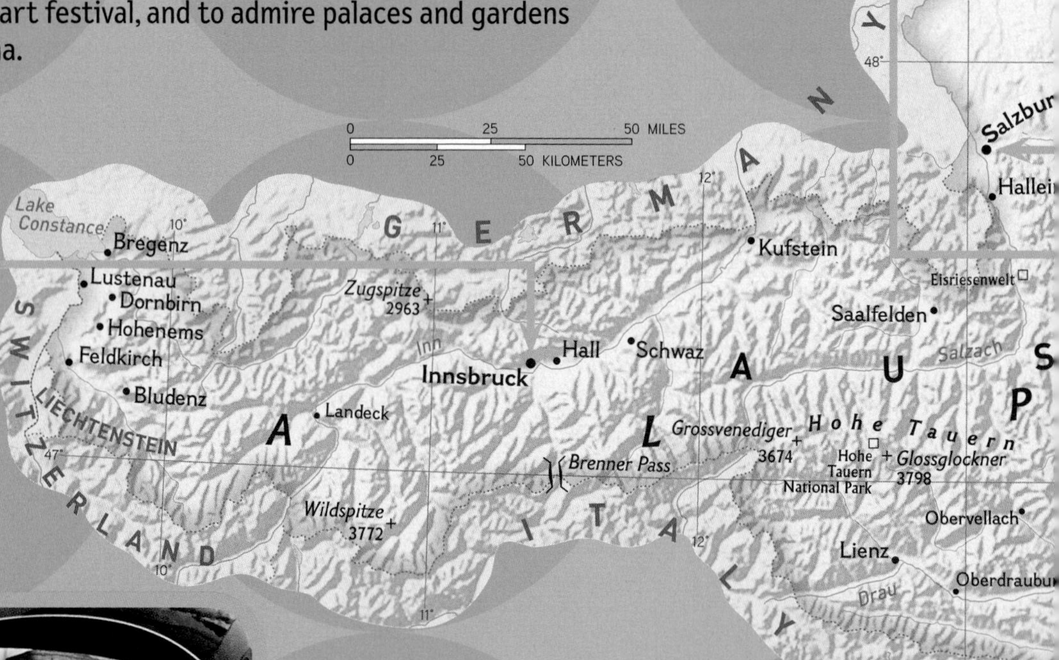

5 ENTER A CRYSTAL WORLD

Innsbruck

Discover 14 underground Chambers of Wonder at Swarovski Crystal Worlds. Watch enormous rooms made of illuminated crystal glass change colors and see crystal animals sparkle.

ID CARD
COUNTRY FACTS

Size: 32,382 sq mi (83,871 sq km)
Population: 8,511,000
Capital: Vienna
Official language: German
Currency: euro
Highest point: Grossglockner, 12,461 ft (3,798 m)
Life expectancy: 81.0 years

5 COOL THINGS TO DO HERE

2 WATCH DANCING HORSES
Vienna

Watch the famed Lipizzaner horses "dance on the air" at Vienna's Spanish Riding School. Attend their morning exercises as they practice their routines to music, or check out a performance. Admire the skill of the riders and horses.

DIGITAL TRAVELER!
The Vienna Boys' Choir is one of the oldest boys' choirs in the world. For nearly 500 years it has been a popular symbol of Austria. Go on the Internet and listen to them sing.

3 TUNE IN TO CLASSICAL MUSIC
Salzburg

Walk through the rooms in two houses: One where Mozart was born and another where he later lived. Learn about Mozart's family and his early music.

EISRIESENWELT ICE CAVES
Called the World of the Ice Giants, these ice caves are the largest in the world. Ice formations change every year, but the average temperature remains below zero Fahrenheit (-18°C).

SCHÖNBRUNN PALACE
This huge palace in Vienna was the home of the Habsburg emperors in the 1700s and 1800s. Its magnificent gardens include a large maze and a labyrinth filled with secrets and games.

HOHE TAUERN NATIONAL PARK
This is the largest nature reserve in the Alps and includes the country's highest peak. Discover glaciers, rock faces, lakes, waterfalls, and pastures.

4 HEAR A DRAGON TALE
Klagenfurt

Take a picture of the statue of the Lindwurm, or winged dragon, in the middle of town. Listen to the legend about a few brave men who killed the dragon to protect the local people and then founded Klagenfurt.

	NATIONAL BIRD:	NATIONAL FLOWER:	NATIONAL MAMMAL:
CZECH REPUBLIC	eagle	*Tilia cordata*	lion
HUNGARY	turul	tulip	vizsla dog
SLOVAKIA	great bustard	rose	Eurasian lynx

CZECH REPUBLIC, HUNGARY, AND SLOVAKIA

Lands of Mountains and Mighty RIVERS

Call the Czech Republic "Czechia" and you'll sound local. Czechs and Slovaks in neighboring Slovakia share a Slavic culture, and were one country (Czechoslovakia) until 1993. The Czech capital Prague and Hungary's capital Budapest are two of Central Europe's most historic cities. In Hungary, visit Lake Balaton, the largest lake in the region and a major tourist destination. Much of the region has a continental climate similar to that of the U.S. Midwest.

5 COOL THINGS TO DO HERE

1 CHECK THE TIME
Prague

Marvel at the performance put on by the Prague Astronomical Clock. Watch statues move on this 600-year-old clock. Check the day, week, month, and year.

2 EXPLORE LABYRINTHS AND MAZES
Lucen

Walk the ten mazes and labyrinths at Castle Lucen in the Czech Republic. Find your way between trees, lights, or rocks.

Globetrotter Attractions

KRKONOŠE MOUNTAINS
This range of mountains is on the border between the Czech Republic and Poland. The range's highest mountain, Mount Snezka, is in the Czech Republic.

KARST CAVES
Belowground, ice caves cover a huge area of the Slovakian region of Slovak Karst. Aboveground, sinkholes, springs, caves, and abysses cover the ground. Careful where you walk!

LAKE BALATON
This lake is known as the "Hungarian Sea." At its many resorts, you can swim, sail, and do other water sports. The surrounding countryside is ideal for cycling and hiking.

DIGITAL TRAVELER!
The capital cities of two of these countries lie on the same major river. What is the name of that river? What two other European capitals also lie on that river? Look at maps and tourist sites on the Internet to find out.

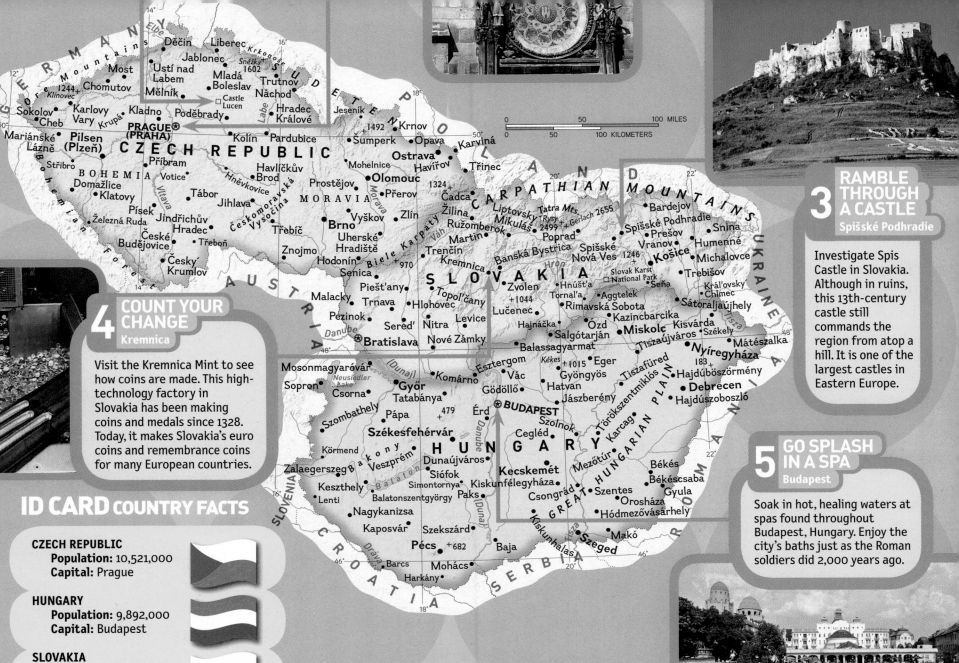

3 RAMBLE THROUGH A CASTLE

Spišské Podhradie

Investigate Spis Castle in Slovakia. Although in ruins, this 13th-century castle still commands the region from atop a hill. It is one of the largest castles in Eastern Europe.

4 COUNT YOUR CHANGE

Kremnica

Visit the Kremnica Mint to see how coins are made. This high-technology factory in Slovakia has been making coins and medals since 1328. Today, it makes Slovakia's euro coins and remembrance coins for many European countries.

5 GO SPLASH IN A SPA

Budapest

Soak in hot, healing waters at spas found throughout Budapest, Hungary. Enjoy the city's baths just as the Roman soldiers did 2,000 years ago.

ID CARD COUNTRY FACTS

CZECH REPUBLIC
Population: 10,521,000
Capital: Prague

HUNGARY
Population: 9,892,000
Capital: Budapest

SLOVAKIA
Population: 5,414,000
Capital: Bratislava

5 COOL THINGS TO DO HERE

1 EXPLORE A GIANT CATHEDRAL
Gdańsk

Feel tiny when you stand in St. Mary's Church, the largest historic brick church in the world. Search its many chapels for tombstones and artwork.

2 MEET WITH A KNIGHT
Malbork

Walk across the drawbridge to meet a knight who's the guide for Malbork Castle. Then start your tour through the largest brick castle in the world and see the armor of many knights.

5 BLAST FROM THE PAST
Cracow

Climb to the top of the highest tower of St. Mary's Basilica from where a trumpeter plays an alarm signal every hour. For 600 years, the trumpet has blared from this location as people look up from Cracow's Grand Square 250 feet (76 m) below.

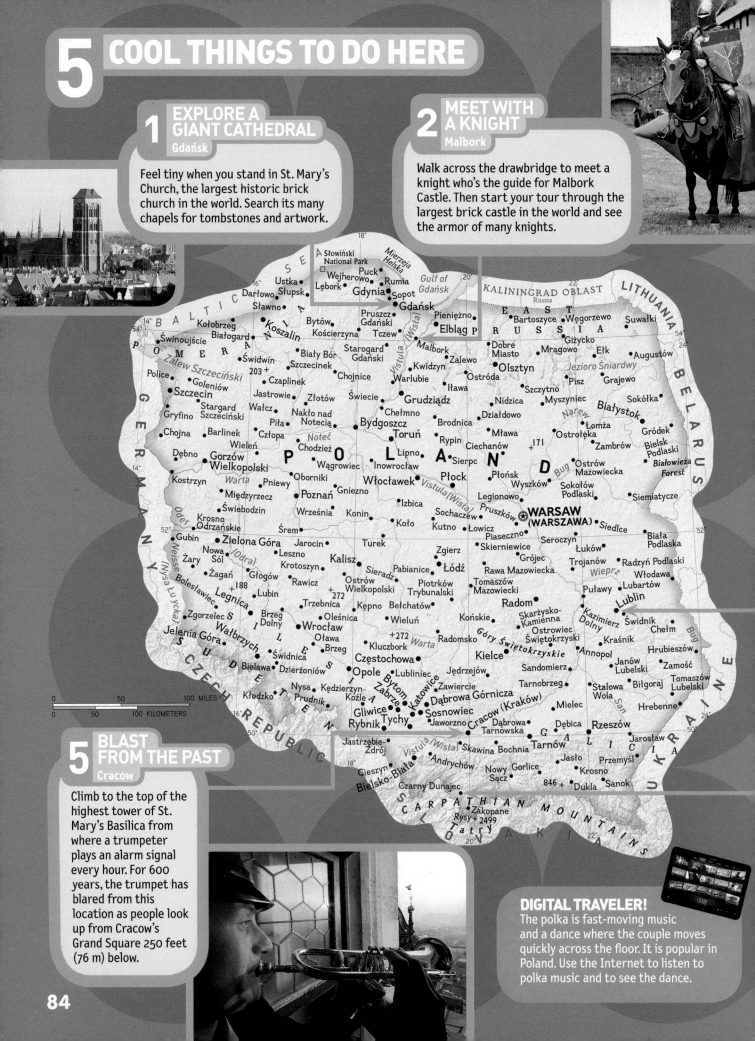

DIGITAL TRAVELER!
The polka is fast-moving music and a dance where the couple moves quickly across the floor. It is popular in Poland. Use the Internet to listen to polka music and to see the dance.

NATIONAL BIRD: white stork

NATIONAL FLOWER: red poppy

NATIONAL MAMMAL: European bison

POLAND

Between Sea and MOUNTAINS

Poland has a Baltic Sea coast and long land borders. Between the Vistula River and the Carpathian Mountains are flat plains and farmland. There are both historic and modern cities, as well as factories and coal mines. Old castles and churches are sprinkled across Poland, and you can see wild bison roaming in an ancient forest. Discover Warsaw, the port of Gdańsk, and the beautiful historic city of Cracow.

3 LEARN ABOUT A WARTIME CAMP
Lublin

Learn about Majdanek, a concentration camp the Nazis built during World War II. Read about the experiences of former prisoners and guards.

4 GO RIPPLE-RAFTING
Czarny Dunajec

Raft down the Dunajec River in Pieniny National Park. Drift through a beautiful river gorge and between huge rock cliffs.

ID CARD
COUNTRY FACTS

Size: 120,728 sq mi (312,685 sq km)
Population: 38,517,000
Capital: Warsaw
Official language: Polish
Currency: zloty
Highest point: Rysy, 8,199 ft (2,499 m)
Life expectancy: 77.0 years

BIALOWIEZA FOREST

The Bialowieza (Białowieża) in northeastern Poland is the last primeval forest in Europe's lowlands. The trees and wildlife are left to grow and die without people's interference. In the 1950s, the European bison was reintroduced to the forest.

GRAND SQUARE, CRACOW

Cracow has one of the largest city squares in Europe. In the Grand Square, people have gathered to shop and celebrate since the 1200s.

SLOWINSKI SAND DUNES

As these sand dunes in Slowinski (Słowiński) National Park in northern Poland shift in the wind, they uncover fossilized tree stumps.

	NATIONAL BIRD:	NATIONAL FLOWER:	NATIONAL MAMMAL:
BELARUS	white stork	wild blue flax	European bison
MOLDOVA	black stork	greater pasque	aurochs
UKRAINE	nightingale	viburnum	particolored bat

EASTERN EUROPE

From Mountains to the BLACK SEA

Eastern Europe is home to two of the continent's largest countries: Ukraine and Belarus. Until the 1990s they and smaller neighbor Moldova were part of the Soviet Union. Belarus is a land full of forests and plains. Ukraine and Moldova have coasts on the Black Sea, into which the Dnieper River flows. Major cities are Kiev (Ukraine), Minsk (Belarus), and Chişinău (Moldova). Ukraine's plains, called steppes, are fertile croplands.

5 COOL THINGS TO DO HERE

1 SPOT THE PUCK
Minsk

Visit the two ice hockey arenas in Minsk, Belarus, host to the 2014 World Hockey Championships. Cheer the home team, the Minsk Dynamo.

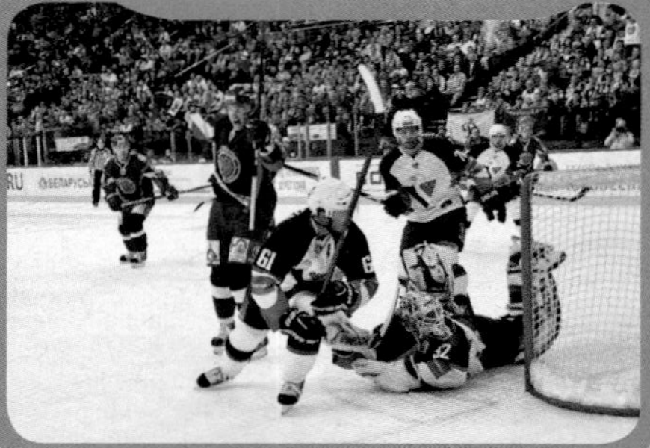

2 WATCH KNIGHTS COMPETE
Mir Castle

Wander through Mir Castle and its park. Then join the festival of medieval culture and wear a knight's armor. Watch archery contests and listen to medieval music, too.

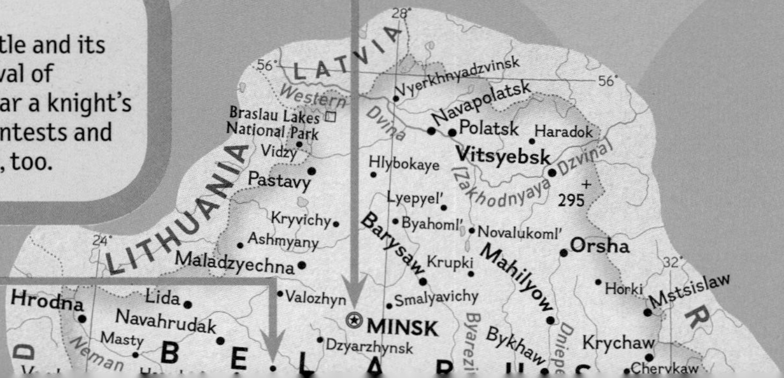

Globetrotter Attractions

BRASLAU LAKES NATIONAL PARK
More than 30 lakes, big and small, are in this park in northwest Belarus, near its border with Lithuania. Search the lakes and pine forests to see elks, lynx, and bears.

BLACK SEA COAST
The Crimea, in the Ukraine, lies along the Black Sea. It is famous for its resorts where you can bathe in mud pools.

CARPATHIAN MOUNTAINS
The Ukraine shares these low mountains with other countries in the region. Tourists hike and bike by forests, farms, and vast meadows.

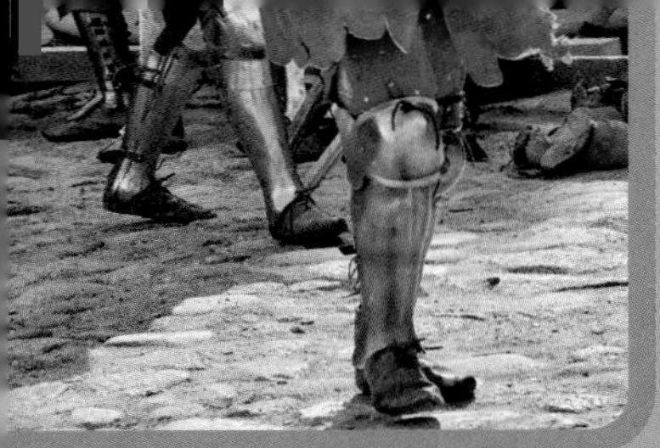

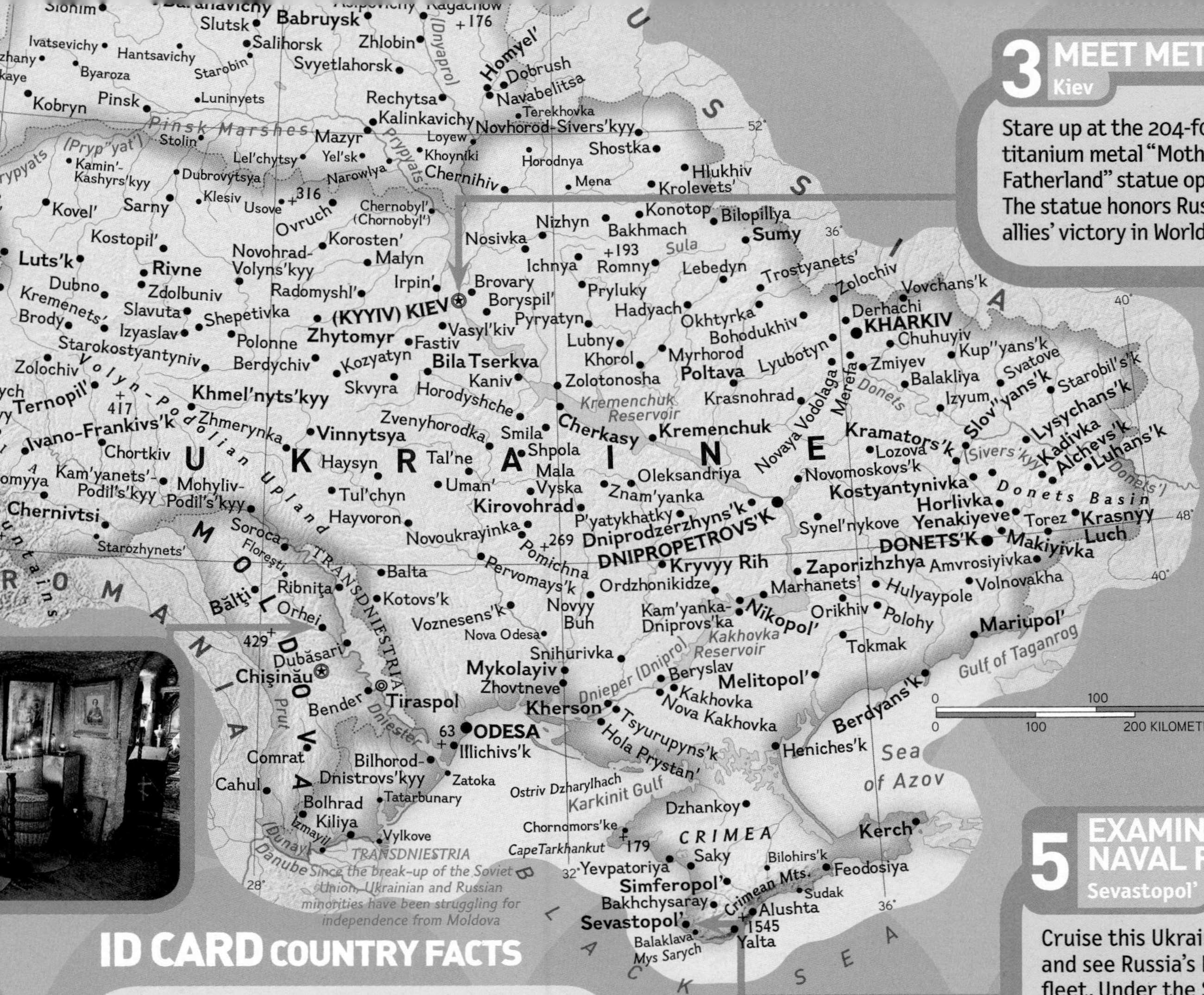

3 MEET METAL MA

Kiev

Stare up at the 204-foot (62-m)-high titanium metal "Mother of the Fatherland" statue opened in 1981. The statue honors Russia and its allies' victory in World War II.

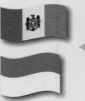

4 ENTER A CAVE MONASTERY

Orhei

Search this cave monastery in wild and remote Moldova. Look down from the cave to the Raut River and follow the paths that lead to other medieval caves.

5 EXAMINE RUSSIA'S NAVAL FLEET

Sevastopol'

Cruise this Ukrainian port and see Russia's Black Sea fleet. Under the Soviet Union the town was closed to visitors, but today tourists can take a harbor tour.

ID CARD COUNTRY FACTS

BELARUS
Population: 9,463,000
Capital: Minsk

MOLDOVA
Population: 4,114,000
Capital: Chișinău

UKRAINE
Population: 45,513,000
Capital: Kiev

DIGITAL TRAVELER!

In 1991, these countries became independent when the Soviet Union broke apart. Make a set of photographs of statues and memorials that celebrate each country's independence.

NATIONAL FLOWER: lavender

NATIONAL TREE: cork oak

NATIONAL MAMMAL: Iberian wolf

PORTUGAL

Cork, Cliffs, and CASTLES

DIGITAL TRAVELER!
Look online for images of two or three Portuguese castles and see if you can re-create them out of craft supplies, or even sand when you're at the beach!

Portugal is Spain's neighbor on the Iberian Peninsula. Along its border with Spain are old fortresses, but the capital Lisbon is a seaport located along the Tagus River. Reminders of a long history linked to sea-voyaging are present all over this city. Western beaches are favored by surfers riding Atlantic waves, and sun-seekers flock to the Algarve region in the south. Portugal is also famous for cork tree bark, which is harvested to make wine stoppers.

ID CARD COUNTRY FACTS

Size: 35,556 sq mi (92,090 sq km)
Population: 10,460,000
Capital: Lisbon
Official language: Portuguese
Currency: euro
Highest point: Ponta do Pico (Azores), 7,713 ft (2,351 m)
Life expectancy: 80.0 years

5 COOL THINGS TO DO HERE

1 STOMP GRAPES
Douro Valley

Participate in the grape harvest in this winemaking region. Pick the grapes and then press the juice out of them by stomping on the fruit in huge vats. Learn how this grape juice is made into a world-famous wine.

2 STAND AMONG EXPLORERS
Lisbon

Explore the Monument to the Discoveries. It honors the explorers who left from Lisbon harbor 500 years ago to explore Asia and the Americas. Enjoy the scenic view of the harbor from its roof.

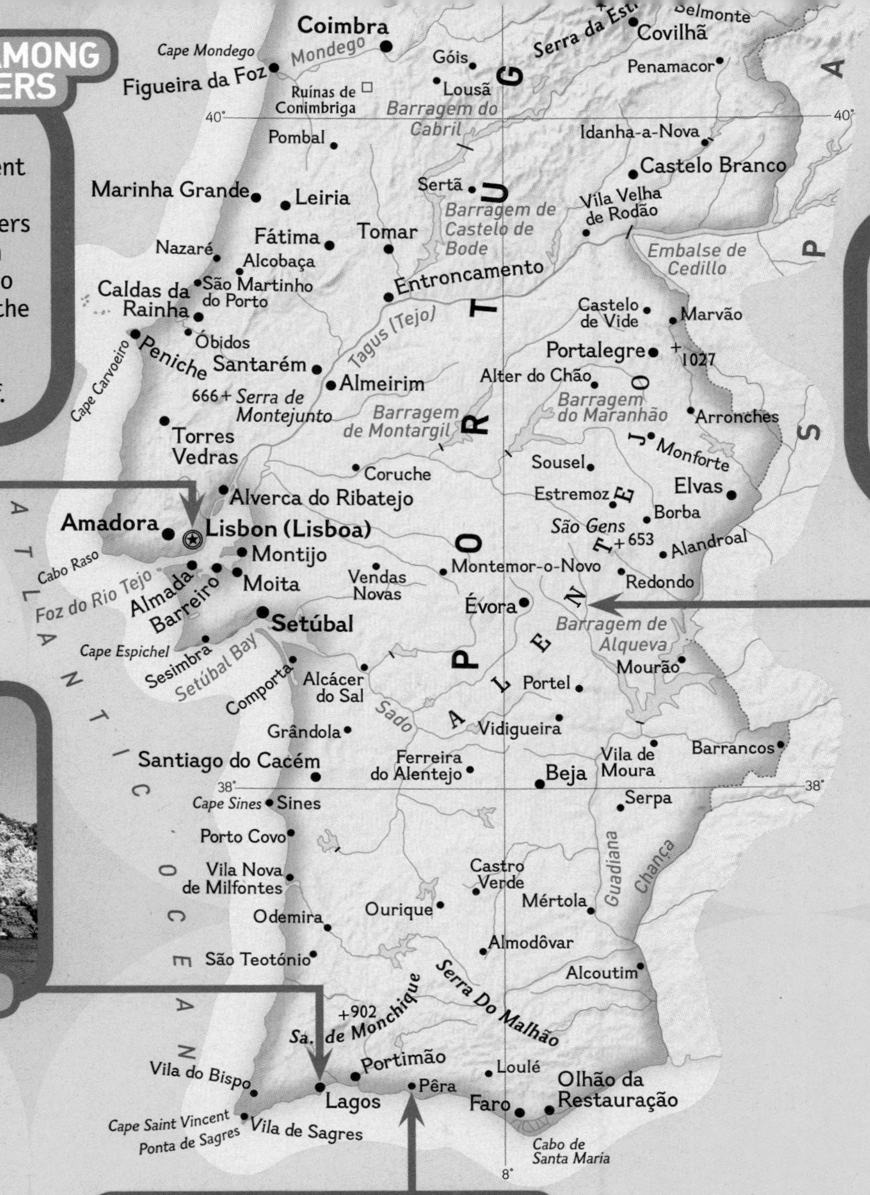

3 TEAR OFF A STRIP
Alentejo

Watch as cork, the bark of the cork oak tree, is stripped from the tree trunks. Cork oak trees live for up to 250 years and the cork is harvested every 9 to 12 years.

4 CRUISE BETWEEN CLIFFS
Lagos

Glide across the water on a fishing boat. Weave between rocks, into caves, and along the water at the bottom of rocky cliffs. Then find a quiet beach where you can relax and paddle in the water.

5 BUILD A SAND CASTLE
Pêra

Create a sand sculpture at Fiesa, a huge sand sculpture festival held each spring. Experts spend weeks making enormous sculptures.

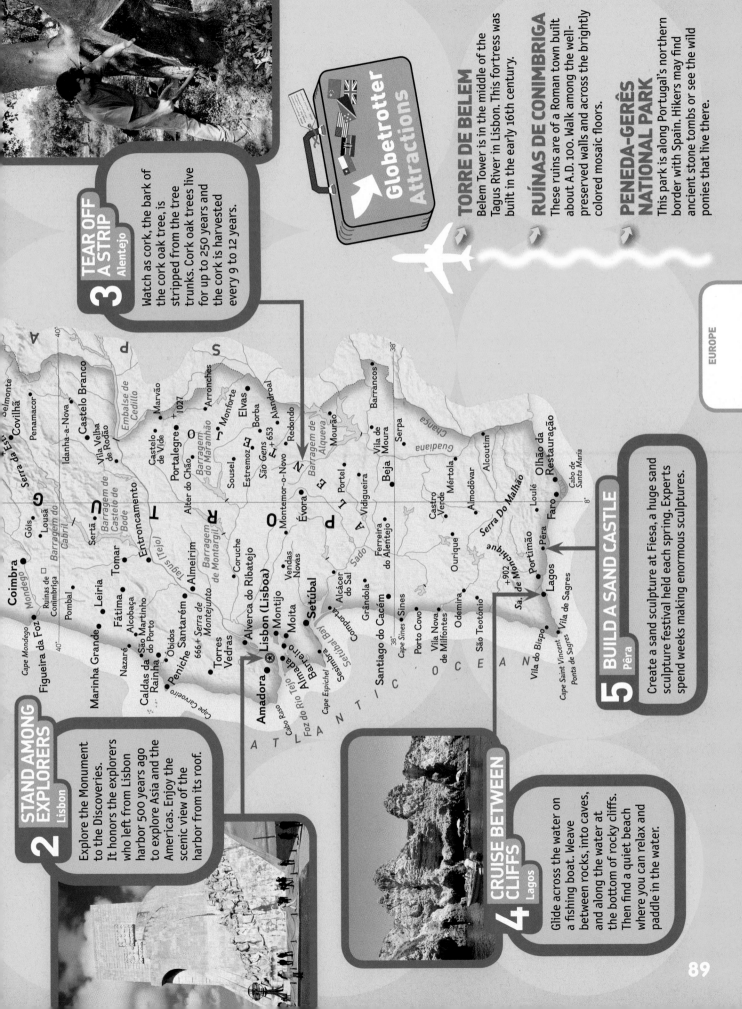

Globetrotter Attractions

TORRE DE BELEM
Belem Tower is in the middle of the Tagus River in Lisbon. This fortress was built in the early 16th century.

RUÍNAS DE CONIMBRIGA
These ruins are of a Roman town built about A.D. 100. Walk among the well-preserved walls and across the brightly colored mosaic floors.

PENEDA-GERÊS NATIONAL PARK
This park is along Portugal's northern border with Spain. Hikers may find ancient stone tombs or see the wild ponies that live there.

	NATIONAL BIRD:	NATIONAL FLOWER:	NATIONAL MAMMAL:
SPAIN	Spanish eagle	red carnation	bull
ANDORRA	lammergeier	violet	boar

SPAIN AND ANDORRA

Beauty, Buildings, and BULLFIGHTS

Landscape and climate in Spain range from the rugged, temperate north to the soft, sandy beaches and sunny Mediterranean weather of the south. There are beautiful cities such as Barcelona, Granada, Toledo, and Madrid with its famous bullfighting ring. Away from the cities, there are traditional and modern farms, as well as tourist hotels and beaches. In the Pyrenees Mountains and landlocked between Spain and France is the tiny country of Andorra.

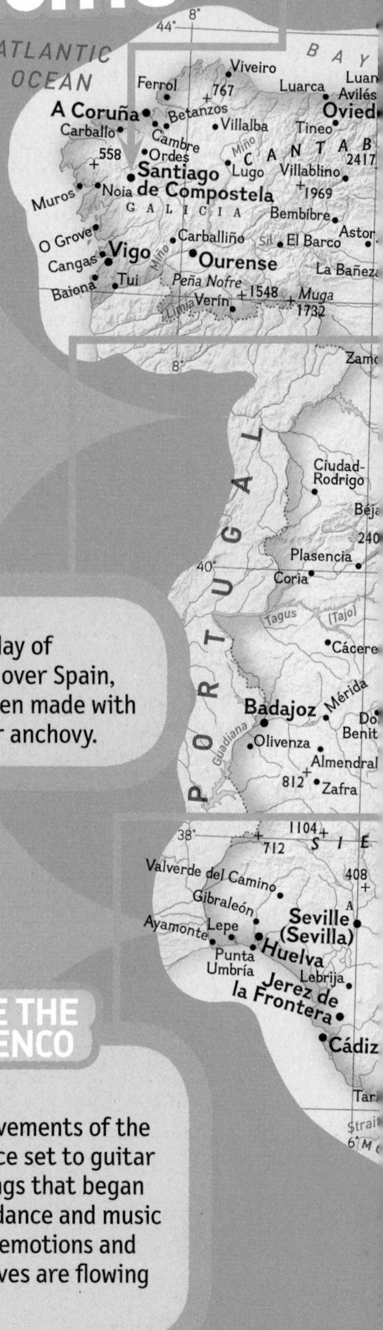

ID CARD COUNTRY FACTS

SPAIN
Population: 46,647,000
Capital: Madrid

ANDORRA
Population: 74,000
Capital: Andorra la Vella

3 TASTE TAPAS
Donostia-San Sebastián

Eat these tasty snacks after a day of sightseeing. Although found all over Spain, tapas in northern Spain are often made with seafood, such as spider crabs or anchovy.

DIGITAL TRAVELER!
Some famous artists came from Spain, such as Pablo Picasso, Salvador Dalí, and Joan Miró. Search the Internet for some paintings by each artist. Pick your favorites and print them out.

4 DANCE THE FLAMENCO
Madrid

Learn the movements of the flamenco dance set to guitar music and songs that began in Spain. The dance and music express deep emotions and the dance moves are flowing and colorful.

5 COOL THINGS TO DO HERE

1 FOLLOW THE SCALLOP SHELLS
Santiago de Compostela

Hike the Way of St. James, a route in northern Spain that Christian pilgrims have walked for more than 1,000 years. It leads to the tomb of St. James at the cathedral in Santiago de Compostela. Scallop shells are used to mark the route.

2 UNLOCK THE SECRET OF THE SEVEN KEYS
Andorra la Vella

Visit the Casa de la Vall in Andorra la Vella. Built as a home, in 1702 it became Andorra's parliament building. Learn how The Cupboard of the Seven Keys got its name.

5 SEARCH AN UNFINISHED CHURCH
Barcelona

This church has been under construction since 1883. Analyze how Antoni Gaudí, the main architect of La Sagrada Familia Church, used nature and religious symbols in his design.

Globetrotter Attractions

THE PYRENEES
These mountains are famous for hiking and winter skiing. They are home to Andorra.

THE ALHAMBRA
It took the Moors more than 130 years to complete this palace and fortress in Granada, Spain. You can visit it today.

CITY OF ARTS AND SCIENCES
Valencia, Spain, drained a river to build this art and science complex. It houses Europe's largest aquarium, a planetarium, and movie theater that shows 3-D movies.

	NATIONAL BIRD:	NATIONAL FLOWER:	NATIONAL MAMMAL:
FRANCE	gallic rooster	iris	European hare
MONACO	peregrine falcon	carnation	European hedgehog

FRANCE AND MONACO

Cafés, Castles, and Coastal BEAUTY

The landscape of France, Western Europe's largest country, is as varied as its food. It has the snowy Alps and Pyrenees, the rugged Atlantic coast and sunny Riviera, ancient volcanoes, and extensive forests. There are beautiful chateaus and vineyards beside the rivers Rhone, Loire, and Seine. Monaco, the world's second-smallest country, is nestled on the French Riviera. It has an area of less than one square mile (2.6 sq km).

1 REFLECT ON ROYALS
Versailles

Pretend to be King Louis XIV as you walk through his Versailles Palace. Kings and queens lived here for more than 100 years. This Hall of Mirrors served as a magnificent setting for lavish parties.

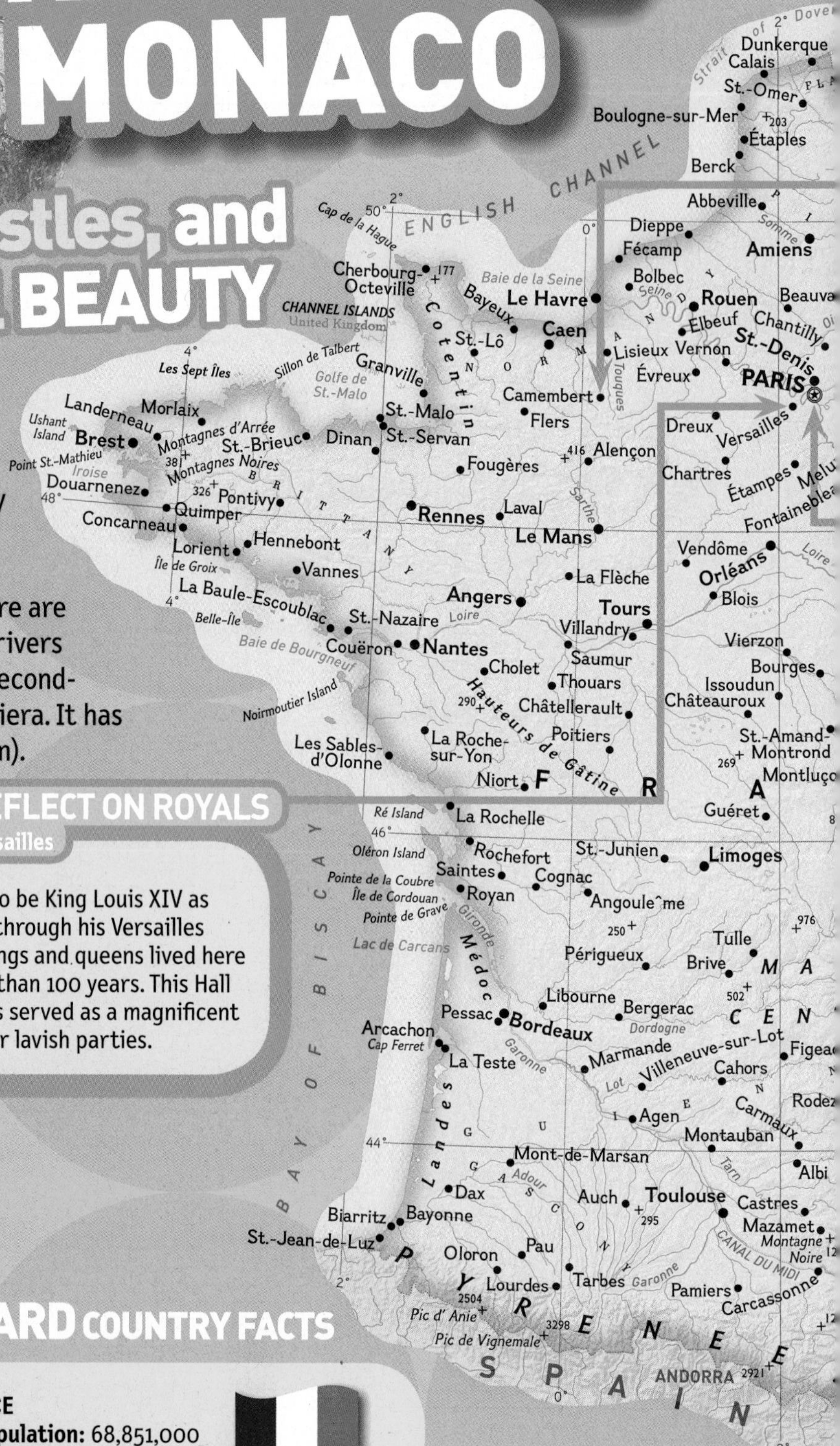

ID CARD COUNTRY FACTS

FRANCE
Population: 68,851,000
Capital: Paris

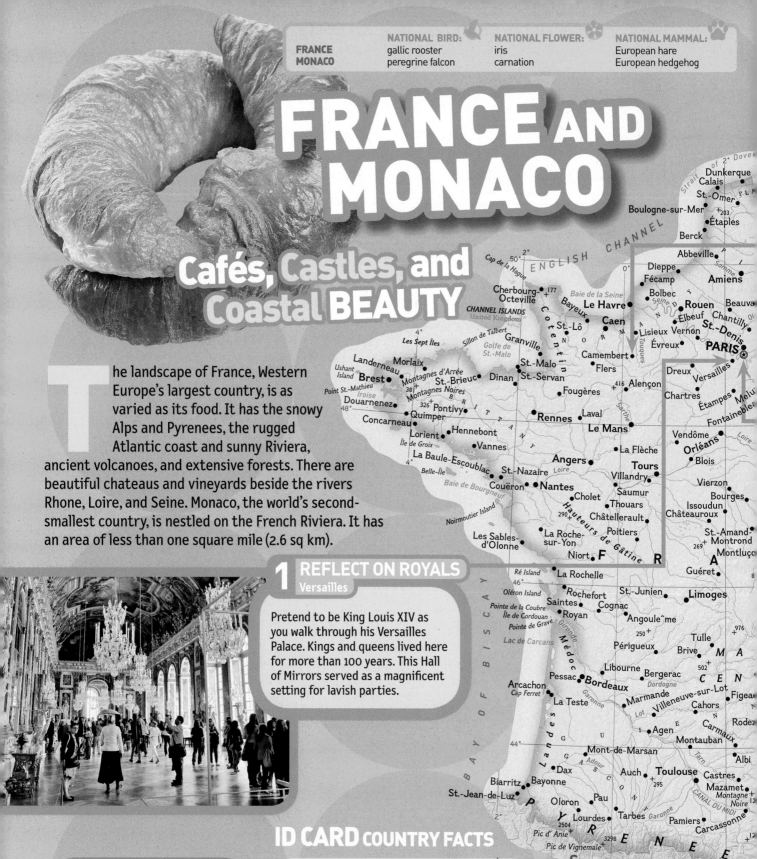

MONACO
Population: 37,000
Capital: Monaco

DIGITAL TRAVELER!
Claude Monet was one of the first Impressionist painters. He was born in Paris and painted French scenes from his home in Giverny. Use the Internet to see examples of his Impressionist art.

5 COOL THINGS TO DO HERE

2 TASTE CHEESE
Camembert Village

Visit a cheese shop and try some Camembert, one of more than 300 kinds of cheese made in France. Stop by the onetime home of Marie Harel, the woman who is believed to have created this creamy treat in 1791.

3 GET A BIRD'S-EYE VIEW
Paris

Climb 704 steps, then take an elevator to the top of the Eiffel Tower. On a clear day, you'll have a panoramic view of the city. The tower is 984 feet (300 m) tall. When it was built in 1889, it was the tallest structure in the world.

4 HEAR THE VA, VA, VROOM
Monte Carlo

Grab a place in the stands to watch the annual Formula One Grand Prix race. Race-car drivers from all over the world zip through Monaco's narrow, curvy streets at speeds of more than 100 mph (161 kph).

THE LOUVRE MUSEUM
This museum in Paris is one of the largest and most visited in the world. You can see famous art, such as Leonardo Da Vinci's painting, the "Mona Lisa," and the Greek statue, "Venus de Milo."

THE PRINCE'S PALACE
This grand castle on the cliffs of Monaco has been in Monaco's royal family since 1341.

CHATEAU VILLANDRY
Many awesome castles dot the Loire Valley. This one has spectacular gardens with a labyrinth, or maze.

5 RIDE THROUGH THE MOUNTAINTOPS
Chamonix-Mont Blanc

Travel across the French Alps in cable cars that transport you from peak to peak. Be sure to take a hike at one of the stops. You can travel in these cable cars all the way to Italy!

See p. 9 for location

5 COOL THINGS TO DO HERE

1 SAIL BY SEALS
Donegal Bay

Take a boat ride on the bay. You'll pass quaint villages, the Bluestack Mountains, and Seal Island where about 200 seals live.

2 EXPLORE A CAVE
Doolin

Put on a hard hat and follow your guide as you descend 120 steps underground into Doolin Cave. The cave was carved by a stream that still flows through it. See the longest free-hanging stalactite found in the Northern Hemisphere. It is 23 feet (7 m) in length.

3 SEARCH A CYBER CASTLE
Limerick

Explore King John's castle. Inside, computer touch screens and 3-D models have been installed to show how the castle survived attacks and warfare.

NATIONAL BIRD: lapwing

NATIONAL FLOWER: shamrock

NATIONAL MAMMAL: Irish wolfhound

IRELAND

The Emerald ISLE

The island of Ireland is shared by the Republic of Ireland and Northern Ireland (part of the United Kingdom). It's known as the Emerald Isle for its lush green pastures. You'll find lakes, called loughs, and mountains dotted with ancient carved stones and prehistoric monuments. There are farms, villages, and Ireland's lively capital city, Dublin. The River Shannon is the longest in the British Isles, at 240 miles (386 km) long.

5 DANCE A JIG
Dublin

First you'll hear fiddles and tin whistles playing lively tunes. Then you'll hear the stamping feet. Join in one of the many Irish dances, including step dancing and the jig. Dance events are held throughout the year at halls, pubs, and clubs.

4 KISS THE BLARNEY STONE
Blarney

Stretch out on the ground and kiss this famous stone (part of Blarney Castle). If you do, legend says that you will always know the right thing to say and have the power to persuade with words.

Globetrotter Attractions

CLIFFS OF MOHER
Sheer cliffs rise 702 feet (214 m) above the churning ocean. A walking trail attracts thousands of tourists.

ROCK OF CASHEL
With its medieval towers and Gothic cathedral, this is one of Ireland's most famous castles. Kings ruled from here for more than 1,000 years. It is located in Tipperary.

NEWGRANGE
These amazingly built tombs and mounds are older than the Egyptian pyramids. The Newgrange temple mound was built more than 5,000 years ago.

ID CARD COUNTRY FACTS

Size: 27,132 sq mi (70,273 sq km)
Population: 4,598,000
Capital: Dublin
Official languages: English and Irish
Currency: euro
Highest point: Carrauntoohil, 3,406 ft (1,038 m)
Life expectancy: 81.0 years

DIGITAL TRAVELER!
Be on the lookout for a Claddagh ring. It will show two hands clasped around a heart with a crown above it. Surf the Internet to find out what the symbol means and how it became popular.

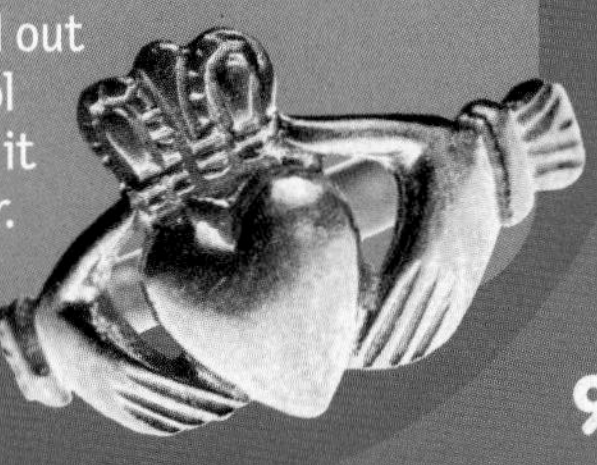

EUROPE

NATIONAL BIRD: robin

NATIONAL TREE: oak

NATIONAL MAMMAL: bulldog

UNITED KINGDOM

Four Nations, One COUNTRY

Four nations make up the United Kingdom: England, Scotland, Wales, and Northern Ireland. Each is represented in the U.K.'s flag and coat-of-arms. The main island, Great Britain, has Scotland's highlands in the north, and more mountains to the west in Wales, while England has lowlands, rolling hills, and a great city, London. Northern Ireland shares a border with Ireland, which is also known as Eire.

Globetrotter Attractions

THE CAIRNGORMS

These eastern Highlands of Scotland are great places for hill walking in summer and skiing in winter.

WHITE CLIFFS OF DOVER

White chalk and black flint give the cliffs their unusual color. They stand at England's closest point to the European mainland.

STONEHENGE

Scientists wonder how in prehistoric times these huge stones near Salisbury, England, were placed in a circle and how some of the huge stones were brought from South Wales, more than 100 miles (160 km) away.

5 COOL THINGS TO DO HERE

1 VISIT GIANT'S LAND

Giant's Causeway

Stand on the cliffs and check out multi-sided stone pillars that look like giant's boots and a giant's harp. Legends say they were once steps for a giant crossing from Northern Ireland to Scotland.

2 ROOT FOR A RUGBY TEAM

Cardiff

Sit in Millennium Stadium and cheer for a Welsh rugby team as it plays an international match. The stadium is the largest in Wales with 74,500 seats.

3 WALK WITH WITCHES

Cornwall

Watch fishing boats come and go through the Cornwall coves, or little inlets. Walk through the narrow village streets. Visit the Witchcraft Museum in Boscastle and the Museum of Smuggling and Fishing in Polperro.

4 BE ON YOUR GUARD

London

At 11:00 in the morning, join the crowd to watch one set of guards replace another in front of Buckingham Palace. The Queen of England lives inside the palace. It has 775 rooms and 240 bedrooms.

5 LISTEN TO BAGPIPES

Edinburgh

See the proud Scottish bagpipe players march by in their plaid kilts at any big event. The sound of bagpipes is like no other instrument. It is the national instrument of Scotland.

ID CARD COUNTRY FACTS

Size: 94,058 sq mi (243,610 sq km)
Population: 64,092,000
Capital: London
Official language: English
Currency: British pound
Highest point: Ben Nevis, 4,409 ft (1,344 m)
Life expectancy: 82.0 years

DIGITAL TRAVELER!

Wizards, dragons, monsters, fantasy and mythical characters are popular in the U.K. Do an Internet search to find out about Nessie, Hogwarts, Y Ddraig Goch, Bilbo Baggins, and Puck.

	NATIONAL BIRD:	NATIONAL FLOWER:	NATIONAL MAMMAL:
BELGIUM	common kestrel	brome	lion
LUXEMBOURG	goldcrest	rose	lion
NETHERLANDS	common spoonbill	tulip	lion

LOW COUNTRIES

The Heart of EUROPE

5 COOL THINGS TO DO HERE

Belgium, the Netherlands, and Luxembourg are known as the Low Countries because they are flat and often below sea level. The Netherlands is famed for flowers, canals, windmills, and farmland. Part of it—known as Holland—is home to Amsterdam with its art museums, and the massive port of Rotterdam. The cities of The Hague (Netherlands), Brussels (Belgium), and Luxembourg (Luxembourg) are the heart of the European Union.

1 CRUISE THE CANALS
Amsterdam

Ride a glass-topped boat through the canals to see some unique sites including Anne Frank's house and the Westerkerk church, with the highest church tower in Amsterdam.

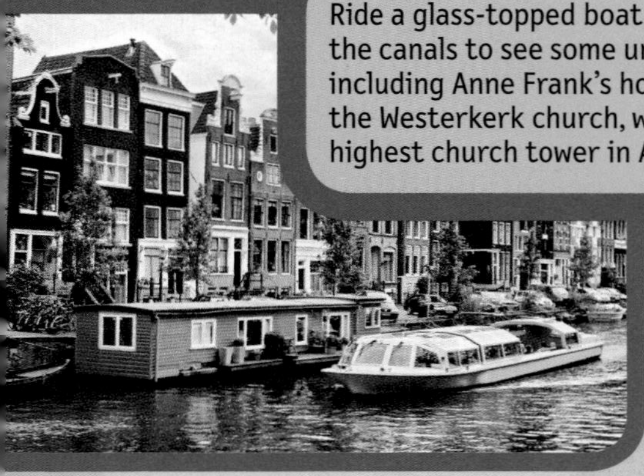

2 STROLL BY WINDMILLS
Zaanstad

Soak up history in the historic village of Zaanse Schans. You'll see windmills, which were once used to power machines that made paint, ground seeds into oil, and sawed lumber.

5 TOUR A TINY COUNTRY
The Hague

Feel like a giant at Madurodam, a minature model of Holland complete with its canals, buildings, and parks.

DIGITAL TRAVELER!

Pierre Marcolini is a world-famous chocolate maker. One of his famous chocolate shops is in Brussels. Use an electronic device to find the location of this shop.

3 SOAR ABOVE THE CITY
Vianden

Sit back and let the chairlift take you 1,476 feet (450 m) above the city. Get a bird's-eye view of city sights and this famous castle where the Counts of Vianden lived 600 years ago.

4 TASTE CHOCOLATE
Brussels

Find out why Belgium is famous for its chocolates. There are excellent chocolate makers in every city. Be sure to try a praline, a chocolate-covered treat with nuts or sweet cream inside.

KEUKENHOF FLOWER GARDEN
More than 7 million tulips, daffodils, and hyacinths fill this garden in Lisse, Netherlands, near Amsterdam, forming what looks like a sea of colors.

GRAND PLACE
The center square in Brussels, Belgium, is surrounded by elegant buildings and statues.

BOCK CASEMATES
This fortress protected Luxembourg against military attacks for many centuries. Its underground passageways had kitchens, horse stables, and sleeping quarters for 1,200 soldiers.

ID CARD COUNTRY FACTS

BELGIUM
Population: 11,164,000
Capital: Brussels

LUXEMBOURG
Population: 543,000
Capital: Luxembourg

NETHERLANDS
Population: 16,798,000
Capital: Amsterdam

	NATIONAL BIRD:	NATIONAL FLOWER:	NATIONAL MAMMAL:
SWITZERLAND	chaffinch	edelweiss	Oberhasli goat
LIECHTENSTEIN	eagle	Alpine rose	fox

SWITZERLAND AND LIECHTENSTEIN

Fresh Air and Fun in the MOUNTAINS

In Switzerland, road and rail tunnels speed visitors on scenic tours through the Alps. Cattle graze in high pastures, tourists flock to ski slopes and to the Cresta Run ice race track in St. Moritz, and experienced climbers tackle peaks such as the Matterhorn. Enjoy a boat trip on Lake Geneva, and explore the cities of Bern, Lausanne, Zurich, and Geneva. Little Liechtenstein is famous for castles, winter sports, and the production of false teeth and textiles.

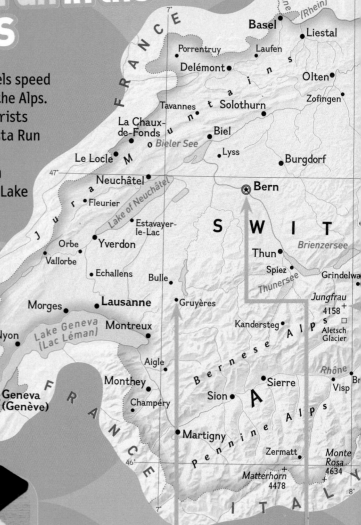

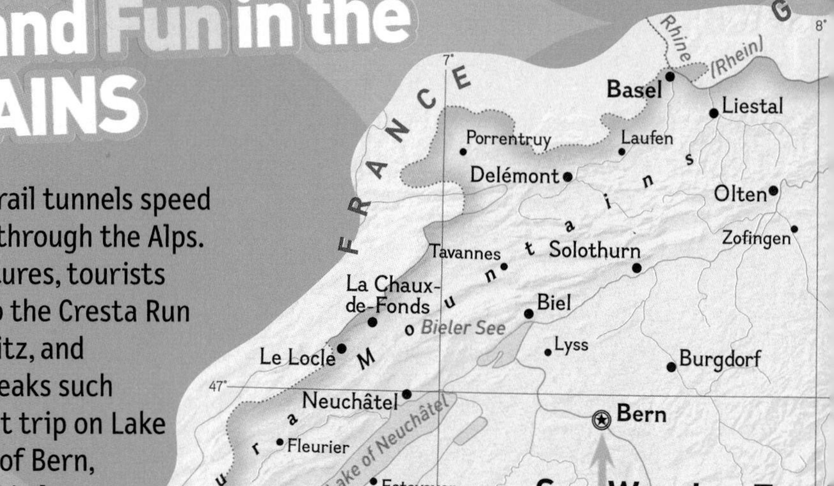

5 VISIT FRANKENSTEIN'S TOWN
Lake Geneva

Stand by the lake where the author Mary Shelley dreamed up the famous monster story, *Frankenstein*. You can swim in and go boating on the lake.

4 EAT CHEESE RACLETTE
Gruyères

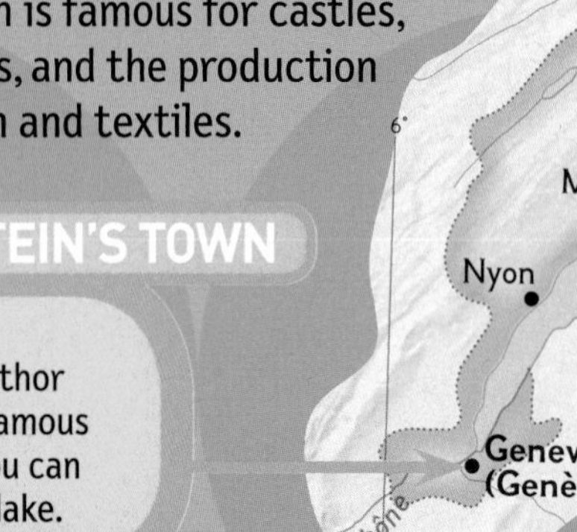

Share a traditional Swiss *raclette* with your friends. This delicious treat is made with melted cheese and whatever additions you like, such as meats, vegetables, or potatoes. The word raclette comes from the French word meaning "to scrape." After you make the raclette, you must scrape the melted cheese onto your plate.

DIGITAL TRAVELER!
Switzerland is famous for a special kind of singing called yodeling. Surf the Internet to find a recording of a yodeler. After you listen, try it yourself!

5 COOL THINGS TO DO HERE

1 SOAR WITH THE EAGLES
Malbun

Ride a chairlift above the treetops where falcons, hawks, and eagles soar. As you walk down the mountain, you'll see the big birds up close.

ID CARD COUNTRY FACTS

SWITZERLAND
Population: 8,078,000
Capital: Bern

LIECHTENSTEIN
Population: 37,000
Capital: Vaduz

THE MATTERHORN
The 14,692-foot (4,478-m)-tall mountain peak in the Swiss Alps is capped with snow all year long. It overlooks the town of Zermatt.

ALETSCH GLACIER
The longest glacier in Europe has an area of 66 square miles (171 sq km). The central part is 15 miles (24 km) long and 1 mile (1.6 km) wide.

VADUZ CASTLE
The Prince of Liechtenstein lives here. Parts of the castle were built in the 1100s, and the royal family has lived here since 1938.

2 TAKE A TRAIN TO A PEAK
Jungfrau

Climb the Alps to Jungfrau peak on a train that chugs through tunnels and climbs to 13,642 feet (4,158 m)—to the highest train station in Europe.

3 WATCH A CLOCK COME ALIVE
Bern

See the Zytglogge zodiacal clock and then climb the spiral staircase to see the insides of the instrument. The clock has chimed every hour since 1405.

5 COOL THINGS TO DO HERE

1 PICK RASPBERRIES
Brankovina

Taste sweet berries right from the bushes that grow on sunny slopes all over Serbia. Serbia is one of the world's top exporters of raspberries.

2 DUCK UNDER BRIDGES
Ljubljanica River

Cruise under several bridges. One is called Cobblers' Bridge because shoemakers set up their shops there by the river. In the 1200s, the bridge was built of wood. Later it was replaced with iron and concrete for strength.

5 VISIT A MOSQUE
Sarajevo

Enter one of the big mosques in the city to admire the colorful decorations on the walls and inside of the dome. Then listen for the call to prayer given from the minaret.

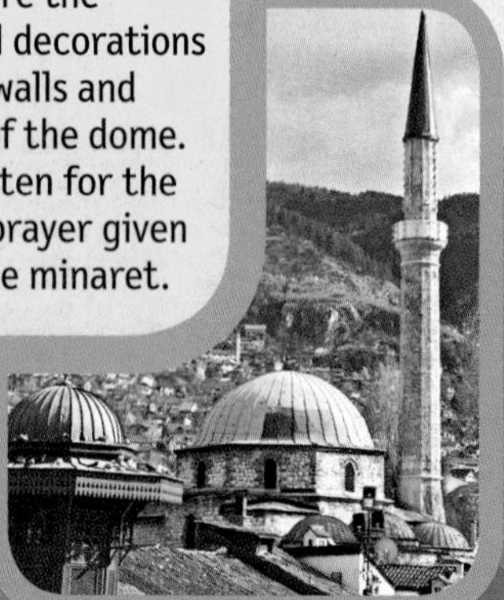

4 GAZE AT A GOAT HEAD
Krujë

Check out the museum inside this castle. You will learn how the mountaintop castle and its soldiers protected Albania from Ottoman Empire troops in 1450, 1466, and 1467. See a replica of the goat-head-topped helmet worn by the Albanian hero Gjergj Kastrioti Skenderbeu.

WESTERN BALKAN COUNTRIES

A Region of Diverse Beauty

Except for Albania, the countries in the western Balkans were part of former Yugoslavia, which broke up between 1991 and the early 2000s. Serbia has the most people, while Montenegro has fewer than a million citizens. Croatia's sunny Adriatic coast and Roman Empire ruins delight tourists. Throughout Bosnia and Herzegovina, Kosovo, Macedonia, and Slovenia, farmers grow and harvest crops among landscapes of mountains, canyons, forests, and ancient fortresses.

OLD BRIDGE OF MOSTAR
The original bridge in Bosnia and Herzegovina was built in 1566 and destroyed by war in 1993. It was rebuilt and reopened in 2004.

RUINS AT BUTRINT
Through history, this has been the site of a Greek colony and city of the Roman Empire. Today visitors to Albania can still see 23 rows of seats of the ancient amphitheater.

DALMATIAN COAST
Croatia's beautiful jagged coast draws people from all over the world for diving, boating, swimming, and enjoying sunny beaches.

ID CARD COUNTRY FACTS

ALBANIA
Population: 2,774,000
Capital: Tirana

BOSNIA AND HERZEGOVINA
Population: 3,834,000
Capital: Sarajevo

CROATIA
Population: 4,253,000
Capital: Zagreb

KOSOVO
Population: 1,824,000
Capital: Prishtina

MACEDONIA
Population: 2,066,000
Capital: Skopje

MONTENEGRO
Population: 623,000
Capital: Podgorica

SERBIA
Population: 7,136,000
Capital: Belgrade

SLOVENIA
Population: 2,060,000
Capital: Ljubljana

3 SHOP IN A BAZAAR
Skopje

Follow the winding cobblestone streets of this immense marketplace. You will pass shops and stalls that sell everything from pastries to jewelry.

DIGITAL TRAVELER!
Choose one of the Western Balkan countries. Then pick a time of year that you would like to travel there. Use your digital device to find out the typical weather at that time of year.

	NATIONAL BIRD:	NATIONAL FLOWER:	NATIONAL MAMMAL:
BULGARIA	snow goose	rose	lion
ROMANIA	great white pelican	dog rose	lynx

EASTERN BALKAN COUNTRIES

Two Friendly NEIGHBORS

The Danube River winds east between the Transylvanian Alps and the Balkan Mountains, separating Bulgaria and Romania. Both countries have coasts on the Black Sea. Bulgaria welcomes tourists to sunny beaches, and grows roses for perfumes, while Romania has gold mines and oil fields. Transylvania, land of the fabled Dracula, has ancient buildings that are left from the time when Romania was part of the Roman Empire.

5 COOL THINGS TO DO HERE

1 CHECK OUT PAINTED CHURCHES
Bucovina

"Read" Bible stories that were painted on church walls in the 15th and 16th centuries. Long ago, artists painted scenes to tell religious stories to the villagers.

5 VISIT DRACULA'S HOMETOWN
Sighișoara

Stroll through a medieval town and stop by the home of Vlad Dracula, a Transylvanian ruler from 1456 to 1462. He inspired the author Bram Stoker to create in 1897 the Gothic horror vampire character, Count Dracula.

4 DISCOVER A BLAST FROM THE PAST

Orşova

Snap a photo of an ancient king, Decebalus, rising from the Danube River. From 1994 to 2004 artists, rock climbers, and construction crews carved the limestone statue with dynamite, air hammers, and pickaxes.

3 EAT YOGHURT, LIVE LONG!

Sofia

At a local café, try true Bulgarian yoghurt made with milk taken from sheep raised on herb-rich pastures, giving it a unique flavor. Bulgarians believe that eating the healthy yoghurt is the reason why the country has the most people living to be more than 100 years old.

2 WATCH A LIGHT SHOW

Veliko Tŭrnovo

As the sun goes down at the Tsarevets Palace complex, spread out a blanket and enjoy the show of laser lights, music, and church bells. The show celebrates key moments in Bulgaria's history.

BELOGRADCHIK ROCKS

Each stone in this stretch of rock in Bulgaria has a name and legend attached to it. They include the Dinosaur, the Lion, the Bear, and the Stone of Thought.

PALACE OF PARLIAMENT

The capital headquarters in Bucharest is the heaviest building in the world. It has more than 2.5 billion tons (2.27 billion tonnes) of steel, bronze, marble, crystal, and wood.

SEVEN RILA LAKES

These lakes in Bulgaria's Rila National Park are named for their shapes, such as Eye Lake, Kidney Lake, and Fish Lake.

ID CARD COUNTRY FACTS

BULGARIA
Population: 7,260,000
Capital: Sofia

ROMANIA
Population: 21,269,000
Capital: Bucharest

DIGITAL TRAVELER!
The Cyrillic alphabet was developed in Bulgaria in the 10th century. Use the Internet to track down the Bulgarian Cyrillic alphabet. Compare it to the alphabet you use.

	NATIONAL BIRD:	NATIONAL FLOWER:	NATIONAL MAMMAL:
GREECE	little owl	laurel	dolphin
CYPRUS	rock dove	Cyprus cyclamen	Cypriot mouflon sheep

GREECE AND CYPRUS

Islands in SEAS

In Greece, ancient and modern buildings are side by side. The ancient Greek civilization arose 2,500 years ago, and spread across the Mediterranean, Ionian, and Aegean seas. Tourists come to admire the Parthenon in Athens, Mt. Olympus, and other historic sites. They also take boat trips around the beautiful Greek islands, including Corfu, Rhodes, and Crete with its Minoan palaces. Farther east is Cyprus, an island with sunny beaches and breathtaking hiking trails.

ID CARD COUNTRY FACTS

CYPRUS
Population: 1,135,000
Capital: Nicosia

GREECE
Population: 11,081,000
Capital: Athens

THE HARBOR OF RHODES

Boats pass between two bronze deer perched high above the harbor. It is believed that a huge statue called the Colossus of Rhodes stood over the harbor until an earthquake toppled it in 226 B.C.

THE PARTHENON

With its famous columns, the remains of this temple in Athens have been standing for more than 2,400 years.

TOMBS OF THE KINGS

Near Paphos harbor in Cyprus, this underground burial chamber is more than 2,000 years old.

5 RIDE A GLASS-BOTTOMED BOAT

Corfu

Float by coastal caves and look for beautiful fish and other sea creatures. Some boats have glass bottoms, which can give you a closer look.

5 COOL THINGS TO DO HERE

1 GO FUTURISTIC IN THE PAST
Athens

Peer into the past at the new Acropolis Museum. Displays are built around the ruins of the ancient Acropolis buildings. Go inside to learn about the past in the virtual reality theater, wearing 3-D glasses.

2 RIDE A DONKEY
Oía

To get up to this village, you can take a donkey ride on the narrow, hilly path. Oía is known for white-washed houses and blue-domed churches.

3 FOLLOW BABY TURTLES
Kyrenia

Watch newly hatched turtles creep into the ocean. Mother turtles visit north Cyprus beaches in May to dig holes and hide their eggs. The eggs hatch in July.

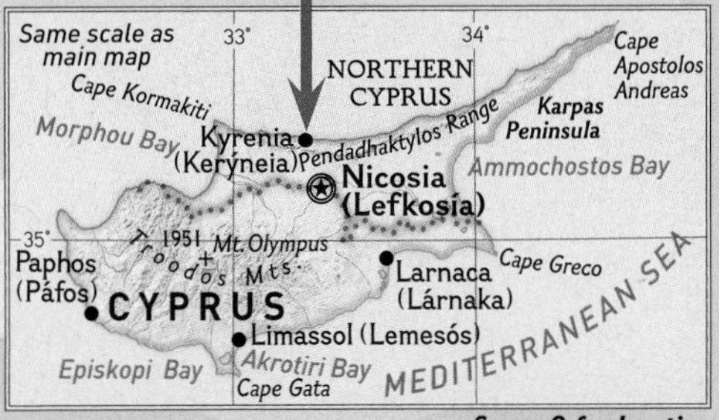

See p. 9 for location

4 HIKE THROUGH A GORGE
Samariá

Walk through Samariá Gorge on Crete, Europe's longest gorge. A river carved this route between the mountains thousands of years ago.

DIGITAL TRAVELER!
Can you guess what is in the special Greek dish called spanokopita? Search the Internet for a recipe to learn the ingredients. Decide if it is a food you'd like to try.

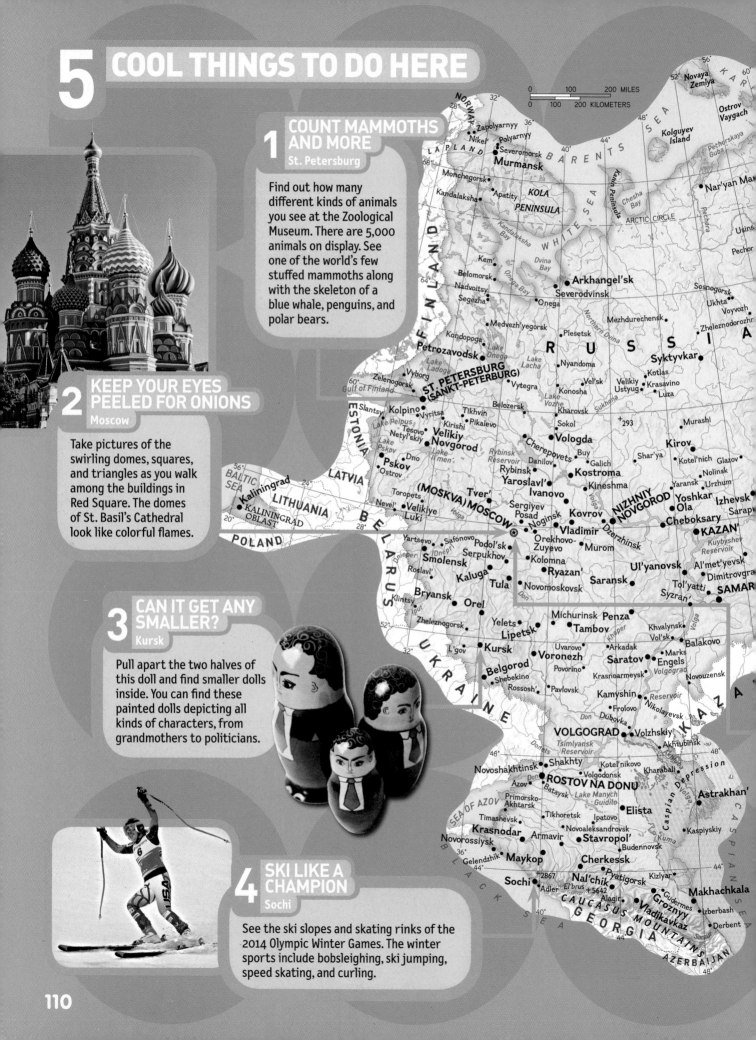

5 COOL THINGS TO DO HERE

1 COUNT MAMMOTHS AND MORE
St. Petersburg

Find out how many different kinds of animals you see at the Zoological Museum. There are 5,000 animals on display. See one of the world's few stuffed mammoths along with the skeleton of a blue whale, penguins, and polar bears.

2 KEEP YOUR EYES PEELED FOR ONIONS
Moscow

Take pictures of the swirling domes, squares, and triangles as you walk among the buildings in Red Square. The domes of St. Basil's Cathedral look like colorful flames.

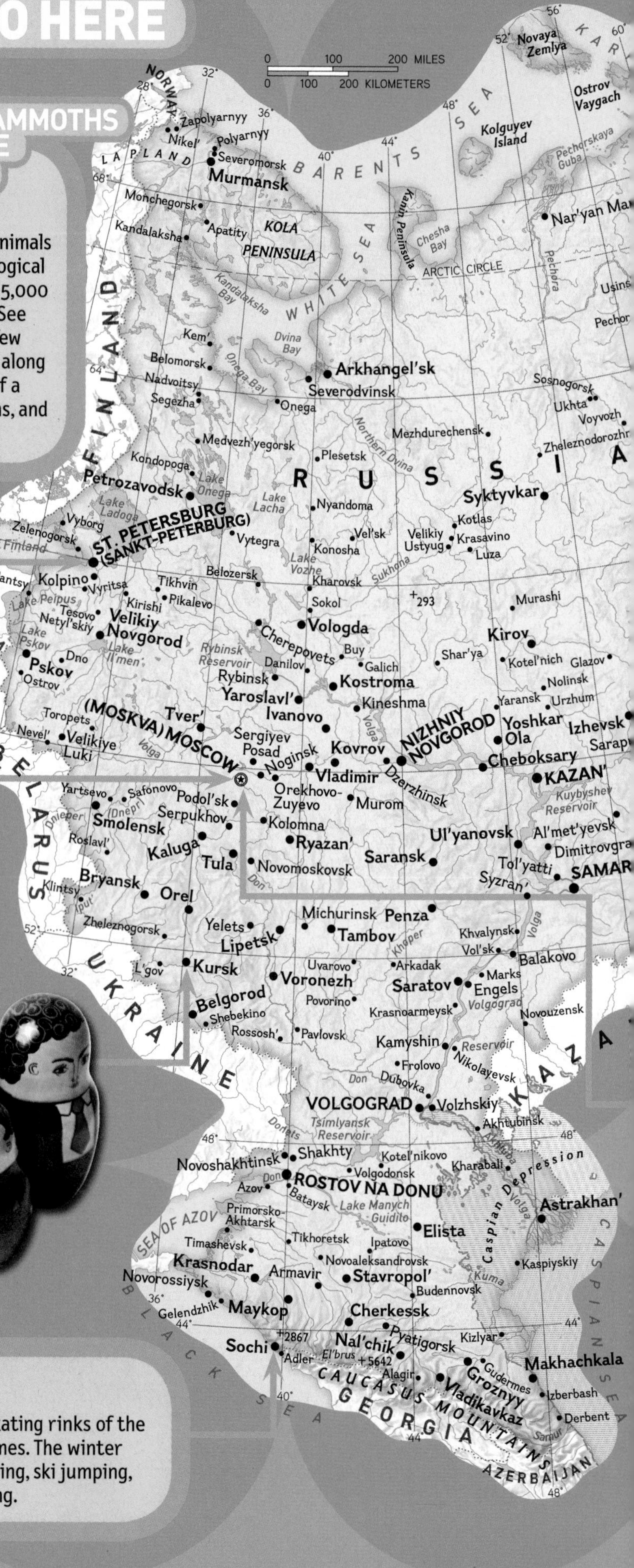

3 CAN IT GET ANY SMALLER?
Kursk

Pull apart the two halves of this doll and find smaller dolls inside. You can find these painted dolls depicting all kinds of characters, from grandmothers to politicians.

4 SKI LIKE A CHAMPION
Sochi

See the ski slopes and skating rinks of the 2014 Olympic Winter Games. The winter sports include bobsleighing, ski jumping, speed skating, and curling.

NATIONAL BIRD: tundra swan
NATIONAL FLOWER: chamomile
NATIONAL MAMMAL: bear

EUROPEAN RUSSIA

In the World's Largest COUNTRY

Russia stretches from Europe across Asia to the Pacific. The Ural Mountains form a natural boundary between Asia and European Russia, which has 80 percent of Russia's people, most of its farms and industries, and the biggest cities—Moscow, St. Petersburg, and Volgograd. Explore the Volga and Don Rivers, and gaze across the Black Sea and the Caspian Sea, a giant lake. Head north to see the polar snows of the Arctic Ocean.

ID CARD COUNTRY FACTS

Size: 6,601,668 sq mi (17,098,242 sq km)*
Population: 143,493,000*
Capital: Moscow
Official language: Russian
Currency: ruble
Highest point: El'brus, 18,510 ft (5,642 m)*
Life expectancy: 70.0 years*
*These figures are for all of Russia. For Asian Russia, see pp. 116–117.

Globetrotter Attractions

MOSCOW'S KREMLIN
These buildings have been tsars' palaces and Soviet government offices, and are now home for the Russian president.

HERMITAGE MUSEUM
This was the St. Petersburg Winter Palace of Russian Emperor Peter I and Catherine the Great in the early 1700s.

MOTHERLAND STATUE
With her sword raised to remember the Battle of Stalingrad, this 170-foot (52-m)-tall statue in Volgograd was the world's largest when it was built in 1967.

5 SEE BEAUTIFUL BALLET
Moscow

Enjoy the beautiful dancers at the Bolshoi Theater. The world-famous Bolshoi Ballet has been around for more than 200 years.

DIGITAL TRAVELER!
Fabergé eggs are beautiful, jeweled eggs that were made as gifts for Russian royalty from 1885 to 1917. Search the Internet for photographs of Fabergé eggs. Find out where you could see one of the originals in Russia today.

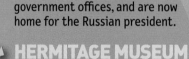

ASIA

Globetrotter GIANT

From the remote, jagged, snowcapped peaks of the Himalaya to the lowest place on Earth, the Dead Sea, Asia is a place of extremes. Spreading almost halfway around the globe, Asia contains enormous rain forests, giant lakes, raging rivers, stunning waterfalls, sprawling deserts, and icy wastelands.

Rice paddy terraces in Chiang Mai, northern Thailand. Rice is the staple grain crop throughout much of eastern Asia.

ASIA

The Most Populated CONTINENT

Asia is a world champion. More people live in Asia than in all the other continents put together. China and India have the two largest populations in the world, each with more than a billion people. Asia has both the most farmers and the most cities with several million inhabitants. Home to more than 40 countries and with a rich diversity of cultures, Asia has a strong influence on world politics and economics.

Globetrotter Attractions

AUNT BERTHA'S TRAVEL TIPS

WHAT'S ON THE MENU?
Across Asia, rice or noodles are eaten with almost everything. Rice is the grain (seeds) of a cereal plant. Noodles are made from dough shaped and cut into long strips, tubes, shells, or folded shapes.

WHAT TO WEAR?
With climates ranging from freezing cold (polar) to very hot and dry (desert), and from seasonal heavy rain (monsoon) to hot and humid (tropical), you may need to change clothes often.

ON THE MOVE
In addition to cars, trains, and planes, Asia has some unusual forms of transportation: rickshaws, tuc tucs, camels, donkey-drawn carts, elephants, junks, and sampans.

EASTERN MEDITERRANEAN

This region is a bridge between Europe and Asia, and it lies between the Black, Caspian, and Mediterranean Seas.

A commonly accepted division between Europe and Asia — here marked by a g_ line — is formed by the Ural Mountain Ural River, Caspian Sea, Caucasus Mountains, and the Black Sea with i_ outlets, the Bosporus and Dardanelle_

| 0 | | 600 | | 1200 MI |
| 0 | 600 | | 1200 KILOMETERS | |

CENTRAL

This region is made up of six countries: the largely Muslim five "stans"—an Iranian word for homelands—and Mongolia, a mainly Buddhist country.

SOUTHWEST

The Arabian Peninsula and countries of the Persian Gulf make up this region. The landscape is mostly deserts and mountains.

INDUSTRY
Japan

Factories in Japan and across the rest of Asia produce most of the world's electronic products including computers, game consoles, smartphones, and televisions.

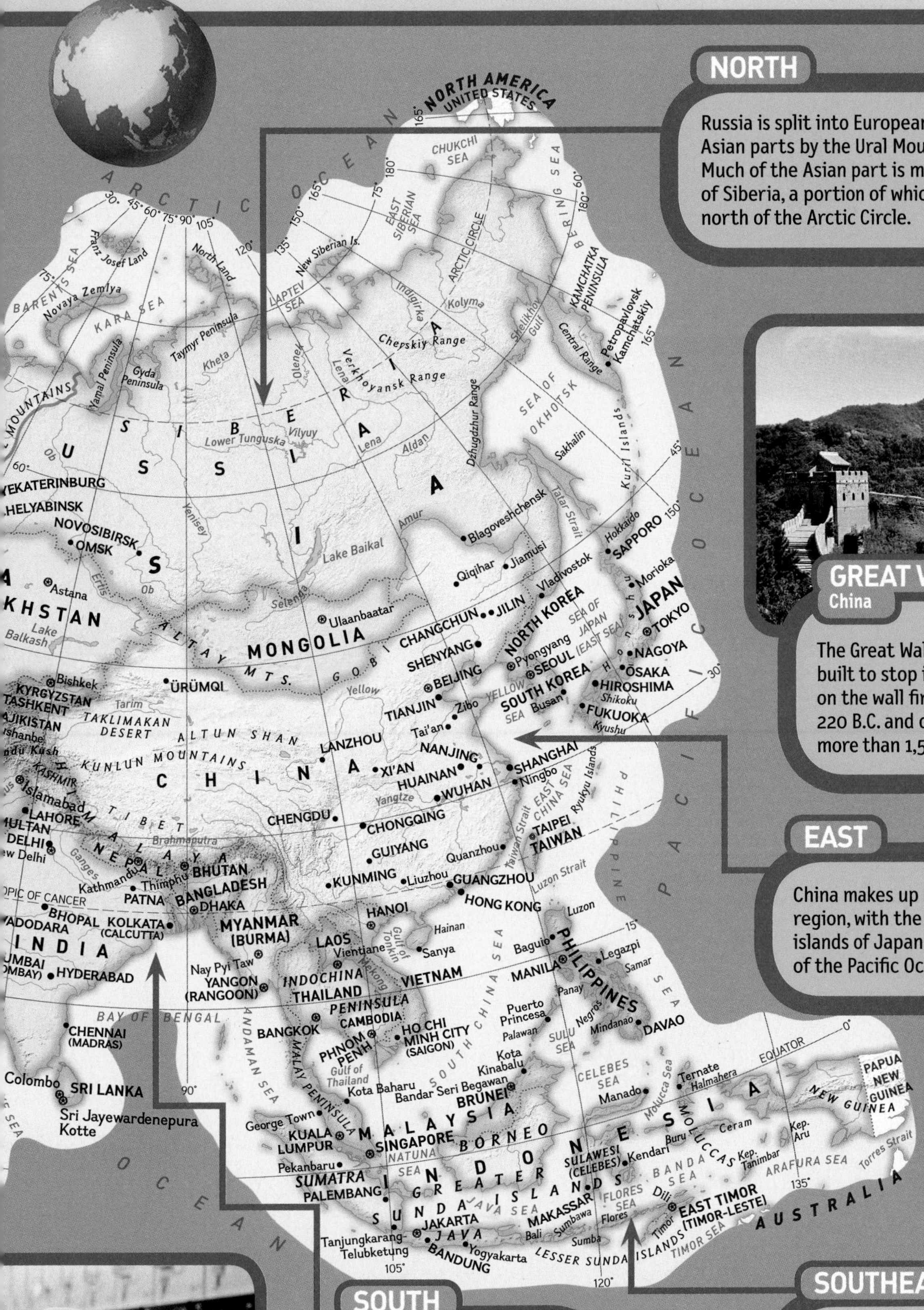

NORTH

Russia is split into European and Asian parts by the Ural Mountains. Much of the Asian part is made up of Siberia, a portion of which lies north of the Arctic Circle.

GREAT WALL
China

The Great Wall of China was built to stop invasions. Work on the wall first began in 220 B.C. and continued for more than 1,500 years.

EAST

China makes up most of this region, with the Koreas and the islands of Japan along the edge of the Pacific Ocean.

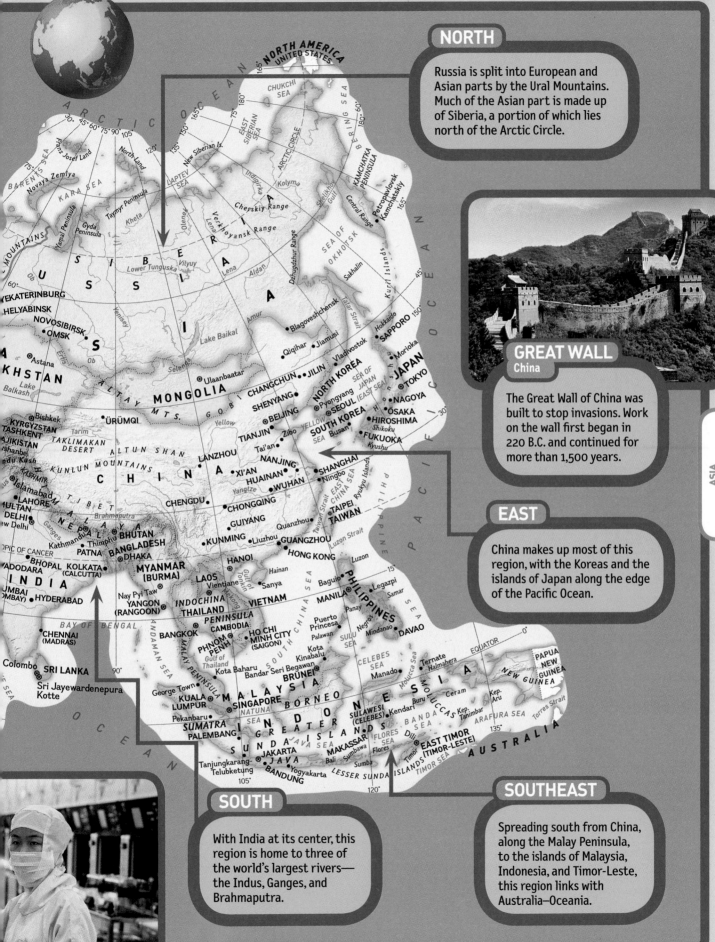

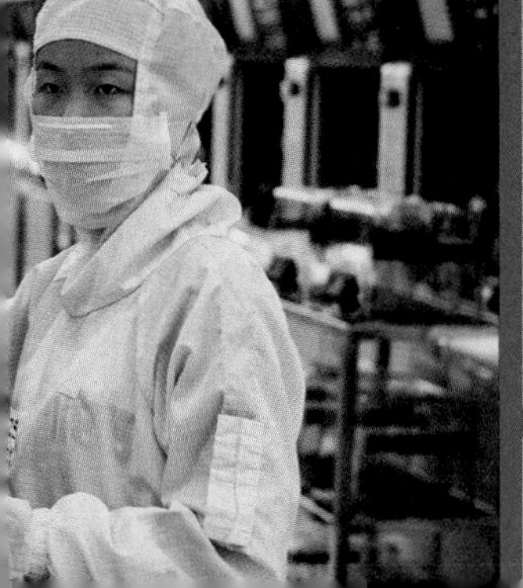

SOUTH

With India at its center, this region is home to three of the world's largest rivers—the Indus, Ganges, and Brahmaputra.

SOUTHEAST

Spreading south from China, along the Malay Peninsula, to the islands of Malaysia, Indonesia, and Timor-Leste, this region links with Australia–Oceania.

NATIONAL BIRD: tundra swan

NATIONAL FLOWER: chamomile

NATIONAL MAMMAL: bear

ASIAN RUSSIA

Rich in Forests, Minerals, and Icy WASTELANDS

By far the biggest part of Russia, Asian Russia stretches from the Ural Mountains east to the volcanic Kamchatka Peninsula and the Bering Sea. It also stretches far north into the Arctic. The world's longest railroad crosses the mineral-rich wilderness of Siberia, the world's biggest plains region. Siberia has conifer forests, or taiga, treeless frozen tundra, long rivers, and lakes. Fish are harvested for caviar (eggs), a favorite delicacy.

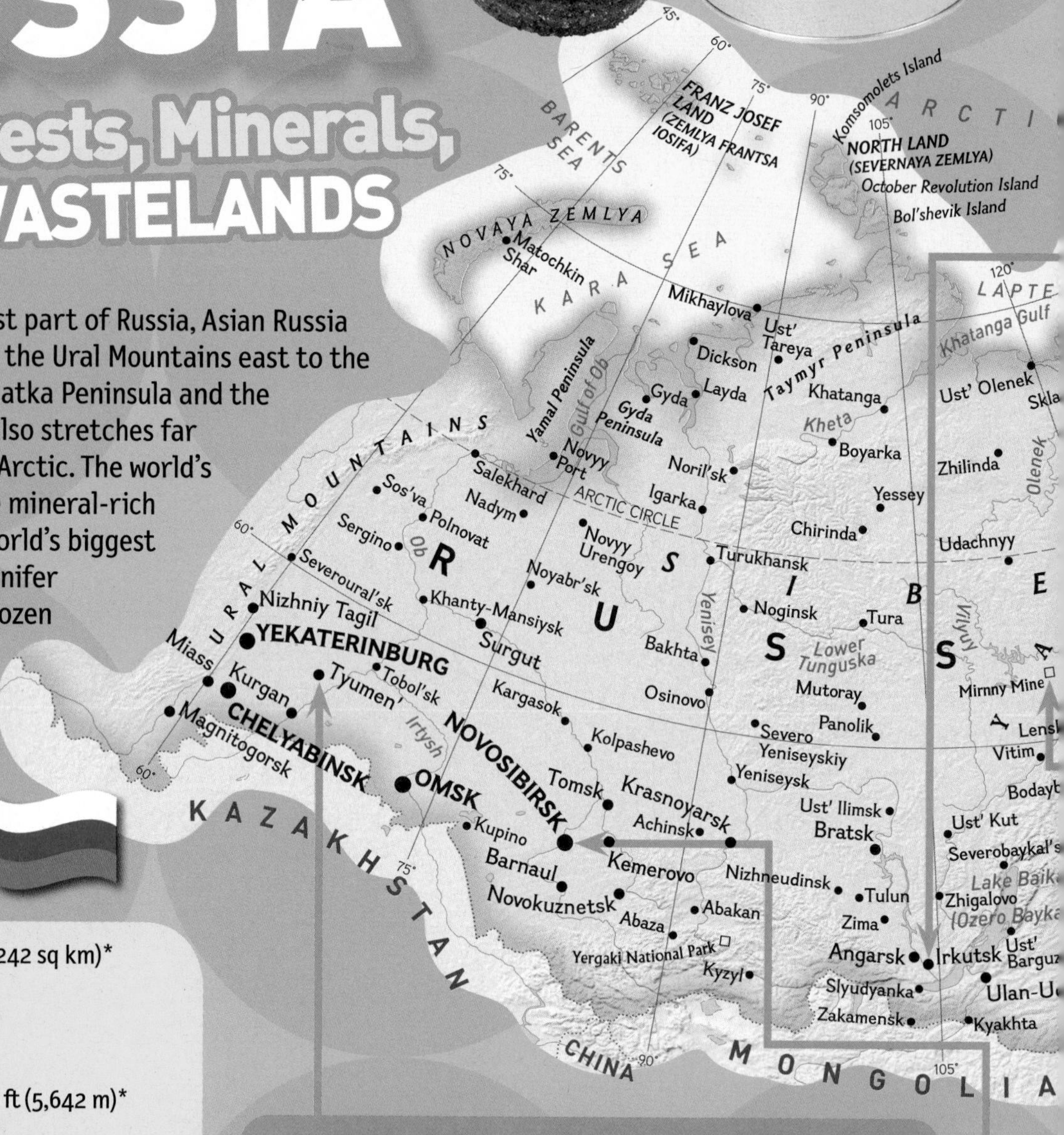

ID CARD
COUNTRY FACTS

Size: 6,601,668 sq mi (17,098,242 sq km)*
Population: 143,493,000*
Capital: Moscow
Official language: Russian
Currency: ruble
Highest point: El'brus, 18,510 ft (5,642 m)*
Life expectancy: 70.0 years*
*These figures are for all of Russia. For European Russia, see pp. 110–111.

5 NOMADS R'US
Tyumen'

Wander through a nomad camp at the Archaeological Museum-Reserve on Lake Andreyevskoye. Eat fish soup and dress in the clothes a northern nomad may wear.

DIGITAL TRAVELER!
In winter, temperatures in parts of Siberia can go down to −58°F (−50°C). This is dangerously cold. Where do you think the lowest temperature ever recorded on Earth was taken? Use the Internet to find out.

5 COOL THINGS TO DO HERE

1 CRUISE ON A LAKE
Irkutsk

Visit the nature reserves of Lake Angara that can only be reached by boat. Stop at an island to see wildlife on the beaches. Admire the forests around the lake.

LAKE BAIKAL
Lake Baikal, in southeast Siberia, is the world's deepest lake. It holds about one-fifth of Earth's surface fresh water.

YERGAKI NATIONAL PARK
Central Siberia's Yergaki National Park is breathtakingly beautiful. Its lakes, mountains, and forests are unspoiled.

YAKUTIA
Yakutia has the coldest temperatures of anywhere that people live. The ground contains many minerals but is permanently frozen below the surface.

2 BLING IT OUT!
Mirnny

Visit the Mirnny Diamond Pit, one of the largest holes, and diamond mines, in the world. Gold is mined here, too. Find jewelry made from local gold and diamonds.

3 TAKE THE LONGEST TRAIN RIDE
Vladivostok

Spend seven nights on one train going from Vladivostok to Moscow. Eat food from the dining car or kiosks at the stations. Make tea in your own cup with hot water from the train car's samovar, or tea urn.

4 SEE RARE ANIMALS
Novosibirsk

Visit the rare liger—half lion and half tiger—at one of Russia's largest zoos. See her babies, called liligers, half liger and half lion.

5 COOL THINGS TO DO HERE

1 TAKE A WILD RIDE
Tbilisi

Ride the giant Ferris wheel as you look out over the city of Tbilisi and the Caucasus Mountains. Play video games or take the waterslide as you enjoy a day atop Georgia's Mtatsminda Mountain. To get there take a funicular, a cable railroad that goes up the mountain.

DIGITAL TRAVELER!
Apricots, the fruit of a small tree, were cultivated in Armenia more than 2,000 years ago. Search the Internet to find the world's largest producers of apricots. Which ones are neighbors of the Caucasus countries?

2 BEWARE MUD POOLS
Gobustan

Go with a guide to mud volcanoes in Azerbaijan near the Caspian Sea to hear mud pools belch and to watch them bubble and explode.

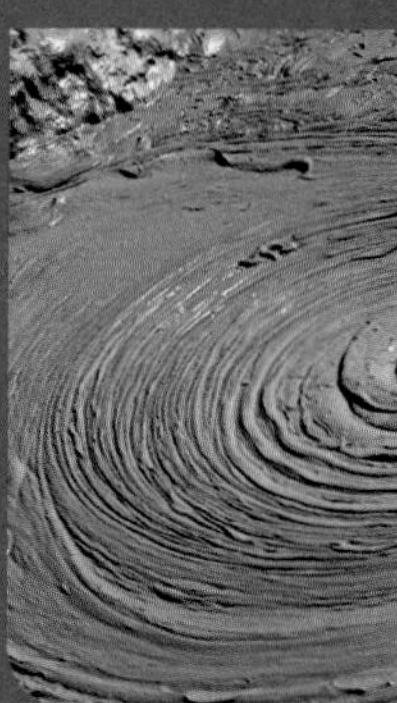

ABKHAZIA & SOUTH OSSETIA
Soon after Georgia seceded from the U.S.S.R in 1991, separatists in Abkhazia and South Ossetia achieved autonomy by defeating Georgian troops. Russia supports these separatist states—recognizing their independence after its 2008 war with Georgia.

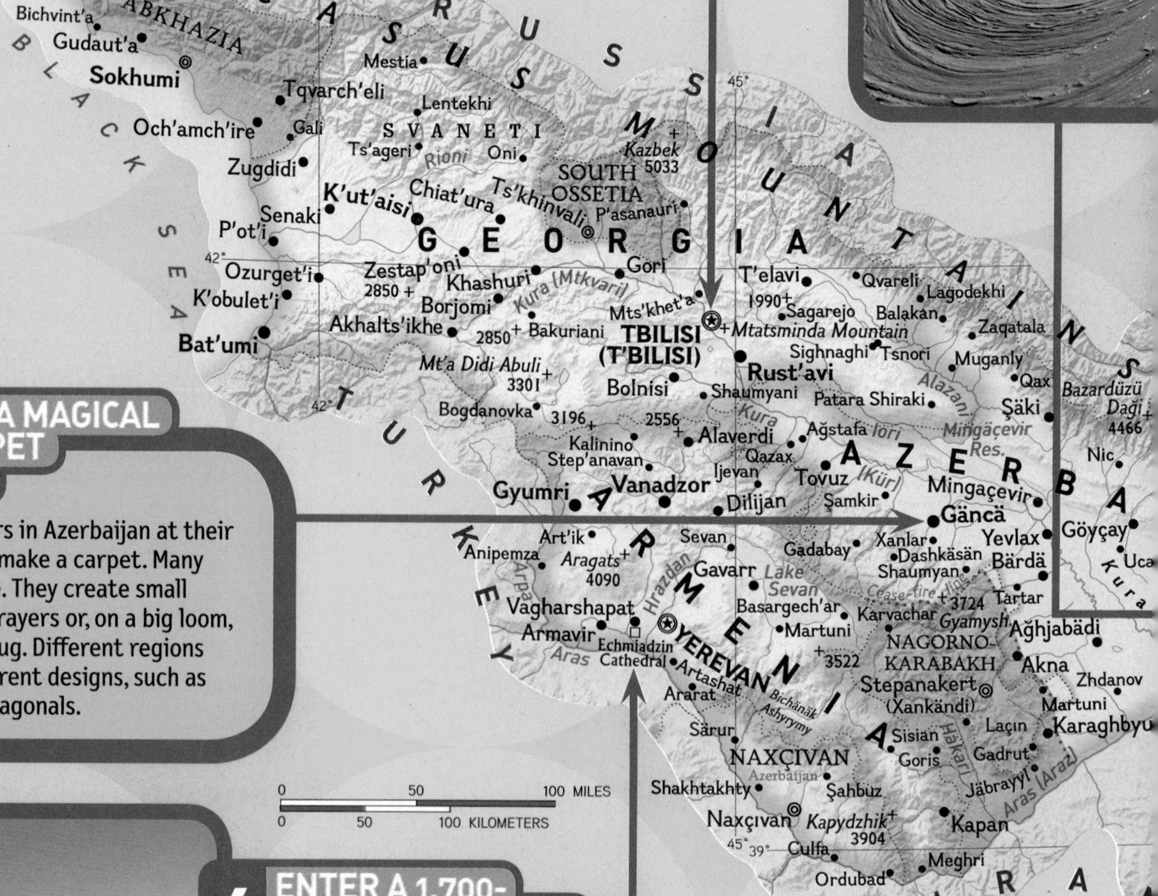

NAGORNO-KARABAKH
This southwestern Azerbaijan region, largely populated by ethnic Armenians, declared independence in 1991. A Russian-brokered cease-fire in 1994 left Karabakh Armenians controlling—but Azerbaijan still claiming—Nagorno-Karabakh

3 BUY A MAGICAL CARPET
Gäncä

Watch weavers in Azerbaijan at their loom as they make a carpet. Many work at home. They create small carpets for prayers or, on a big loom, a room-size rug. Different regions produce different designs, such as shields and diagonals.

4 ENTER A 1,700-YEAR-OLD CHURCH
Echmiadzin

Enter Echmiadzin Cathedral, founded in 303. This ancient church in Armenia has been remodeled over the centuries, but remains the center of the Armenian Christian (Orthodox) religion.

	NATIONAL BIRD:	NATIONAL FLOWER:	NATIONAL MAMMAL:
ARMENIA	eagle	*Althaea armeniaca*	lion
AZERBAIJAN	golden eagle	water fringe	Karabakh horse
GEORGIA	common pheasant	white nettle	Caucasian shepherd dog

CAUCASUS COUNTRIES

Mountains Between Two SEAS

Separating southeast Europe from Asia are the Caucasus Mountains. In the southern Caucasus are Armenia, Azerbaijan, and Georgia, lands that lie between the Black and Caspian seas. Their neighbors are Russia, Turkey, and Iran. The northern Caucasus is a disputed region. Oil-rich Azerbaijan, noted for handmade rugs, borders the Caspian Sea, and Georgia has a sunny Black Sea coast. Armenia has many lakes, the largest being Lake Sevana.

ID CARD COUNTRY FACTS

ARMENIA
Population: 3,048,000
Capital: Yerevan

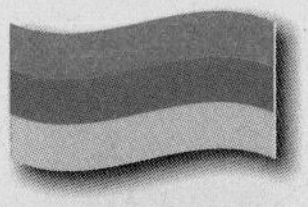

AZERBAIJAN
Population: 9,418,000
Capital: Baku

GEORGIA
Population: 4,541,000
Capital: Tbilisi

5 CLIMB AN ANCIENT TOWER
Baku

Find the Maiden's Tower in the Walled City in Baku, Azerbaijan. Climb to the top of this ancient eight-story tower. Gaze across the old city and along the coast of the Caspian Sea.

LAKE RITSA
Deep forest covers the three mountains that surround this beautiful lake in Abkhazia, Georgia.

ARMENIAN PLATEAU
These highlands in Armenia include mountains, deep river valleys, extinct volcanoes, and giant plateaus formed as flowing lava cooled.

SVANETI
This high, mountainous region of Georgia still has many medieval villages and tower houses.

NATIONAL BIRD: redwing

NATIONAL FLOWER: tulip

NATIONAL MAMMAL: gray wolf

TURKEY

A Bridge Between Europe and ASIA

Turkish delight is a delicacy in Turkey, a country that is often said to be a bridge between Europe and Asia. The national capital is Ankara, on the high rocky plateau of Anatolia. But the largest city is Istanbul, formerly Constantinople, on the Bosporus Strait. With the Sea of Marmara and the Dardanelles, the Bosporus forms a key waterway linking the Mediterranean and Black seas.

5 STAND UNDER AN ANCIENT DOME
Istanbul

Gaze up at the huge dome in Hagia Sophia, a church completed in 537 and once used as a mosque. The dome is held up by half-domes and arches.

4 STAGE A PLAY FOR A DAY
Ephesus

Climb the steps in this huge amphitheater. The Romans built it so that 25,000 people could watch concerts, plays, political discussions, and gladiator battles.

3 GET SHIPSHAPE
Selimiye

Wander down a road lined with boatyards. Watch the huge wooden boats, called *gulets*, being built using traditional methods. Taste the local figs, almonds, and honey.

5 COOL THINGS TO DO HERE

1 RIDE IN A GLASS ELEVATOR
Ankara

Travel on the glass elevator to the top of Atakule, Ankara's highest building. At the tower's top, stand in one place and let the rotating room change the view.

MOUNT ARARAT
This mostly treeless mountain rises above the plains in eastern Turkey, near the border with Iran and Armenia. Many believe Noah's Ark came to rest here.

CAPPADOCIA
Wind and rain shaped the soft rock of this region, located largely in the Nevsehir Province between Yozgat and Niğde. Then people carved tunnels to form underground towns. Some underground buildings are still used today.

PATARA BEACH
Swim at this beach, but don't forget to check out the birds and endangered turtles that nest here, and nearby ancient ruins.

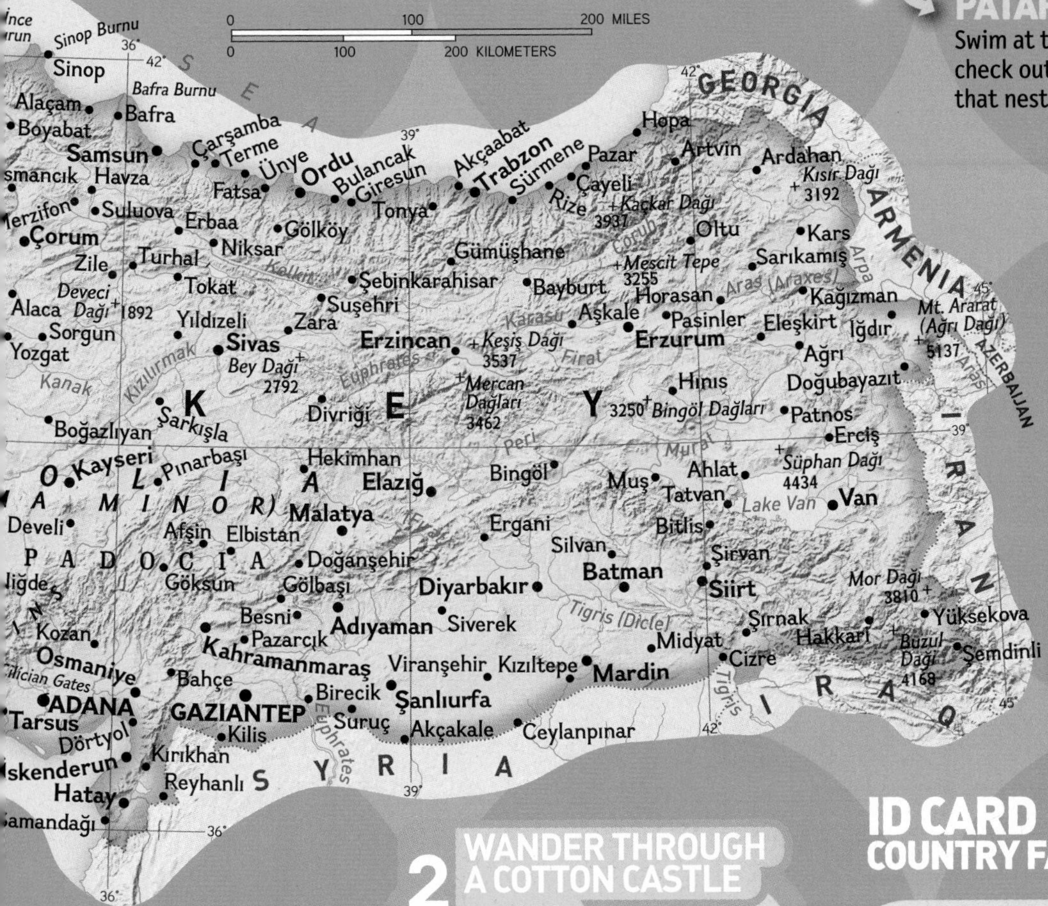

DIGITAL TRAVELER!
What is the name of the bridge in Istanbul that links the European and Asian parts of Turkey? Use the Internet to find out.

2 WANDER THROUGH A COTTON CASTLE
Pamukkale

See why this bizarre landscape is called the Cotton Castle. Trickling warm mineral water has left white deposits that form stone waterfalls and forests.

ID CARD COUNTRY FACTS

Size: 302,535 sq mi (783,562 sq km)
Population: 76,083,000
Capital: Ankara
Official language: Turkish
Currency: Turkish lira
Highest point: Mount Ararat, 16,854 ft (5,137 m)
Life expectancy: 73.0 years

	NATIONAL BIRD:	NATIONAL FLOWER:	NATIONAL MAMMAL:
LEBANON	Dunn's lark	starflower	striped hyena
SYRIA	eagle	poppy anemone	Tsolov's hamster
JORDAN	Sinai rosefinch	black iris	Arabian oryx

LEBANON, SYRIA, AND JORDAN

Land Between Seas and DESERTS

Syria is the biggest of these three Middle Eastern states, with deserts, mountains, and dry wadis (valleys), but highways and modern cities, too.

Lebanon and Syria have greener Mediterranean Sea coasts. In Jordan, you can wade in the River Jordan and in the salty Dead Sea. There are farm villages, and bustling cities, too, such as Amman, Damascus, and Beirut. In recent times these countries have been troubled by conflicts.

5 COOL THINGS TO DO HERE

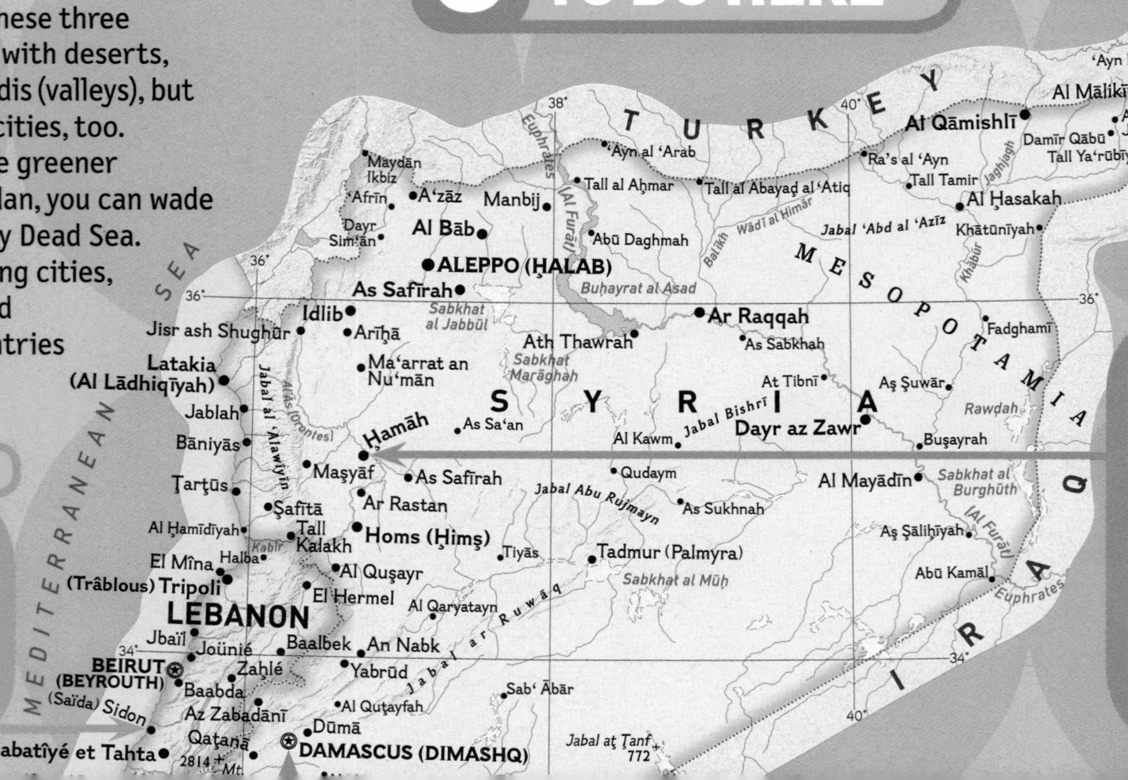

1 SEE GIANT WATERWHEELS
Ḩamāh

Marvel at the huge *noria*, or waterwheels, in Syria. These brought water to aqueducts, or artificial water paths, for hundreds of years. The water went to fields in the desert and to the city of Ḩamāh. The biggest waterwheel brought water to the Great Mosque in Ḩamāh.

5 GET A WHIFF OF SOAP
Sidon

Wander through the Sidon Soap Museum in an ancient town in Lebanon. See how handmade olive oil soap has been made for hundreds of years. Smell the sweet soaps drying in the factory.

4 EXPLORE A WALLED CITY
Damascus

Visit Syria to see one of the oldest continually inhabited cities in the world. Walk to the ancient gates. Visit the varied ancient religious sites and homes around the city. Careful, though—some of the buildings are not in good repair.

2 ROOT AROUND IN ROCKS
Petra

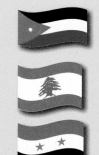

Explore the ancient buildings and caves carved into the rocks at Petra, Jordan. Camel caravans stopped here when traveling between the Red Sea and the Dead Sea.

3 SNORKEL CORAL REEFS
Gulf of Aqaba

Watch the coral reef as you drift on this arm of the Red Sea in Jordan. Snorkel or take a glass-bottomed boat or underwater craft to see the sea turtles, dolphins, and multicolored fish.

Globetrotter Attractions

PALMYRA
This oasis and ancient city in Syria's desert was on a trade route that linked Persia, India, China, and the Roman Empire.

WADI RUM
Among interesting desert formations, this site in Jordan has evidence that humans have lived here for 12,000 years.

QADISHA VALLEY
For more than 1,000 years, religious holy men have hidden away in the caves and monastaries in this valley in Lebanon.

ID CARD COUNTRY FACTS

JORDAN
Population: 7,309,000
Capital: Amman

LEBANON
Population: 4,822,000
Capital: Beirut

SYRIA
Population: 21,898,000
Capital: Damascus

DIGITAL TRAVELER!
The cedar of Lebanon is a conifer tree that grows in mountain regions of these countries. Search the Internet to find photographs of the tree. Then find out how timber from the tree was used in ancient times.

5 COOL THINGS TO DO HERE

1 CIRCLE AN ANCIENT CITY BY BOAT
Acre

View this ancient city from the sea. See the city walls from boats, just as the Crusaders first saw them. Wander along the winding alleys and through underground passages in the old city of Acre.

2 REPLANT A FOREST
Carmel

Volunteer to help park rangers plant trees to reforest Mount Carmel where a forest fire burned more than 8,000 acres (3,237 ha) of woodland in 2010. Learn how the forest is coming back to life.

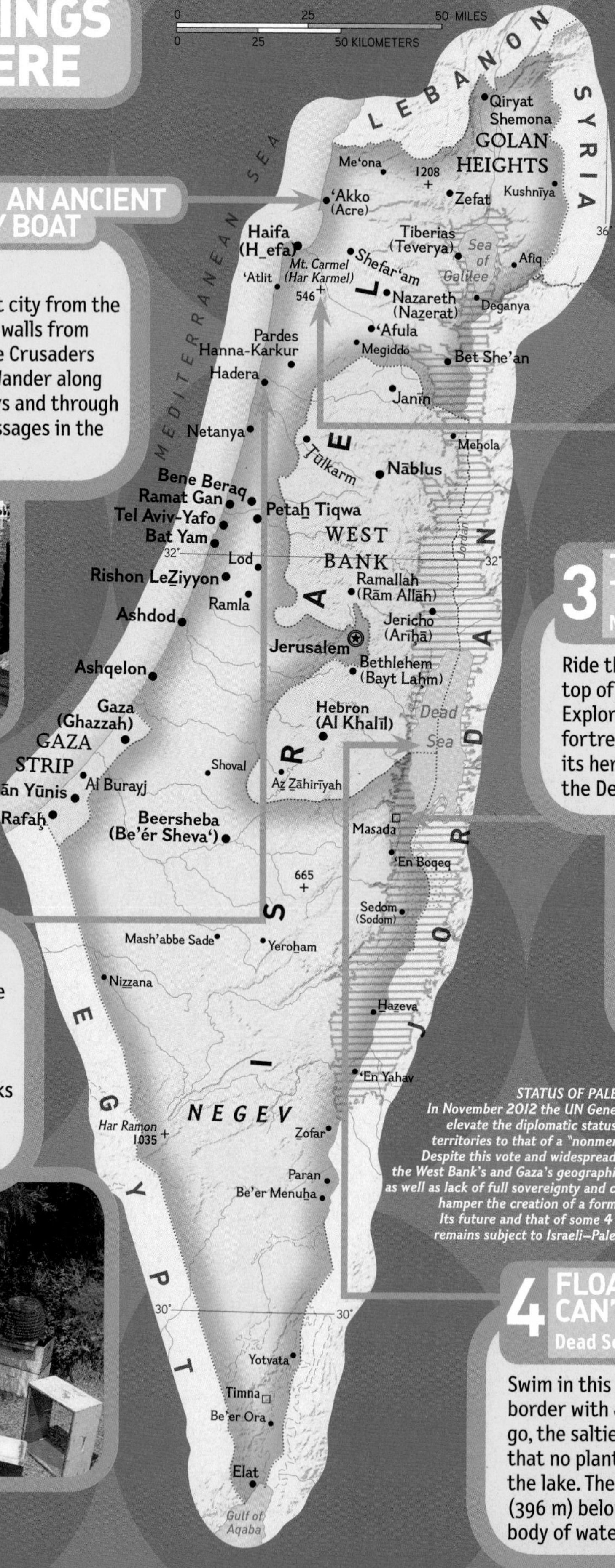

STATUS OF PALESTINE

In November 2012 the UN General Assembly voted to elevate the diplomatic status of the Palestinian territories to that of a "nonmember observer state." Despite this vote and widespread international support, the West Bank's and Gaza's geographical and political separation, as well as lack of full sovereignty and control over these territories hamper the creation of a formal Palestinian state. Its future and that of some 4 million Palestinians remains subject to Israeli–Palestinian negotiations.

3 TAKE A CABLE CAR TO A FORTRESS
Masada

Ride the cable car to the flat top of this steep mountain. Explore the remains of the fortress and learn the story of its heroes. See the desert and the Dead Sea far below.

5 MEET A KIBBUTZNIK
Hadera

Chat with kibbutzniks who make farming a way of life by sharing everything. In 1927 Polish pioneers began a kibbutz as a lifestyle experiment. Kibbutzniks raise animals, grow crops, and keep bees to make honey.

4 FLOAT WHERE FISH CAN'T SWIM
Dead Sea

Swim in this salty lake on Israel's border with Jordan. The deeper you go, the saltier the water—so salty that no plants or animals can live in the lake. The lake is about 1,300 feet (396 m) below sea level, the lowest body of water on Earth's surface.

NATIONAL BIRD: hoopoe

NATIONAL MAMMAL: Israeli gazelle

NATIONAL FLOWER: rakefet (cyclamen)

ISRAEL

Desert and Seas in a HOLY LAND

Israel has a Mediterranean coast, borders the Sea of Galilee in the north, and touches the Red Sea (at the Gulf of Aqaba). In the southwest is the Negev desert. Israel shares the Dead Sea with Jordan, but the West Bank of the River Jordan is disputed territory. Jerusalem is a city holy to Jews, Christians, and Muslims as can be seen by their religious symbols in the city: Jewish menorah candleholder, Christian cross, and Muslim star and crescent Moon.

JERUSALEM

The ancient city of Jerusalem is the capital of Israel, as well as being important to three religions: Judaism, Christianity, and Islam.

TIMNA PARK

At this lake in the desert, tour the first copper mine and check out ancient rock drawings. Visit incredible rock formations and take a pedal boat out on the lake.

SEA OF GALILEE

This sea, filled by the Jordan River, provides Israel with drinking water and beaches. Visit its many natural, historic, and holy sites.

DIGITAL TRAVELER!
The region of Israel is known as the "Holy Land." The country is home to religious sites of three major religions. Use the Internet to find out who were their spiritual leaders.

ID CARD COUNTRY FACTS

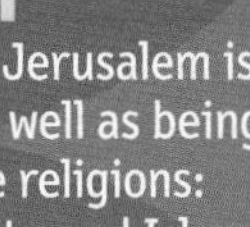

Size: 8,019 sq mi (20,770 sq km)
Population: 8,054,000
Capital: Jerusalem
Official languages: Hebrew and Arabic
Currency: new Israeli shekel
Highest point: Har Meron, 3,963 ft (1,208 m)
Life expectancy: 82.0 years

ASIA

NORTHERN ARABIAN PENINSULA

Surrounded by Seas and GULFS

People in the Arabian Peninsula love horses and camels. Their desert land lies between seas and gulfs important for commerce. Oil-rich Saudi Arabia is larger than its neighbors Qatar, Bahrain, Kuwait, and the United Arab Emirates, which is made up of states that border the Persian Gulf sea route. Much of Arabia is barren desert, but oil money and technology have transformed society, with skyscrapers, expressways, and airports in what was once desert.

5 STARE AT THE WORLD'S TALLEST WATER FOUNTAIN

Jeddah

Search the sky of Jeddah, Saudi Arabia, and you'll find the plume from Jeddah's Fountain. Admire the tallest water fountain in the world. It shoots water more than 1,000 feet (305 m) into the air.

ASIR NATIONAL PARK
Mountains, foggy forests, and even occasional snow are found in this protected area in Saudi Arabia.

RUB' AL KHALI
The largest sand desert in the world, the Rub' al-Khali is in four countries.

PALM ISLANDS
The largest artificial islands in the world, Palm Islands in the United Arab Emirates, are in the shape of palm trees.

ID CARD COUNTRY FACTS

Saudi Arabia
Population: 30,054,000
Capital: Riyadh

Qatar
Population: 2,169,000
Capital: Doha

Bahrain
Population: 1,131,000
Capital: Manama

Kuwait
Population: 3,459,000
Capital: Kuwait City

United Arab Emirates
Population: 9,346,000
Capital: Abu Dhabi

DIGITAL TRAVELER!
This region is the world's largest producer of crude oil, or petroleum. What products do you think are made from petroleum? Check your list by finding out about crude oil on the Internet.

5 COOL THINGS TO DO HERE

1 CHOOSE A WINNER
Kuwait City

Cheer your favorite camel and robot rider at the camel races in Kuwait. Race alongside the camels in cars with the owners and their remote rider controls.

2 WALK ACROSS A SKY BRIDGE
Riyadh

Zoom on fast elevators to the 99th floor of Kingdom Center. Walk across the bridge at the top. Enjoy the view of the city and desert from this unusual building.

3 RIDE, BOUNCE, BUMP AT A PARK
Adhari

Climb aboard rides at Adhari Park. Ride a flying carousel. Bounce on trampolines or whirl in teacups. Drive bumper cars. Eat food from all over the world before you go bowling or golfing.

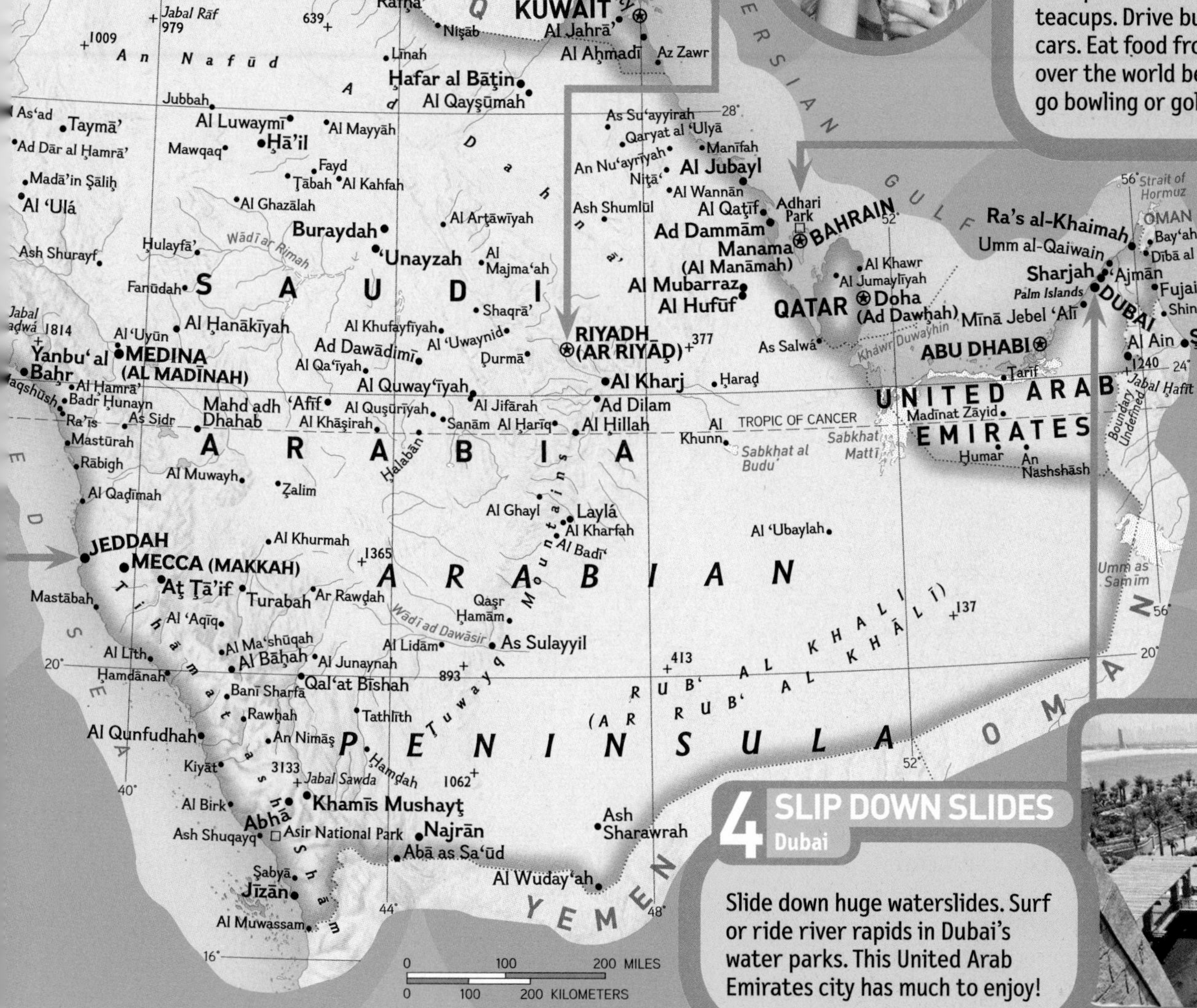

4 SLIP DOWN SLIDES
Dubai

Slide down huge waterslides. Surf or ride river rapids in Dubai's water parks. This United Arab Emirates city has much to enjoy!

ASIA

	NATIONAL BIRD:	NATIONAL FLOWER:	NATIONAL MAMMAL:
OMAN	ostrich	frankincense	Muscat gazelle
YEMEN	eagle	coffea arabica	Arabian leopard

SOUTHERN ARABIAN PENINSULA

Deserts, Wadis, and COASTS

Dates are grown by farmers in Oman and Yemen, at the southern tip of Arabia. For hundreds of years, people here have lived by fishing and trading in the Arabian Sea and Indian Ocean. In the cities, traditional homes stand beside modern buildings. Inland are mountains, dry wadis or valleys, and a hot, sandy desert called (in Arabic) Rub' Al Khali, meaning "the Empty Quarter."

5 VISIT A MOUNTAIN VILLAGE
Al Hajjarah

Trek the mountain path to the stone buildings in this Yemeni town. Admire how buildings and mountains blend one into another.

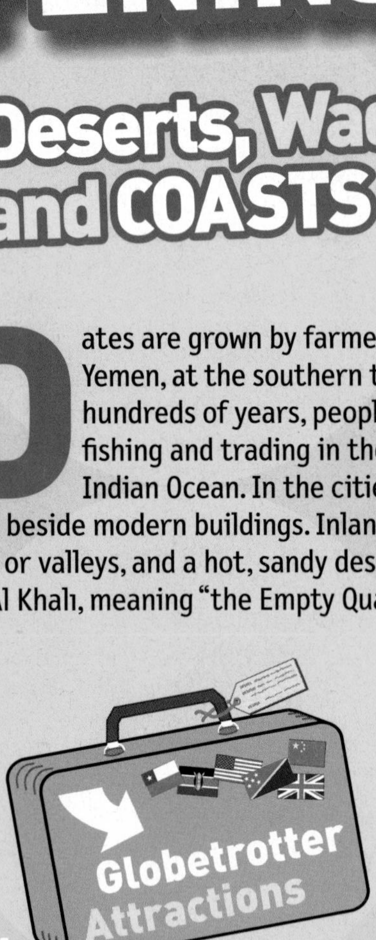

AL JABAL AL AKHDAR
Oman's Green Mountain rises from rocky, dusty land. Agriculture and villages can be seen on its terraces.

SOCOTRA
Many of the plants and animals that live on Yemen's Socotra Islands, such as the dragon's blood trees, do not exist anywhere else on Earth.

DHOFAR SPRINGS
In the Dhofar region of Oman, the 360 springs in and near the mountains are fed by the June to September rains.

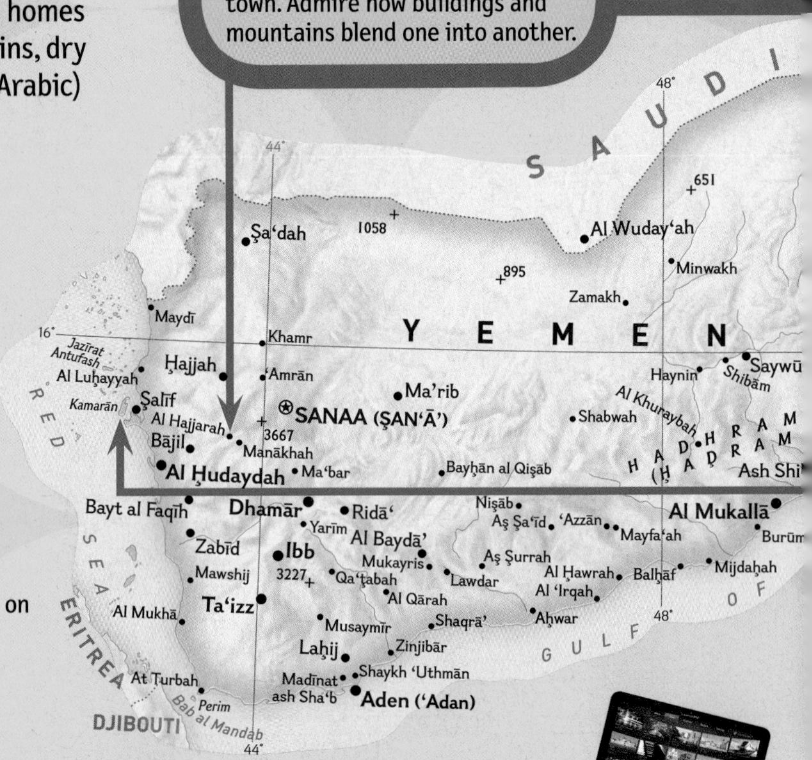

DIGITAL TRAVELER!
Date palms are used for food, shelter, clothing, and fuel. Which countries do you think produce the most date palm fruit? Search the Internet to find out.

5 COOL THINGS TO DO HERE

1 SPY THE LAND
Nizwá

Pass the date palms in Oman's oasis Nizwá on the way to the fort that protected the town for hundreds of years. Locate the huge central tower with such a good view that no sneak attack was possible.

2 CLIMB AN INCENSE BURNER
Maţraḩ

Climb to the top of the giant incense burner in Maţraḩ, Oman's Riyam Park. View the historic harbor where Arab dhows sailed in with trade goods for Maţraḩ's huge souk or marketplace.

3 SEE AN ENDANGERED ANIMAL
Oman

Enjoy Oman's Arabian Oryx Sanctuary. The oryx disappeared in the wild and are slowly being reintroduced. These were brought here from zoos.

4 EXPLORE A DESERT ISLAND
Kamarān Island

Sit on a Red Sea beach on Yemen's Kamarān, or Two Moons, Island. Watch the sky: For two weeks each month, it seems like two moons shine at the same time.

ID CARD
COUNTRY FACTS

OMAN
Population: 3,983,000
Capital: Muscat

YEMEN
Population: 25,235,000
Capital: Sanaa

NATIONAL BIRD: chukar partridge

NATIONAL FLOWER: rose

NATIONAL MAMMAL: sand gazelle

IRAQ

Early Civilization Between Two RIVERS

Iraq is mostly flat plains and desert with the Zagros Mountains in the northeast. Traces remain of the ancient civilization of Mesopotamia between the rivers Tigris and Euphrates. Today, oil-rich Iraq still uses the rivers, which join as the Shatt al Arab to flow into the Persian Gulf. Troubled by war since 2003, Iraq's main cities are Baghdad, Mosul in the north, and Basra in the south.

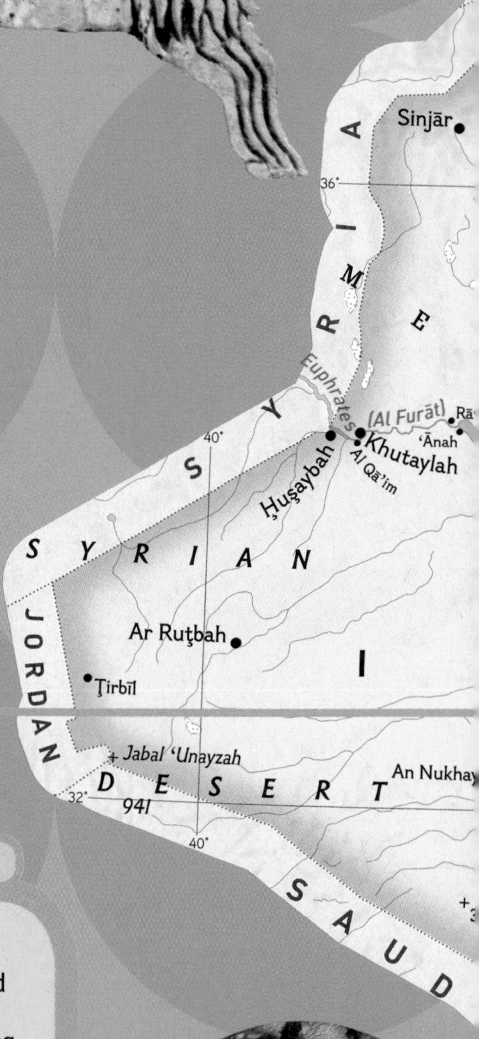

MOSUL

Mosul is built along the Tigris River. Across the river from it are the ruins of the ancient city of Nineveh.

NATIONAL PARK OF THE MARSHLAND

Iraq's first national park is a reclaimed marshland. Native reeds, animals, and local people have returned to live there.

MESOPOTAMIA

This region, the fertile valley between the Tigris River and the Euphrates River, is where the first civilization developed.

5 WANDER UNDER A WONDER

Madain

Be amazed that no pillars hold up this brick arch, one of the largest arches in the world. Taq Kisra is all that is left of an ancient palace. Built in the city of Ctesiphon, now Madain, most of the palace was destroyed over the years.

DIGITAL TRAVELER!

The Hanging Gardens of Babylon, one of the Seven Wonders of the Ancient World, were built in Iraq about 2,500 years ago. But where was Babylon? Find out the most likely sites using the Internet.

5 COOL THINGS TO DO HERE

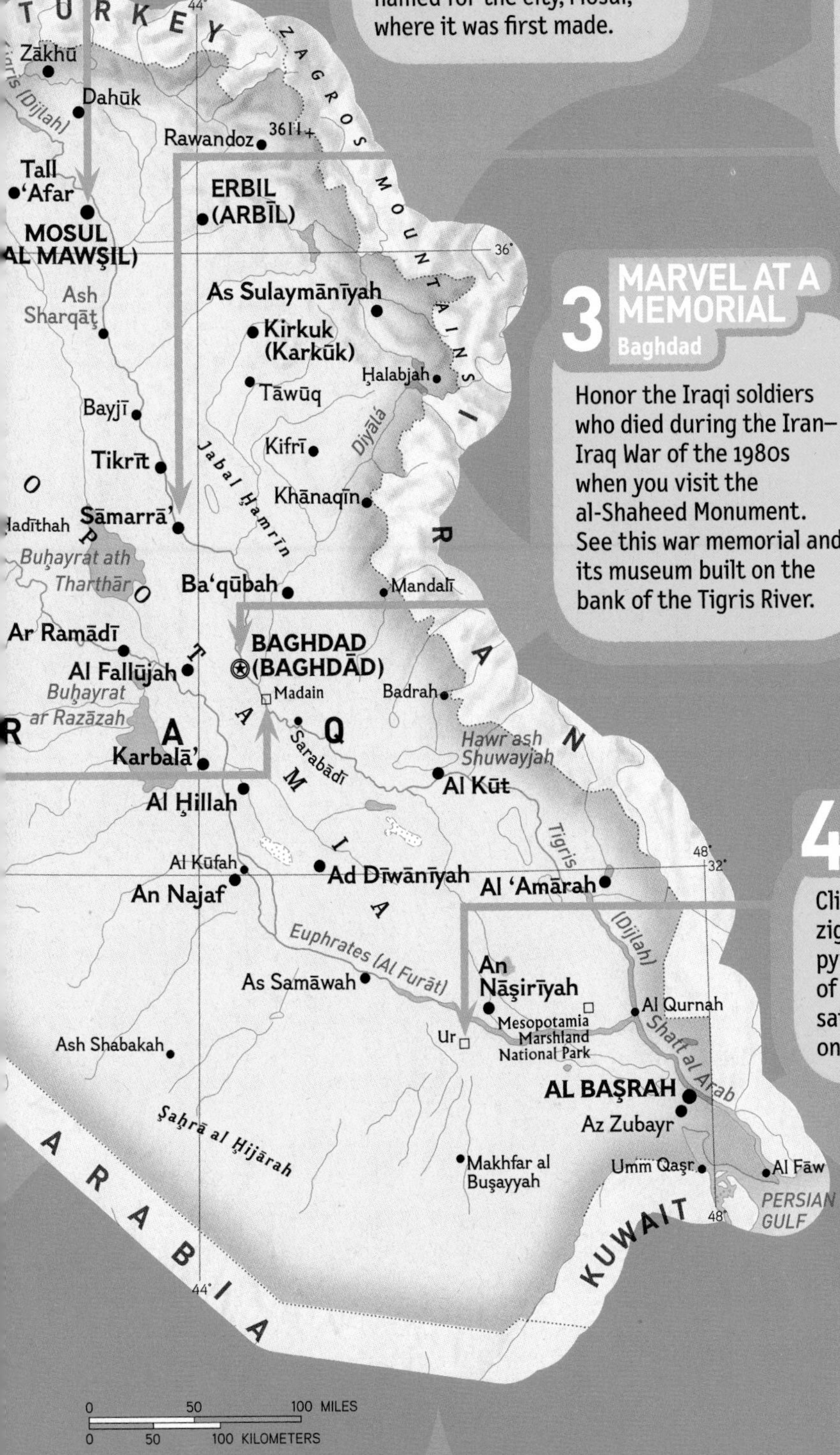

1 BUY MUSLIN CLOTHING
Mosul

Admire the plain cotton cloth that comes in a variety of weights. Muslin cloth was named for the city, Mosul, where it was first made.

2 SEE A SPIRAL MINARET
Sāmarrā

Locate Sāmarrā's Great Mosque and its spiral minaret. Built more than 1,000 years ago, it has survived many wars.

3 MARVEL AT A MEMORIAL
Baghdad

Honor the Iraqi soldiers who died during the Iran–Iraq War of the 1980s when you visit the al-Shaheed Monument. See this war memorial and its museum built on the bank of the Tigris River.

4 GAZE AT A ZIGGURAT
Ur

Climb the steps on Ur's ziggurat, a 4,000-year-old pyramid-shaped tower made of mud bricks. Imagine what sat on this huge base. No one knows for sure.

ASIA

ID CARD COUNTRY FACTS

Size: 169,235 sq mi (438,317 sq km)
Population: 35,095,000
Capital: Baghdad
Official languages: Arabic and Kurdish
Currency: New Iraqi dinar
Highest point: Cheeka Dar, 11,847 ft (3,611 m)
Life expectancy: 69.0 years

NATIONAL BIRD: see-see partridge

NATIONAL TREE: cypress

NATIONAL MAMMAL: Persian leopard

IRAN

From Mountains to PLATEAUS

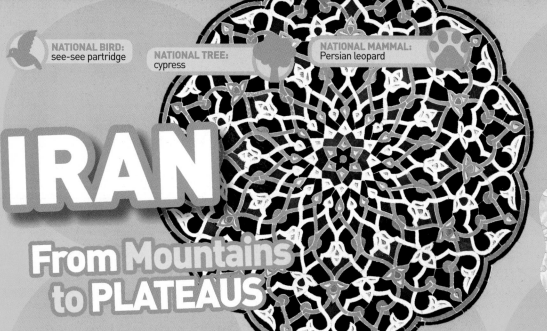

Iran's history dates back to the Persian Empire, and its people speak Farsi, or Persian. Today's Islamic republic has oil fields, modern cities, domed mosques with geometric art, and rural villages of mud-brick houses. Iran has a Caspian Sea coast north of the capital Tehran. Inland are some of the world's most desolate deserts, and mountain ranges that are formidable barriers.

5 GO UP TALL TOWERS

Tehran

Take the trip to the top of the Azandi Tower, built in 1971 to celebrate the Persian Empire. Then look in the distance for the newer Milad Tower, the world's sixth tallest tower.

ID CARD COUNTRY FACTS

Size: 636,372 sq mi (1,648,195 sq km)
Population: 76,521,000
Capital: Tehran
Official language: Persian
Currency: Iranian rial
Highest point: Kuh-e Damavand, 18,406 ft (5,610 m)
Life expectancy: 73.0 years

4 DISCOVER A WATER CAVE

Ali-Sadr

Tour one of the largest caves in the world by boat! Ride along the rivers and walk across an underground island.

DIGITAL TRAVELER!
Mosques (Islamic houses of worship) in Iran have tiles and carvings with beautiful repeating geometric patterns. Search the Internet to find a variety of geometric patterns and then invent your own on paper or your computer.

5 COOL THINGS TO DO HERE

1 SHOP IN A BAZAAR
Tabrīz

Shop at the Tabrīz Historic Bazaar. It began as a trade center along the Silk Road from China. Today, merchants still sell rugs and spices there.

MOUNT DAMAVAND
This inactive volcano is the highest peak in Iran and the highest volcano in Asia. Its top is often covered in snow and visible for miles.

DASHT-E KAVĪR
Almost no one lives in the Kavīr Desert. This great salt desert has a salt crust and seldom gets rain, but it does have salt marshes that act like quicksand!

GOLESTAN NATIONAL PARK
Located in the mountains, this protected area includes rivers and waterfalls and has many rare birds and mammals.

2 WATCH CARPETS BEING MADE
Mashhad

Inspect the Persian carpets made in this city. Carpets have been woven here for hundreds of years. Many are dark red or blue-black with a medallion in the center.

3 EXPLORE A 2,500-YEAR-OLD PALACE
Persepolis

Wander through the ruins of this palace complex. Find the carved pictures, statues, remaining columns, throne hall, and even the king's bath.

5 COOL THINGS TO DO HERE

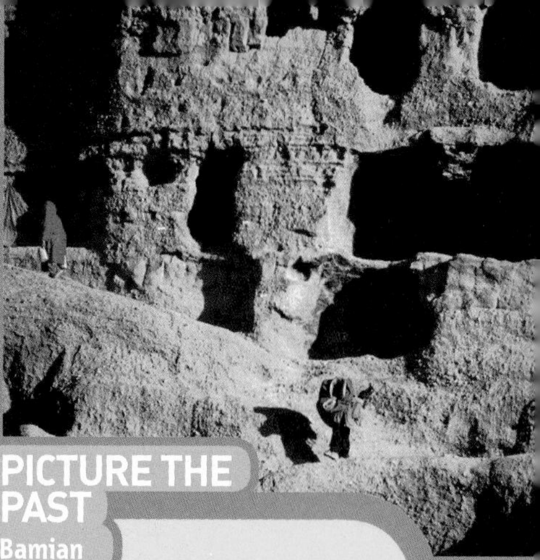

1 EXPLORE A FORT
Herat

Explore the restored ancient fortress overlooking Herat. Wander the winding ramps and huge rooms of this fort, built on the Silk Road from China. Examine the museum's ancient items.

2 GO ON A PICNIC
Kandahar

Eat on the green terraces around the Baba Wali Shrine in Kandahar. Walk the steps and wander in the pomegranate gardens around this famous shrine located on the banks of the Arghandab River.

3 PICTURE THE PAST
Bamian

Investigate the Bamian caves. Find the remains of recently destroyed ancient carved statues of Buddha. Admire the murals on the cave walls, some of the world's first oil paintings.

DIGITAL TRAVELER!
What large animals do you think live in Afghanistan? Use the Internet to find out and to learn in what part of the country each lives.

NATIONAL BIRD: spotted eagle

NATIONAL FLOWER: tulip

NATIONAL MAMMAL: snow leopard

AFGHANISTAN

A Landlocked, Mountainous COUNTRY

Afghanistan has deserts, rolling plains, and the high Hindu Kush mountains, which rise along the border with Pakistan. The country has ancient ruins, historic routes such as the Khyber Pass, and fertile valleys, where village farmers grow crops. Nomads herd Karakul sheep, prized for hides and wool. Kabul is the biggest city in Afghanistan, which has been troubled by war since the 1980s.

5 WATCH KITE-FIGHTING
Kabul

Cheer the colorful kites controlled from the ground by boys and men. Watch kites crash to the ground when the specially prepared strings of one kite cut another's strings. Find the kite-flyers on rooftops and in the nearby hills. Catch a falling kite to become a kite runner.

4 TRACE TILES AT TOWERS
Ghazni

Locate the Ghazni towers as they rise above the barren plain. The outsides of the towers are covered with intricate tile decorations. The towers were built during the Ghaznavid Empire in the 1200s.

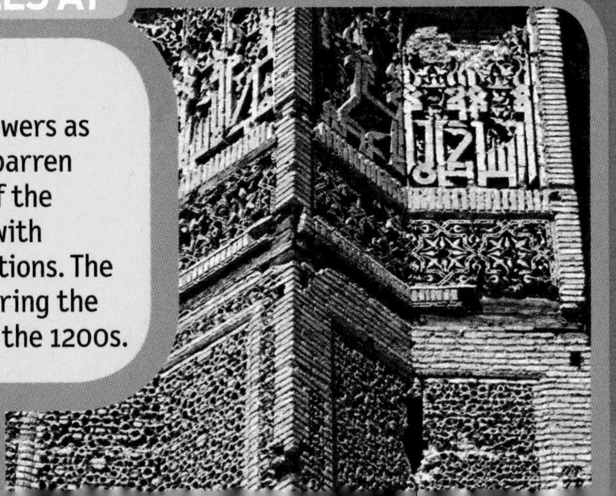

KHYBER PASS
Roads, hiking paths, and trains use this pass through the Khyber Hills to go from Afghanistan to Pakistan.

HINDU KUSH
The Hindu Kush is a Central Asian mountain system in both Pakistan and Afghanistan. In Afghanistan, lower rounded mountains are in the west with higher mountains to the east.

BAND-E AMIR NATIONAL PARK
This chain of six deep lakes was formed when minerals created natural dams to hold back the water in this desert region.

ID CARD
COUNTRY FACTS

Size: 251,827 sq mi (652,230 sq km)
Population: 30,552,000
Capital: Kabul
Official languages: Afghan Persian (Dari) and Pashto
Currency: afghani
Highest point: Nowshak, 24,580 ft (7,492 m)
Life expectancy: 60.0 years

NATIONAL BIRD: chukar partridge

NATIONAL FLOWER: poet's jasmine

NATIONAL MAMMAL: markhor

PAKISTAN

A Mix of LANDSCAPES

Separated from British India in 1947, Pakistan has northern mountains where the Hindu Kush and Karakoram ranges meet the Himalaya. Central and southern plains are watered by the Indus and other rivers. Baluchistan in the west is arid, and so is the Thar Desert in the southeast. Most cities, including Islamabad and Lahore, are in the greener, wetter north, but the biggest is Karachi on the Arabian Sea.

5 EAT POTATOES MASALA

Islamabad

Smell the spices. Make your own masala, which is a mix of local spices— any that you like. Each region and house has its own favorite combination. It may include coriander, cumin, and cinnamon.

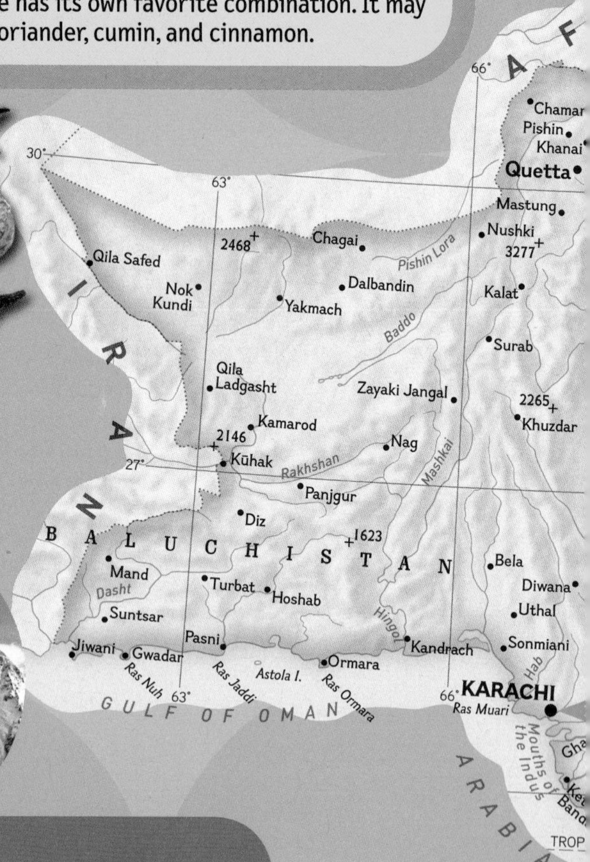

Globetrotter Attractions

KARAKORAM HIGHWAY

This highway from China to Pakistan is about 500 miles (800 km) long. It goes across high mountains and deep valleys.

PUNJAB PROVINCE

Most of this province is on a plain used to grow crops. The Indus River and four others flow across it and often change course due to annual floods.

MOHENJO-DARO

This was once the largest city of the Indus civilization. Its ruins show well-planned streets and a drainage system built nearly 4,500 years ago. It is located in the southeastern part of Pakistan near the city of Larkana.

DIGITAL TRAVELER!

Five of the fourteen highest mountains in the world are found in Pakistan. Use the Internet to find these mountains. Make a list from highest to lowest, in both meters and feet.

5 COOL THINGS TO DO HERE

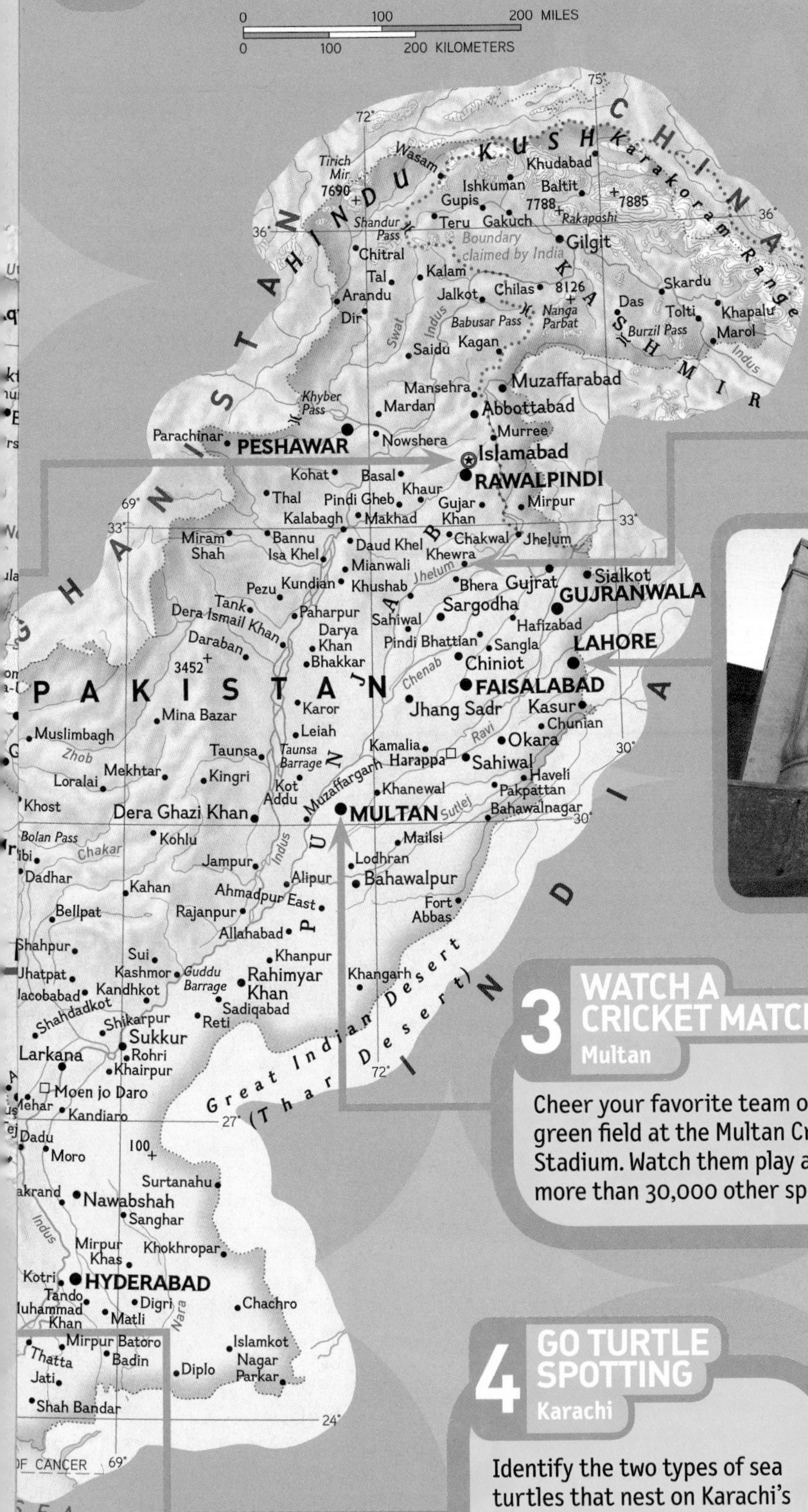

1 TOUR A SALT MINE

Khewra

Ride a train through the second largest salt mine in the world. Travel into the mines used by Alexander the Great 2,300 years ago. See bridges of rock salt stretching across ponds.

2 FIGURE OUT A FORT

Lahore

View the marble palaces and mosques inside the fort. Compare the red sandstone, baked bricks, and marble that were used for the buildings. Examine the elaborate mosaics. Wander in the elegant water gardens with terraces, waterfalls, and ponds.

ASIA

3 WATCH A CRICKET MATCH

Multan

Cheer your favorite team on the lush green field at the Multan Cricket Stadium. Watch them play along with more than 30,000 other spectators.

4 GO TURTLE SPOTTING

Karachi

Identify the two types of sea turtles that nest on Karachi's beaches. Watch them come ashore from August to February when they nest in the sand. Keep the beach clean for the turtles.

ID CARD COUNTRY FACTS

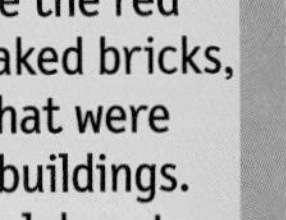

Size: 307,374 sq mi (796,095 sq km)
Population: 190,709,000
Capital: Islamabad
Official languages: Urdu and English
Currency: Pakistani rupee
Highest point: K2 (Mt. Godwin-Austen), 28,251 ft (8,611 m)
Life expectancy: 66.0 years

	NATIONAL BIRD:	NATIONAL FLOWER:	NATIONAL MAMMAL:
INDIA	peacock	Indian lotus	lion
NEPAL	Himalayan monal	rhododendron	cow
MALDIVES	gray heron	pink rose	flying fox (bat)
SRI LANKA	jungle fowl	blue water lily	Sri Lankan elephant

SOUTH ASIA

Land of High Peaks and Mighty RIVERS

India, seventh largest country in area, and second biggest in population, dominates South Asia. It has mountains, deserts, plains, jungles, a long sea coast, and both historic and modern cities. The Ganges and Brahmaputra rivers rise in the Himalaya, where Nepal is India's small neighbor. Sri Lanka is an island off India's southern tip, and the Maldives are islands west of India, in the Indian Ocean.

ID CARD COUNTRY FACTS

India
Population: 1,276,508,000
Capital: New Delhi

Maldives
Population: 360,000
Capital: Male

Nepal
Population: 26,810,000
Capital: Kathmandu

Sri Lanka
Population: 20,501,000
Capital: Colombo

5 TOUR BOLLYWOOD FILM CITY
Hyderabad

Visit Ramoji Film City's sets where many of India's famous Bollywood movies are made. Watch the actors and directors working as they shoot a movie in a garden, house, or village.

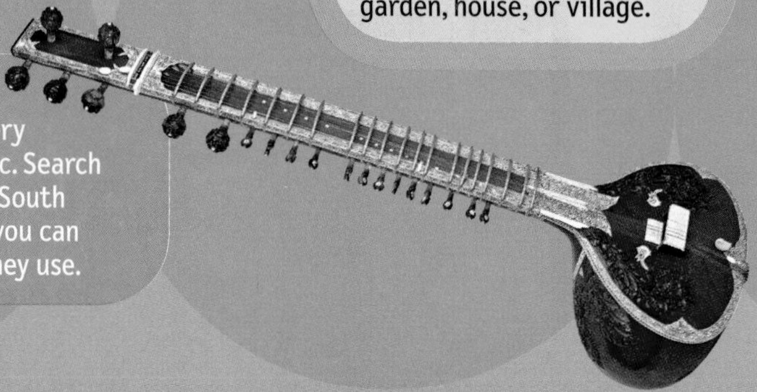

DIGITAL TRAVELER!
The music of South Asia is very different from Western music. Search the Internet for songs from South Asian countries. Then see if you can find out what instruments they use.

5 COOL THINGS TO DO HERE

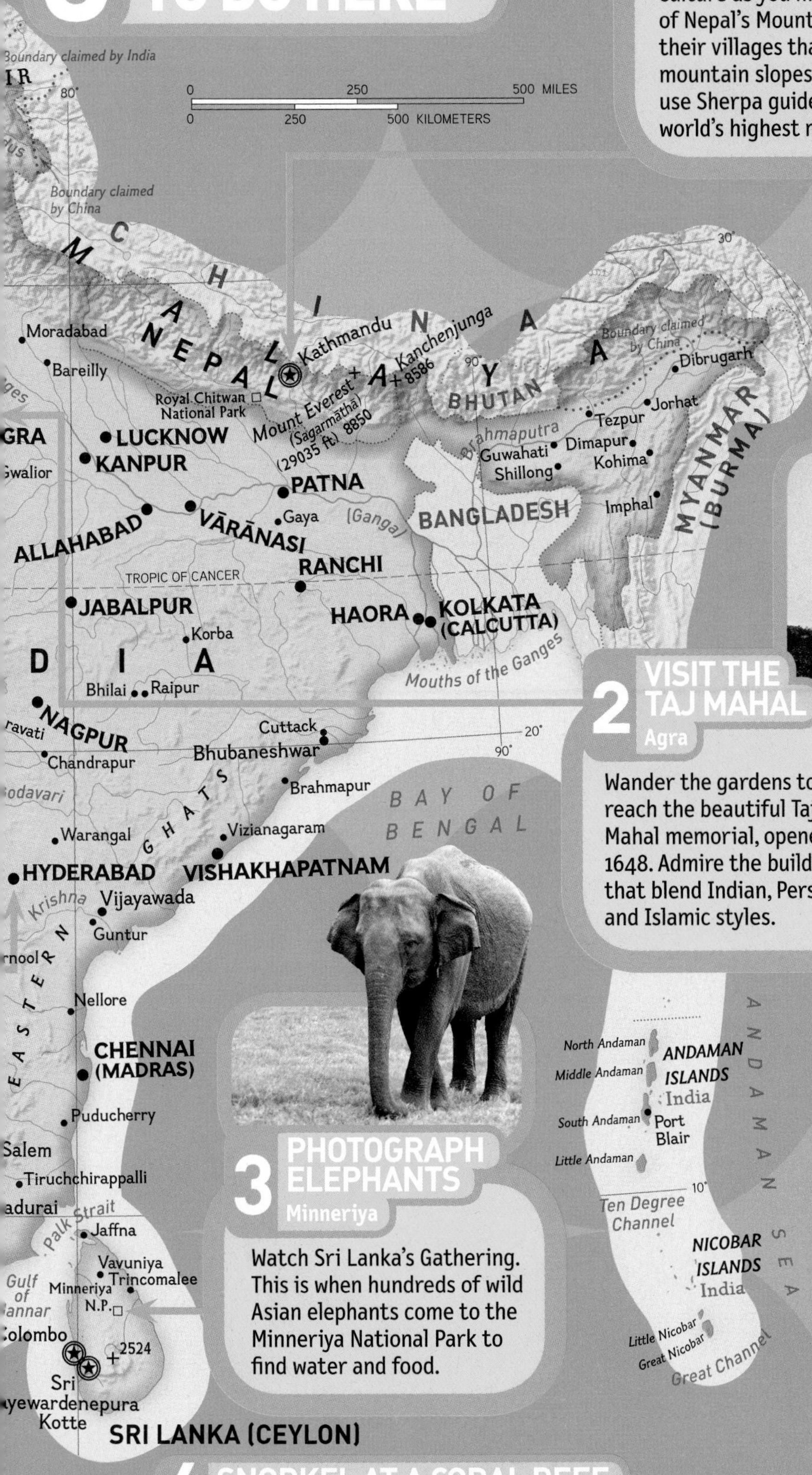

1 BE GUIDED BY SHERPAS
Kathmandu

Learn about the Sherpa culture as you hike at the base of Nepal's Mount Everest. Visit their villages that cling to the mountain slopes. Outsiders use Sherpa guides to climb the world's highest mountains.

2 VISIT THE TAJ MAHAL
Agra

Wander the gardens to reach the beautiful Taj Mahal memorial, opened in 1648. Admire the buildings that blend Indian, Persian, and Islamic styles.

3 PHOTOGRAPH ELEPHANTS
Minneriya

Watch Sri Lanka's Gathering. This is when hundreds of wild Asian elephants come to the Minneriya National Park to find water and food.

4 SNORKEL AT A CORAL REEF
Maldives

Wonder at the colorful fish, other underwater creatures, and the coral reefs around these islands.

Globetrotter Attractions

THAR DESERT
This desert crosses the India and Pakistan border. Its sand dunes are often very tall or move in the wind, taking different shapes.

CHITWAN NATIONAL PARK
This Nepal park has wild Bengal tigers and the last population of horned Asiatic rhinoceroses.

GANGES RIVER
The Ganges begins in the high Himalaya and crosses a fertile region of India until it reaches the Bay of Bengal.

	NATIONAL BIRD:	NATIONAL FLOWER:	NATIONAL MAMMAL:
BANGLADESH	magpie-robin	shapia	royal Bengal tiger
BHUTAN	raven	blue poppy	takin

BANGLADESH AND BHUTAN

From Mangrove Forests to a MOUNTAIN NATION

East of India is Bangladesh, so flat and low-lying that cyclone storms cause floods as the sea surges inland from the Bay of Bengal. The Ganges and Brahmaputra rivers flow into the bay, forming a vast delta. Bangladeshi people farm, fish, and work in factories. In Dhaka city, "baby taxis" jostle for passengers. Bhutan is a rugged Himalayan mountain kingdom, between India and Chinese-ruled Tibet.

DIGITAL TRAVELER!
Weather in Bangladesh is influenced by monsoons—wind systems that change directions on a seasonal basis. Find out when the monsoons come to Bangladesh. Which month gets the highest average rainfall in Dhaka? On average, how much rain falls during that month?

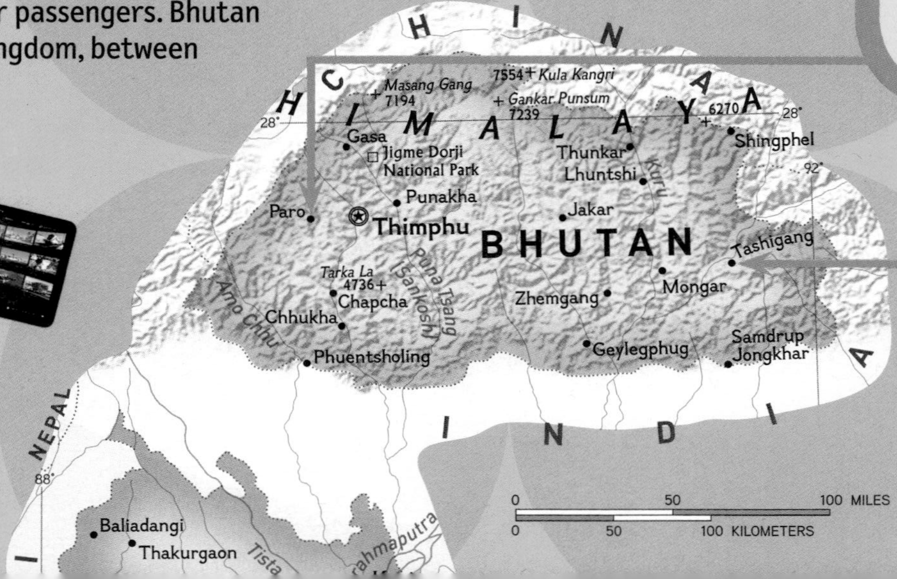

5 COOL THINGS TO DO HERE

1 HIKE A HOLY TRAIL
Paro

Climb from the valley floor along the cliff to find Bhutan's small Paro Taktsang or Tiger's Nest Monastery. Admire the views across the canyon before you take the trail down the cliff to a waterfall.

2 WATCH AN ARCHERY COMPETITION
Tashigang

Watch the archers in any village in Bhutan. Archery is the national sport and this small country is proud to take part in only one Olympic sport: archery.

Globetrotter Attractions

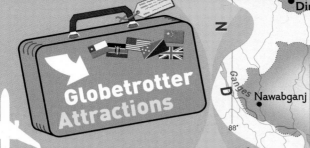

THE SUNDARBANS
This mangrove forest in Bangladesh is one of the largest in the world. It extends across islands and along waterways that empty into the Bay of Bengal.

JIGME DORJI NATIONAL PARK
Snow leopards and tigers live in this Bhutan protected area. Meltwater from mountain glaciers fills lakes and rivers.

GANGES DELTA
The Ganges and Brahmaputra rivers flow into the Bay of Bengal. The Ganges Delta is where the rivers' flowing waters have left fertile land. It is the largest delta in the world.

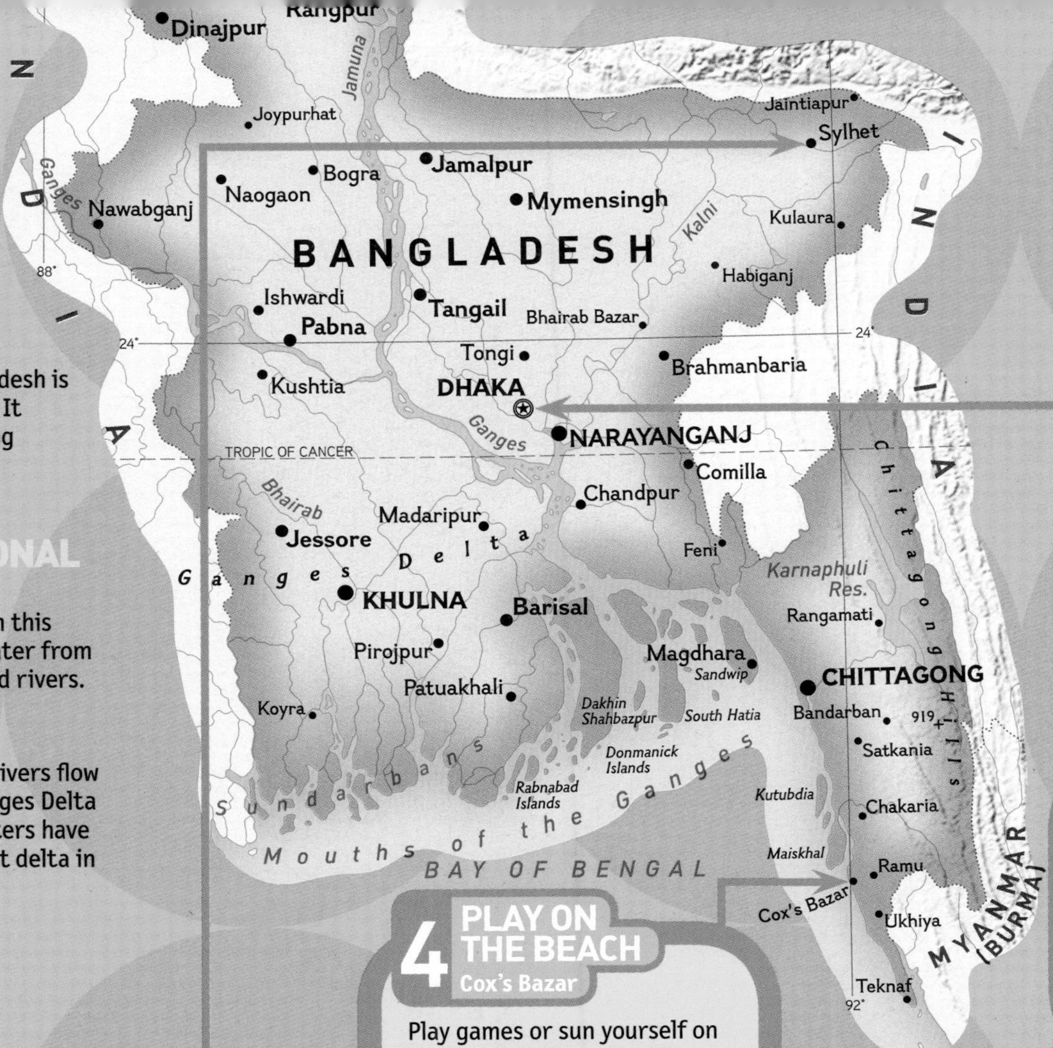

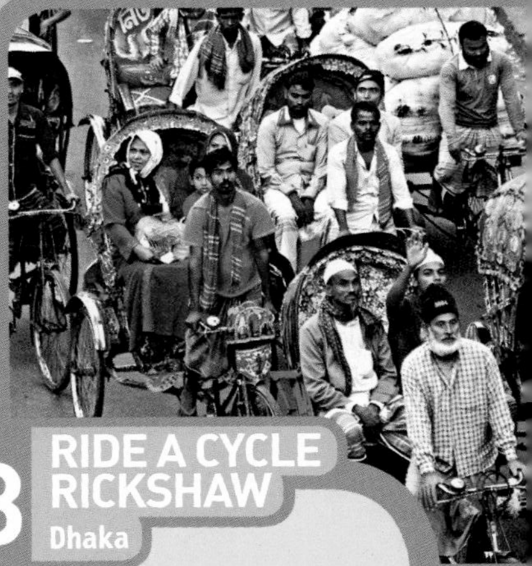

3 RIDE A CYCLE RICKSHAW
Dhaka

Choose a cycle rickshaw to get around Bangladesh's capital, called "The Rickshaw Capital of the World." While stuck in a rickshaw traffic jam, admire the paintings on those rickshaws nearby.

4 PLAY ON THE BEACH
Cox's Bazar

Play games or sun yourself on the beach in this town in Bangladesh. Enjoy the tropical weather and sandy shore on this, the world's longest uninterrupted natural beach.

5 TASTE TASTY TEA
Sylhet

Drive through lush, green tea gardens near Sylhet. See how the tea growers have made terraces on the hillside. At the Bangladesh Tea Research Institute, taste teas and learn how tea is grown and processed.

ID CARD COUNTRY FACTS

BANGLADESH
Population: 156,595,000
Capital: Dhaka

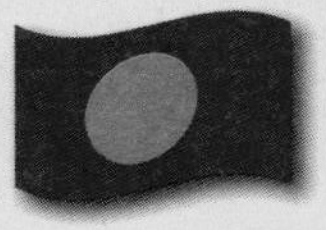

BHUTAN
Population: 733,000
Capital: Thimphu

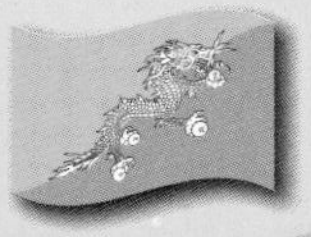

5 COOL THINGS TO DO HERE

1 SEE THE TERRA-COTTA ARMY
Xi'an

Admire the Terra-cotta Army buried about 2,200 years ago. See how workers today have pieced together the broken bits of clay to rebuild the warriors, their horses, and chariots. Hundreds of warriors with different faces but the same body stand in rows, protecting China's first emperor.

2 HIKE ALONG A GREAT WALL
Badaling

Hike along the Great Wall of China. Built over hundreds of years, the wall protected China. Imagine the soldiers marching along the steep winding path that is high on the mountain ridge.

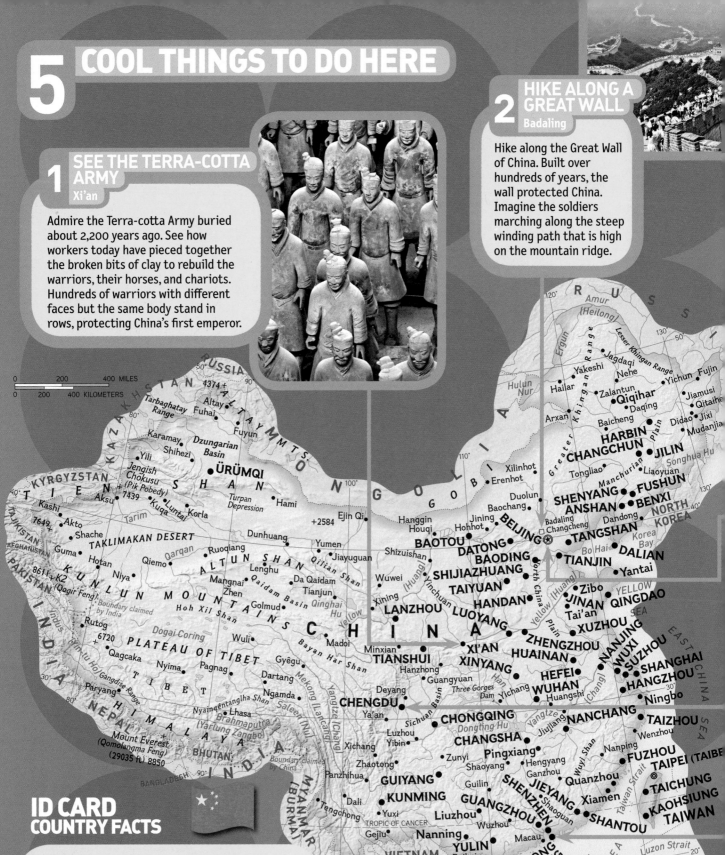

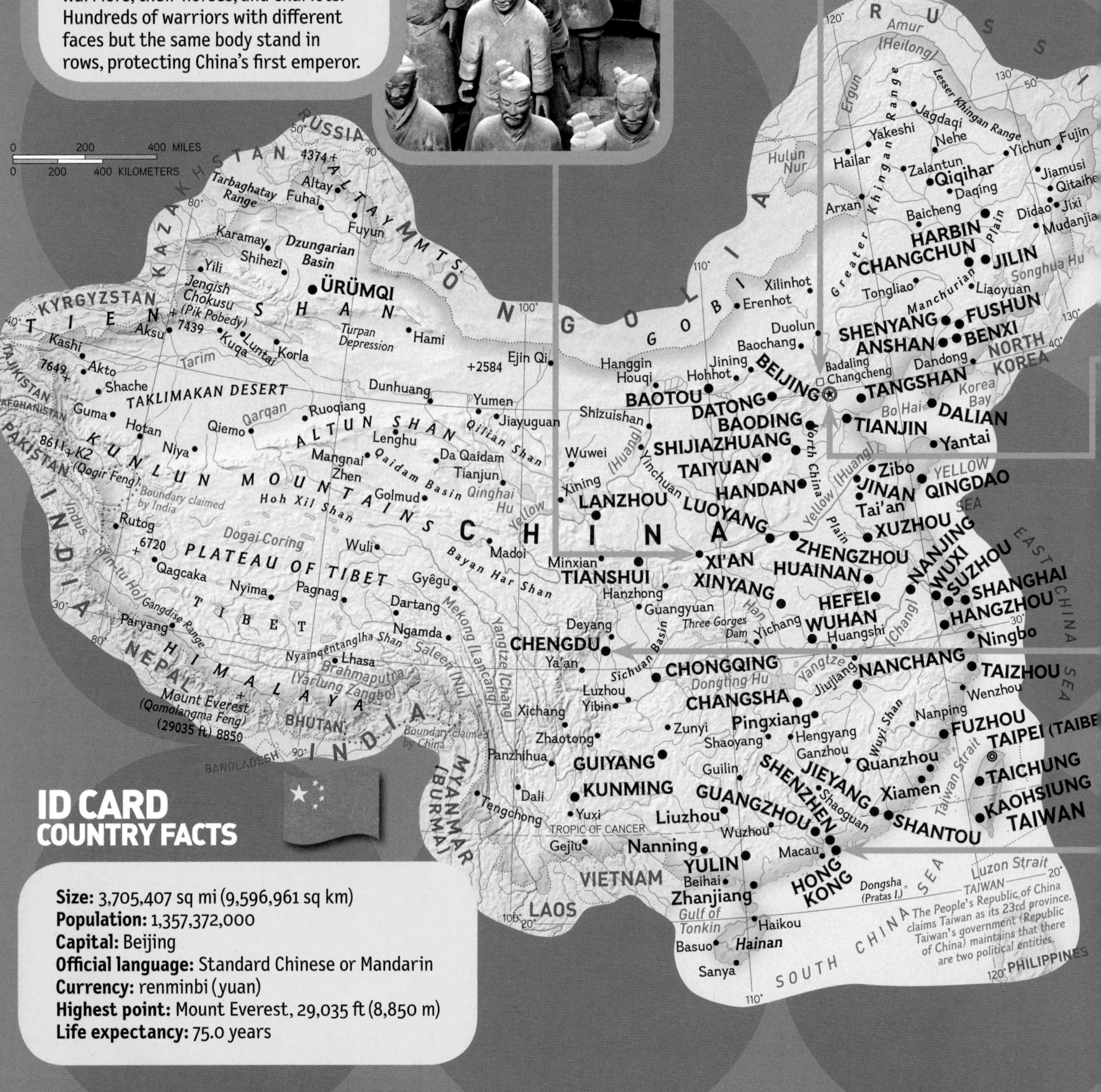

ID CARD
COUNTRY FACTS

Size: 3,705,407 sq mi (9,596,961 sq km)
Population: 1,357,372,000
Capital: Beijing
Official language: Standard Chinese or Mandarin
Currency: renminbi (yuan)
Highest point: Mount Everest, 29,035 ft (8,850 m)
Life expectancy: 75.0 years

NATIONAL BIRD: red-crowned crane

NATIONAL MAMMAL: giant panda

NATIONAL FLOWER: peony

CHINA

Land of the GREAT WALL

No country has more people than China. Civilization in the ancient land of fabled dragons grew around rivers, such as the Huang He and Yangtze. To the west are Tibet and the Himalaya. To the north lie the Tien Shan and Altai mountains, and the Gobi Desert. Ships ply the Yellow, East China, and South China seas. Northern winters are cold, but south China is subtropical, with monsoon rains.

3 ENTER A FORBIDDEN CITY
Beijing

Wander through this huge palace complex where emperors and their families lived. Search for designs using animals and flowers.

4 FEED A GIANT PANDA
Chengdu

Admire, photograph, and feed a giant panda. In Southwest China the Chengdu Research Base of Giant Panda Breeding allows visitors to meet the giant pandas in their specially designed environment.

5 VISIT DISNEYLAND
Hong Kong

In this Chinese city, visit the Wild West in Grizzly Gulch. Enjoy Mystic Manor. Play in Toy Story Land. Journey into the jungle.

DIGITAL TRAVELER!
Yaks are important animals for the people of Tibet, an autonomous region of China. Search the Internet to learn how Tibetans use the yak.

THE GOBI
This desert, shared with Mongolia, is mostly bare rock. Very little water is found here, except deep underground. Parts of the Gobi get less than four inches (102 mm) of rain a year. It is a very cold desert in winter, but has very hot summers.

HONG KONG
A view from the hills shows the city's skyscrapers, its excellent harbor, and the New Territories in the distance.

THREE GORGES DAM
This concrete dam on the Yangtze River creates electricity and protects many people from river flooding.

NATIONAL BIRD: green pheasant

NATIONAL FLOWER: chrysanthemum

NATIONAL MAMMAL: raccoon dog

JAPAN

A Rugged ISLAND CHAIN

Japan is a country of islands in the Pacific Ocean. The islands lie on the Pacific "Ring of Fire" where earthquakes, tsunamis, and volcanic eruptions occur. The four main islands are Honshu, Hokkaido, Kyushu, and Shikoku. The capital, Tokyo, is on Honshu, as is Mount Fuji. About 80 percent of Japan is mountain and forest, so most people live in cities along the coastal plains.

DIGITAL TRAVELER!
Manga comics are popular in Japan among people of all ages. Use your digital device to look for manga kids' comics and choose your favorites to read.

5 COOL THINGS TO DO HERE

1 VISIT A PEACE MEMORIAL
Hiroshima

At Hiroshima Peace Memorial Park, remember those who died from the nuclear bomb attack in 1945 at the end of World War II.

2 SOAK IN HOT SPRINGS
Beppu

Go to a resort or public bath to relax in pools of hot water. Hot volcanic water gushes into hot springs throughout Beppu. People also use this resource for heating buildings.

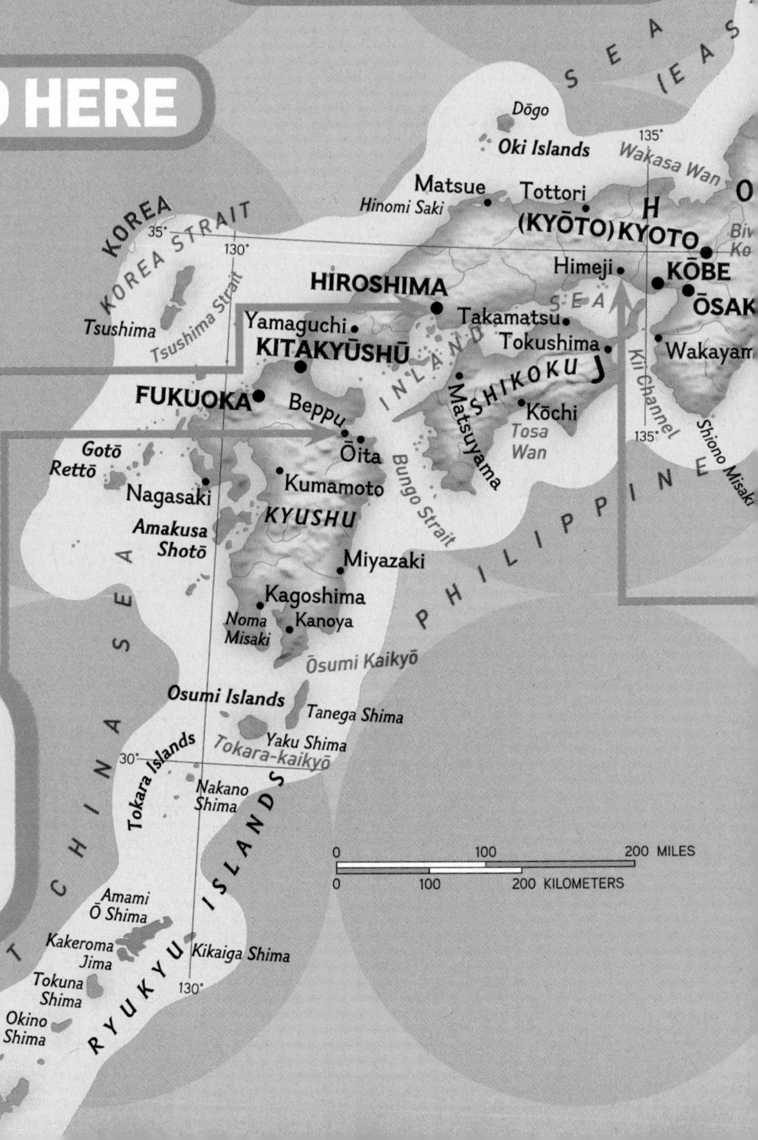

Globetrotter Attractions

MOUNT FUJI

Japan's highest mountain is called an active volcano, though it last erupted in 1707. Its cone-shaped peak is visible from Tokyo and Yokohama.

LAKE BIWA

Japan's largest lake is most likely the oldest one. It probably is more than five million years old.

KUSHIRO-SHITSUGEN NATIONAL PARK

Endangered Japanese cranes are protected here. You may see pairs of cranes dancing together.

3 MAKE YOUR OWN NOODLES

Yokohama

Create your own ramen noodles at the Cupnoodle Museum. Learn how Momofuku Ando invented his first instant meal in 1958 and ramen for space flights in 2005.

4 HOLD ON TO YOUR SEAT!

Tokyo

Speed from Tokyo to Aomori at 199 miles an hour (320 kph) on the super-fast Shinkansen train. The train's pointy front prevents "tunnel boom" caused by air pressure changing as the train enters a tunnel at high speed.

ASIA

5 CROSS SWORDS WITH SAMURAI

Himeji

Discover one of the few surviving wooden castles in Japan. With watchtowers, moats, and residences for samurai warriors, Himeji Castle protected this area in the 1600s.

ID CARD COUNTRY FACTS

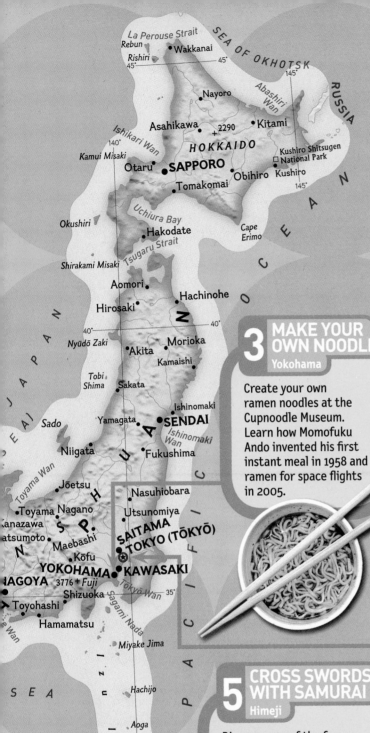

Size: 145,913 sq mi (377,915 sq km)
Population: 127,301,000
Capital: Tokyo
Official language: Japanese
Currency: yen
Highest point: Fuji, 12,388 ft (3,776 m)
Life expectancy: 83.0 years

5 COOL THINGS TO DO HERE

1 GET TO GRIPS WITH GIANTS
Erdenet

Wrestling is the country's most popular sport. Fans watch competitions in stadiums and on television. The wrestler who wins the most rounds in a competition is ranked "Giant."

2 DON'T GET THE HUMP!
Yol Valley

Explore the Gobi desert by camel. Guided camel rides take you over the desert's highest sand dunes. The two-humped camels are unique to this region.

5 WALK WITH DINOSAURS
Nemegt Basin

Explore the land where dinosaurs once roamed. See fossils and footprints here. A great collection of dinosaur eggs and nests were sent to a museum in Ulaanbaatar.

4 SLEEP IN A GER
Terelj

Stay with a nomadic family and learn about their lives. Many Mongolians still live in *gers*. These are sturdy tents that can be built and taken down in under an hour.

NATIONAL BIRD: Saker falcon

NATIONAL TREE: saxaul

NATIONAL MAMMAL: Bactrian camel

MONGOLIA

A Vast and Barren LAND

Warm clothes and hats are essential in windswept Mongolia. In the Gobi Desert it can get very cold, and very hot. Though smaller than neighbors Russia and China, Mongolia is a vast country, sparsely populated, with few cities. Most of the land is treeless steppe plains, where nomads herd livestock, and there is little farmland. The snow-topped Altay Mountains rise in western Mongolia, where there are many lakes.

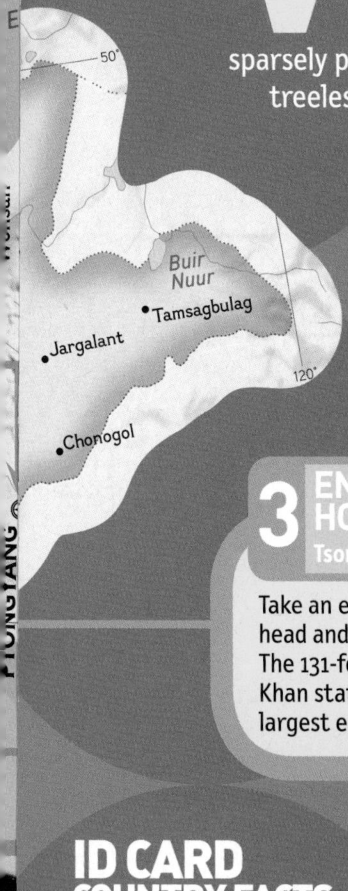

3 ENTER A GIANT HORSE

Tsonjin Boldog

Take an elevator to the horse's head and see a beautiful view. The 131-foot (40-m) Genghis Khan statue is one of the world's largest equestrian statues.

ALTAY RANGE

This mountain range stretches through China, Mongolia, Russia, and Kazakhstan. Humans lived in this region more than a million years ago. Many small groups of people still live here.

THE GOBI

In Mongolian, *gobi* means "waterless place." Much of the Gobi desert is covered in rocks, not sand. There are even a few ice-filled canyons.

HUSTAI NATIONAL PARK

The protected grasslands here made this a suitable place to reintroduce wild Przewalski's horses. The endangered horse is Mongolia's national symbol.

ID CARD COUNTRY FACTS

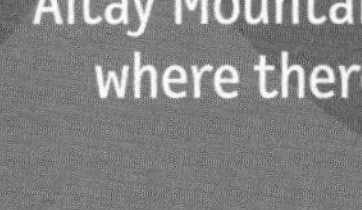

Size: 603,908 sq mi (1,564,116 sq km)
Population: 2,792,000
Capital: Ulaanbaatar
Official language: Khalkha Mongol
Currency: togrog (tugrik)
Highest point: Tavan Bogd Uul, 14,350 ft (4,374 m)
Life expectancy: 69.0 years

DIGITAL TRAVELER!
Mongolia is one of the most sparsely populated countries in the world. Use the Internet to find out its population density. How does that compare to the population density in the United States and other highly populated countries, such as India and Brazil?

	NATIONAL BIRD:	NATIONAL FLOWER:	NATIONAL MAMMAL:
MYANMAR	Burmese peacock	paduak	elephant
THAILAND	Siamese fireback	rachapruek	Thai elephant

MYANMAR AND THAILAND

The Heart of SOUTHEAST ASIA

Myanmar, also known as Burma, is a mountainous, forested country with rice-growing lowlands such as the Irrawaddy Delta. To the south and east is Thailand, called Siam until 1939. Northern Thailand is hilly, but the southern plains offer rich farmland. The main river is the Chao Phraya. People use the rivers for transportation. Monsoon rains sweep both these countries in the rainy season. Away from the cities, tribal groups live in mountain villages.

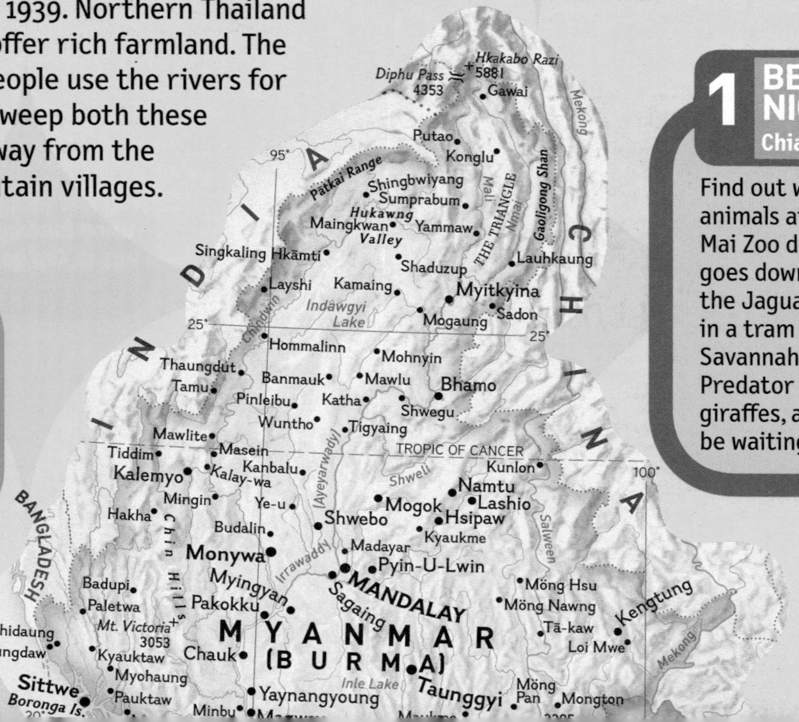

5 COOL THINGS TO DO HERE

1 BE A NIGHT OWL
Chiang Mai

Find out what the animals at the Chiang Mai Zoo do after the sun goes down. Walk along the Jaguar Trail. Or, ride in a tram through the Savannah Safari and the Predator Prowl. Zebras, giraffes, and tigers will be waiting for you.

2 SLINK WITH SNAKES
Bangkok

Get acquainted with snakes of all kinds, including a poisonous king cobra. Staff at Bangkok Snake Farm will show you how they handle snakes safely. Learn which snakes are dangerous.

DIGITAL TRAVELER!
Pad Thai is a popular food eaten throughout Thailand. Go online to find out what this is and how to cook it. Ask your family to help you prepare it at home.

3 TOUR AN ANCIENT PAGODA
Yangon

Stroll up the long stretch of walkway—or take an elongated elevator—to the 2,500-year-old Shwedagon Pagoda. This is a sacred Buddhist site, covered with hundreds of gold plates and 4,531 diamonds.

4 SHOP AT A FLOATING MARKET
Damnoen Saduak

See the pyramids of fruits and vegetables stacked in boats. Watch the boats float along the canal and pull over so that the merchants can sell to shoppers who are waiting on the banks.

PHONG NGA BAY
The bay is dotted with sheer-cliff islands. Some look as if they will topple over. One island was featured in a 1974 James Bond movie.

AYUTTHAYA
Palace towers sit among the ruins of a royal city dating from the 1400s.

INLE LAKE
This beautiful lake in Myanmar is known for the Intha people who row boats with their legs.

5 GET WET WITH WILDLIFE
Ko Adang

Glide through the water in Tarutao National Marine Park and count how many kinds of fish you see.

ID CARD
COUNTRY FACTS

MYANMAR
Population: 53,259,000
Capital: Rangoon

THAILAND
Population: 66,185,000
Capital: Bangkok

	NATIONAL BIRD:	NATIONAL FLOWER:	NATIONAL MAMMAL:
LAOS	bare-faced bulbul	plumeria	Indian elephant
VIETNAM	Vietnamese waterbird	red lotus	water buffalo
CAMBODIA	giant ibis	romduol	kouprey

LAOS, VIETNAM, AND CAMBODIA

Ancient Temples, Powerful Rains, and AMAZING FOOD

In these Southeast Asian countries, forested uplands, plateaus, and mountains rise above lowland plains. The people of Laos, Vietnam, and Cambodia (formerly Kampuchea) rely on seasonal rains and the Mekong and other rivers for rice-growing. Houses are built on stilts beside rivers. Cambodia has a lake-river, the Tonle Sap, while Vietnam's long coastline extends from the Gulf of Tonkin in the north to the South China Sea.

5 COOL THINGS TO DO HERE

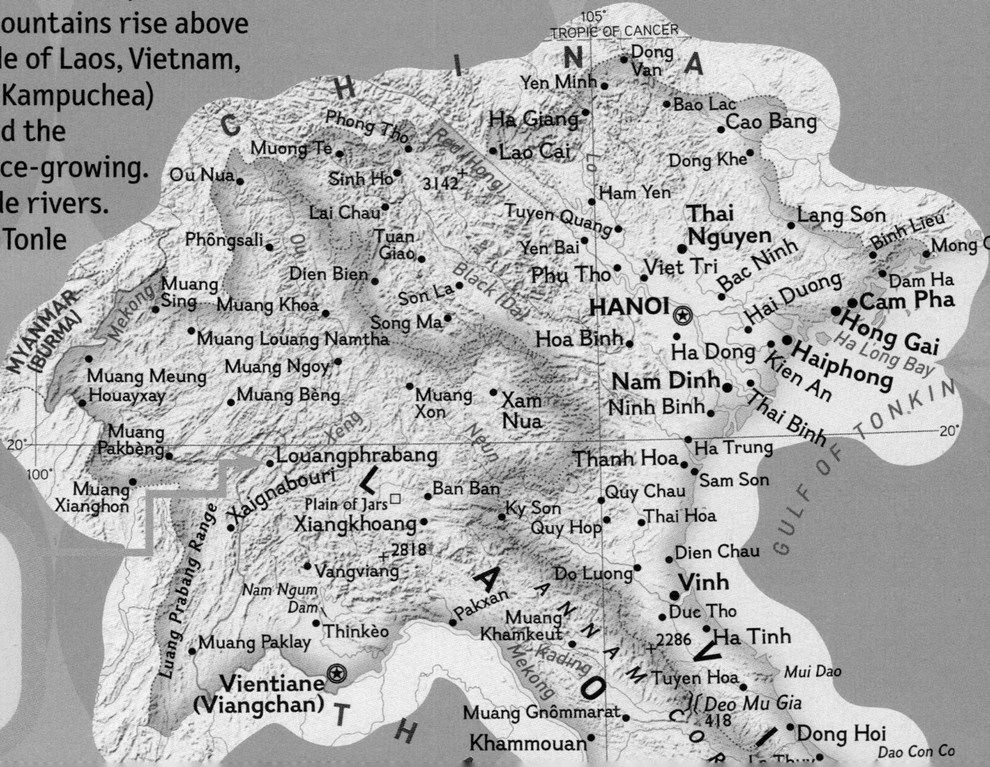

1 GO BOATING ON A BAY
Ha Long Bay

Float by some of the thousands of jungle islands. Some are hollow with huge caves. About 1,000 people live in the bay on boats and floating houses. They support themselves by fishing.

2 HARVEST RICE
Louangphrabang

Visit a farm and help cut the rice stalks and separate the grains. Learn about the tools farmers use in the rice paddies. Your host may cook a delicious dish for you to eat.

3 MEANDER WITH MYTHS
Angkor

Walk through the remains of temples dating back to the 800s. Angkor Wat Temple has stone carvings of mythological stories and historic events.

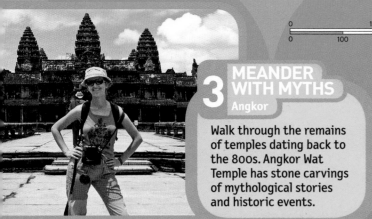

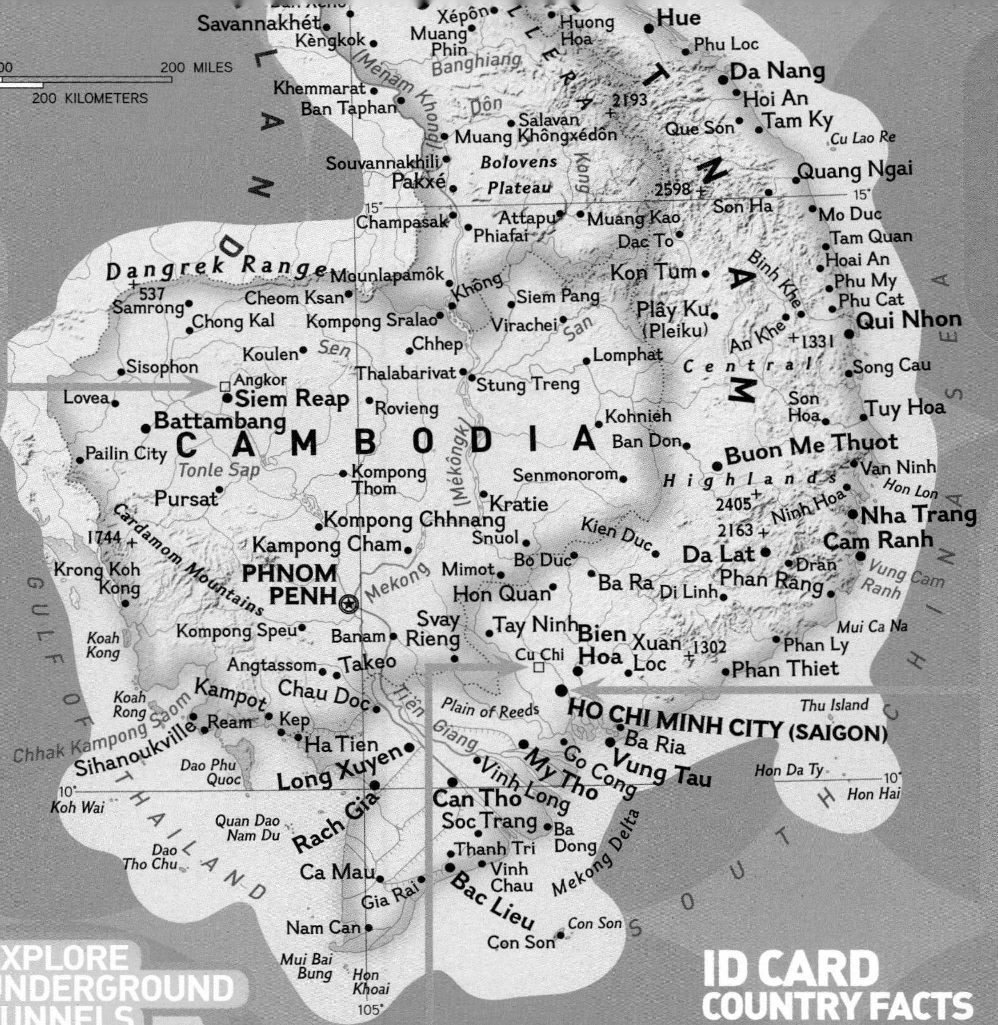

DIGITAL TRAVELER!
Buddhism is an important religion in Laos, Vietnam, and Cambodia. Use the Internet to find out more about Buddhism. Who was Buddha, and when did he live? What are some main beliefs of the faith?

4 SWIM, SLIP, AND SLIDE
Ho Chi Minh City

Ride on a turtle-shaped boat in Suoi Tien Cultural Theme Park, a water park devoted to Buddhism. Swim in a pool surrounded by dragon statues. Climb up the face of a Buddhist sage figure and slip down his beard on a waterslide.

ANNAMESE CORDILLERA
This beautiful mountain range forms the boundary between Laos and Vietnam. Its forests are home to the long-horned Vu Quang ox.

PLAIN OF JARS
Stone jars are scattered in these fields in Laos, sometimes in clusters of several hundred. Scientists think these prehistoric jars may have been part of local burial customs.

TONLE SAP
This lake in Cambodia increases in size and flows into a river after the rainy monsoon season.

5 EXPLORE UNDERGROUND TUNNELS
Cu Chi

Crawl through a tunnel as a guide explains how the Viet Cong lived here during the 1960s war. The tunnels had meeting rooms, hospitals, and sleeping quarters.

ID CARD COUNTRY FACTS

LAOS
Population: 6,736,000
Capital: Vientiane

VIETNAM
Population: 89,721,000
Capital: Hanoi

CAMBODIA
Population: 14,406,000
Capital: Phnom Penh

5 COOL THINGS TO DO HERE

1 TOUR GIANT TWIN TOWERS
Kuala Lumpur

The Petronas Twin Towers are among the tallest buildings in the world. They are 1,483 feet (452 m) high. There are 88 floors in each building. The Skybridge connects the two towers on the 42nd floor.

Globetrotter Attractions

MOUNT KINABALU
Strong mountain climbers hike to the top of Malaysia's highest mountain. Other visitors have fun below, walking across swinging bridges and soaking in hot springs.

TAMAN NEGARA NATIONAL PARK
People say that Malaysia's largest national park is also the world's oldest jungle. The plants and animals have survived the Ice Age and other major world changes.

TASEK MERIMBUN
Brunei's largest lake has black water. The tannin from falling leaves stains the water. Scientists found rare white-collared fruit bats near the lake.

2 STEP BACK IN TIME
Singapore

Walk around the Chinatown Heritage Center and see kitchens, bedrooms, and streets that have been re-created to look like the past.

3 CLIMB 272 STEPS
Selangor

Explore the three Batu Caves where you'll probably see monkeys frolicking. The main cave can be found at the top of the tall staircase. You won't miss the huge Hindu statue outside.

4 PARTY WITH PINK DOLPHINS
Sentosa

Watch pink dolphins perform at a water show. Stand at underwater level and follow the sharks on the other side of the glass. Wade into a pool and swim with shovel-nosed rays. It's all at Underwater World and Dolphin Lagoon.

	NATIONAL BIRD:	NATIONAL FLOWER:	NATIONAL MAMMAL:
BRUNEI	crested fireback	simpoh ayer	pygmy treeshrew
MALAYSIA	rhinoceros hornbill	Chinese hibiscus	Malayan tiger
SINGAPORE	crimson sunbird	vanda "Miss Joaquim"	merlion (mythical animal)

BRUNEI, MALAYSIA, AND SINGAPORE

Lowlands and Mountains Surrounded by WATER

Forested west Malaysia occupies most of the Malay Peninsula, shared with Thailand. To the west across the Strait of Malacca is Sumatra, part of Indonesia. In the far south is Singapore, a city-state with a busy trade port, which separated from Malaysia in 1965. Travelers cross the South China Sea to the island of Borneo to reach east Malaysia, including Sarawak and Sabah. Also on Borneo is the small oil-rich state of Brunei.

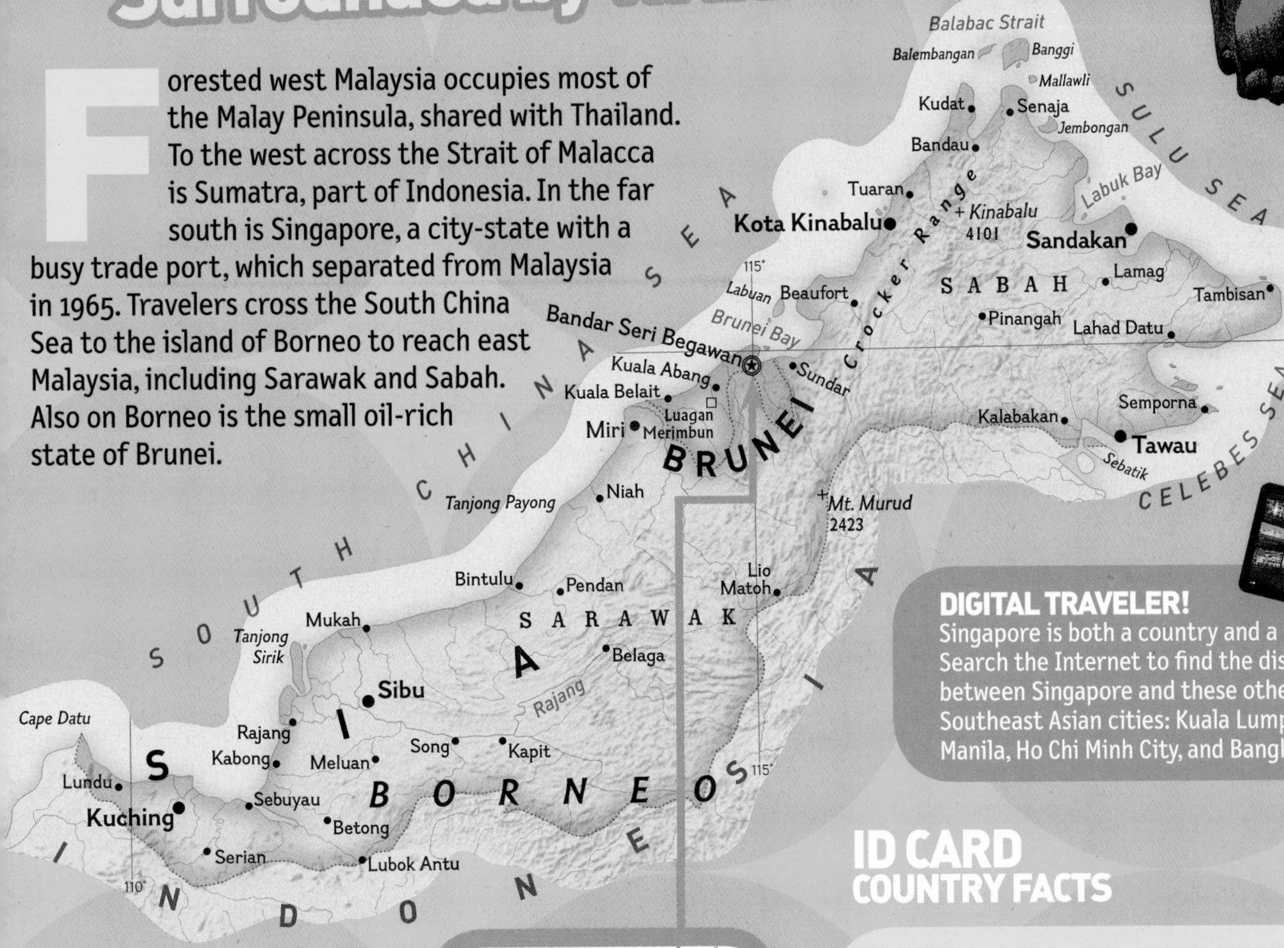

DIGITAL TRAVELER!

Singapore is both a country and a city. Search the Internet to find the distance between Singapore and these other Southeast Asian cities: Kuala Lumpur, Manila, Ho Chi Minh City, and Bangkok.

ID CARD
COUNTRY FACTS

BRUNEI
Population: 407,000
Capital: Bandar Seri Begawan

MALAYSIA
Population: 29,794,000
Capital: Kuala Lumpur

SINGAPORE
Population: 5,444,000
Capital: Singapore

5 WALK ON STILTS
Bandar Seri Begawan

Ride a tour boat to these water villages where more than 30,000 people live. Their houses sit above the river on stilts. Wooden bridges connect the homes, schools, shops, and restaurants.

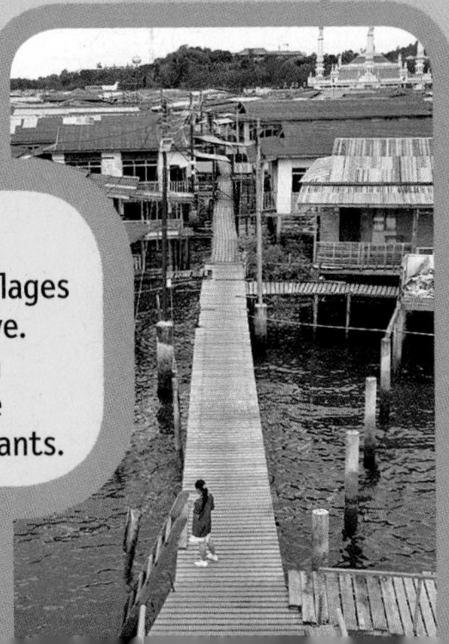

5 COOL THINGS TO DO HERE

ID CARD
COUNTRY FACTS

TIMOR-LESTE
Population: 1,108,000
Capital: Dili

INDONESIA
Population: 248,527,000
Capital: Jakarta

1 TIE-DYE A T-SHIRT
Yogyakarta

Learn to make a batik pattern on a shirt. Batiks have been around for centuries. Trace a pattern with glue or wax. Then paint over it. When you wash off the glue or wax, the pattern shows up.

2 HANG IN A HAMMOCK
Atauro Island

Ride a ferry to the island for a quiet vacation. Islanders built eco-friendly bamboo cabins that encourage tourists to relax without disturbing the natural beauty.

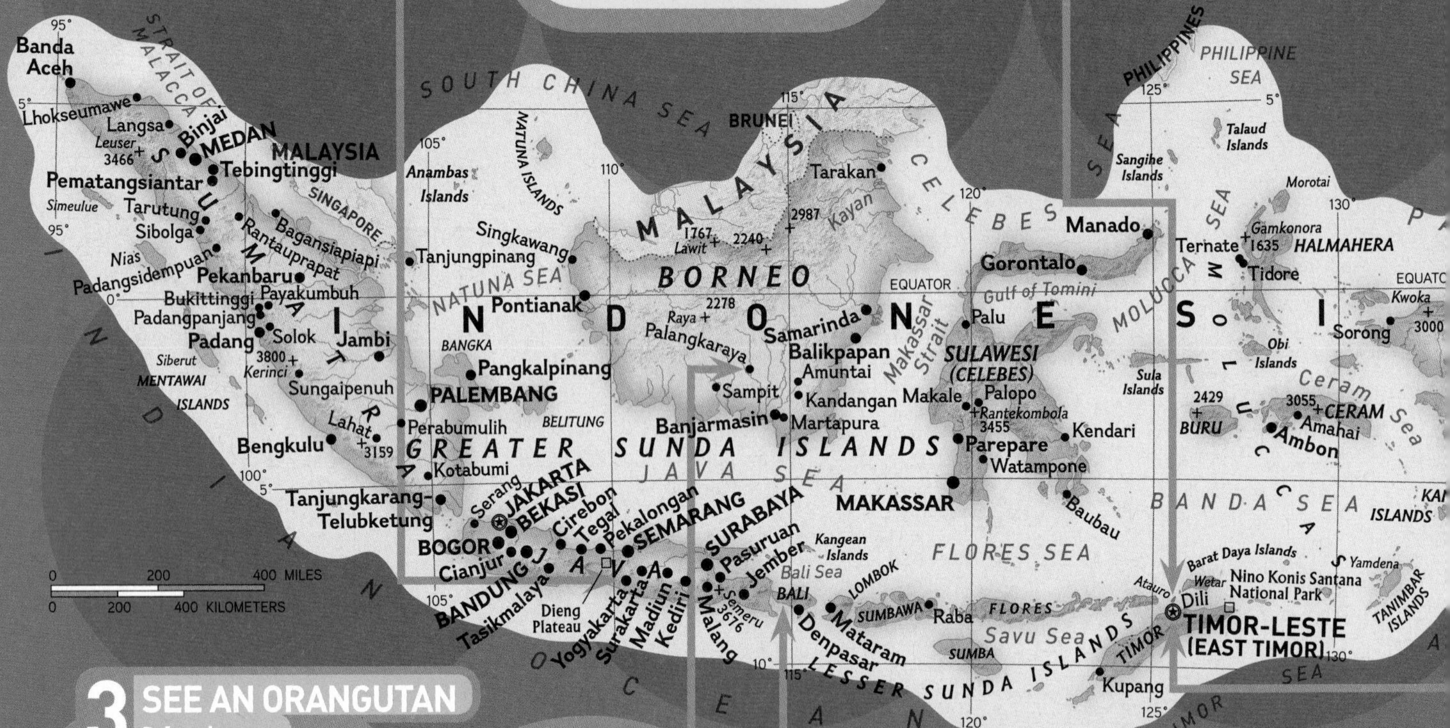

3 SEE AN ORANGUTAN
Palangkaraya

Learn about orangutans and how the B.O.S. Nyaru Menteng Reintroduction Center saves and cares for injured and orphaned animals. It is the world's largest orangutan conservation facility. Since the animals are wild, people cannot stand close to them.

4 GO NUTS UP A TREE
Bali

Stand back from the palm trees and shout when you see a coconut drop. Workers climb the tall trees to chop down the coconuts. Indonesia is one of the world's top producers of coconuts. Coconut is a popular food by itself and in sauces and desserts.

	NATIONAL BIRD:	NATIONAL FLOWER:	NATIONAL MAMMAL:
TIMOR-LESTE	iris lorikeet	puspa pesona	crocodile
INDONESIA	Javan hawk-eagle	jasminum sambac	Asian palm civet

TIMOR-LESTE AND INDONESIA

Wildlife, Islands, and RAIN FORESTS

Indonesia has more than 13,000 islands, including Java, Sumatra, and Sulawesi. Parts of New Guinea and Borneo are also in Indonesia. About half the islands are inhabited. Java has most of Indonesia's cities and industries. The island of Timor is shared between Indonesia and independent Timor-Leste (East Timor). The rugged landscape includes volcanoes, mountains, and rain forests with rare animals, like orangutans, but also fertile farmlands.

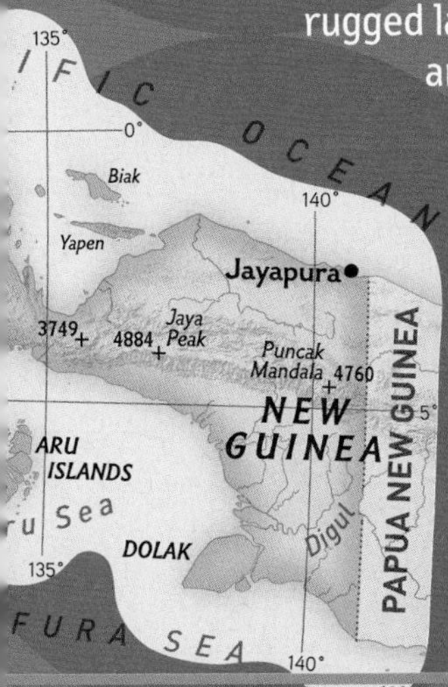

5 GO WHALE WATCHING
Dili

Stand at the railing of a tour boat and look for pilot whales, melon-headed whales, and many other kinds. The coast of Timor-Leste has one of the world's highest concentrations of whales.

PUNCAK MANDALA
This mountain peak in Papua, Indonesia, is popular with mountain climbers and scientists. The peak's melting ice cap was last seen in 1989.

DIENG PLATEAU
This land in Java, Indonesia, was once a sacred Hindu temple complex. Eight temples still stand there today. The plateau is a volcano's crater that was once filled with water.

NINO KONIS SANTANA NATIONAL PARK
Timor-Leste's first national park is home for several endangered birds, such as the yellow-crested cockatoo and the Timor green-pigeon.

DIGITAL TRAVELER!
One of the world's greatest volcanic eruptions took place in Indonesia, on the island of Krakatau. Search the Internet to find out more about this eruption. When did it happen? What happened to the island? How did the eruption affect the world?

NATIONAL BIRD: Philippine eagle

NATIONAL FLOWER: sampaguita

NATIONAL MAMMAL: swamp water buffalo

PHILIPPINES

An Archipelago NATION

Like its neighbor Indonesia, the Philippines has many islands. It's an archipelago, or chain, of more than 7,000 islands. Eleven large islands are where most Filipino people live. The capital, Manila, and most other major cities are on Luzon island. There are mountains and volcanoes, and earthquakes sometimes occur. Dense forest formerly covered most islands, but much of it has been cut for lumber and cleared for farmland.

5 TOUR AN OLD-WORLD CITY
Vigan

Step back in time in a city that people from Spain settled in 1572. Ride in a horse-drawn carriage. See how old-world houses are now museums, inns, and stores. Churches and the Archbishop's Palace are as splendid as ever.

Globetrotter Attractions

CHOCOLATE HILLS (CHOCLOATE HILLS)
There are at least 1,260 nearly identical dirt hills in Bohol. Scientists can't agree how they got here. Legends say that two giants threw sand and stones at each other.

MOUNT MAYON
The most active volcano in the Philippines is also called the world's most symmetrical volcano. Mount Mayon in Luzon has erupted 47 times in the last 400 years.

BANAUE RICE TERRACES
Almost 2,000 years ago, the Ifugao people carved out giant, steplike layers of rice fields. How they did so remains a mystery. The Ifugao continue to grow rice here.

4 GET INTERACTIVE AND INSIDE
Manila

Pick up a magnifying glass and examine an ant colony. Crawl through models of body organs to understand how they work. The Museo Pambata wants you to get up close and touch the exhibits.

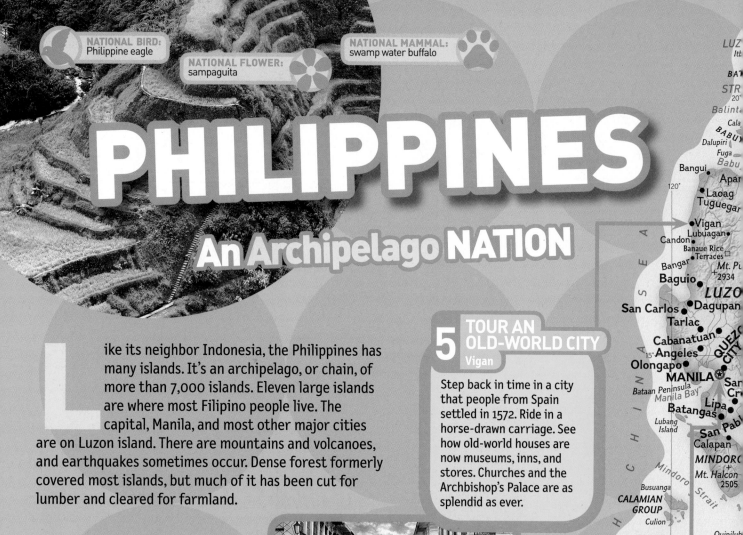

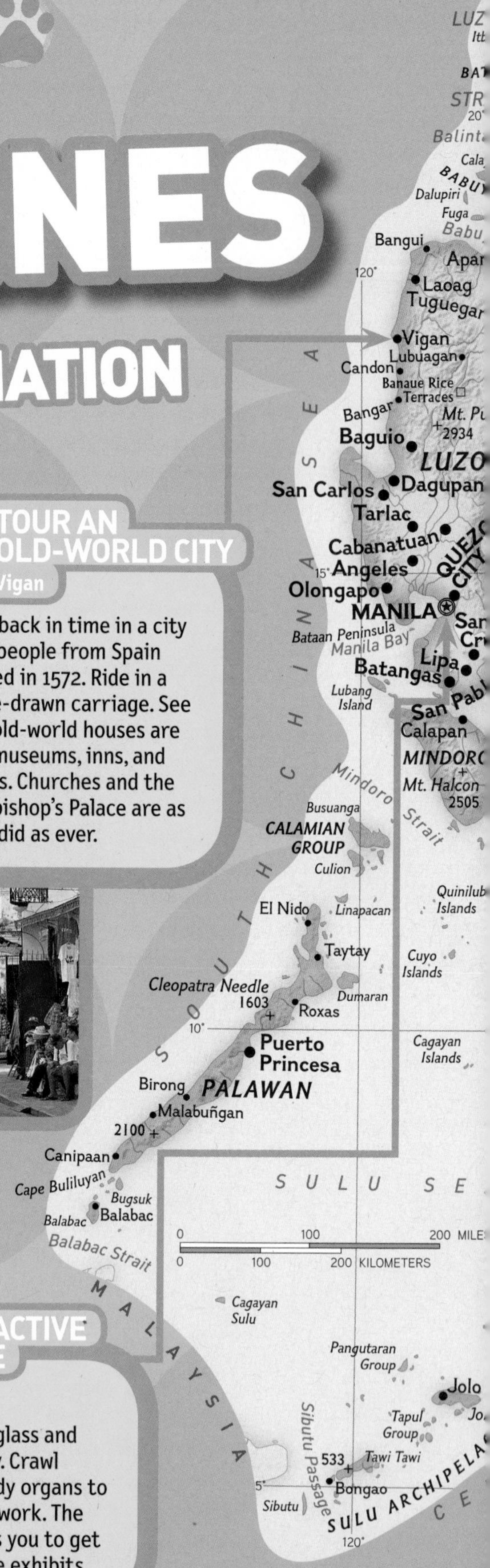

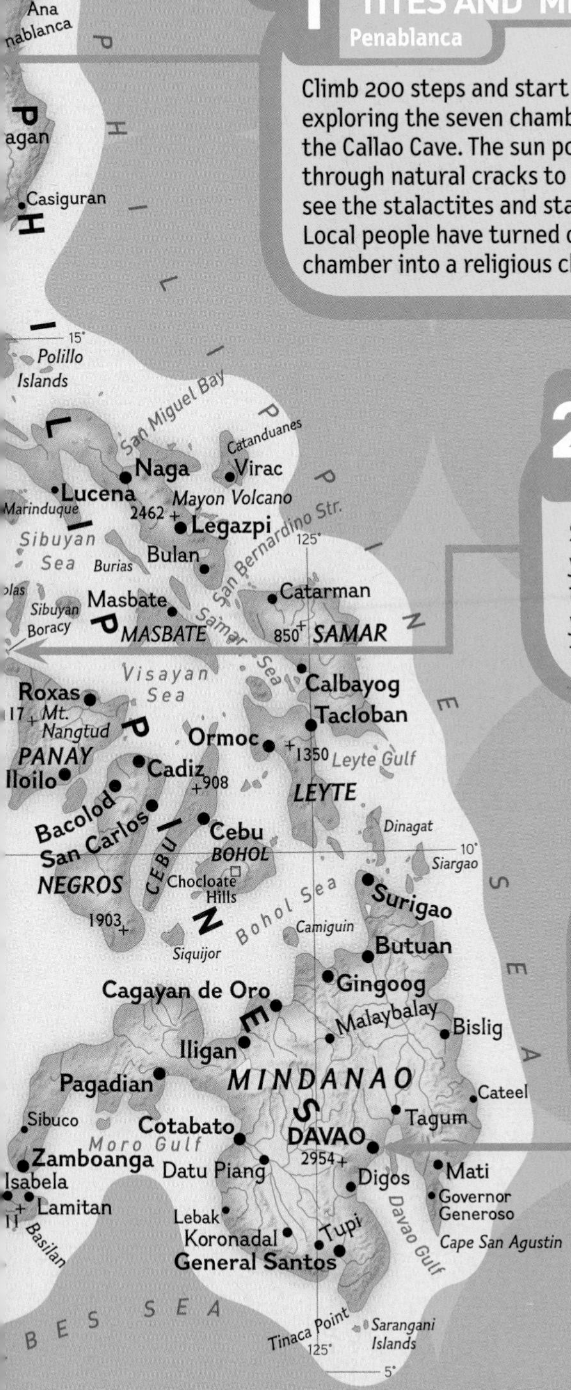

5 COOL THINGS TO DO HERE

1 BEWARE 'TITES AND 'MITES!

Penablanca

Climb 200 steps and start exploring the seven chambers of the Callao Cave. The sun pokes through natural cracks to let you see the stalactites and stalagmites. Local people have turned one chamber into a religious chapel.

2 SQUISH, SPLISH, AND SPLASH

Boracy Island

Squish your toes in the softest sand you've ever felt! White Beach is famous for its powdery sand. When you want to cool off, take a sail along the island in a boat called a paraw.

ASIA

3 TAKE A LOOK AT THOSE TEETH!

Davao

Meet Crocodile Park's biggest resident, a 19-foot (5.8-m)-long crocodile named Pangil. Learn how the staff care for newborn crocodiles.

DIGITAL TRAVELER!

The word *yo-yo* may have come from the Philippines. Use the Internet to find out when and how people in the Philippines first used yo-yos.

ID CARD COUNTRY FACTS

Size: 115,831 sq mi (300,001 sq km)
Population: 96,209,000
Capital: Manila
Official languages: Filipino and English
Currency: Philippine peso
Highest point: Mount Apo, 9,692 ft (2,954 m)
Life expectancy: 69.0 years

AFRICA

A Banded Continent Straddling the Equator

Seen from space, Africa is marked by the Great Rift Valley—an enormous 3,700-mile (5,955-km)-long trench in the continent created by a fault in Earth's crust. Its landscape changes in bands, with a Mediterranean coastline and mountains in the north, then desert, grassland, tropical rain forest, and more grassland and desert in the south. There are mighty rivers, giant waterfalls, and huge lakes. Second only to Asia in size, Africa stretches some 4,600 miles (7,400 km) east to west and 5,000 miles (8,050 km) north to south.

In the background is Mount Kilimanjaro, the highest point in Africa. In the foreground, a herd of elephants migrates across the African savanna, which is also home to fierce members of the cat family, including lions, leopards, and cheetahs.

AFRICA

A Diverse GIANT

Africa has more countries (54), cultures, and languages (some 1,600) than any other continent. Most of the people live in small villages and towns, but there are booming cities such as Cairo, Lagos, and Johannesburg. Africa is the poorest continent, and many of its countries suffer unrest, corruption, and disease. In the last few years, several of the countries in the northwest and northeast regions of Africa have been troubled by civil wars and ethnic tensions.

NORTHWEST

From the Atlas Mountains in the north to the Gulf of Guinea coast in the south, this region has lots of natural resources such as oil and natural gas. At its center is the Sahara—the world's largest desert. This region also has many countries with fast-growing populations.

CENTRAL

The Congo, the region's longest river and major transportation route, flows through rain forest. To the east are Africa's great lakes and the savanna with its rich diversity of wildlife.

AUNT BERTHA'S TRAVEL TIPS

TASTY TREATS
Sample dates, olives, and rice dishes in North Africa, millet (cereal), cassava (also known as manioc), and plantain (bananas) in East and West Africa, and sweet potatoes in southern Africa.

WILDLIFE WONDERS
Go on safari in one of eastern or southern Africa's national parks to see some of the world's greatest concentrations of wildlife.

SHOPPING
Railway stations and road junctions are often packed with booths and stalls where local farmers and traders sell to visitors and passersby. These are great places to buy handicrafts and souvenirs.

GREAT CITIES

Nairobi

Nairobi is one of Africa's most modern cities. Skyscrapers fill the center of the city.

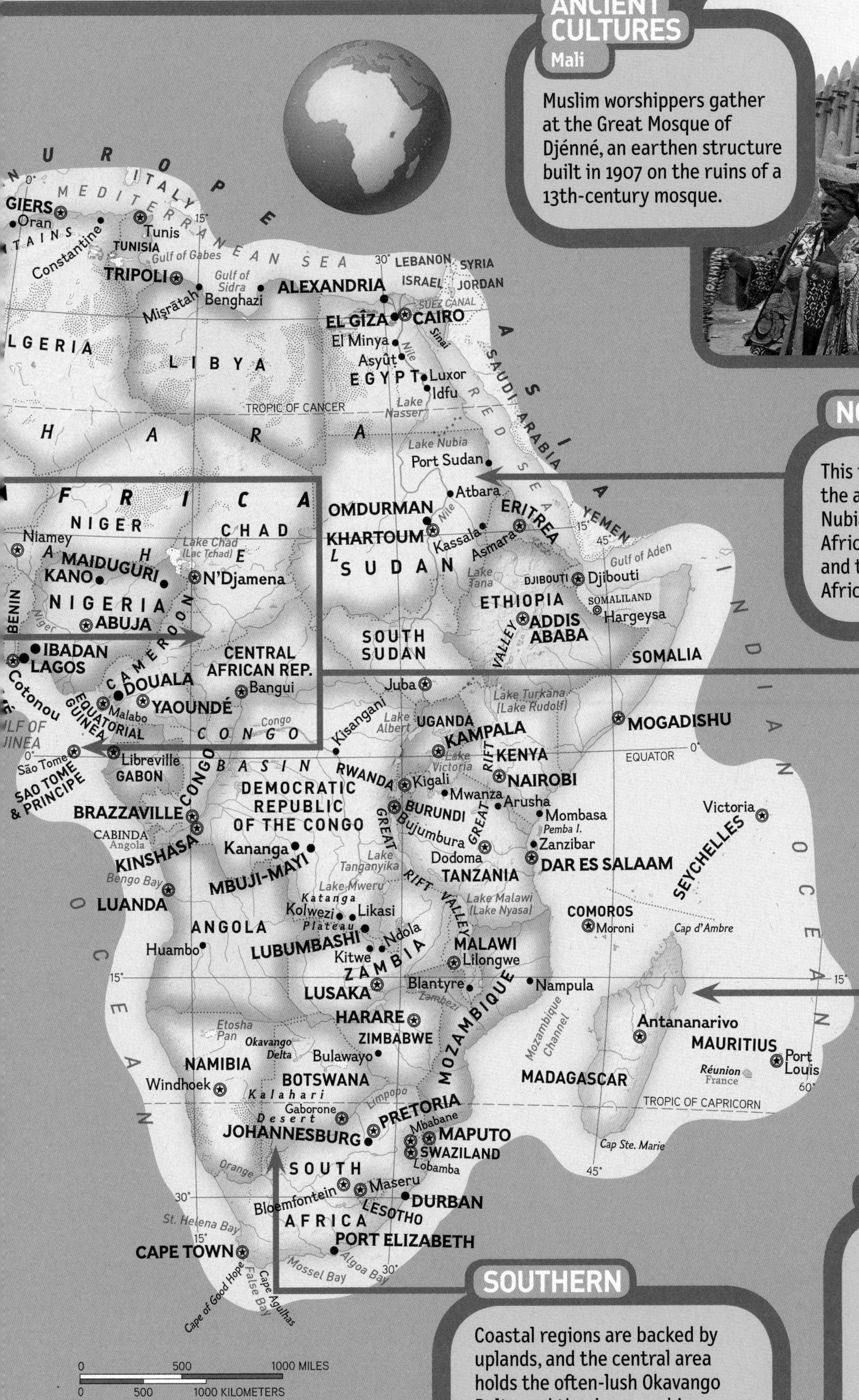

ANCIENT CULTURES
Mali

Muslim worshippers gather at the Great Mosque of Djénné, an earthen structure built in 1907 on the ruins of a 13th-century mosque.

NORTHEAST

This is made up of lands of the ancient Egyptians and Nubians, the "horn" of Africa on the eastern tip, and the countries of East Africa around Lake Victoria.

ISLANDS

In the Indian Ocean lies a series of island African countries, the largest of which is Madagascar. Cape Verde and Sao Tome and Príncipe are island countries off the west coast of Africa.

SOUTHERN

Coastal regions are backed by uplands, and the central area holds the often-lush Okavango Delta and the dry, scorching Kalahari Desert.

AFRICA

NATIONAL BIRD: northern bald ibis

NATIONAL TREE: argan

NATIONAL MAMMAL: Barbary macaque

MOROCCO

Mysterious and MAGICAL

At the northwest corner of Africa, separated from Europe by the Strait of Gibraltar, lies Morocco, land of magical buildings, spices, and ancient traditions. The fertile Mediterranean coastal strip is where most Moroccans live, in villages and cities such as Casablanca. South of the Atlas Mountains that rise to more than 13,000 feet (3,962 m), the vast Sahara desert begins. Here are rocky plains, giant sand dunes, and oases. Western Sahara is a disputed desert region, claimed by Morocco.

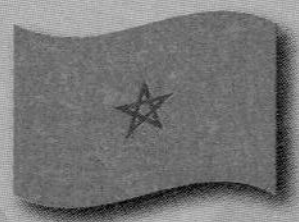

ID CARD COUNTRY FACTS

Size: 275,117 sq mi (712,550 sq km)*
Population: 32,950,000
Capital: Rabat
Official language: Arabic
Currency: Moroccan dihram
Highest point: Jebel Toubkal, 13,665 ft (4,165 m)
Life expectancy: 70.0 years
* includes Western Sahara

5 COOL THINGS TO DO HERE

1 SHOP 'TIL YOU DROP
Fez

Smell the sweet fruit. Hear shopkeepers greeting you. As you wander the maze-like streets, you can shop for everything from candy to carpets.

2 SAIL A STRAIT
Tangier

You can take a one-hour ferry ride from the northern tip of Africa to Spain in Europe. You'll cross the Strait of Gibraltar, where the Atlantic Ocean meets the Mediterranean Sea.

3 SEEK OUT SNAKE CHARMERS
Marrakech

Go to a busy marketplace and watch snake charmers perform their acts. They pretend to hypnotize their snakes by playing music. You will probably see fortune-tellers and jugglers, too.

WESTERN SAHARA
Western Sahara, formerly Spanish Sahara, was divided by Morocco and Mauritania in 1976. Morocco has administered the territory since Mauritania's withdrawal in August 1979. The United Nations does not recognize this annexation, and Western Sahara remains in dispute.

4 GO BLUE FOR A DAY
Chechaouene

Stroll through the old streets in this town and snap photos of the blue houses. Stop in a blue-tinted cafe and sip a cup of famous Moroccan mint tea.

5 RIDE A CAMEL
Merzouga

Sit tall on the back of a camel as it ambles through the sand in the Sahara. Camels are the main way to travel in the Sahara, a desert almost the size of the United States.

Globetrotter Attractions

GORGES DU TODRHA
In the High Atlas Mountains, a hiking trail stretches between steep cliff walls.

HASSAN II MOSQUE
About 25,000 worshippers can fit in this beautiful Casablanca mosque.

KASBAH AT AÏT BEN HADDOU
This is Morocco's most famous and oldest kasbah (old city). Visitors can see earthen homes, stores, and mosques. *Lawrence of Arabia* and other movies were filmed here.

DIGITAL TRAVELER!
In Morocco, you may see a man wearing a *fez*. This is a round, red, felt hat. It often has a tassel on top. Where do you think the hat originated? Go on the Internet to check.

	NATIONAL BIRD:	NATIONAL FLOWER:	NATIONAL MAMMAL:
ALGERIA	Algerian nuthatch	rosy garlic	fennec fox
TUNISIA	house bunting	jasmine	lion

ALGERIA AND TUNISIA

Hot Desert DESTINATIONS

Both Algeria and Tunisia have a Mediterranean coast with a pleasant climate and fertile farmland. Along the coast are many seaside resorts popular with tourists. Most Algerians and Tunisians live along the coast, in cities such as Algiers and Tunis. Here, too, are ruins of ancient towns. Algeria—Africa's largest country—features the High Atlas Mountains and the rock, sand, and scattered oases of the vast Sahara.

5 HAVE A SWEET DATE
M'Zab Valley

Taste a date that was just picked off the date palm tree. Enjoy this tiny, sweet fruit. Northern Africa has just the right warm, sunny climate to grow dates. One tree can produce 180 pounds (82 kg) of dates each year.

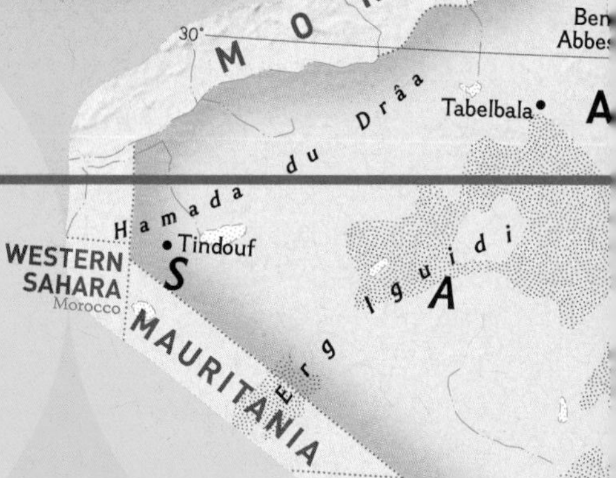

TASSILI-N-AJJER
Between 8,000 and 1,000 years ago, cave-dwellers drew pictures on cave walls in what is now south-eastern Algeria. Today, you can still see more than 15,000 of these drawings.

MONUMENT DES MARTYRS
An eternal flame sits in the center of this monument in Algiers that honors soldiers who fought in Algeria's war for independence.

EL JEMM
In A.D. 238, El Jemm, Tunisia, was a small Roman village with one of the world's largest amphitheaters. More than 35,000 people gathered for sporting events with animals and gladiators.

ID CARD COUNTRY FACTS

ALGERIA
Population: 38,290,000
Capital: Algiers

TUNISIA
Population: 10,882,000
Capital: Tunis

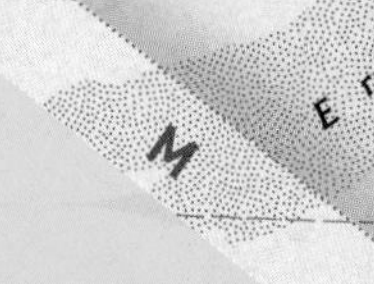

DIGITAL TRAVELER!
Search the Internet for a map of the Sahara. List all the countries that the Sahara crosses.

5 COOL THINGS TO DO HERE

1 SMELL SPICES
Algiers

Wander the Africaine Market and see if your nose knows the difference between ginger and cinnamon.

2 CRISS-CROSS CLIFF BRIDGES
Constantine

Cross some of Constantine's many bridges. The Rhumel River has carved a deep gorge through the city. The bridges allow cars and people to cross the gorge. Some bridges are suspended from cliffs.

3 GO FISHING
Tabarqa

See what you catch when you ride in a fishing boat from Tabarqa's harbor. Learn about coral fishing as you watch divers drag small nets to pick up pieces from coral reefs.

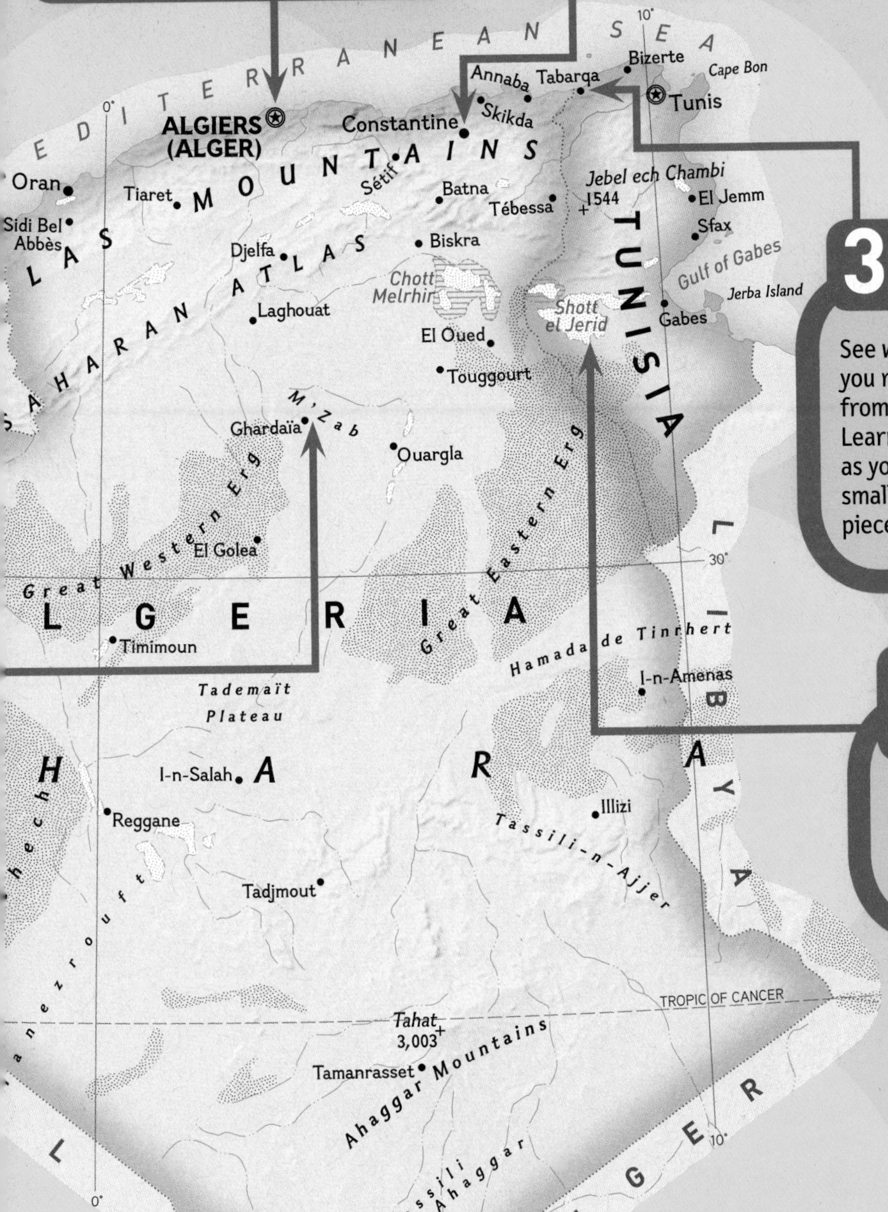

4 STEP INTO THE STAR WARS SET
Shott el Jerid

Visit the place where Luke Skywalker grew up. In 1977, George Lucas picked the desert of Tunisia for his *Star Wars* setting.

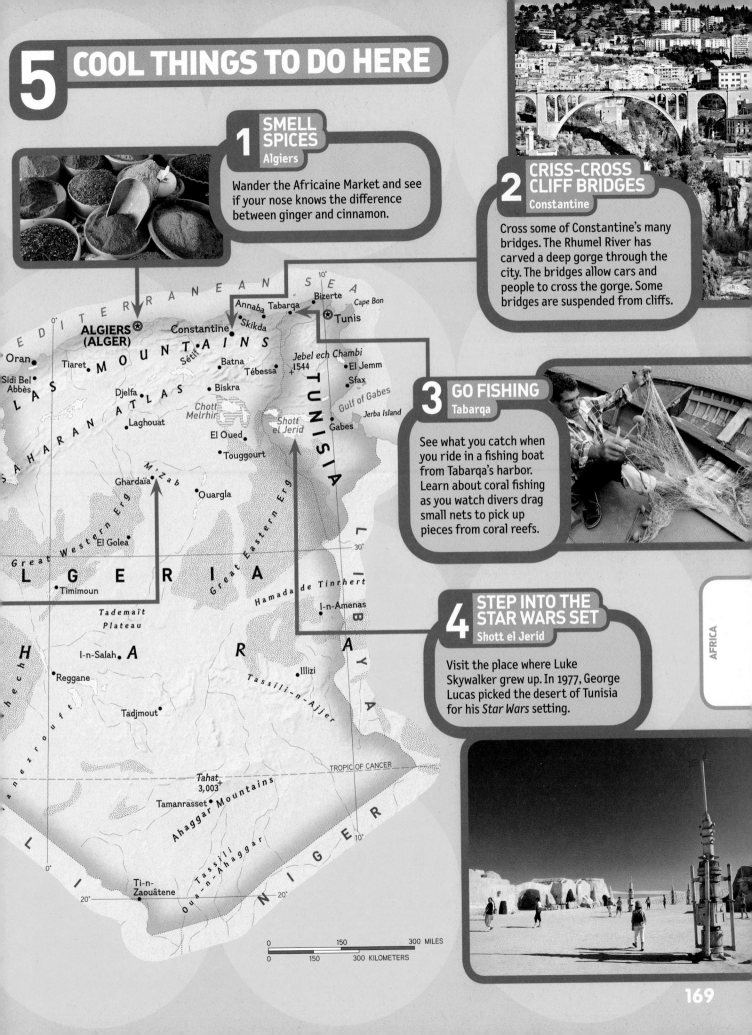

NATIONAL BIRD: rough-legged hawk

NATIONAL TREE: date palm

NATIONAL MAMMAL: dromedary camel

LIBYA

Vast Deserts and SEASHORES

Like its neighbors, Libya is a land of contrasts. Most Libyans farm or live in cities in the coastal regions of Cyrenaica and Tripolitania, on either side of the Gulf of Sidra. Very few people live in the other 90 percent of Libya—mostly the Libyan Desert of the Sahara, with vast tracts of sand dunes and low mountains. Even oases are scarce, but beneath the sand are rich reserves of oil.

1 YOU RULE THE TOWN!
Tripoli

Stand on the balcony of the historic Yusuf Karamanli House. This was once the home of Tripoli's ruling family. Now it is a museum where you can see clothing, furniture, and everyday objects from the 1800s.

5 FLOAT IN SALTY LAKES
Ubari Sand Sea

Splash in a lake in the middle of the Sahara. Because of the high level of carbonation and salt in the water, swimmers can float easily. The water is five times saltier than ocean water.

DIGITAL TRAVELER!
Among the early people of Libya were Berbers. They were nomads, moving with their herds of sheep and goats to find new grazing land. Berbers are well known for making dishes in a pot called a tajine. Look on the Internet for pictures of tajines and find a recipe you would like to make.

4 SEE 12,000-YEAR-OLD PAINTINGS
Jebel Acacus

Take a tour through a cave in the Jebel Acacus mountain range. Look at the prehistoric rock paintings and carvings and try to retell their stories.

5 COOL THINGS TO DO HERE

ID CARD
COUNTRY FACTS

Size: 679,362 sq mi (1,759,540 sq km)
Population: 6,518,000
Capital: Tripoli
Official language: Arabic
Currency: Libyan dinar
Highest point: Bikku Bitti, 7,434 ft (2,166 m)
Life expectancy: 75.0 years

2 TAKE TEA AND TUNES
Tripoli

Nibble on a date and sip a cup of tea at Magha as-Sa'a, a popular teahouse. Sit outdoors, but be sure to go inside to see the collection of musical items, such as an old electric guitar and jukebox.

3 VAMOOSE TO SEE ZEUS
Shaḩḩāt

Imagine how the Greeks built this Temple of Zeus in the fifth century B.C. It was even bigger than the Parthenon in Athens. It was part of the ancient city of Cyrene.

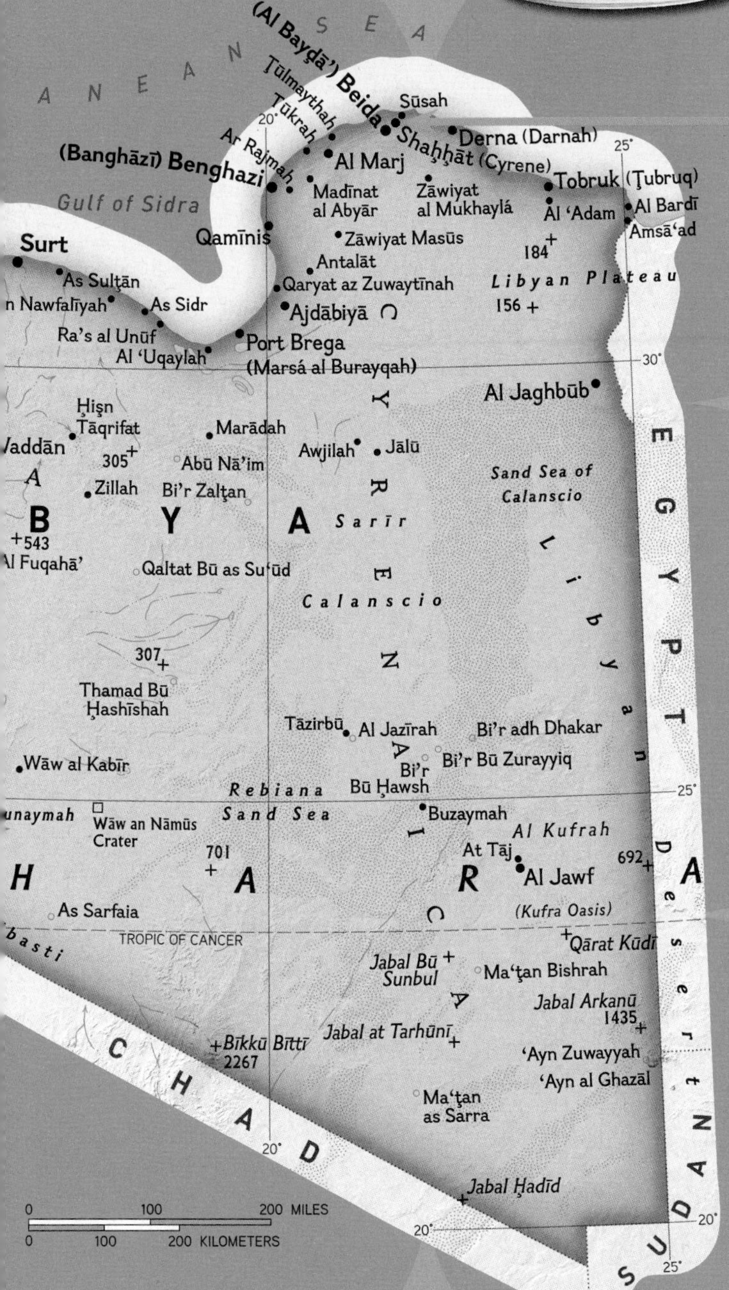

Globetrotter Attractions

LEPTIS MAGNA
Here are the ruins of one of the most beautiful cities of the Roman Empire. In 190 B.C. the city had a harbor, monuments, stores, and homes.

GURGI MOSQUE
The main prayer hall of this mosque in Tripoli is decorated with marble from Italy, tiles from Tunisia, and carved stones from Morocco.

WĀW-AN-NĀMŪS CRATER
This prehistoric volcano is located in the Sahara, surrounded by lakes.

NATIONAL BIRD:
golden eagle

NATIONAL FLOWER:
Egyptian lotus

NATIONAL MAMMAL:
fennec fox

EGYPT

Crossroads of CONTINENTS

1 OPEN A BOOK TO HISTORY
Alexandria

Stand in this library and look up through the high glass-panelled roof. The shelves can hold eight million books. The first library here was destroyed in a war in the third century B.C.

The Nile River and its delta nurture Egypt's farmland and cities, as they have since the time of the pyramids. The Aswan Dam's Lake Nasser provides extra irrigation for a hot, dry land. To the west of the Nile is the Libyan Desert, to the east are the Red Sea and the Sinai Peninsula joining Asia and Africa. The Suez Canal links the Red Sea to the Mediterranean, providing a route between Europe and Asia.

PYRAMIDS OF GIZA
More than 4,500 years ago, three Egyptian rulers ordered these pyramids built. After the rulers died, their bodies were placed inside their pyramids.

VALLEY OF THE KINGS
Egyptians built underground tombs for their kings. People placed clothes, furniture, and food next to the kings' bodies for the afterlife.

CAIRO MUSEUM
King Tutankhamun's mask (see above) and mummies of other kings are in the museum.

5 SNORKEL IN THE RED SEA
Dahab

Put on a mask and fins and wade into the water of the Red Sea. The coral reefs are home to colorful fish, dolphins, and turtles.

DIGITAL TRAVELER!
The Suez Canal is an important modern transportation route in Egypt. Go online and find a picture of the canal. Then read how long it takes ships to sail through the canal.

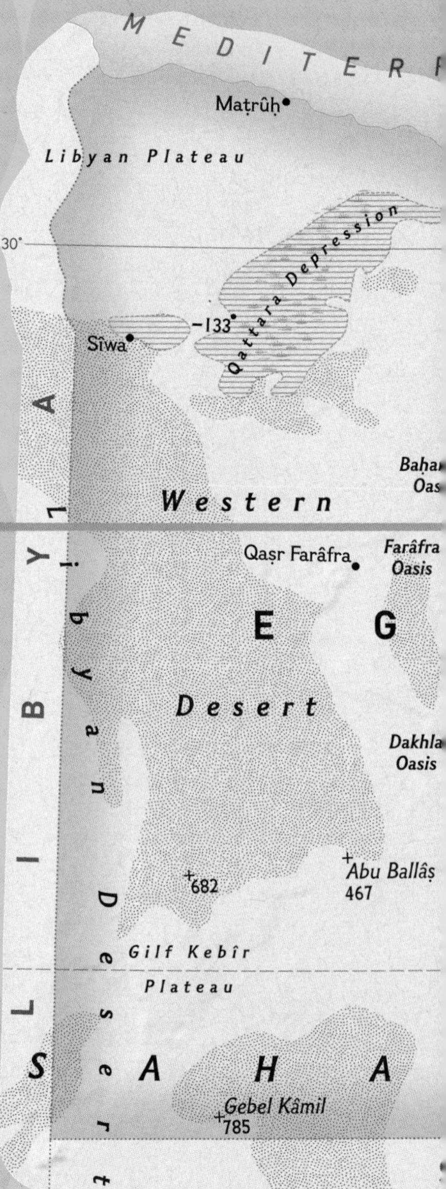

5 COOL THINGS TO DO HERE

2 RIDE A CAMEL TO THE SPHINX

El Gîza

Ride from the pyramids to the biggest and oldest statue in Egypt. Decide where the lion's body ends and the human head begins. The Sphinx is 66 feet (20 m) high and 240 feet (73 m) long.

3 CLIMB MOSES' MOUNTAIN

Mount Sinai

Hike in a special place to Muslims, Christians, and Jews. Traditionally, some people call this the place in the Bible where Moses received the Ten Commandments.

ID CARD COUNTRY FACTS

Size: 386,662 sq mi (1,001,450 sq km)
Population: 84,667,000
Capital: Cairo
Official language: Arabic
Currency: Egyptian pound
Highest point: Mount Catherine, 8,652 ft (2,637 m)
Life expectancy: 70.0 years

4 SAIL ON A SLOW BOAT

Aswân

Feel the wind take your felucca sailboat along the Nile River, the longest river in the world. Sail by the Tombs of the Nobles and stop at the Aswân Botanic Gardens.

MEDITERRANEAN SEA
ALEXANDRIA (EL ISKANDARÎYA)
Port Said (Bûr Sa'îd)
GAZA STRIP
ISRAEL
JORDAN
Nile Delta
Ṭanta
Ismâ'ilîya
Suez Canal
SHUBRA EL KHEIMA
EL GÎZA
CAIRO (EL QÂHIRA)
Pyramids of Giza
SINAI
El Faiyûm
Gulf of Suez
Gulf of Aqaba
SAUDI ARABIA
Gebel el Galâla el Qiblîya 1218
Mt. Sinai 2285
Mt. Catherine 2637
Dahab
El Minya
Nile (An Nil)
Gebel Ghârib 1751
Sharm el Sheikh
Râs Muḥammad
Mallawi
Eastern Desert
Asyûṭ
Gebel Shâyib el Banât 2187
Hurghada
Bûr Safâga
EGYPT
Girga
Abu Muharik
RED SEA
Quṣeir
Valley of the Kings
Gebel el Sibâ'i 1484
El Khârga
Luxor
Khârga Oasis
Idfu
Gebel Nugruṣ 1505
Gebel Ḥamâta 1977
Aswân
1st Cataract
Aswan High Dam
Berenice
Râs Banâs
Foul Bay
Gebel el Farâid 1366
TROPIC OF CANCER
Lake Nasser
Marsa Sha'ab
Siyal Islands
SAHARA
Boundary claimed by Sudan
Gebel Siri 420
Halayeb
Cape Elba (Râs Hadarba)
SUDAN
Nile
30°
0 100 200 MILES
0 100 200 KILOMETERS

AFRICA

5 COOL THINGS TO DO HERE

1 WELCOME THE FISHING BOATS
Nouakchott

Hurry to the water in the late afternoon and watch the fishermen unload their fish-filled nets. Children scurry to help by sorting the fish on trays.

2 THUMP A DRUM
Dakar

Follow the beat of your drumming teacher. One kind of African drum is called a *djembe*. Use your hands to slap and tap your djembe.

3 LEARN KITE SURFING
Cape Verde Islands

Let the wind fill your kite, and hold on tight! The kite will carry you through the water. After you take a lesson, relax on the beach.

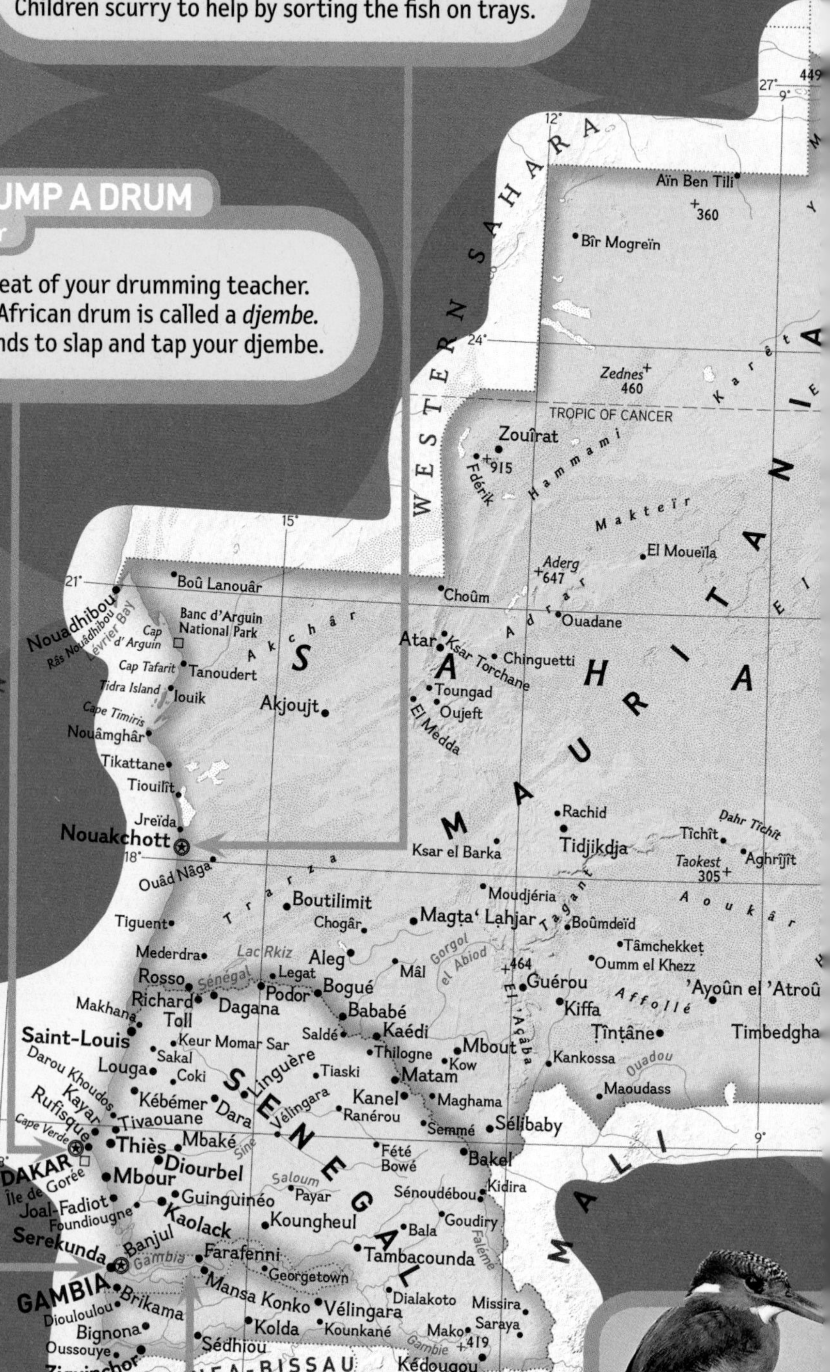

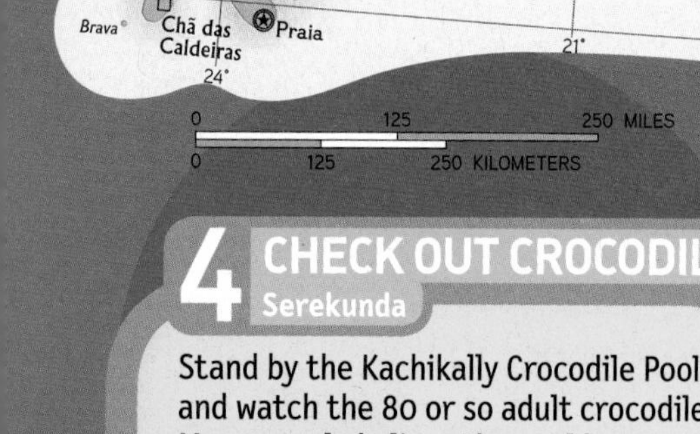

4 CHECK OUT CROCODILES
Serekunda

Stand by the Kachikally Crocodile Pool and watch the 80 or so adult crocodiles. Many people believe the pool has supernatural healing powers and the water can bring good luck.

NORTHERN WEST AFRICA

The Atlantic Meets the SAHARA

Mauritania is bigger than its southern neighbors, Senegal and Gambia. Most of Mauritania is in the Sahara, with southern grasslands near the Senegal River. The river forms a border with Senegal, which has desert, forest, and savanna. Gambia, named for the Gambia River, is enclosed by Senegal, but has an Atlantic coast. Some 400 miles (643 km) west, the dry, volcanic Cape Verde islands rise from the ocean.

ID CARD COUNTRY FACTS

CAPE VERDE
Population: 515,000
Capital: Praia

GAMBIA
Population: 1,884,000
Capital: Banjul

MAURITANIA
Population: 3,712,000
Capital: Nouakchott

SENEGAL
Population: 13,497,000
Capital: Dakar

Globetrotter Attractions

CHÃ DAS CALDEIRAS
This village is set inside a volcano's crater on Fogo Island in Cape Verde. Villagers grow grapes in the rich volcanic soil. The steaming volcano peak is almost always in view.

HOUSE OF SLAVES
In the late 1700s, thousands of captured Africans were forced into this Goree Island (Île de Gorée) building in chains. They left Senegal through the Door of No Return to become slaves in the Americas.

BANC D'ARGUIN NATIONAL PARK
Mauritania's island beaches and sand dunes attract migrating sandpipers, pelicans, and flamingos to spend the winter.

5 TWEET ABOUT WILD BIRDS
Gambia River

Listen to bird calls as your *pirogue* glides on the Gambia River. A pirogue is like a canoe. This colorful bird is called a malachite kingfisher.

DIGITAL TRAVELER!
Kora, *tabala*, and *balafon* are three kinds of African instruments. Do some digital research to find out what each instrument looks and sounds like.

CENTRAL WEST AFRICA

Wetlands and WILDLIFE

Five states occupy the Atlantic coast of West Africa from Senegal south and then east to the Gulf of Guinea. They are Guinea-Bissau, Guinea, Sierra Leone, Liberia (Africa's oldest republic), and Côte d'Ivoire (Ivory Coast). Central West Africa is warm and wet, with coastal forest and mangrove swamps, rivers flowing through coastal plains, and amazing wildlife. Inland are savanna grasslands and mountains rising more than 6,000 feet (1,829 m).

ID CARD COUNTRY FACTS

CÔTE D'IVOIRE (IVORY COAST)
Population: 21,142,000
Capital: Yamoussoukro

GUINEA
Population: 11,793,000
Capital: Conakry

GUINEA-BISSAU
Population: 1,677,000
Capital: Bissau

LIBERIA
Population: 4,357,000
Capital: Monrovia

SIERRA LEONE
Population: 6,242,000
Capital: Freetown

Globetrotter Attractions

ORANGO ISLANDS NATIONAL PARK
The park in Guinea-Bissau covers several islands. A rare kind of saltwater hippo lives here.

YAMOUSSOUKRO BASILICA
This church in Côte d'Ivoire may be the largest Christian house of worship in the world. It can hold 18,000 people inside and 300,000 outside.

NIMBA MOUNTAINS
Some unusual animals live here, including goliath frogs, which can weigh seven pounds (3 kg). The mountains straddle Guinea, Liberia, and Côte d'Ivoire.

5 FLIP OUT! Conakry
Catch a performance by the children of Conakry. After school, many of them learn acrobatics. They perform in parks and in their gym. Some have become circus stars.

DIGITAL TRAVELER!
When Ellen Johnson Sirleaf was elected president of Liberia in 2005, she was the first woman president of any African country. Use your electronic device to find out how many other countries have had women presidents.

5 COOL THINGS TO DO HERE

1 BUY KORHOGO CLOTH
Korhogo

Choose the pictures that you like best. Artists paint large scenes on cloth. People hang the cloths on their walls or sew them into shirts and jackets.

2 KEEP YOUR EYES ON THE BALL
Abidjan

See teams play at the stadium called "Le Felicia," which also hosts athletic events. The Ivory Coast soccer team often plays here.

4 CHECK OUT THE CHIMPS
Bossou Forest

Visit the chimpanzee research station and find out why studies show that these chimps are the smartest in the world.

3 LOOK FOR RUBBER TREES
Buchanan

Visit a rubber farm and watch the milky latex drip from the trees. Workers collect the latex and turn it into rubber for tires and other products.

EASTERN WEST AFRICA

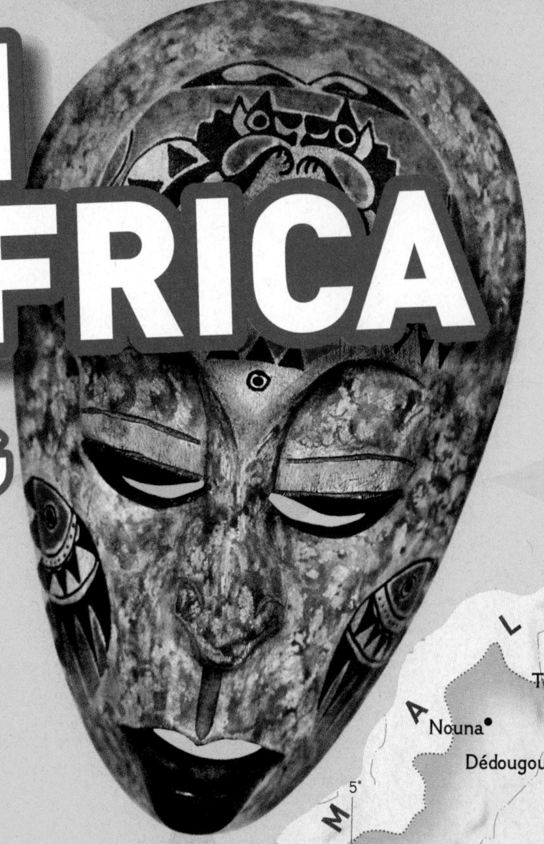

Warm and WELCOMING

Ghana, Togo, and Benin have coasts on the Gulf of Guinea. To the north is landlocked Burkina Faso. These four warm countries share historic cultures and a landscape of mostly plains and forest plateaus. The highest peak (in Togo) is only 3,235 feet (986 m). Building the Akosombo Dam in the 1960s created Lake Volta and many rivers that water land for farming. English is the official language of Ghana, but French is spoken in Benin, Burkina Faso, and Togo.

ID CARD COUNTRY FACTS

BENIN
Population: 9,645,000
Capital: Porto-Novo

BURKINA FASO
Population: 18,015,000
Capital: Ouagadougou

GHANA
Population: 26,088,000
Capital: Accra

TOGO
Population: 6,168,000
Capital: Lomé

DIGITAL TRAVELER!
A lithophone is a traditional percussion instrument in Togo and other African places. Search the Internet to find a picture of a lithophone. Then find a sample of lithophone music.

Globetrotter Attractions

STONE SCULPTURES OF LAONGO

Sculptors from around the world come to Laongo, in Burkina Faso, to carve the large granite stones.

LAKE VOLTA

This is one of the world's largest artificial lakes. It provides much of the water for Ghana and serves as a transportation route, a source of electric power, and a resource for fishing.

OUIDAH MUSEUM OF HISTORY

The museum tells the story of slave trading. It is located by the Benin port where slaves were forced onto ships.

5 COOL THINGS TO DO HERE

1 SPOT A HIPPO
Wechiau

Peer through binoculars to spot the hippos at the Wechiau Community Hippo Sanctuary. This river is home to one of the two remaining hippo groups in Ghana.

2 SHOP AT THE MARKETPLACE
Ouagadougou

Join the crowds of locals and tourists at the market where you'll find vegetables and fruits, pottery and baskets, clothing, and jewelry. Musicians often entertain the shoppers.

3 SPLASH UNDER WATERFALLS
Badou

Let the Akloa Falls gush down around you as you cool off in its natural pool. The falls drop down from a cliff that is 115 feet (35 m) above the pool.

4 LIVE LIKE ROYALTY
Abomey

Learn about the powerful Benin Empire and the kings who ruled it from these palaces from 1695 to 1900. In addition to being homes for the kings, the ten palaces stored the treasures of the kingdom. Modern reenactments show how the royal families lived.

5 HANG ON TIGHT!
Cape Coast region

Step carefully on this rope bridge suspended 98 feet (30 m) above the forest floor in Kakum National Park.

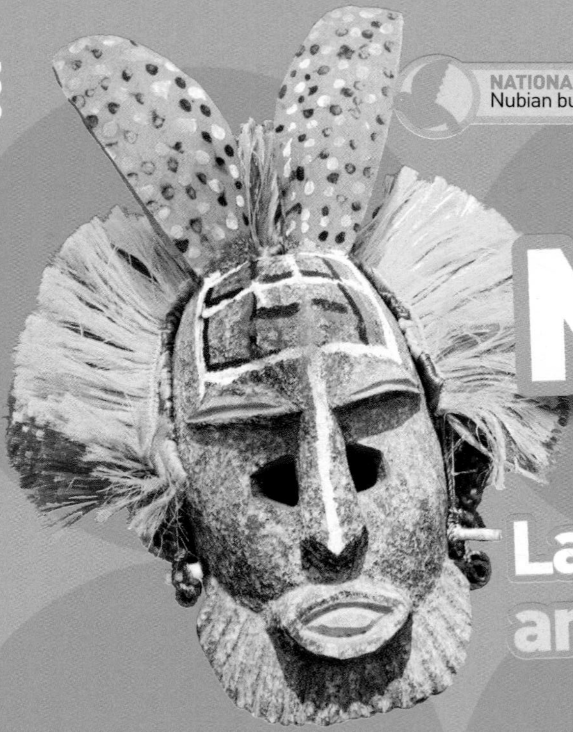

NATIONAL BIRD: Nubian bustard

NATIONAL TREE: nere

NATIONAL MAMMAL: African wild frog

MALI

Land of Music and MASKS

Mali has no seacoast, is mostly flat, and has two distinct regions. In the hot, dry north, the Sahara merges into the Sahel, a drought-prone, treeless expanse where nomads herd livestock. In the south, the Niger River waters the landscape for trees and crops. Mali, once a rich empire, has a fascinating culture, and ancient trade routes link historic cities such as Timbuktu.

ID CARD COUNTRY FACTS

Size: 478,841 sq mi (1,240,192 sq km)
Population: 15,461,000
Capital: Bamako
Official language: French
Currency: Communaute Africaine Financiere franc
Highest point: Hombori Tondo, 3,789 ft (1,155 m)
Life expectancy: 54.0 years

5 COOL THINGS TO DO HERE

1 MEET PEOPLE ON THEIR WAY TO MARKET
Mopti

Greet the Fulani people as they go to trade goods at the market. The people are nomadic. They move from place to place with their cattle. The women and girls wear colorful clothing.

2 FOLLOW THE HUMPBACK ROAD
Timbuktu

Pretend you are a trader crossing the Sahara. Tourists can take short camel rides, but real traders still travel on camels to make deliveries from the salt mines.

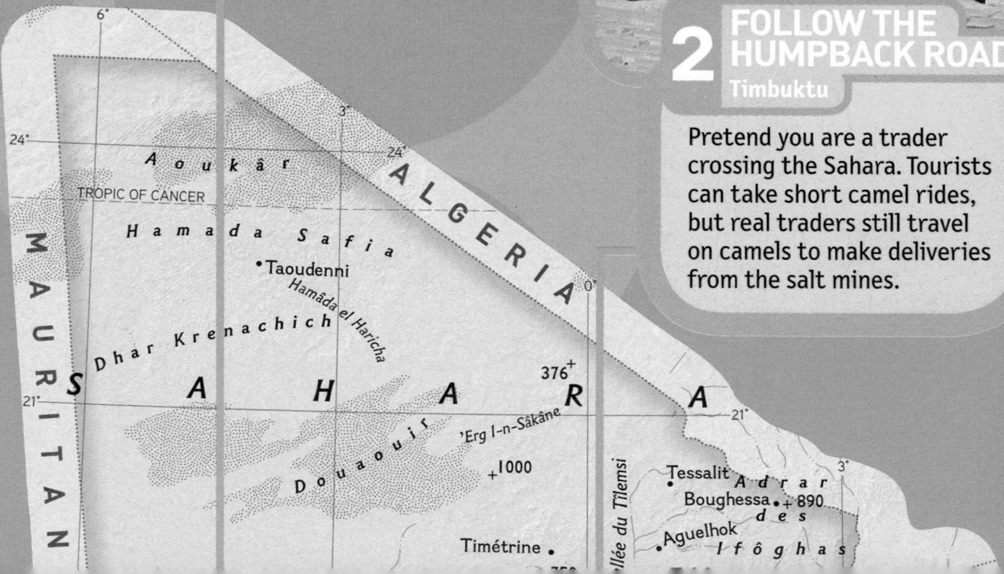

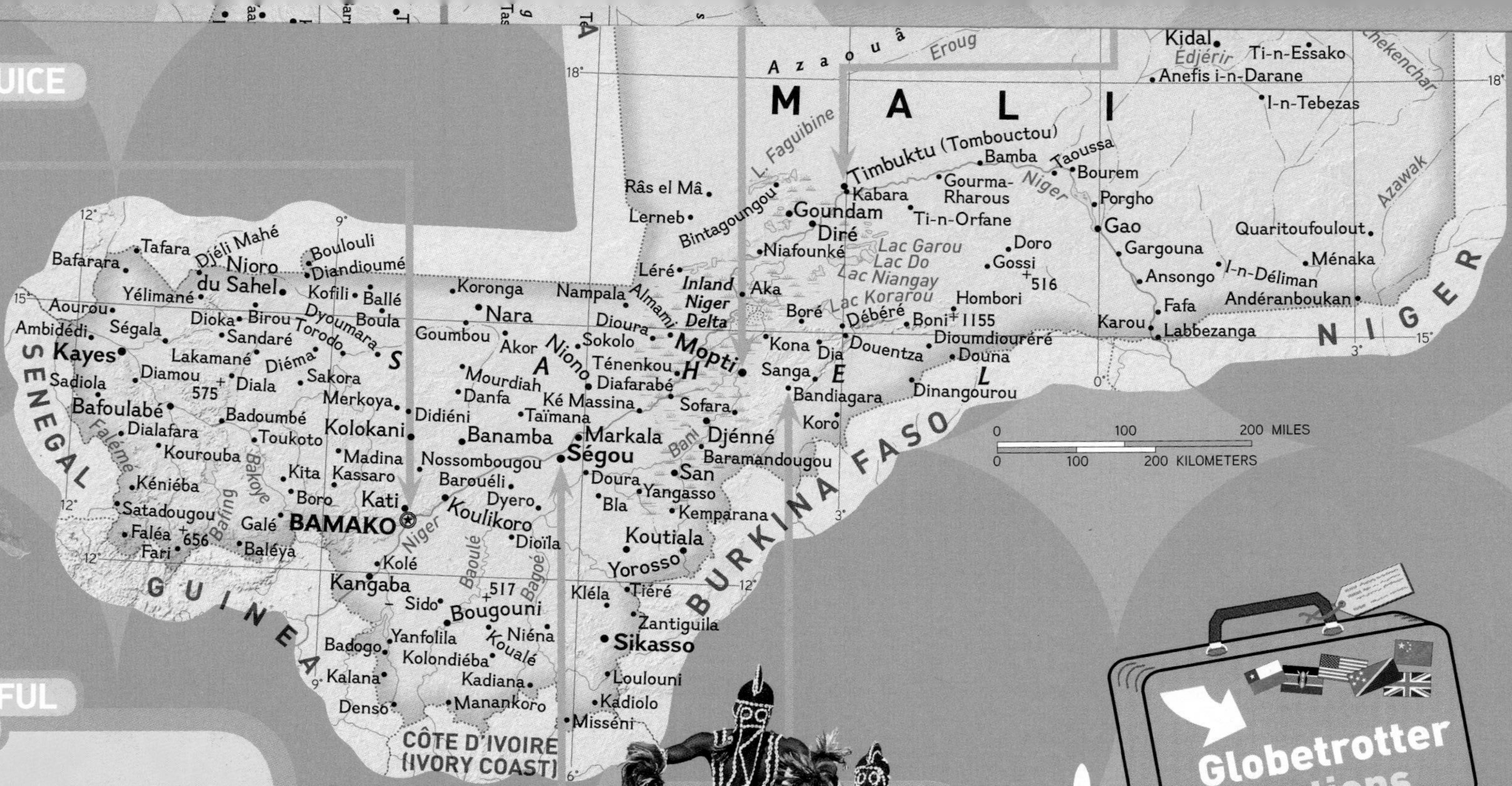

3 SIP FLOWER JUICE
Bamako

Drop by a restaurant and enjoy a djablani drink. It is made from the petals of a hibiscus flower.

4 MAKE BEAUTIFUL MUD CLOTHS
Ségou

Start with a colorful fabric. Use a stick and mud to draw pictures that tell a story. The Mali people will show you how to dry the mud and rinse it off. Then your mud cloth will be ready!

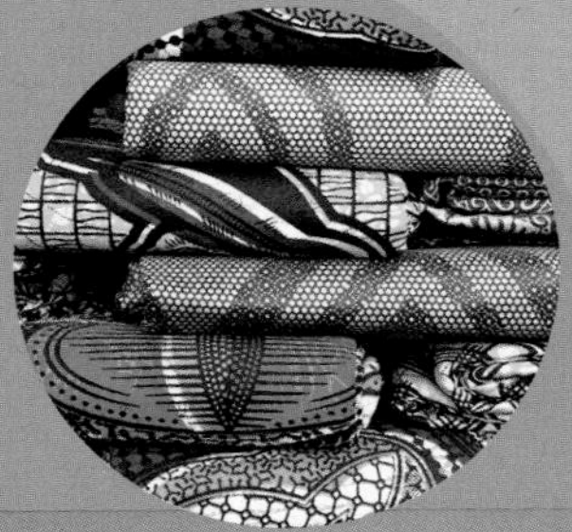

DIGITAL TRAVELER!
Bright, colorful fabrics are everywhere in Mali. Take photographs of the fabrics you like best and use them in a scrapbook about your globetrotter journey.

5 MARVEL AT MASKED DANCERS
Bandiagara

Celebrate with the Dogon people as they put on masks and colorful clothes and dance on stilts during religious ceremonies and festivals.

Globetrotter Attractions

ETHNOLOGICAL MUSEUM
The collections of clothing, jewelry, games, and musical instruments tell what life was like in Timbuktu hundreds of years ago.

GREAT MOSQUE OF DJENNE
It is said that this Islamic house of worship is the largest mud-built structure in the world.

BANDIAGARA CLIFFS
More than 600 years ago, the Dogon people carved their villages into the cliffs of Bandiagara. These communities are still alive today.

5 COOL THINGS TO DO HERE

1 SEE GODDESS SCULPTURES
Oshogbo

Follow the forest path into this sacred grove. The Yoruba people have made shrines, statues, and artwork for the goddesses they believe in.

2 STOP AT THE STONE
Abuja

Shout out when the rock comes into view! This huge boulder is called the "Gateway to Abuja." Its picture is on the 100 naira bill, Nigerian money.

3 RIDE A BOAT TO THE BEACH
Lagos

Head for Tarkwa Beach, one of the most popular beaches in Lagos. You can only reach it by boat, but the ride is worth it for a fun day of swimming.

4 SPOT A CUTE CRITTER
Rhoko Forest

Look out for bush babies jumping from tree to tree. These noctural primates are about the size of a squirrel and have supersharp night vision.

NATIONAL BIRD: black crowned crane

NATIONAL FLOWER: costus

NATIONAL MAMMAL: Cross River gorilla

NIGERIA

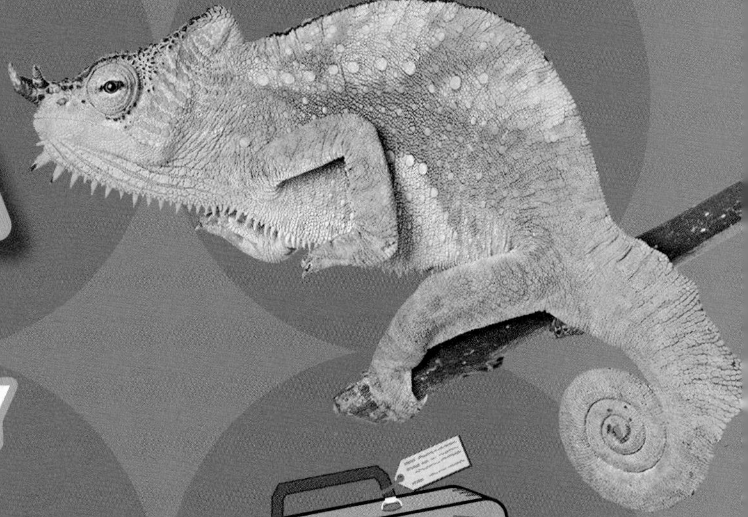

Africa's Most Populated COUNTRY

Africa's population giant, Nigeria, is a prosperous country, thanks to oil fields in the south and offshore in the Gulf of Guinea. The country has distinct regions, each with its own cultures and wildlife, and large, lively cities. The landscape includes grassy plains and highlands, rivers, lakes including artificial Kainji Reservoir, rocky mountains, lowland forest, and mangrove swamps in the Niger River Delta. Northern Nigeria is hotter and drier than the south.

5 READ MESSAGES FROM MONKEYS

Calabar

Try to figure out what these animals are communicating to one another at the Drill Monkey Rehab Center. A grin usually is a friendly gesture. They make sounds to keep their group together and rub their chests on trees to keep others away.

Globetrotter Attractions

ABUJA NATIONAL MOSQUE

This gold-domed mosque attracts worshippers and visitors throughout the year.

OLUMO ROCK

During an 1830s war, the Egba people hid from their enemies by this rock. After the war, the rock became a sacred place. Visitors can reach the top of the 449-foot (137-m)-high rock in Abeokuta by elevator or stairs.

YANKARI NATIONAL PARK

This large park has swamps, floodplains, bush, and grasslands—a comfortable home for baboons, giraffes, hyenas, hippos, and others.

AFRICA

ID CARD COUNTRY FACTS

Size: 356,669 sq mi (923,768 sq km)
Population: 173,615,000
Capital: Abuja
Official language: English
Currency: naira
Highest point: Chappal Waddi, 7,936 ft (2,419 m)
Life expectancy: 52.0 years

DIGITAL TRAVELER!

The currency of Nigeria is *naira* and *kobo*, with 100 kobo to 1 naira. Find a website that converts 10 U.S. dollars into Nigerian money. How many naira and kobo would you have?

NATIONAL BIRD: marabou stork

NATIONAL TREE: date palm

NATIONAL MAMMAL: red river hog

CHAD

From Desert to SAVANNA

Northern deserts and central savanna grasslands where elephants roam—that's most of Chad. Only in the south of this sub-Saharan country is there land suitable for farming. It's still hot in the south, though in the highlands of the Tibesti Mountains it is cool, and the Ennedi Plateau is temperate. Chad's farmers and herders rely on rivers such as the Chari and Logone, and on Lake Chad, which is shallow and shrinking so fast it may disappear.

Globetrotter Attractions

GUELTA D'ARCHEI

Far out in the Sahara is this *guelta*, or oasis. Between canyon walls, water bubbles up to form a pool. Camels drink near the home of the last Nile crocodiles.

LAKE CHAD

The size of this large lake changes with each season but is getting smaller.

EMI KOUSSI

This large and broad volcano is the highest mountain in the Sahara, but it no longer erupts.

ID CARD COUNTRY FACTS

Size: 495,755 sq mi (1,284,000 sq km)
Population: 12,209,000
Capital: N'Djamena
Official languages: French and Arabic
Currency: Cooperacion Financière en Afrique Central franc
Highest point: Emi Koussi, 11,204 ft (3,415 m)
Life expectancy: 50.0 years

5 COOL THINGS TO DO HERE

1 GET INTO MUSIC AND MASKS
N'Djamena

Examine this museum's many musical instruments used by Chad's people over the years. Find the masks people used throughout Chad's history.

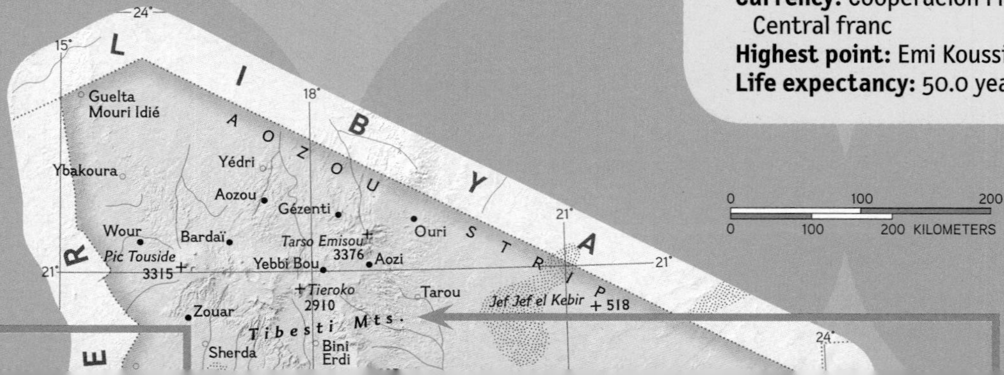

2 TAKE A WALK ON SANDY STREETS
Mao

Wander the sandy streets and meet with friendly children. Admire the bright clothes worn by girls. Visit their one-room school. Travel down the dusty streets on a horse. Shop at street vendors.

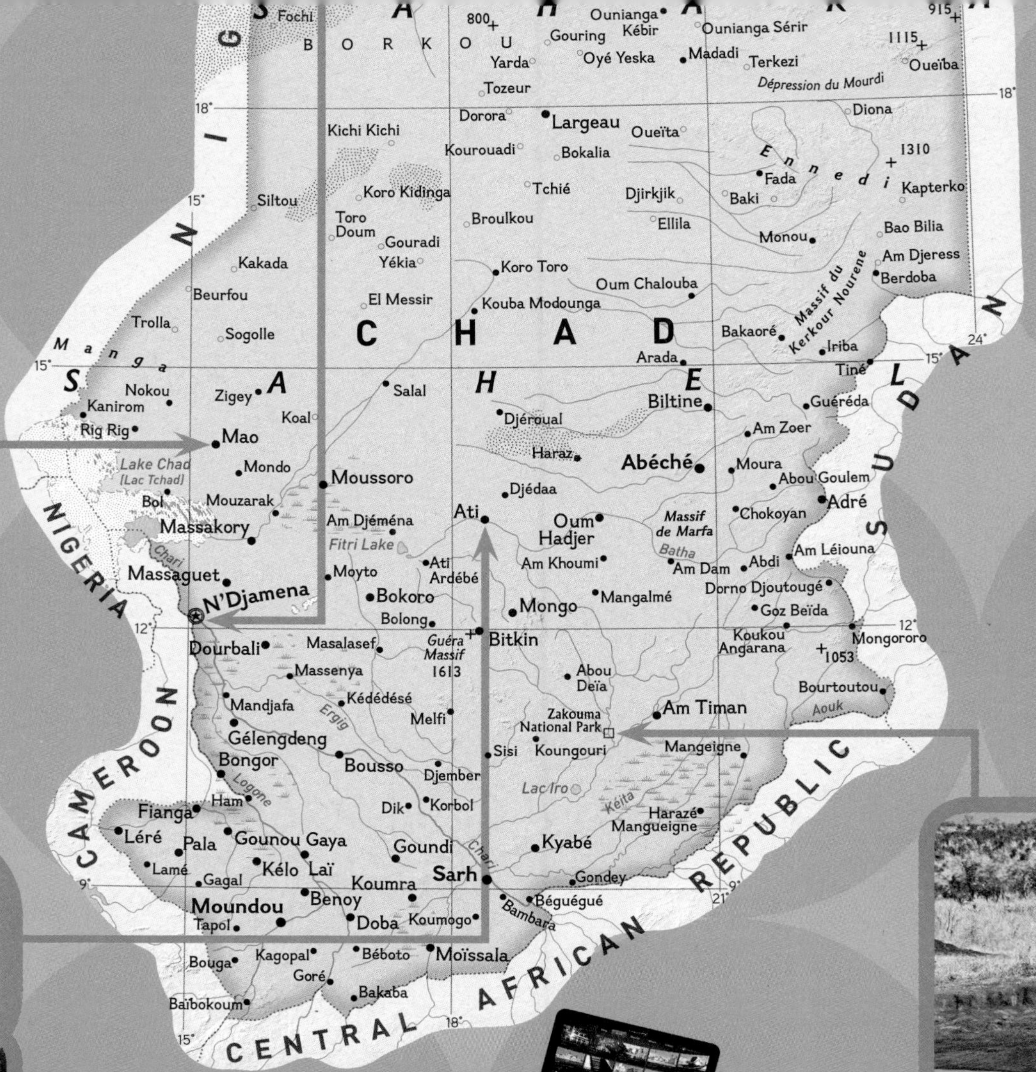

3 GET WATER FROM A WELL
Ati

Join villagers as they get the water they need for drinking, cooking, and washing from the local well. Try carrying water in a jug on your head.

4 TREK OVER AN OLD VOLCANO
Tibesti Massif

Walk the Tibesti Mountains and see several inactive volcanoes. Visit canyons and hot springs. Find the rock paintings and carvings made long ago. Meet the Toubou people who now live on oases in the nearby desert.

5 BE AN ELEPHANT CONSERVATIONIST
Zakouma National Park

Watch rangers protect the elephants in Chad's first national park. Elephants almost disappeared until better protection allowed their numbers and those of other wild animals to increase.

DIGITAL TRAVELER!
Lake Chad provides water to millions of people in Chad and three other neighboring countries. Go online to figure out which countries these are. Then see if you can find out how deep Lake Chad is.

	NATIONAL BIRD:	NATIONAL FLOWER:	NATIONAL MAMMAL:
SUDAN	secretary bird	oleander	Burton's gerbil
SOUTH SUDAN	African fish eagle	*Bidens chipli*	kob

SUDAN AND SOUTH SUDAN

Desert, Rivers, and the RED SEA

South Sudan broke from Sudan in 2011. Until the split, Sudan was Africa's biggest country. It's mostly desert. To the west is the Sahara, while the Nubian Desert borders the Red Sea. Yet through this hot land of sand and camels flows the Nile, Africa's mightiest river. On its banks stands Khartoum, capital of Sudan. In South Sudan is a vast wetland formed by the White Nile, known as the Sudd.

ID CARD COUNTRY FACTS

SUDAN
Population: 34,186,000
Capital: Khartoum

SOUTH SUDAN
Population: 9,782,000
Capital: Juba

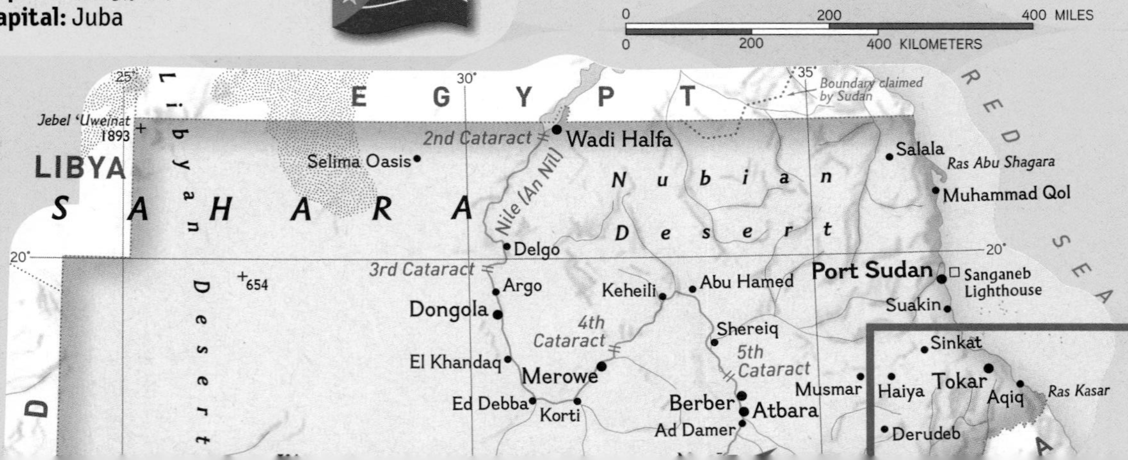

5 COOL THINGS TO DO HERE

1 GET THE POINT OF PYRAMIDS
Meroë

Visit Sudan's Meroë, once the capital of the Kingdom of Kush. Wander through its royal cemetery, which includes about 100 small pyramids.

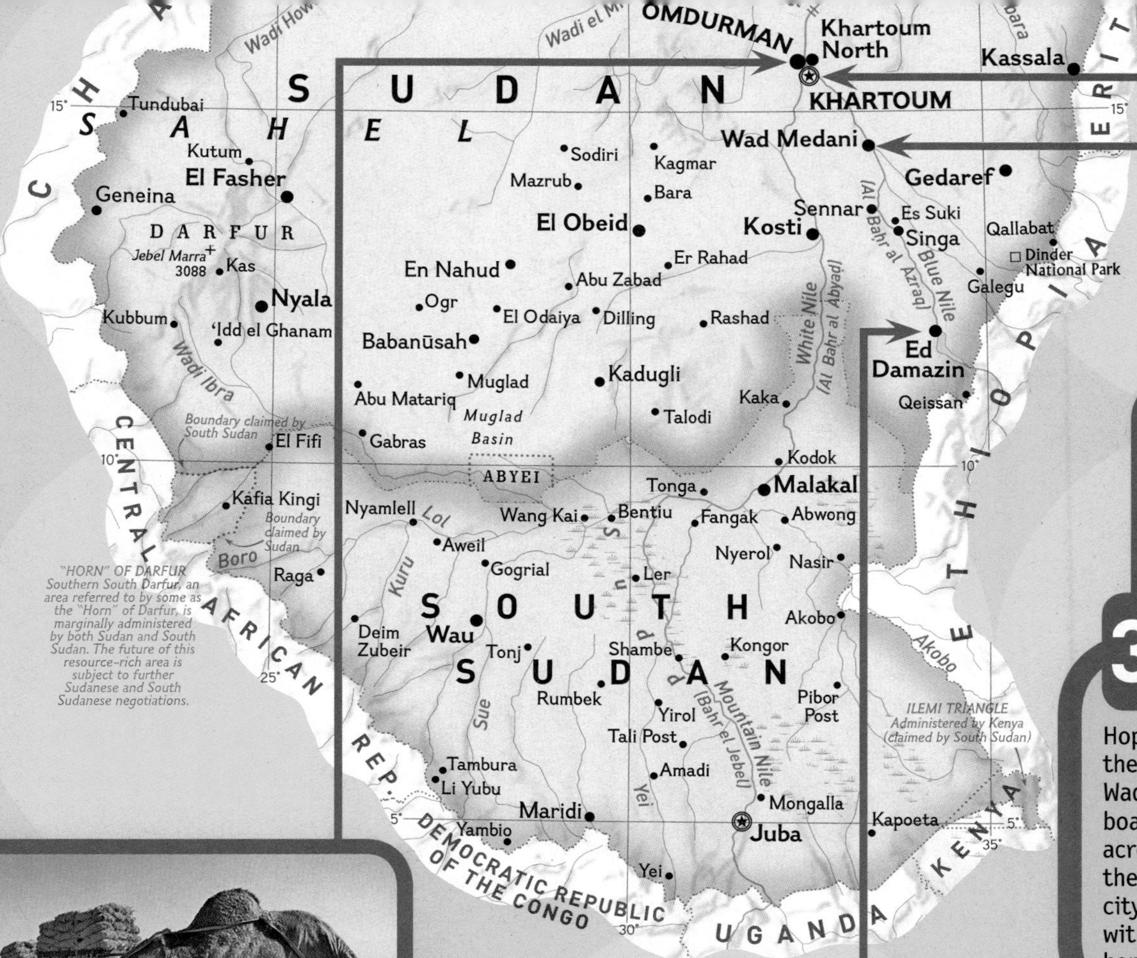

2 TOUR TEMPLES AND TOMBS
Khartoum

Visit ancient temples and tombs outside the Sudan National Museum. These buildings and ruins were moved from the Nubia area when it was flooded for Egypt's Aswan High Dam.

3 SAIL FOR A MILE ON THE BLUE NILE
Wad Medani

Hop a boat to travel on the Blue Nile in Sudan's Wad Medani. Take a boat to the beach just across the river from the city. Explore the city, which is a favorite with visitors and honeymooning couples.

5 PACK UP A CAMEL
Omdurman

Admire camels from South Sudan that are for sale in this camel market. Find one that is fast, one that can carry a heavy load, or one that can do both!

4 WATCH WATER MAKE ELECTRICITY
Ed Damazin

Watch the water move through the Ar-Rusayris Dam. Enjoy the green land it waters and the electricity its hydroelectric plant creates.

DIGITAL TRAVELER!
Do online research to learn about the traditional foods in Sudan and South Sudan. What would you eat if you traveled there?

Globetrotter Attractions

SANGANEB LIGHTHOUSE
This Sudan lighthouse stands on a coral reef in the Red Sea. There are great views from the top.

DINDER NATIONAL PARK
Many different animals live on the grasslands and in woodlands and forests of this park in Sudan.

AL-MOGRAN PARK
This Sudan amusement park is where the Blue Nile and White Nile rivers come together.

	NATIONAL BIRD:	NATIONAL FLOWER:	NATIONAL MAMMAL:
ERITREA	lemon dove	prickly acacia	Arabian camel
ETHIOPIA	African firefinch	calla lily	lion

ERITREA AND ETHIOPIA

Two Contrasting COUNTRIES

Eritrea separated from Ethiopia in 1993. Ethiopia, one of Africa's oldest countries, is almost ten times larger than Eritrea, which occupies a strip of Red Sea coast. In the mountains and plateaus of the Great Rift Valley are grasslands, forests, and many farms. There is also a wealth of wildlife. Rivers rise here, including the Blue Nile, and Tana is a large lake in Ethiopia. The lowlands are hot and barren, with severe droughts.

SIMIEN MOUNTAINS NATIONAL PARK

This Ethiopian national park has many animals found nowhere else in the world. The weather has shaped its mountains, deep valleys, and high sharp cliffs.

THE ROYAL ENCLOSURE

The Ethiopian fortress-city of Fasil Ghebbi in Gonder has several castles surrounded by a wall. Ethiopian emperors of the 1600s and 1700s built these unique palaces and churches.

DAHLAK ARCHIPELAGO

Only 4 of these 210 Eritrean islands have people living on them. Many divers come to explore the Red Sea around them with its many fish and birds.

5 COUNT THE CHERUBS
Gonder

Look up from the wall paintings to find the cherubs painted on the ceiling of Debre Berhan Selassie, an Ethiopian church.

4 INSPECT WAR TANKS
Taulud Island

Wander around Eritrea's Massawa War Memorial. Visit the three captured tanks and see the fountain spouting water.

ID CARD COUNTRY FACTS

ERITREA
Population: 5,765,000
Capital: Asmara

ETHIOPIA
Population: 89,209,000
Capital: Addis Ababa

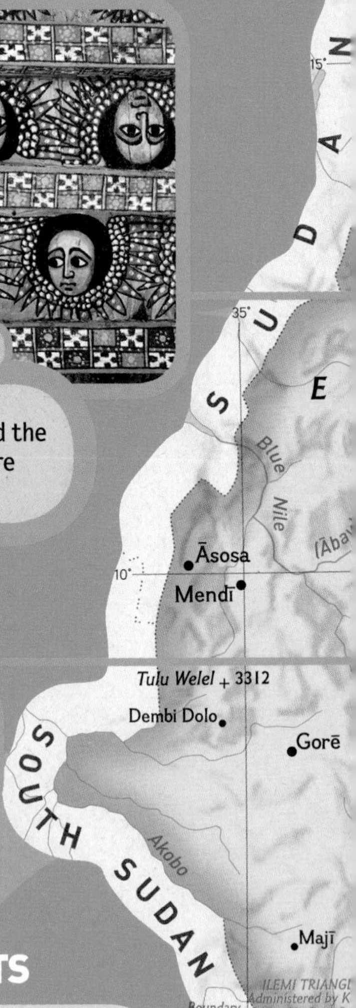

5 COOL THINGS TO DO HERE

1 SNAP A FUTURISTIC GAS STATION
Asmara

Admire this unusual service station in Eritrea, built in the shape of a 1930s airplane.

2 EAT YOUR PLATE
Adi Ugri

Sit around a table in Eritrea. Eat the stew that comes on a spongy pancake called *injera.* Tear a piece of injera and wrap it around the meat. No forks, just pop it into your mouth!

3 EXPLORE CAVE CHURCHES
Lalībela

Look down into a pit to find a church carved from one piece of rock. See all 11 of Lalībela, Ethiopia's rock cave churches. Admire how the rock was cut away for doors and windows.

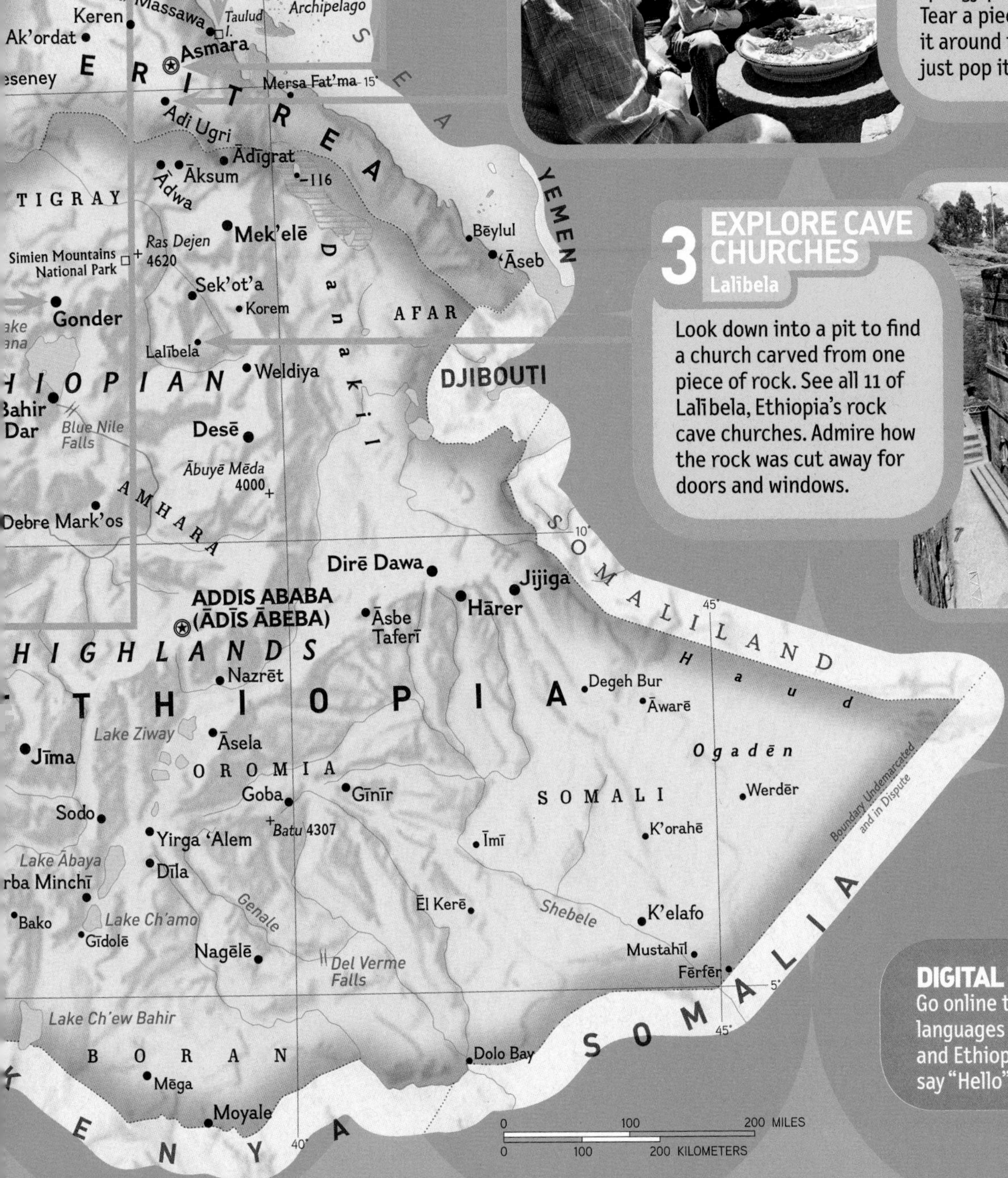

DIGITAL TRAVELER!
Go online to search for the languages spoken in Eritrea and Ethiopia. Find out how to say "Hello" in both countries.

	NATIONAL BIRD:	NATIONAL FLOWER:	NATIONAL MAMMAL:
DJIBOUTI	Djibouti francolin	Egyptian starcluster	gerenuk
SOMALIA	Somali lark	*Euphorbia noxia*	leopard

HORN OF AFRICA

Neighbors by the SEA

Neighbors on the jutting Horn of Africa are Djibouti and Somalia. The climate is hot and dry, and there are few rivers. Tiny Djibouti is separated from the Arabian Peninsula by a narrow seaway, part of the Red Sea and Gulf of Aden. To the east, Somalia, possibly the "Land of Punt" of legend, stretches south from Cape Gwardafuy along the Indian Ocean. Somalia has been strife-torn, with civil war and piracy.

5 COOL THINGS TO DO HERE

1 WATCH WHALE SHARKS
Gulf of Tadjoura

See the world's largest fish when it comes to feed on tiny plankton in this Djibouti gulf. Some whale sharks weigh more than an elephant but they don't bite, even though they are sharks not whales.

2 JOIN IN A JAM SESSION
Berbera

Instead of walking through the streets of Berbera in Somalia, ride in a *bajaj*, a three-wheeled motorized rickshaw. Listen for music and street singers, and hear songs that tell a story.

5 IMAGINE YOU ARE ON THE MOON
Ābhē Bid Hāyk'

Wander between the limestone chimneys that dot this flat plain in Djibouti. Wake early to see flocks of pink flamingos on the shores of the lake. Maybe they'll take off to fly over the tall pillars and dry land.

ID CARD
COUNTRY FACTS

DJIBOUTI
Population: 939,000
Capital: Djibouti

SOMALIA
Population: 10,383,000
Capital: Mogadishu

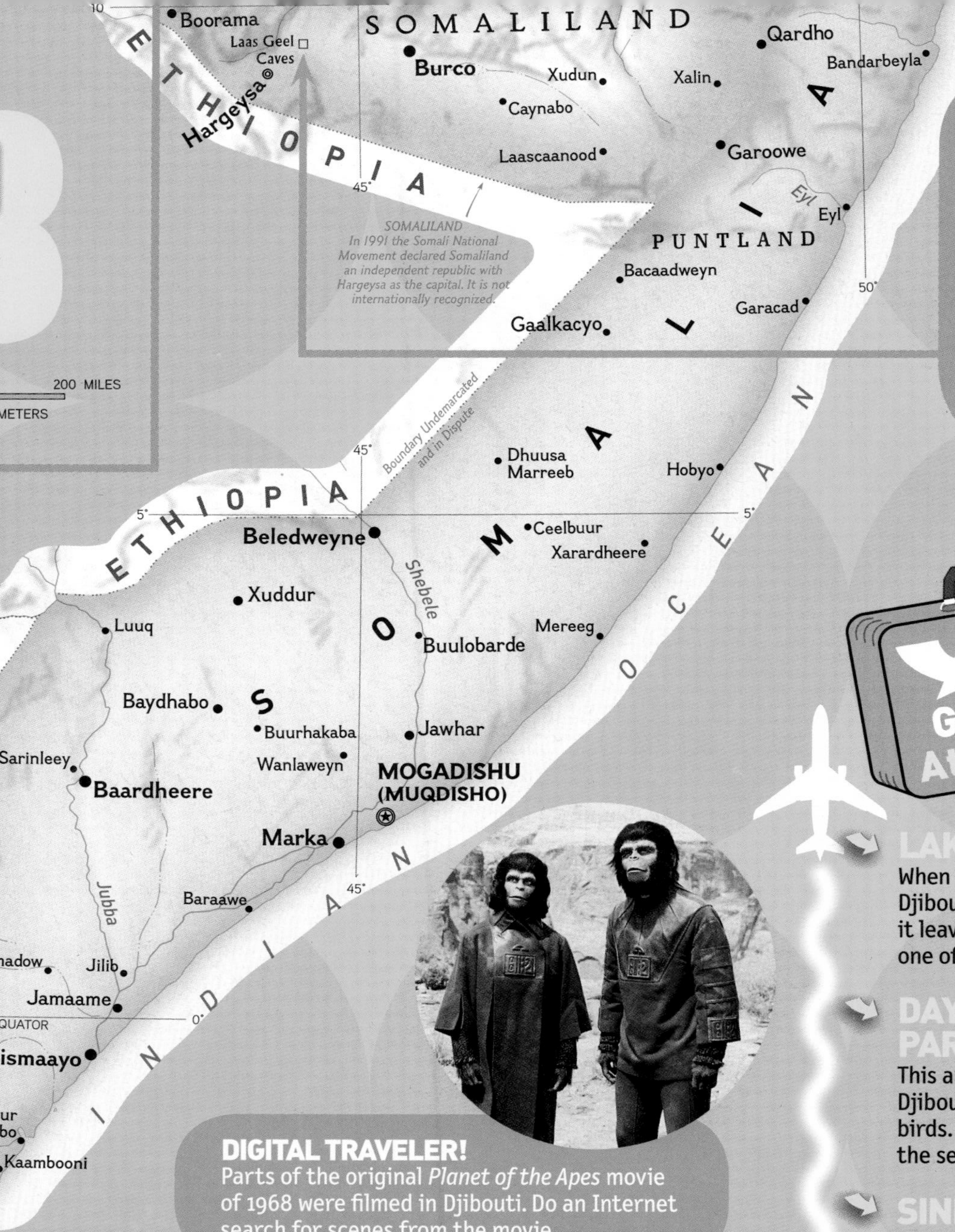

4 SHOP AT THE MARKET
Djibouti City

Buy what you need at the Central Market in the city of Djibouti in Djibouti. Visit stores and street vendors with their goods spread out under an umbrella. Go in the morning, as it gets very hot and quiet in the afternoon.

3 BE ARTISTIC IN CAVES
Laas Geel

See some of Africa's best-preserved cave paintings on a guided tour of Laas Geel in Somalia. The paintings were made between 7,000 and 5,000 years ago and show people and both domesticated and wild animals.

DIGITAL TRAVELER!
Parts of the original *Planet of the Apes* movie of 1968 were filmed in Djibouti. Do an Internet search for scenes from the movie.

LAKE ASSAL
When the warm, salty water of Djibouti's Lake Assal (Lac 'Assal) dries, it leaves a crust of salt. The lake is in one of the hottest places on Earth.

DAY FOREST NATIONAL PARK
This ancient forest in northern Djibouti has a variety of trees and birds. The land is very different from the semi-desert and deserts nearby.

SINBUSI BEACH
The coastline near Marka has many small beach resorts where tourists can do various watersports.

5 COOL THINGS TO DO HERE

1 COUNT FLAMINGOS
Lake Nakuru

Count the thousands of flamingos eating in the lake. Search for the other 450 types of birds found here. Watch for rhinoceroses and giraffes.

2 GREET A GIRAFFE
Nairobi National Park

Watch these gentle-looking giants stretch their long tongues to reach the best leaves at the top of trees. See zebras, lions, baboons, and hippopotamuses as you are guided through this park of grasslands. All these animals live very close to Kenya's capital city of Nairobi.

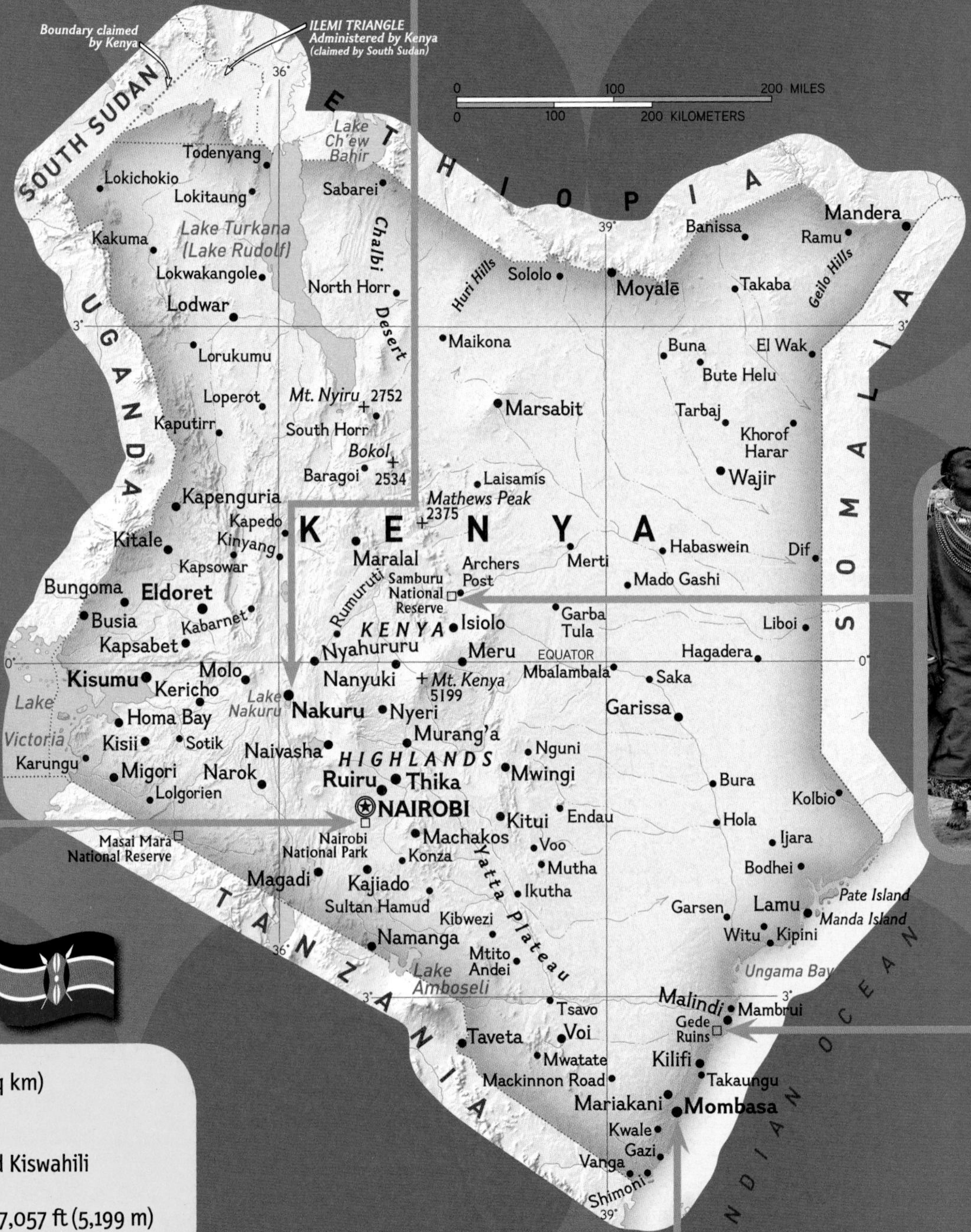

ID CARD
COUNTRY FACTS

Size: 224,081 sq mi (580,367 sq km)
Population: 44,184,000
Capital: Nairobi
Official languages: English and Kiswahili
Currency: Kenyan shilling
Highest point: Mount Kenya, 17,057 ft (5,199 m)
Life expectancy: 60.0 years

NATIONAL BIRD: pink flamingo

NATIONAL TREE: acacia

NATIONAL MAMMAL: lion

KENYA

Sand, Cities, and SAFARIS

Wildlife-rich savanna plains, forest highlands, desert scrub, the Great Rift Valley, Indian Ocean beaches, and mangrove swamps make Kenya a globetrotter's delight. Nairobi and other cities, and most big farms, are in the southern highlands, topped by Mount Kenya. Mombasa on the coast is popular with tourists. Kenya's main lake is Turkana (formerly called Lake Rudolf), though it shares Africa's largest lake, Victoria, with Tanzania and Uganda.

MASAI MARA NATIONAL RESERVE

This preserve is home to the biggest and wildest animals in Africa, including the Cape buffalo, elephant, leopard, lion, and rhinoceros.

LAKE TURKANA

This lake is the largest desert lake in the world. Little lives in the desert around it, but some hippopotamuses and crocodiles live in or near its salty water.

MOUNT KENYA

This ancient extinct, or dead, volcano is Africa's second highest mountain. It is near the Equator with glaciers at its top.

3 DANCE TO THE BEAT

Samburu National Reserve

Enjoy watching the Samburu people dance in circles. Men and women dance separately to singing, not instruments. Admire the elaborate beaded necklaces used in their dances.

4 WATCH SNAPPERS SNAP

Mombasa

Watch the crocodiles at Mamba Village jump high into the air to snap meat at feeding time. Learn as you see crocs at different ages.

5 IMAGINE GHOSTS OF GEDE

Gede Ruins

Wander through the palace, mosque, and houses built of coral bricks. Puzzle over why the people abandoned the town hundreds of years ago.

DIGITAL TRAVELER!

Take a digital safari. Go online and find photographs of some of the most popular animals native to Kenya: elephants, Cape buffalo, lions, leopards, and rhinoceroses.

AFRICA

NATIONAL BIRD: ostrich

NATIONAL FLOWER: African blackwood

NATIONAL MAMMAL: giraffe

TANZANIA

From Mountains to GRASSLANDS

In Tanzania snow-topped Mount Kilimanjaro towers above the Serengeti Plains, teeming with big game. Most of the country is high plateau, with western lakes including Tanganyika, Malawi (Nyasa), and Rukwa. Tanzania also shares Lake Victoria, on its northern border. In the Indian Ocean, the islands of Zanzibar and Pemba are part of Tanzania. Most people are farmers, but minerals and tourism are vital to the economy.

5 SPOT LIONS IN THE TREES

Lake Manyara National Park

Drive along the rugged roads to see baboons and hear birds. Continue through the woodland where lions hang out in trees and elephants trumpet. Watch for the hippo pools.

Globetrotter Attractions

MOUNT KILIMANJARO

The highest mountain in Africa is also the tallest in the world that is not part of a mountain chain. Its weather is tropical at the bottom and arctic at the top.

NGORONGORO CRATER

A large volcano exploded and left this bowl-shaped depression. Today, many African animals and the cattle of the Maasai people live on its grasslands.

SELOUS GAME RESERVE

This huge game reserve protects many elephants, lions, and other big animals.

ID CARD COUNTRY FACTS

Size: 365,754 sq mi (947,300 sq km)
Population: 49,122,000
Capital: Dar es Salaam
Official languages: Kiswahili and English
Currency: Tanzanian shilling
Highest point: Kilimanjaro, 19,340 ft (5,895 m)
Life expectancy: 60.0 years

5 COOL THINGS TO DO HERE

1 EAT WALI MAHARAGE
Kigoma

Order *wali maharge*—rice and beans—for lunch or dinner. The beans are cooked with spices, sugar, and coconut milk.

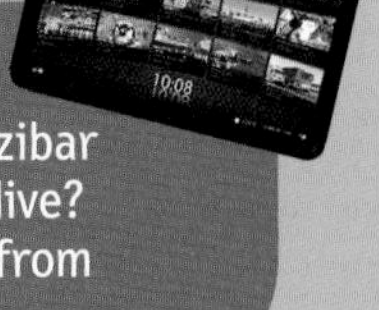

2 WATCH WILDEBEESTS
Serengeti National Park

Count the huge herds of migrating wildebeests and zebras as they race across the grasslands of the Serengeti and Ngorongoro Conservation Area.

3 JUMP FOR JOY
Arusha

Visit a Masai village to try milking their cattle or collecting firewood. Hear traditional stories and ride a donkey. See their school and learn the games these children play.

4 CHEER AT A DHOW RACE
Zanzibar

Watch the local fishermen race their traditional sailing boats, called dhows. Cheer them during the Stone Town harbor races.

DIGITAL TRAVELER!

Search online to learn about the Zanzibar red colobus monkeys. Where do they live? How are people trying to keep them from becoming extinct? Download a photo.

AFRICA

	NATIONAL BIRD:	NATIONAL FLOWER:	NATIONAL MAMMAL:
BURUNDI	Goliath heron	orchid	lion
RWANDA	winding cisticola	water lily	African leopard
UGANDA	gray crowned crane	African tulip	mountain gorilla

GREAT LAKES REGION

A Nature-Rich LANDSCAPE

The great lakes of Central Africa's Rift Valley are important to several countries, including Burundi, Rwanda, and Uganda. Lake Victoria is partly in southern Uganda, Lake Tanganyika on Burundi's southwest border, and Lac Kivu on Rwanda's western border. Mountain slopes are planted with coffee and other crops. Gorillas survive in forests, and game roams Uganda's northern savanna. Uganda is on the Equator but the altitude means it's seldom too hot for comfort.

ID CARD
COUNTRY FACTS

BURUNDI
Population: 10,892,000
Capital: Bujumbura

RWANDA
Population: 11,116,000
Capital: Kigali

UGANDA
Population: 36,890,000
Capital: Kampala

5 COOL THINGS TO DO HERE

1 VIEW CHEETAHS
Kidepo Valley National Park

Locate lions, leopards, and cheetahs on the grasslands of Uganda's isolated park. When water is scarce, find the animals near wetlands and pools.

2 FIND FRESH TEA AND COFFEE
Rubavu

Walk through a tea or coffee field in Rwanda. Visit one of the thousands of small farms that grow these crops.

3 SPEND A DAY BY THE SEA
Bujumbura

Visit the capital of Burundi at the northeast end of this lake, the longest freshwater lake in the world. Enjoy the sun and water at its beaches, but watch for a hippo walking on the beach!

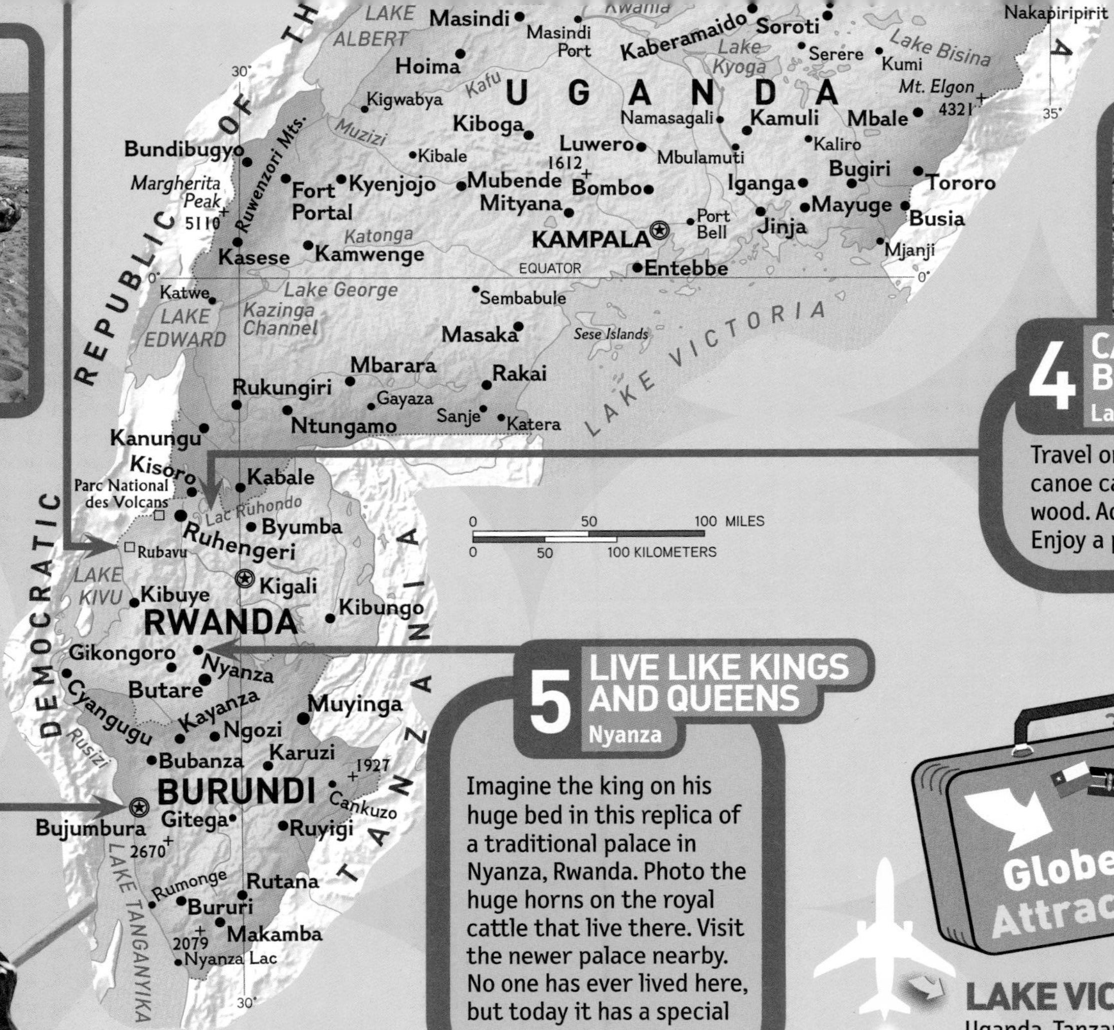

4 CANOE PAST BIRD PARADISE
Lac Ruhondo

Travel on this Rwandan lake in a canoe carved from one piece of wood. Admire the rare water birds. Enjoy a picnic on one of its islands.

DIGITAL TRAVELER!
Burundi drummers are famous for the music they play at festivals and other important events. Search the Internet to find a video clip of the Drummers of Burundi. They are also called *Les Tambourinaires*.

5 LIVE LIKE KINGS AND QUEENS
Nyanza

Imagine the king on his huge bed in this replica of a traditional palace in Nyanza, Rwanda. Photo the huge horns on the royal cattle that live there. Visit the newer palace nearby. No one has ever lived here, but today it has a special art museum.

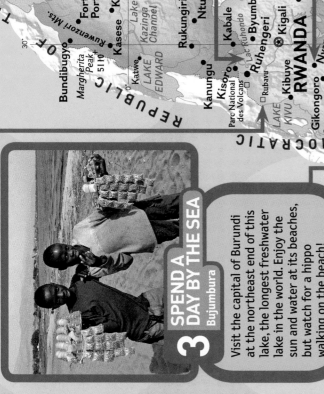

Globetrotter Attractions

LAKE VICTORIA
Uganda, Tanzania, and Kenya border this lake, the largest lake in Africa. Its waters flow into the Nile River.

PARC NATIONAL DES VOLCANS
This park in Rwanda has beautiful scenery, active volcanoes, and mountain gorillas.

"MOUNTAINS OF THE MOON"
In Uganda, the Ruwenzori Mountains, with their glaciers and lakes, descend into the Rift Valley. Their tops are often covered in clouds and are always snow-covered.

	NATIONAL BIRD:	NATIONAL FLOWER:	NATIONAL MAMMAL:
CEN. AF. REPUB.	Sangha Forest robin	*Pleiocarpa mutica*	African elephant
CONGO	Ituri batis	orchid	lion
D.R. CONGO	Congo peafowl	coffee flower	okapi

CENTRAL AFRICA

The Heart of the CONTINENT

The mighty Congo River, and other rivers such as the Ubangi (or Oubangui), flow across Central Africa. Two countries use the name Congo: Congo (Congo-Brazzaville) and the Democratic Republic of the Congo (Dem. Rep. Congo, or Congo-Kinshasa, formerly Zaire). Their northern neighbor is the Central African Republic (Cen. Af. Rep.). There are equatorial rain forests and savanna, and grassy plateaus in the drier north. The Democratic Republic of the Congo's eastern border passes through several of Africa's great lakes.

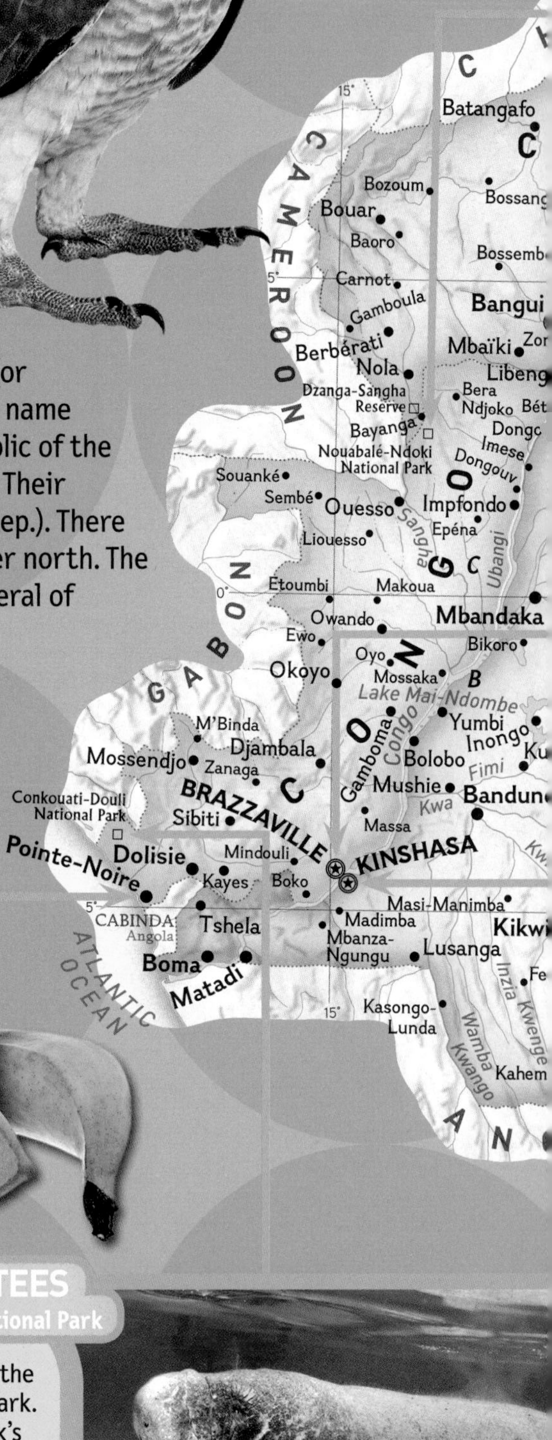

5 EAT FRIED BANANAS
Pointe-Noire

Order fried plantains, a type of banana. In the Congo enjoy them with meat, often goat. Eat plantains fried, boiled, or baked, but not raw.

CONGO RIVER
This river, the second longest in Africa, forms the border between the Democratic Republic of the Congo and Congo. Its waters take six months to go from its source to the Atlantic Ocean.

DZANGA-SANGHA SPECIAL RESERVE
This rain forest reserve in the Central African Republic is home to many lowland gorillas and forest elephants.

VOLCAN NYIROGONGO
The city of Goma in the Democratic Republic of the Congo lies in the path of lava from this very active volcano.

4 MEET MANATEES
Conkouati-Douli National Park

Watch the manatees in the lagoons of this Congo park. The manatee is the park's symbol because this endangered animal is protected here.

5 COOL THINGS TO DO HERE

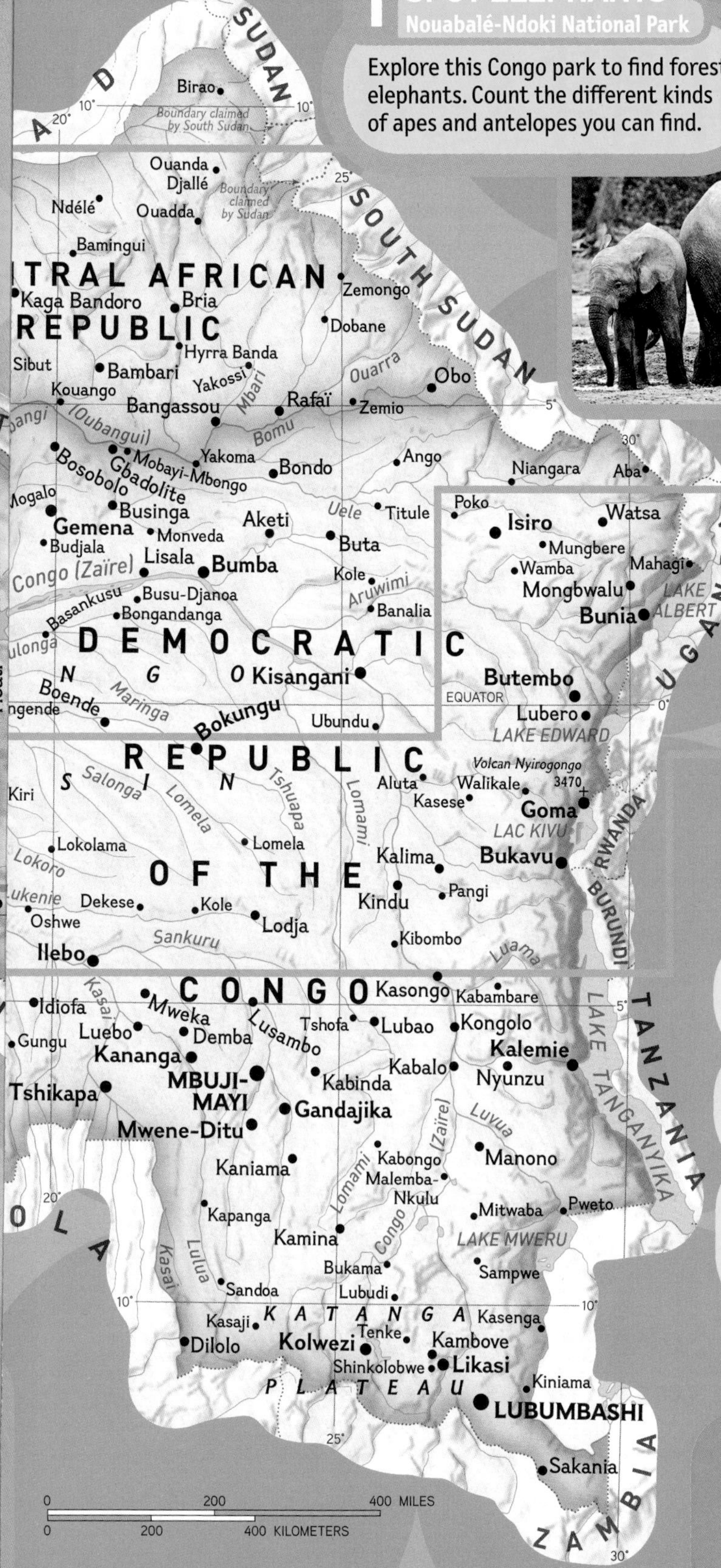

1 SPOT ELEPHANTS
Nouabalé-Ndoki National Park

Explore this Congo park to find forest elephants. Count the different kinds of apes and antelopes you can find.

2 HAVE A FISH FEAST
Brazzaville

Watch the Congo River that flows alongside Brazzaville in the Congo. Eat fish from the river's waters. Take a water taxi across the river to Kinshasa in another country!

3 PLAY BASKETBALL
Kinshasa

Cheer the women and men as they play basketball in the Dem. Rep. Congo. Meet the boys and girls who practice in the hope of joining international basketball teams.

ID CARD
COUNTRY FACTS

CENTRAL AFRICAN REPUBLIC
Population: 4,476,000
Capital: Bangui

CONGO
Population: 4,355,000
Capital: Brazzaville

DEMOCRATIC REPUBLIC OF THE CONGO
Population: 71,128,000
Capital: Kinshasa

AFRICA

DIGITAL TRAVELER!
Hundreds of kinds of butterflies live in Central African Republic. Go online and find photographs of the country's butterflies. Compare them to photographs of butterflies where you live.

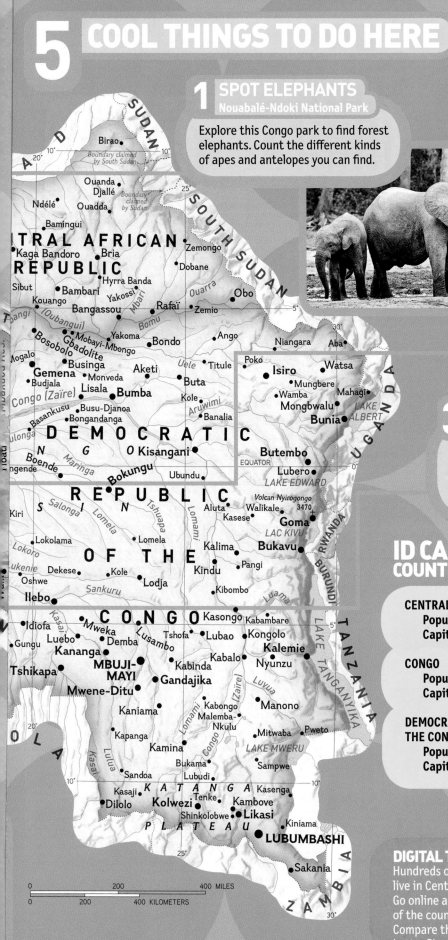

5 AMUSE AN ANTELOPE
Quiçama National Park

Find the secretive giant sable antelope in Angola's national parks. Once thought extinct, this antelope with long horns that curve toward its back has been spotted by researchers.

ID CARD
COUNTRY FACTS

Size: 481,354 sq mi (1,246,700 sq km)
Population: 21,635,000
Capital: Luanda
Official language: Portuguese
Currency: kwanza
Highest point: Morro de Moco, 8,596 ft (2,620 m)
Life expectancy: 51.0 years

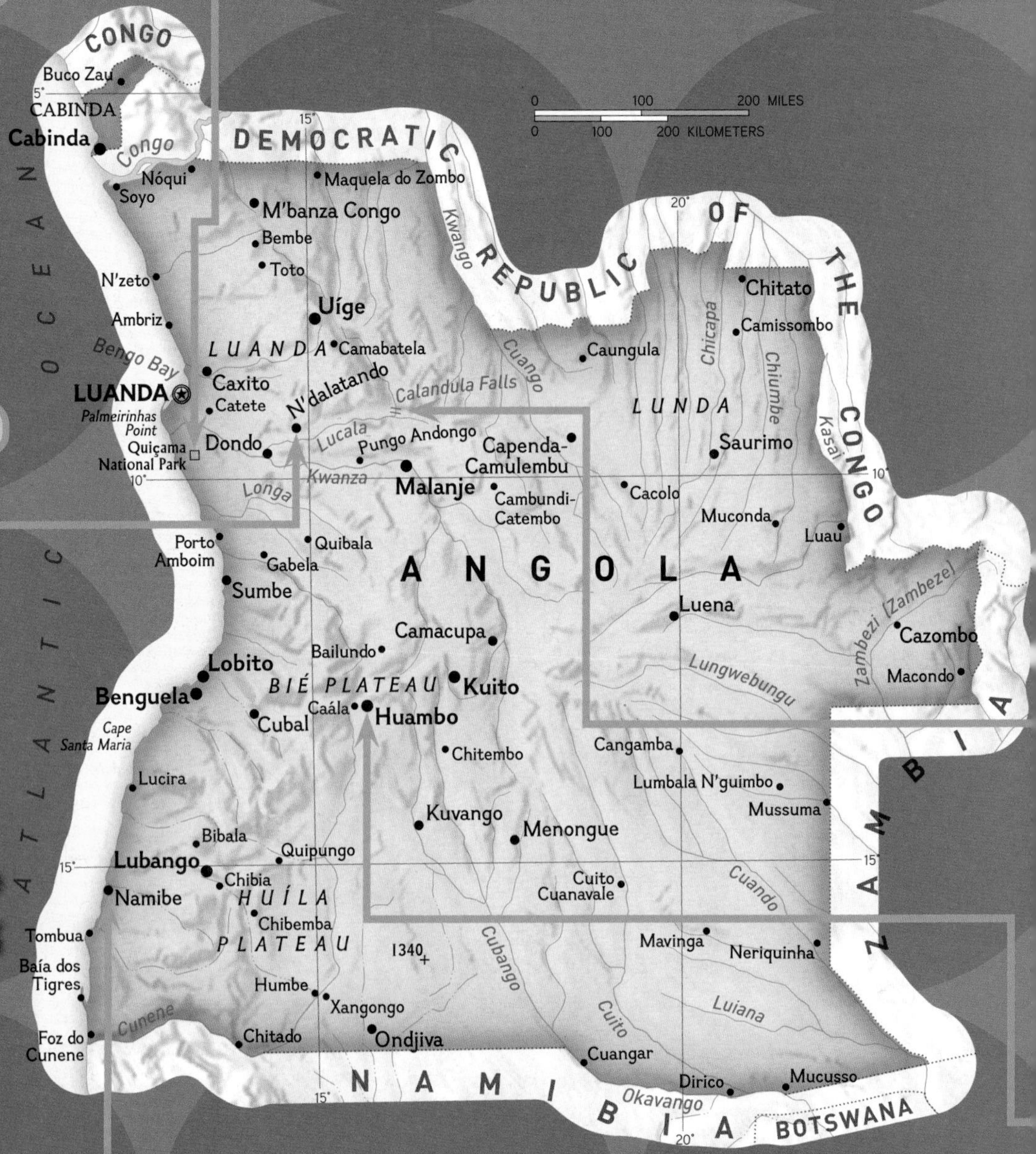

4 SNIFF A SPICY FLOWER
N'dalatando

Check out the Porcelain Rose, a sweet-smelling ginger plant that is unique to the region. Wander under giant bamboo plants that grow in the botanical garden just outside this small city.

3 GO FISHING
Namibe

Observe the fishermen who bring in most of the fish Angolans love to eat. Identify the factories where the fish are processed.

NATIONAL BIRD: peregrine falcon

NATIONAL TREE: acacia

NATIONAL MAMMAL: leopard

ANGOLA

Building a BRIGHT FUTURE

Angola is a land of hills, rivers, and grasslands, with forests in the north and desert in the south toward Namibia. Separate, but part of Angola, is Cabinda to the north. Portuguese sailors explored this coast in the 1500s, and today Angola's national capital Luanda is an international port. Portuguese is the official language. Natural resources include diamonds and oil, but most Angolans are village farmers.

5 COOL THINGS TO DO HERE

1 VISIT AN AMAZING WATERFALL
Calandula Falls

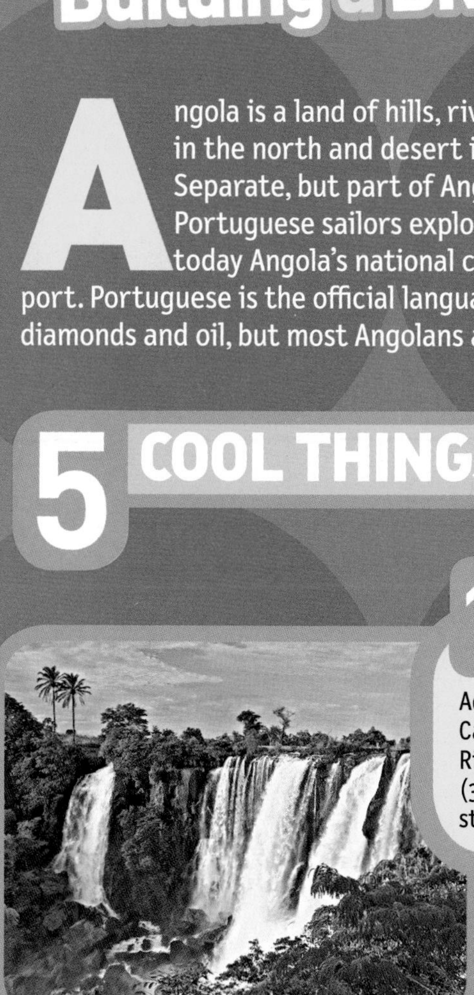

Admire the horseshoe-shaped Calandula Falls on the Lucala River. It usually spans 1,300 feet (396 m) but after seasonal floods stretches 2,000 feet (606 m).

2 GET ON TRACK
Huambo

Ride the only train that goes from the Atlantic Coast to central Africa. This train, built in 1929, needed major repairs. It is now carrying goods and passengers once again.

DIGITAL TRAVELER!
People in Angola enjoy eating fish *calulu*, or fish stew. Do an Internet search for a fish calulu recipe and find out its ingredients. Is this something you would order in Angola?

THE BLACK ROCKS
These huge rocks near Pungo Andongo are more than 656 feet (200 m) high and are unlike the rest of the grassland region where they are found.

SHIPWRECK BEACH
The shore of Bengo Bay (Baía do Bengo), north of Angola's capital, Luanda, is home to old, rusting ships. Huge metal ships stand at a tilt along the beach or on their side in the water.

FORTALEZA DE SÃO MIGUEL
This star-shaped fort was built by the Portuguese in 1576. It's the oldest building in the city and still watches over the port of Luanda. It now houses the Museum of the Armed Forces.

	NATIONAL BIRD:	NATIONAL FLOWER:	NATIONAL MAMMAL:
ZAMBIA	African fish eagle	mangrove flower	black rhinoceros
MALAWI	bar-tailed trogon	water mint	Thomson's gazelle

ZAMBIA AND MALAWI

Buffalo, Bats, and MONKEY BREAD

3 MEET MILLIONS OF BATS

Kasanka National Park

Observe the largest mammal migration in the world. Each October, about eight million fruit bats arrive. They swarm the sky and hang upside down in trees.

Much of Zambia is high plateau, with the Muchinga Mountains near the border with Malawi, which is a land of forests and savanna. There are large lakes, including Bangweulu in Zambia and Malawi (Nyasa) on Malawi's eastern border with Tanzania. Zambia has copper mines, but farming is the chief activity in both countries. The Victoria Falls on the Zambezi River, the Kariba Dam, and amazing wildlife attract tourists.

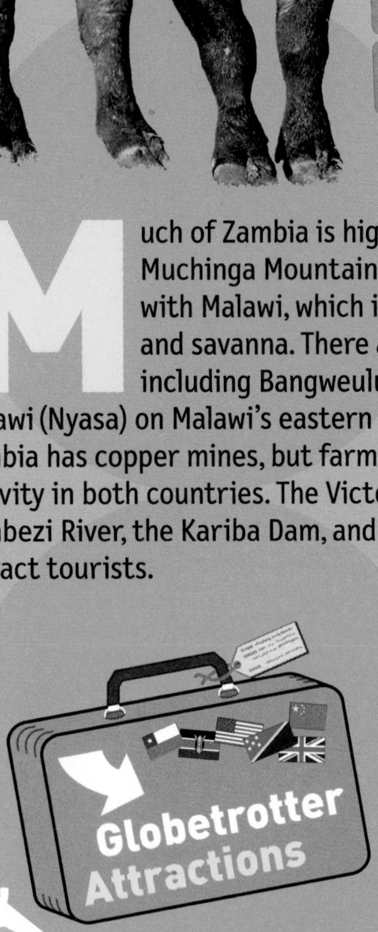

Globetrotter Attractions

LAKE MALAWI

This is one of the African Great Lakes and one of the deepest lakes in the world. It is home to hundreds of colorful cichlid fish, called *mbuna*.

KAFUE NATIONAL PARK

Whether you go on a night drive or daytime boat cruise here in Zambia, there is a good chance you will see elephants, leopards, crocodiles, rhinos, and much more.

VICTORIA FALLS

Some people call this the "Greatest Curtain of Falling Water in the World." It is on the Zambia–Zimbabwe border.

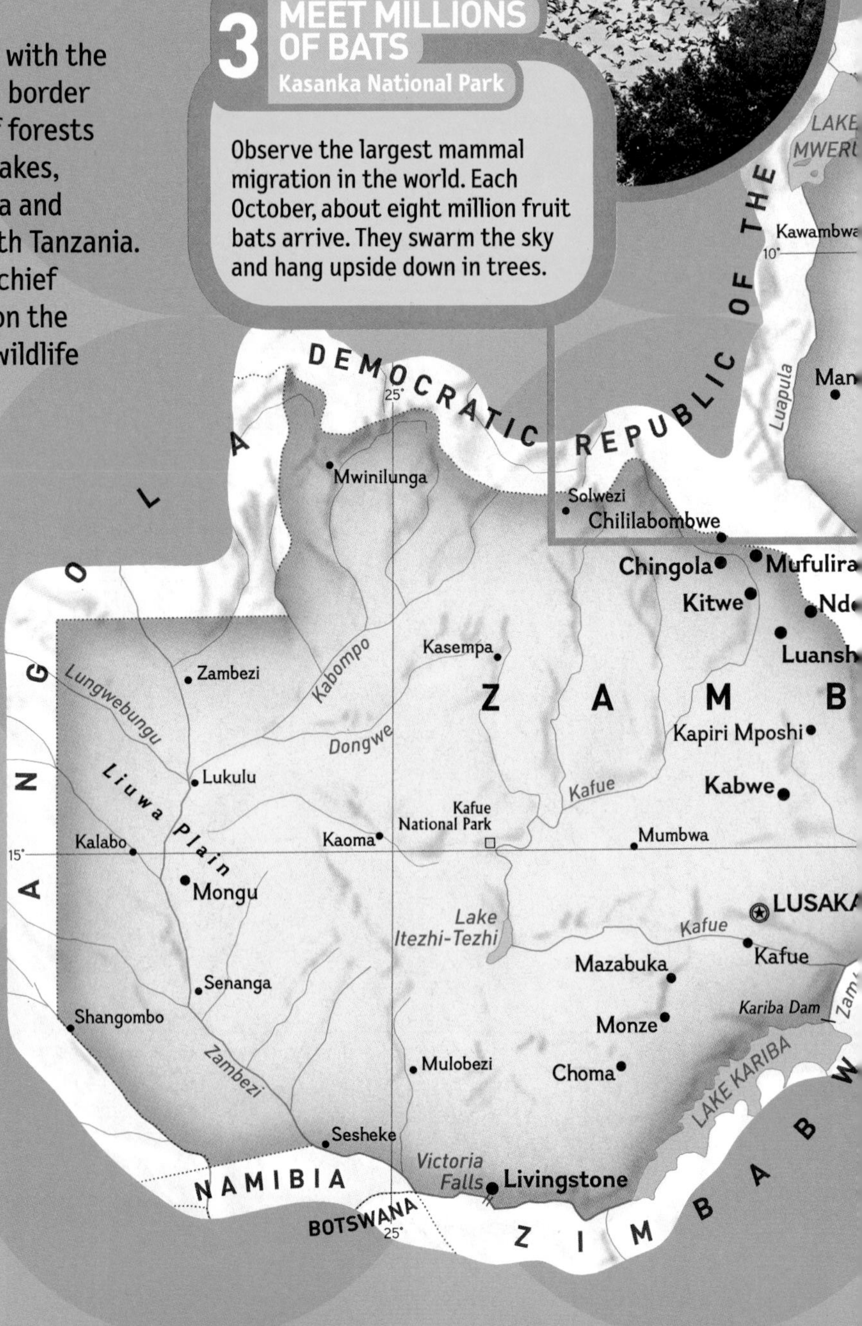

5 COOL THINGS TO DO HERE

1 CANOE PAST BUFFALO
Lower Zambezi National Park

Snap lots of photos on your canoe tour of the Zambezi River. You may see Cape buffalo quenching their thirst or hippos taking a bath. Keep your distance!

2 EAT MONKEY BREAD
Likoma Island

Taste the coconut-looking fruit of the baobab tree. Its nickname is "monkey bread." It tastes like a mix of pear, grapefruit, and vanilla.

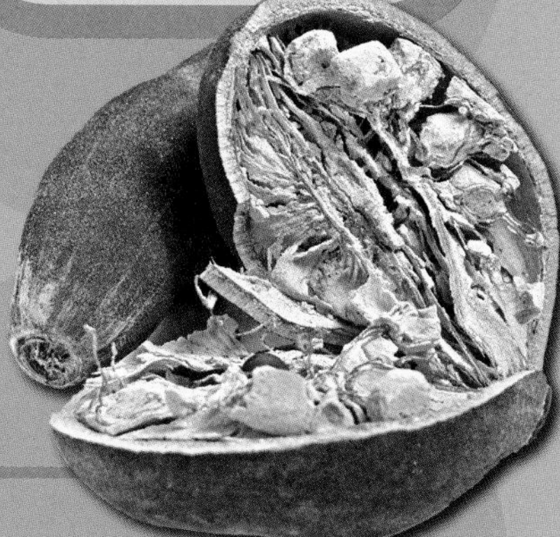

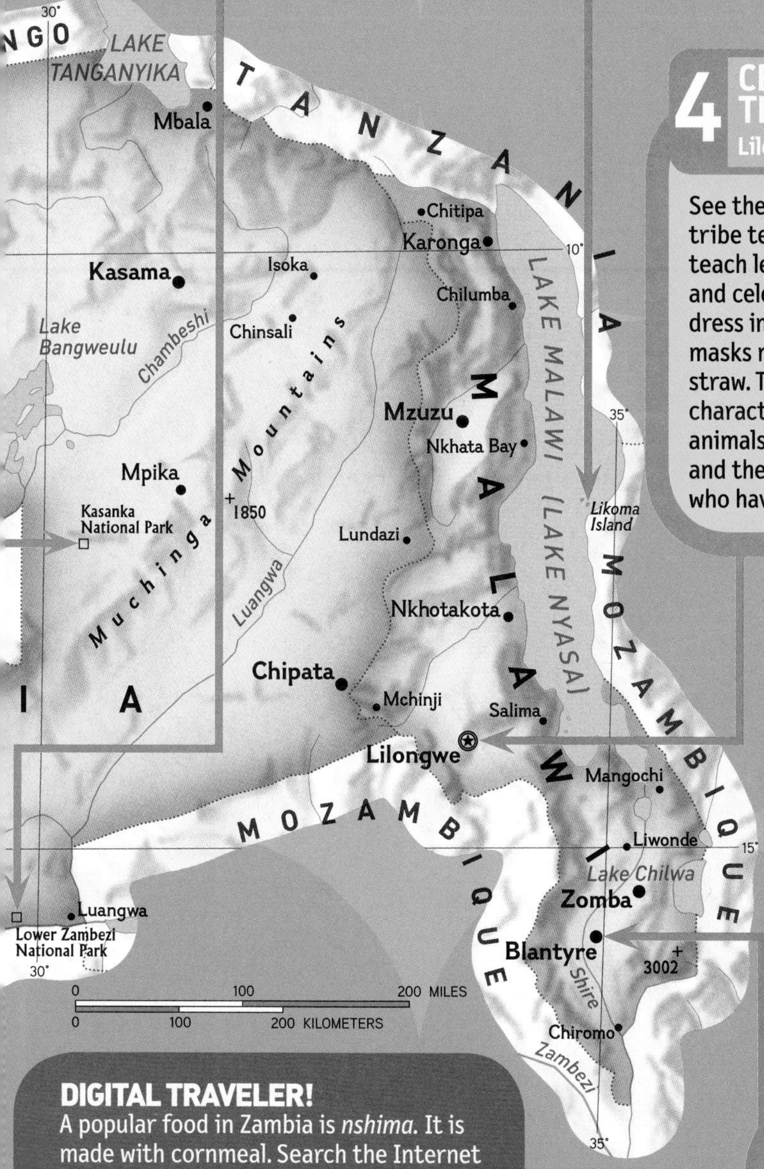

4 CELEBRATE WITH THE CHEWA
Lilongwe

See the men of the Chewa tribe tell stories and teach lessons at festivals and celebrations. They dress in costumes and masks made of wood and straw. They dance as characters, such as wild animals, slave traders, and the spirits of those who have died.

AFRICA

ID CARD
COUNTRY FACTS

ZAMBIA
Population: 14,187,000
Capital: Lusaka

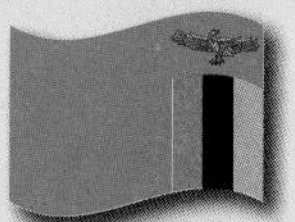

MALAWI
Population: 16,338,000
Capital: Lilongwe

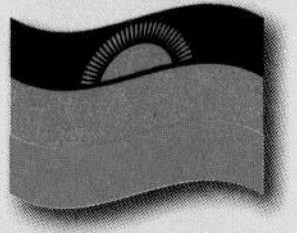

DIGITAL TRAVELER!
A popular food in Zambia is *nshima*. It is made with cornmeal. Search the Internet to find pictures, a recipe, and what it is typically eaten with. Try a meal with nshima and find out if you like it.

5 KEEP SCORE AT A NETBALL GAME
Blantyre

Hear the crowd roar when the ball swishes through the hoop! Malawi's national women's netball team has played in international games. Netball is like basketball.

NATIONAL BIRD: flamingo
NATIONAL TREE: baobab
NATIONAL MAMMAL: African elephant

MOZAMBIQUE

Land of Sky-Blue WATERS

Mozambique is a land of sand and water: It has plains, swamps, grassy plateaus, and forested hills. There are rivers such as the Limpopo and the Zambezi, which fills a lake behind the Cahora Bassa Dam. Lake Malawi (Nyasa) in the north is one of Africa's great natural lakes. Mozambique, with its valuable fisheries, borders the warm, blue Indian Ocean. The seaway off the coast is called the Mozambique Channel.

ID CARD
COUNTRY FACTS

Size: 308,642 sq mi (799,380 sq km)
Population: 24,336,000
Capital: Maputo
Official language: Portuguese
Currency: metical
Highest point: Monte Binga, 7,992 ft (2,436 m)
Life expectancy: 50.0 years

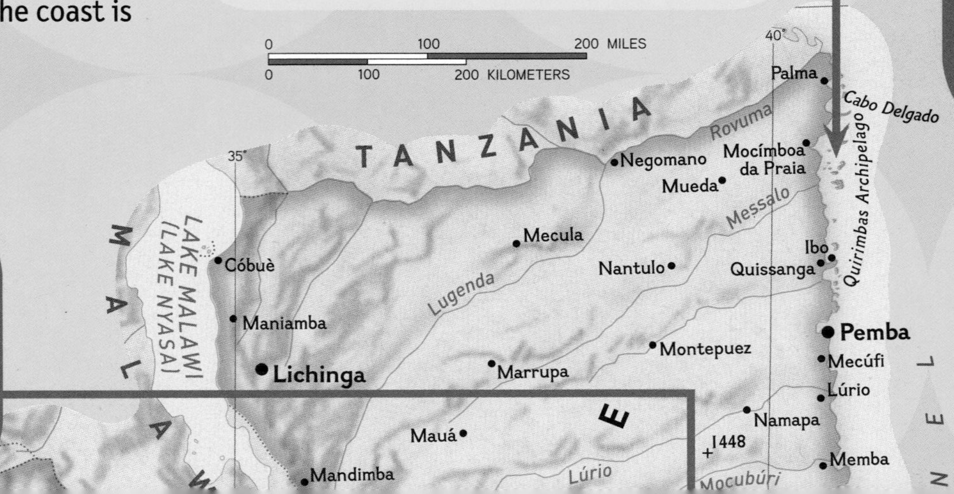

5 COOL THINGS TO DO HERE

1 GO ISLAND HOPPING
Quirimbas Archipelago

Sail on a boat called a dhow to some of the 12 islands in this archipelago. Ibo Island was a trading post in the 1500s. Now it has resorts.

2 TAKE A TRAIN RIDE
Nampula

Travel from Nampula to Cuamba on one of the country's few railroad routes. Recently there have been big improvements in reducing the trip from 10 hours to 7 (27 stops to 9). The distance is the same as Boston to New York.

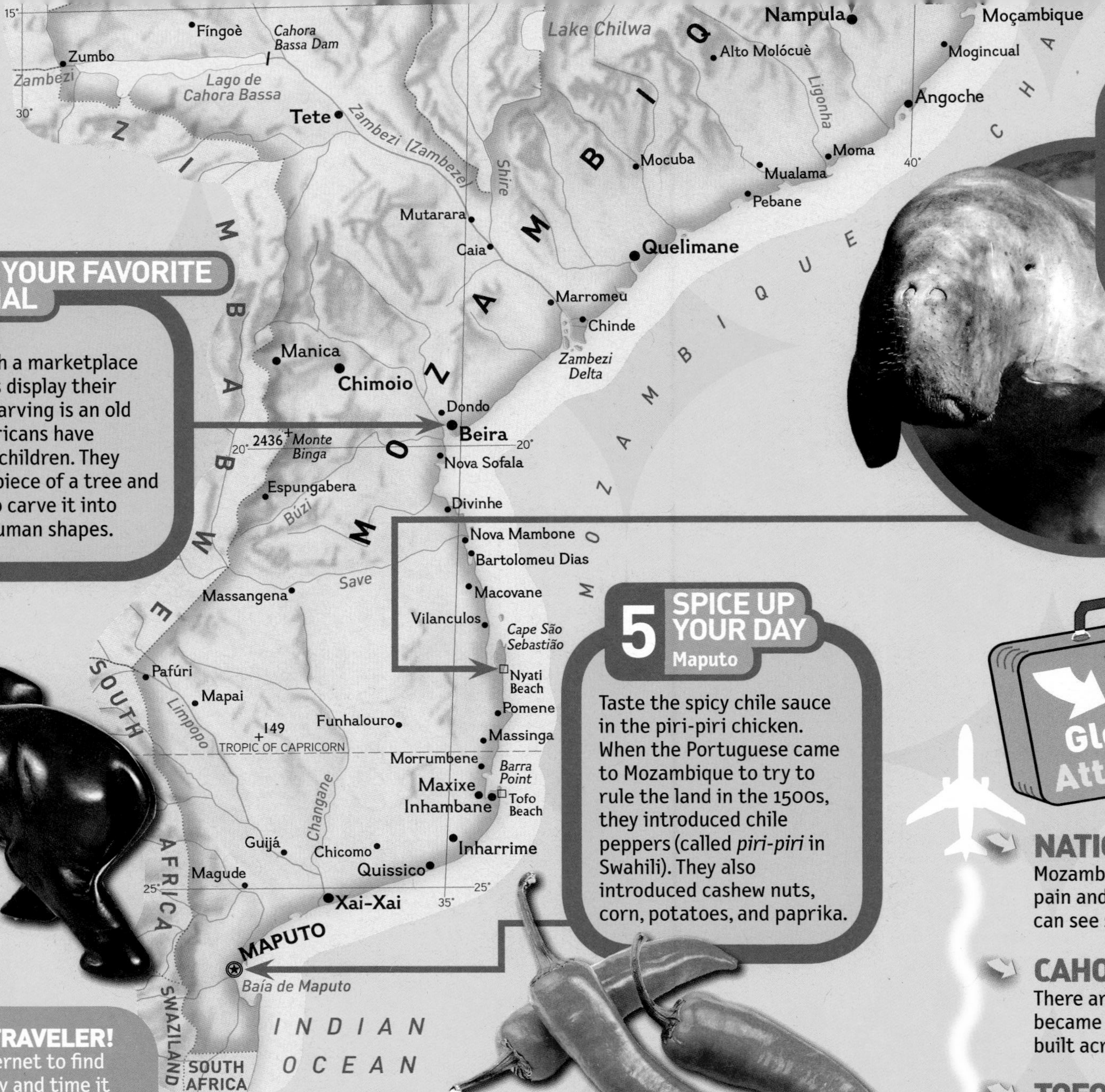

3 SEARCH FOR DUGONGS
Nyati Beach

Stay in the shallow water and you could see a huge dugong poke its head up for air. Dugongs are also called sea cows because they walk on the ocean floor and pull up grass to eat.

4 FIND YOUR FAVORITE ANIMAL
Beira

Stroll through a marketplace where artists display their work. Wood carving is an old craft that Africans have taught their children. They start with a piece of a tree and use a knife to carve it into animal and human shapes.

5 SPICE UP YOUR DAY
Maputo

Taste the spicy chile sauce in the piri-piri chicken. When the Portuguese came to Mozambique to try to rule the land in the 1500s, they introduced chile peppers (called *piri-piri* in Swahili). They also introduced cashew nuts, corn, potatoes, and paprika.

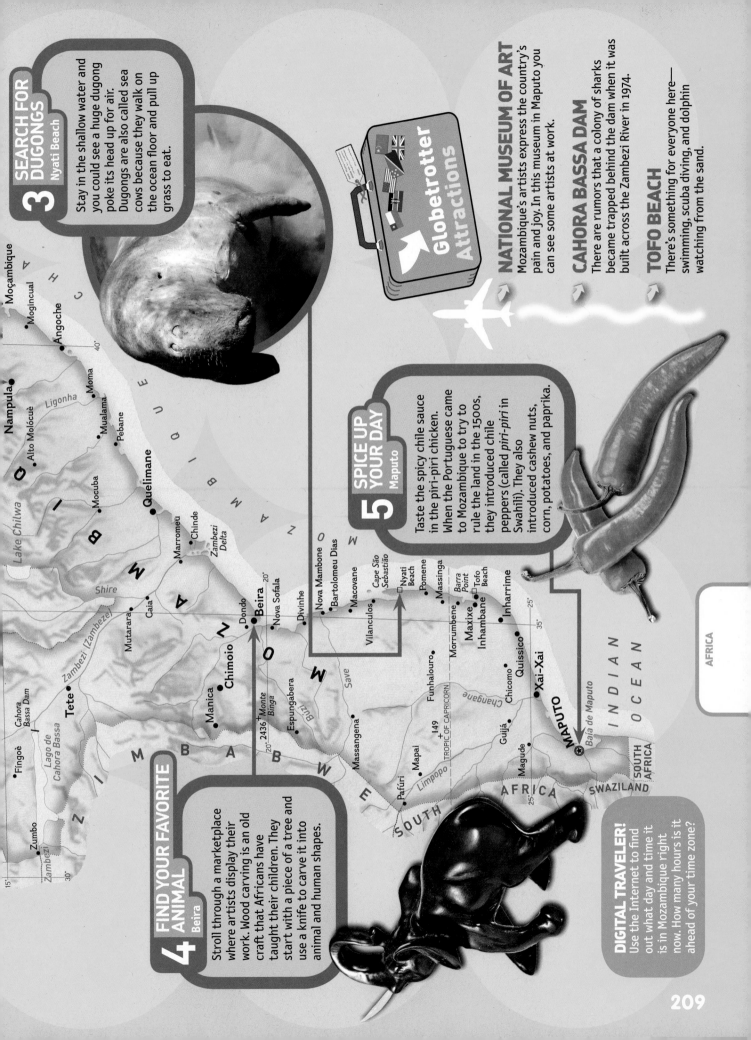

Globetrotter Attractions

NATIONAL MUSEUM OF ART
Mozambique's artists express the country's pain and joy. In this museum in Maputo you can see some artists at work.

CAHORA BASSA DAM
There are rumors that a colony of sharks became trapped behind the dam when it was built across the Zambezi River in 1974.

TOFO BEACH
There's something for everyone here—swimming, scuba diving, and dolphin watching from the sand.

DIGITAL TRAVELER!
Use the Internet to find out what day and time it is in Mozambique right now. How many hours is it ahead of your time zone?

NATIONAL BIRD: African fish eagle

NATIONAL FLOWER: flame lily

NATIONAL MAMMAL: sable antelope

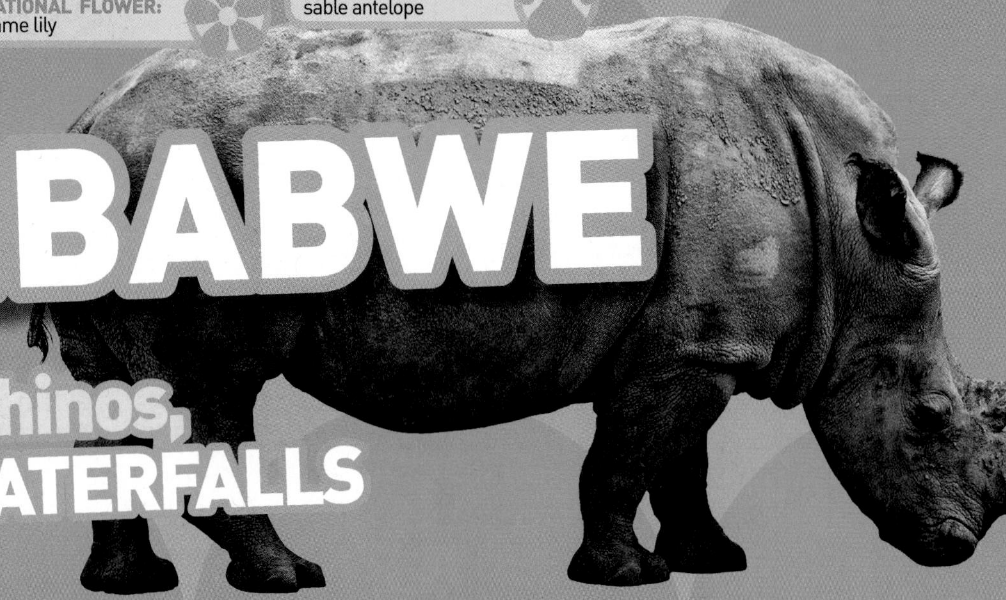

ZIMBABWE

Ruins, Rhinos, and WATERFALLS

Zimbabwe is a land of ancient history, traditional crafts, modern cities and farms, and wildlife roaming national parks. The central highlands, or high veld, rise to rocky hills in the south. In the north, Zimbabwe shares with Zambia the hydroelectric dam and lake at Kariba on the Zambezi River. The spectacular Victoria Falls in the northwest have the African name Mosi oa Tunya ("Smoke that Thunders").

5 CRAFT WITH CLAY
Bulawayo

Watch the pottery wheel spin as people shape soft clay into bowls. The Mzilikazi Art and Crafts Center trained many famous African artists.

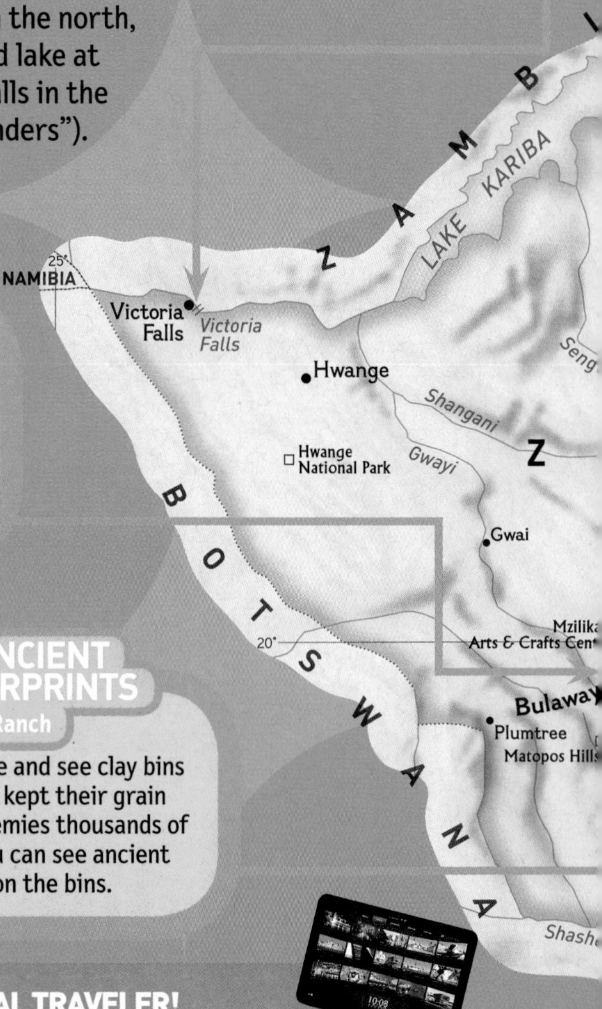

4 SEE ANCIENT FINGERPRINTS
Sentinel Ranch

Explore a cave and see clay bins where people kept their grain safe from enemies thousands of years ago. You can see ancient fingerprints on the bins.

ID CARD COUNTRY FACTS

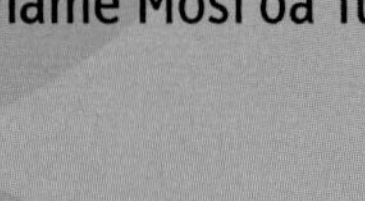

Size: 150,872 sq mi (390,757 sq km)
Population: 13,038,000
Capital: Harare
Official language: English
Currency: Zimbabwean dollar
Highest point: Mt. Inyangani, 8,504 ft (2,592 m)
Life expectancy: 56.0 years

DIGITAL TRAVELER!
Search online to learn about the name of Zimbabwe. What does it mean? What other name did the country have from the 1890s to 1980? How did it get that name?

5 COOL THINGS TO DO HERE

1 BRIDGE THAT GAP
Victoria Falls

Start at Victoria Falls, Zimbabwe, and walk the bridge over the Zambezi River. At the other end, you will be in Livingston, Zambia. Enjoy the view of rushing water at Victoria Falls.

GREAT ZIMBABWE
Massive stone walls remind us of a great city built about A.D. 1200 to 1400 with more than 10,000 people.

MATOPOS HILLS
Awesome shapes of boulders stretch for miles. Stone Age people lived here and left an abundance of rock paintings.

HWANGE NATIONAL PARK
More than 35,000 elephants live here. Each year people must pump water into dry waterholes so that there is enough for the elephants to drink.

2 FOLLOW BLACK RHINOCEROSES
Matusadona National Park

See this endangered rhino in the wild. Learn how the park is trying to protect the rhinos from hunters and increase the population. The park also has the second largest group of wild lions in Africa.

3 BUY A COLORFUL BASKET
Harare

Arrive early at the Mbare flea market and look at the woven baskets. Craftspeople are proud of their work.

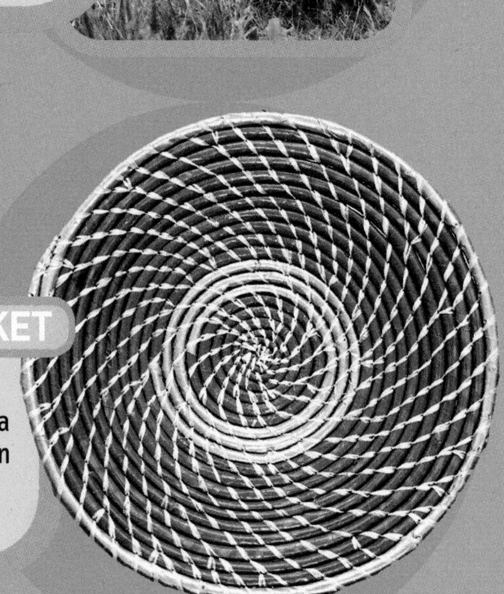

	NATIONAL BIRD:	NATIONAL FLOWER:	NATIONAL MAMMAL:
BOTSWANA	lilac-breasted roller	red spiderling	zebra
NAMIBIA	African fish eagle	welwitschia	oryx

BOTSWANA AND NAMIBIA

Sparkling Sea, Sunshine, and DESERT SANDS

Botswana's rolling-hill landscapes are fine for cattle-raising, while in the north the Okavango River floods wetlands. It is much more barren in the southwestern Kalahari Desert. In mineral-rich Namibia, the Namib Desert receives hardly any rain. The bleak Atlantic coastline was called by early sailors the "Skeleton Coast." Wildlife herds make seasonal migrations, and many people travel outside the country, too, finding jobs in the cities of neighboring South Africa.

SKELETON COAST PARK

Through history, this Namibia beach was littered—first with whalebones, and later shipwrecks.

CENTRAL KALAHARI GAME RESERVE

Twice the size of Massachusetts, this park's grasslands seem to go on forever. After a strong rain the wild animals flock to the watering holes.

TULI BLOCK FARMS

This narrow piece of Botswana has beautiful views, especially from a cliff called Solomon's Wall.

5 STROLL AROUND A METEORITE

Grootfontein

See Earth's largest meteorite, the Hoba. Scientists say it fell to Earth less than 80,000 years ago. A farmer found it in 1920.

4 CLIMB A SAND DUNE

Sossusvlei

Enjoy the soft, deep sand as you climb up Dune 45 for a spectacular view of the sand and water. Some people sand-ski down the steep slope by zigzagging. Others sit down and slide.

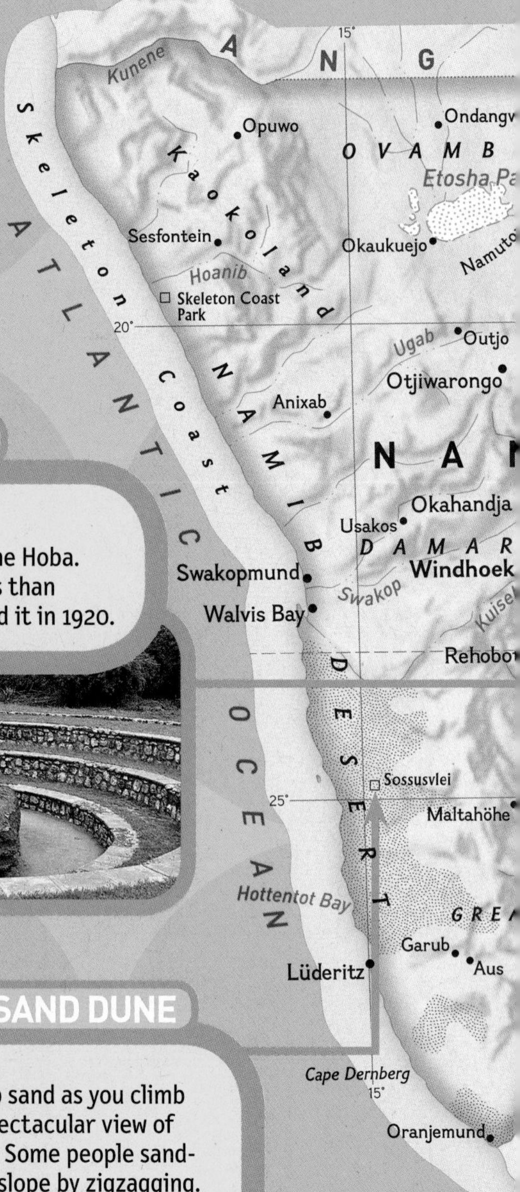

5 COOL THINGS TO DO HERE

ID CARD
COUNTRY FACTS

BOTSWANA
Population: 1,866,000
Capital: Gaborone

NAMIBIA
Population: 2,410,000
Capital: Windhoek

1 DELVE IN A DELTA
Okavango Delta

Step into a canoe, called a *mokoro*. Glide through the water and look for some of the 122 kinds of mammals and 64 kinds of reptiles in the delta. Some of the islands there have been built by termites.

2 ZOOM IN ON ZEBRAS
Makgadikgadi Pans Game Reserve

Observe the zebras that migrate to the rivers after heavy rain. In prehistoric time the park was a giant lake, but it has dried up.

DIGITAL TRAVELER!
Search the Internet for photographs of sand dunes in Namibia. How many different shapes can you find? Make a drawing or painting of your favorite sand-dune photo.

3 GO ON A QUIVER TREE QUEST
Keetmanshoop

Walk among trees that store water in their trunks. Past hunters made quivers (bags to hold arrows) from the branches.

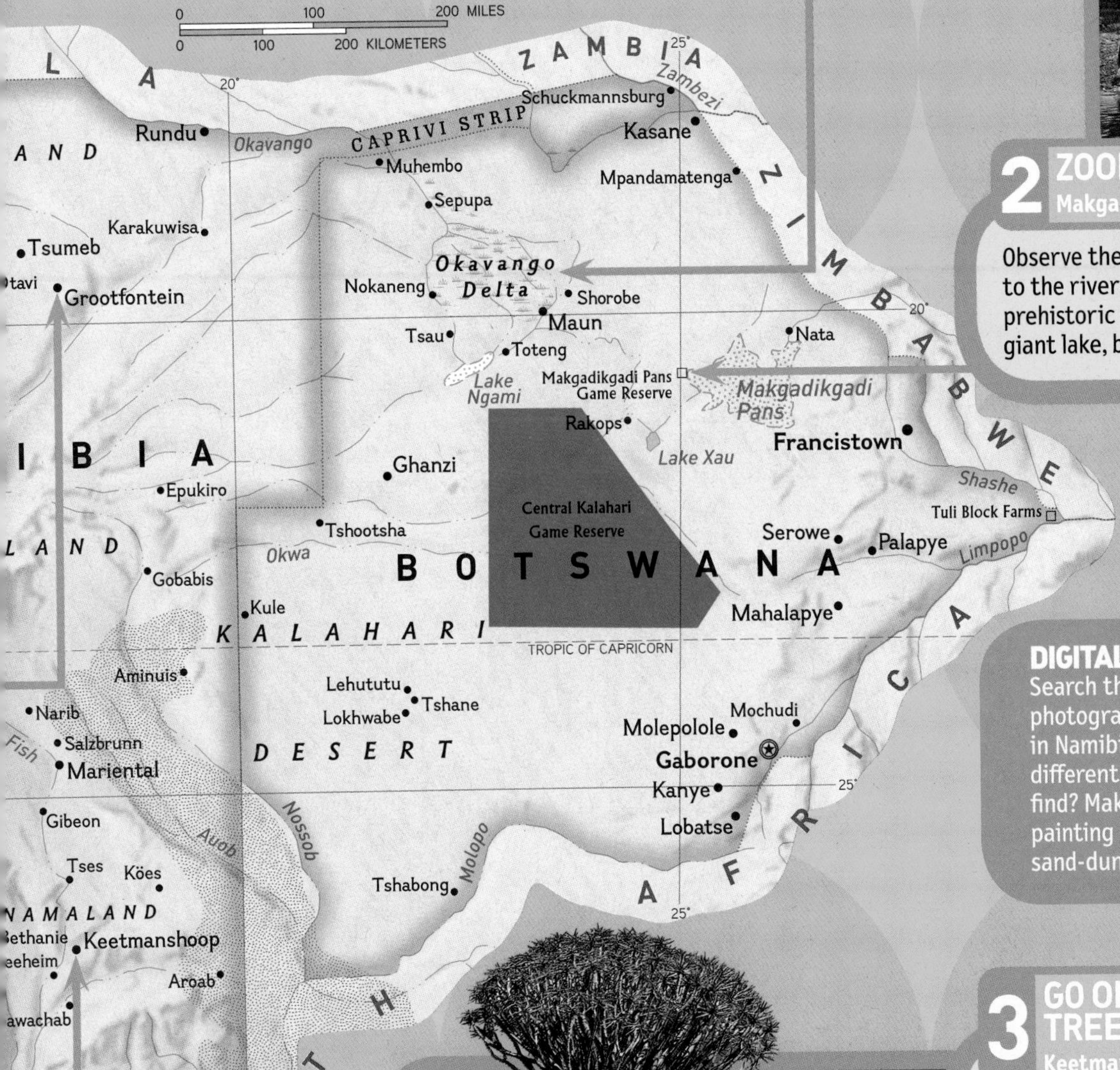

Globetrotter Attractions

5 COOL THINGS TO DO HERE

NGYWENYA MINE

The iron ore mine in Swaziland is the world's oldest mine. People began using the mine's iron about 43,000 years ago. Ngywenya locally means "crocodile," and that is the shape of the mountain above the valley.

KRUGER NATIONAL PARK

This South African park, a leader in protecting animals and the environment, is home to 34 kinds of amphibians, 114 reptiles, and 147 mammals.

CAPE OF GOOD HOPE

Sir Francis Drake passed the Cape of Good Hope when he sailed around the world in 1580. To get a good view of it today, people can ride cable cars to the top of Table Mountain.

DIGITAL TRAVELER!
Find a map online that shows the most southern point of South Africa. What is the name of that cape? How far away is it from where you live?

1 WATCH A RUGBY MATCH
Johannesburg

See the Springboks, South Africa's team, play top-notch rugby at Ellis Park Stadium.

2 LISTEN TO PENGUINS
Boulders Beach

Listen for the braying sound of these African penguins. They sound like donkeys. The colony of black-and-white birds lives on the beach, but residents can hear the noise in their homes nearby.

	NATIONAL BIRD:	NATIONAL FLOWER:	NATIONAL MAMMAL:
LESOTHO	African rock pipit	spiral aloe	black rhinoceros
SOUTH AFRICA	blue crane	king protea	springbok
SWAZILAND	purple turaco	sugarbush	Thomson's gazelle

SOUTHERN AFRICA

The Tip of a Vast CONTINENT

South Africa surrounds its mountainous neighbor, Lesotho, and almost envelops Swaziland's grassland and forests. It lies at Africa's tip, and ships sail east around the Cape of Good Hope from the Atlantic into the Indian Ocean. The interior is a saucer-shaped plateau, with veld or grassy plains behind coastal mountains, including the Drakensberg. Rivers include the Orange, Limpopo, and Tugela. Major cities include Cape Town, Johannesburg, and Pretoria.

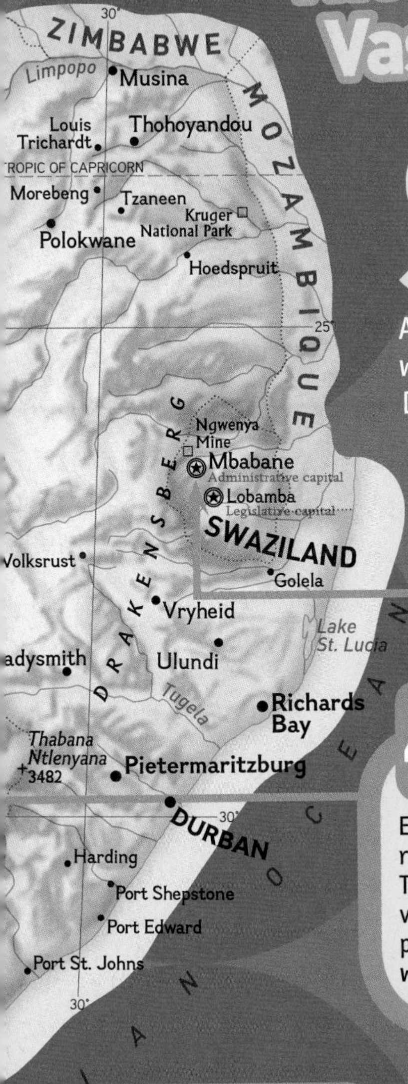

5 BUY SWAZI CANDLES
Mbabane

Discover that no two Swazi candles are alike. In the candle shop, see the variety of colorful patterns. More than 200 local candle-makers produce candles that are sent all over the world.

AFRICA

4 RIDE A PONY ON A TREK
Malealea

Enjoy the scenery as you ride a pony along the trail. Teenagers from local villages will walk beside the ponies to help you and they will point out the sites.

3 BE A FOSSIL HUNTER
Quthing

Look carefully on the road to Quthing and you could find dinosaur footprints. These are tracks of many different dinosaurs.

ID CARD
COUNTRY FACTS

LESOTHO
Population: 2,242,000
Capital: Maseru

SOUTH AFRICA
Population: 52,982,000
Capital: Pretoria

SWAZILAND
Population: 1,238,000
Capital: Mbabane

AFRICAN ISLANDS

Jewels in the INDIAN OCEAN

Africa's Indian Ocean islands were stopovers for old-time sailors, and today are glittering tourist destinations. The island countries are Madagascar (the largest African island), Mauritius, Seychelles, and Comoros. These are precious natural jewels, for their stunning wildlife is threatened as the island ecosystems are unbalanced. Madagascar's lemurs, for example, are unique to the island, but much of their forest habitat has been felled for farms and development.

5 STOP AND SMELL YLANG YLANG

Mohéli

Sniff the sweet smell of the ylang ylang flower. Comoros exports most of the world's supply of ylang ylang oil. It is the main ingredient of many fine perfumes.

STONE FOREST

At the heart of Tsingy de Bemaraha National Park on Madagascar is a labyrinth of knife-edged stone towers, canyons, and wet caves. The stone forest is home to many unusual plants and animals.

KARTHALA

Here on Comoros, one of the world's largest active volcanoes also has one of the largest craters.

COUSIN ISLAND

Many rare birds live here in Seychelles. Sometimes the sky gets dark because of all the birds soaring together.

DIGITAL TRAVELER!
There are about 115 islands in Seychelles. Go online and find a list of these islands. Are there any island names that start with the same letter as your first name?

5 COOL THINGS TO DO HERE

1 MEET GIANT TORTOISES
Victoria

Snap some photos of the Aldabra giant tortoises at the Botanical Gardens. These tortoises also live in the wild on islands in Seychelles. They can weigh up to 550 pounds (249 kg).

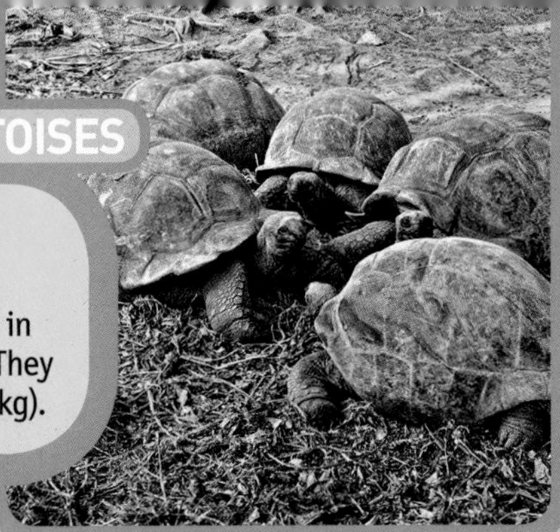

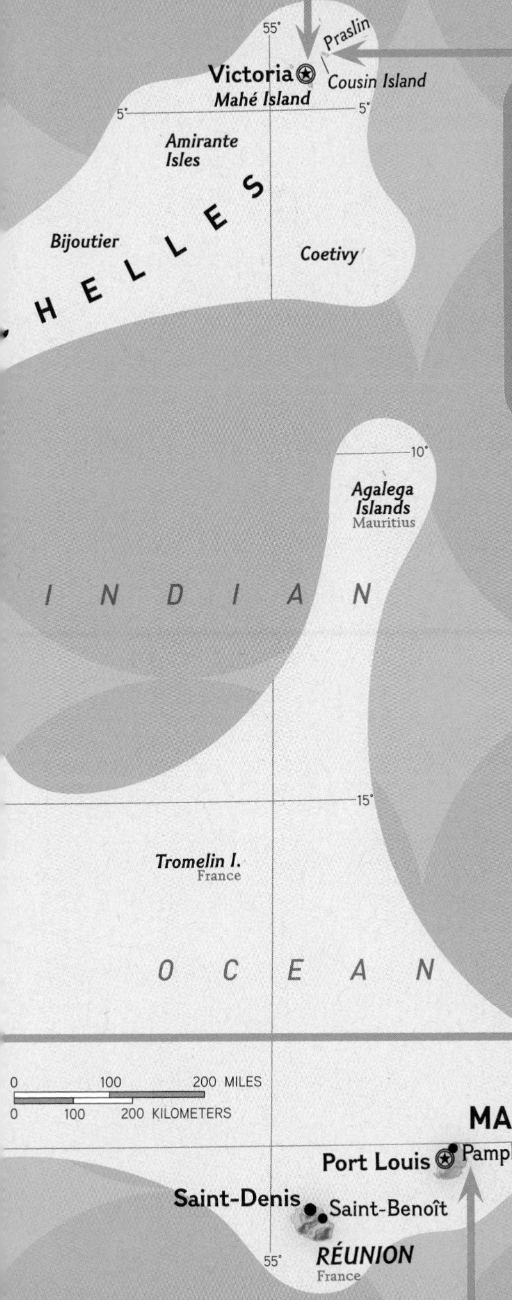

2 PHOTOGRAPH SUPER HUGE FRUIT
Praslin

Find a coco de mer tree and be impressed by the world's heaviest seeds. One can weigh 50 pounds (23 kg).

ID CARD COUNTRY FACTS

COMOROS
Population: 792,000
Capital: Moroni

MADAGASCAR
Population: 22,550,000
Capital: Antananarivo

MAURITIUS
Population: 1,297,000
Capital: Port Louis

SEYCHELLES
Population: 93,000
Capital: Victoria

3 SPY ON AN AYE-AYE
Madagascar

Join a night-walk group as they try to spot aye-ayes. These creatures are found only in Madagascar. You may hear them tapping on branches and listening for insects that they can dig out with their pointy fingers.

4 GET A TASTE OF SUGAR
Pamplemousses

Taste a sample as you learn why sugar was once as valuable as gold. The museum site was once a sugar factory surrounded by sugarcane fields.

AUSTRALIA AND OCEANIA

Islands of all SIZES

This vast region includes Australia—a huge island continent—New Zealand, Papua New Guinea, and about 25,000 islands scattered across the Pacific Ocean. These islands make up the cultural areas of Melanesia, Micronesia, and Polynesia. While Australia, New Zealand, and Papua New Guinea have mountain ranges, many of the other islands are low-lying. Stretching in an arc from the north island of New Zealand to Papua New Guinea is a series of volcanoes, many of them active.

The dry, inland plains of Australia are home to kangaroos, the world's largest pouched mammals. The huge Uluru, also called Ayers Rock, is a sacred place for the Aboriginal people.

AUSTRALIA AND OCEANIA

From Ancient Peoples to Modern CULTURES

Aboriginal Australians first arrived about 50,000 years ago, sailing from southeast Asia. Many thousands of years later, other Asian people spread to the islands of Oceania. Maoris were Polynesians who reached New Zealand about 4,000 years ago. Today, the region has 11 independent countries and 21 island groups that are territories of the United States, France, Australia, New Zealand, the United Kingdom, and Chile.

MELANESIA

This area stretches from Papua New Guinea to Fiji and includes the Solomon Islands and Vanuatu.

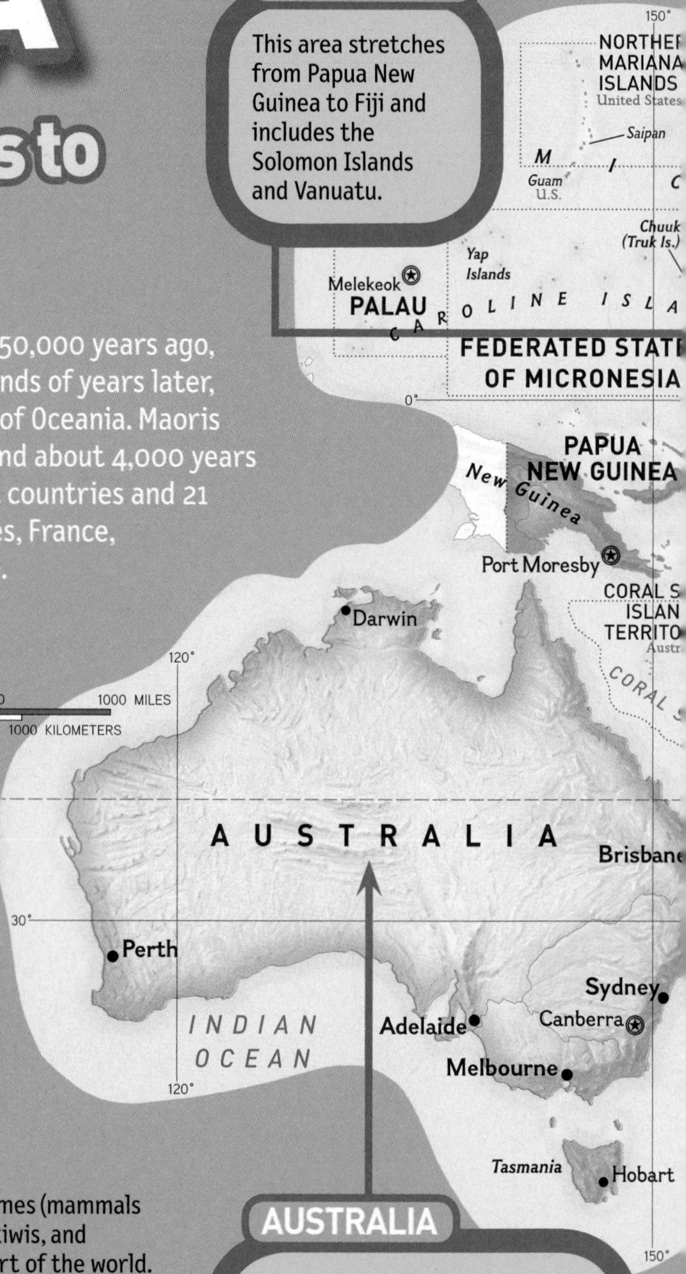

AUSTRALIA

This is the world's smallest continent and its largest island. Most of the cities lie along the coast. The remote, sparsely populated interior is called the Outback. The Great Barrier Reef is off the northeast coast.

AUNT BERTHA'S TRAVEL TIPS

UNUSUAL ANIMALS

Look out for marsupials (pouched mammals), monotremes (mammals that lay eggs), and flightless birds that include emus, kiwis, and ostriches. Many of these animals are unique to this part of the world.

DOWN UNDER

Australia and New Zealand are often said to be "Lands Down Under." Being in the Southern Hemisphere, their seasons are reversed, so summer begins in December and winter begins in June.

"HAVING A BAR-B"

Particularly in Australia, where the climate is mostly tropical, people love to have their meals outdoors. They often use barbecues for cooking meat and fish.

MICRONESIA
The Caroline Islands, Marshall Islands, and other island groups mostly north of the Equator make up this region.
SEA LIFE
Polynesia
On the many thousands of small islands in the region, people face problems of limited living space and fresh water. Along seashores, houses are built on stilts.
POLYNESIA
The largest Pacific Ocean island group, this region includes the Samoa, Cook, Society, and Austral islands. Together with Micronesia and Melanesia it forms Oceania.
FARMING
New Zealand
In New Zealand, sheep outnumber people. Preparing and selling sheep's wool and meat are major industries in the country.
NEW ZEALAND
Twelve hundred miles (1,931 km) across the Tasman Sea from Australia lie the islands of New Zealand. The country is more mountainous, cooler, and wetter than its "neighbor."
AUSTRALIA & OCEANIA
30°
180°
30°
Midway Is.
U.S.
Hawaiian Islands
TROPIC OF CANCER
NORTH PACIFIC OCEAN
POLYNESIA
Honolulu
HAWAI'I
United States
Wake Island
U.S.
Johnston Atoll
U.S.
Bikini Atoll
MARSHALL ISLANDS
Ralik Chain
Ratak Chain
Majuro
Palikir
MICRONESIA
150°
Kingman Reef
U.S.
Palmyra Atoll
U.S.
Howland Island
U.S.
Baker Island
U.S.
Tarawa
(Bairiki)
Gilbert Islands
Kiritimati
LINE ISLANDS
Jarvis I.
U.S.
EQUATOR
0°
Yaren
NAURU
Phoenix Islands
KIRIBATI
MELANESIA
SOLOMON ISLANDS
TUVALU
Funafuti
Tokelau
N.Z.
Marquesas Islands
Honiara
Solomon Islands
Santa Cruz Islands
SAMOA
AMERICAN SAMOA
U.S.
Apia
Pago Pago
Îles Wallis
France
Îles de Horne
VANUATU
Port Vila
COOK ISLANDS
New Zealand
TUAMOTU ARCHIPELAGO
Tahiti
Society Is.
NEW CALEDONIA
France
Suva
FIJI
TONGA
NIUE
N.Z.
FRENCH POLYNESIA
France
Nouméa
Nuku'alofa
Austral Islands
TROPIC OF CAPRICORN
SOUTH PACIFIC OCEAN
Pitcairn Island
United Kingdom
150°
Norfolk Island
Australia
Kermadec Islands
New Zealand
30°
Lord Howe Island
Australia
Auckland
North Island
TASMAN SEA
NEW ZEALAND
Wellington
Christchurch
Chatham Islands
New Zealand
South Island
180°

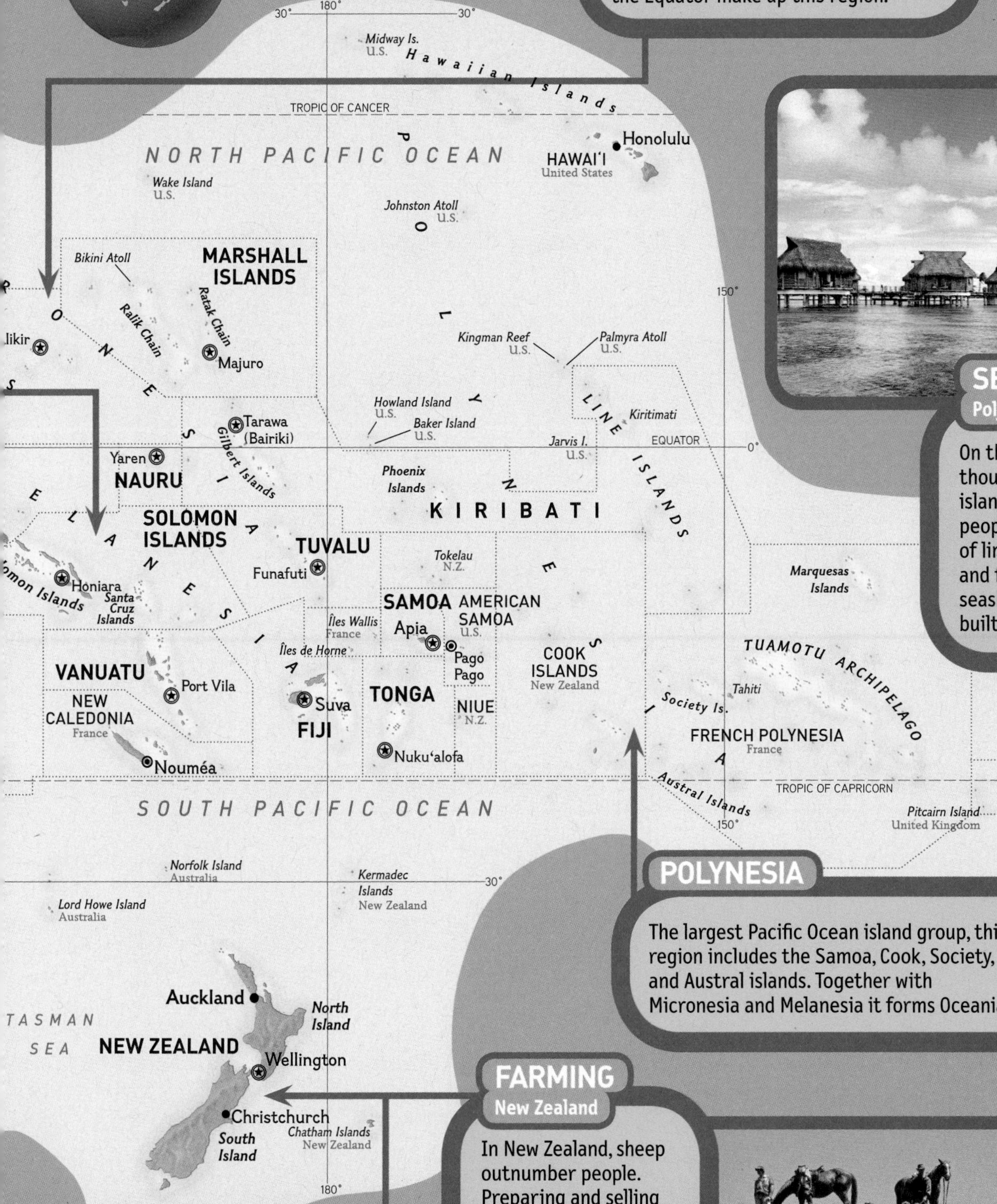

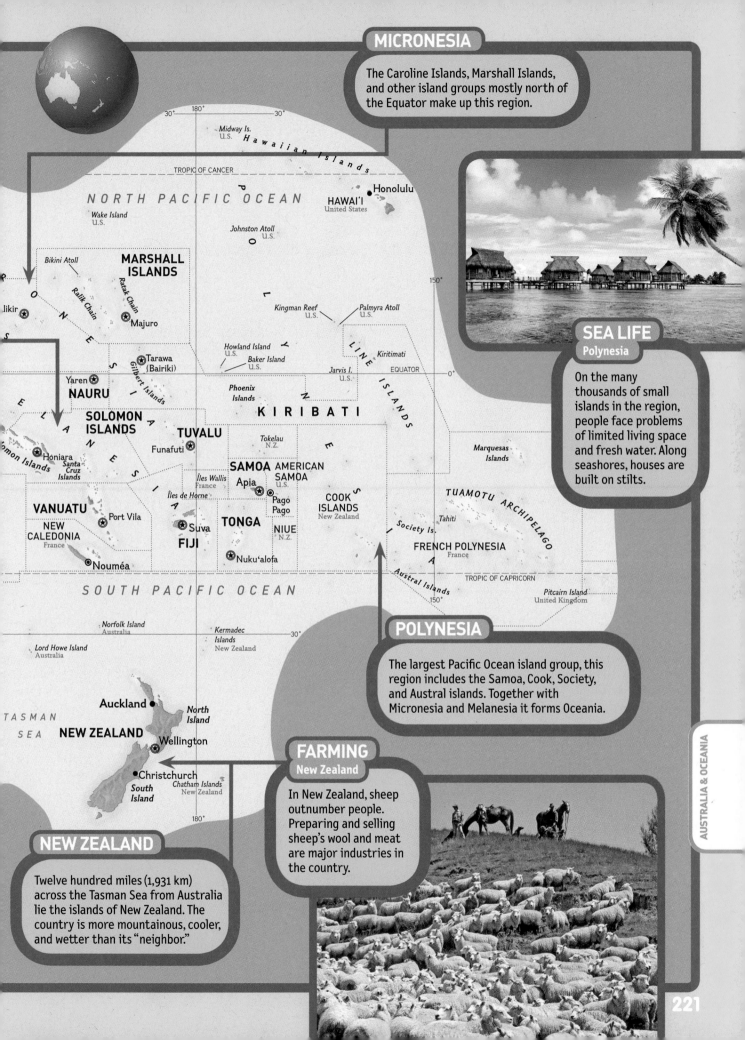

NATIONAL BIRD: emu

NATIONAL TREE: golden wattle

NATIONAL MAMMAL: red kangaroo

AUSTRALIA

A Land DOWN UNDER

Australia covers an entire continent, and includes the island of Tasmania. Much of the interior is dry desert, mountains, and "bush," but the land is rich in minerals and there are forests, farms, and huge sheep and cattle ranches or "stations." Australia's people come from all over the world, but many of its plants and animals are unique to this giant island.

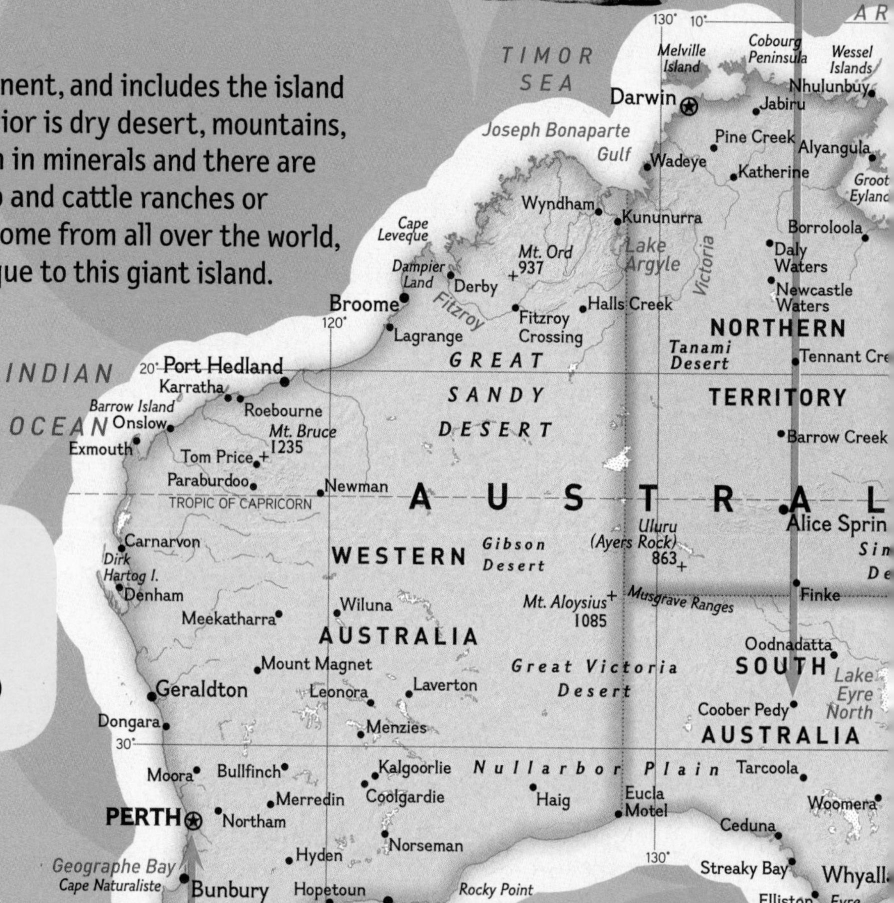

ID CARD COUNTRY FACTS

Size: 2,969,906 sq mi (7,692,024 sq km)
Population: 23,106,000
Capital: Canberra
Official language: English
Currency: Australian dollar
Highest point: Mt. Kosciuszko, 7,310 ft (2,215 m)
Life expectancy: 82.0 years

5 START A LONG TRAIN RIDE

Perth

The 2,704-mile (4,352-km)-long Indian Pacific passenger train journey from Perth to Sydney takes 65 hours. It runs along coasts and across deserts.

DIGITAL TRAVELER!
Australians drive on the left-hand side of the road. Surf the Internet to find other countries that do this.

5 COOL THINGS TO DO HERE

1 GO UNDERGROUND
Coober Pedy

Visit opal miners' homes called "dugouts." They are built underground so families can escape outside temperatures of more than 120°F (48.9°C).

Globetrotter Attractions

SYDNEY OPERA HOUSE
This is one of the most photographed buildings in the world. It took 30 years to figure out how to build the "sails" on the roof.

ULURU
Rising 1,142 feet (348 m), this huge mass of sandstone is the largest single slab of rock in the world.

AUSTRALIA ZOO
Many of the world's pouched mammals can be seen at this zoo in Beerwah, Queensland. They include kangaroos, possums, bandicoots, and koalas.

2 SEE GREAT WHITE SHARKS
Great Barrier Reef

The 1,429-mile (2,300 km)-long coral reef off the east coast is the world's largest living structure. It is home to several kinds of sharks.

3 RIDE THE WAVES
Boomerang Beach

Some of the world's best surfing beaches are along the coast of New South Wales. Like a boomerang, the waves always come back to you!

4 WALK ON GLASS
Melbourne

At the Eureka Tower, you can step into a glass cube almost 1,000 feet (305 m) above street level for a bird's-eye view of the city.

5 COOL THINGS TO DO HERE

1 SOAK IN HOT SPRINGS
Great Barrier Island

Dip into the warm water of Kaitoke Hot Springs. The water is heated by thermal activity underground. It feels especially good after a hike on New Zealand's fourth largest island.

2 HANG OUT ON A HARBOR BRIDGE
Auckland

Walk across the harbor bridge for a great view of the city. Get strapped into the safety gear and stroll the walkway high above water. See how tiny the boats look!

3 FLOAT THROUGH FIORDS
Milford Sound

Take a two-hour cruise from the top of this fiord to the ocean. Stare at the sheer cliffs on both sides of your boat. Look for seals resting on cliffs.

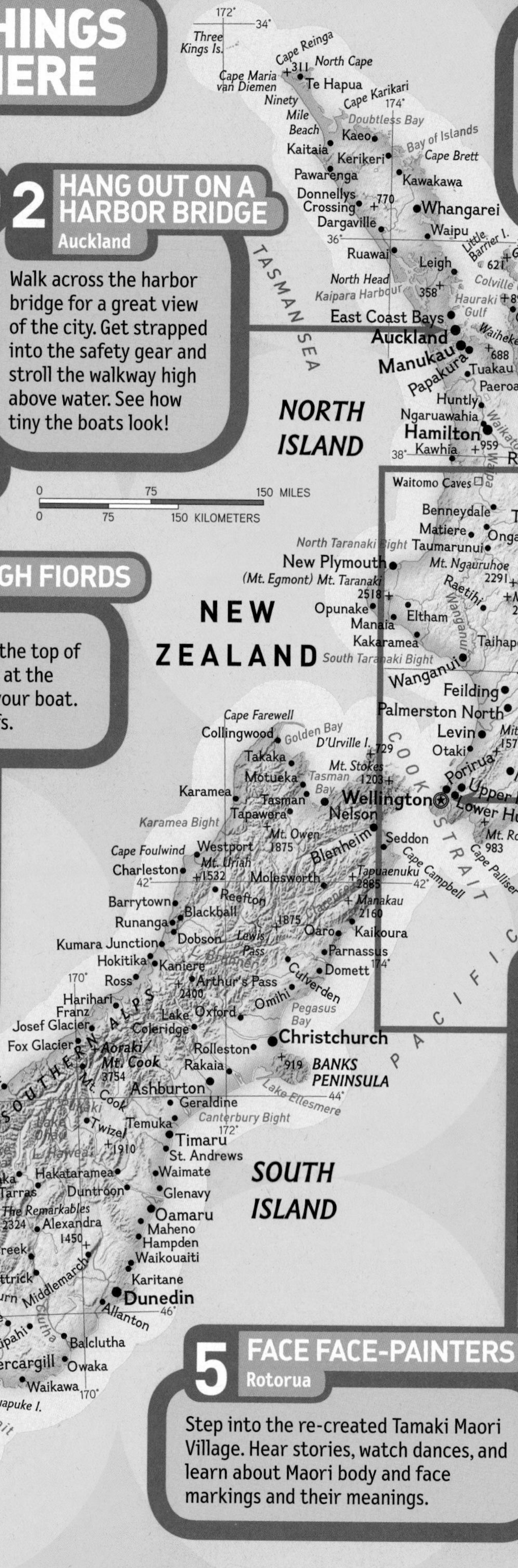

5 FACE FACE-PAINTERS
Rotorua

Step into the re-created Tamaki Maori Village. Hear stories, watch dances, and learn about Maori body and face markings and their meanings.

NATIONAL BIRD: kiwi

NATIONAL TREE: silver fern

NATIONAL MAMMAL: long-tailed bat

NEW ZEALAND

Land of the KIWI

Unique island wildlife such as the kiwi and spectacular scenery make New Zealand (named by Dutch explorers) a land not to miss. North Island, with volcanoes, hot springs, and grassy plains, is where most New Zealanders live. South Island is rugged, with snow-capped Southern Alps' peaks, lakes, glaciers, and fiords. New Zealand has more sheep than people, and the seas around its coastline and islands are rich in fish.

ID CARD COUNTRY FACTS

Size: 103,363 sq mi (267,710 sq km)
Population: 4,450,000
Capital: Wellington
Official languages: English and Maori
Currency: New Zealand dollar
Highest point: Aoraki (Mt. Cook), 12,316 ft (3,754 m)
Life expectancy: 81.0 years

4 ENJOY A SWEET PAVLOVA

Wellington

Stop in a café and order their most popular dessert. A pavlova is a crunchy, sweet shell filled with whipped cream, meringue, and delicious fruit.

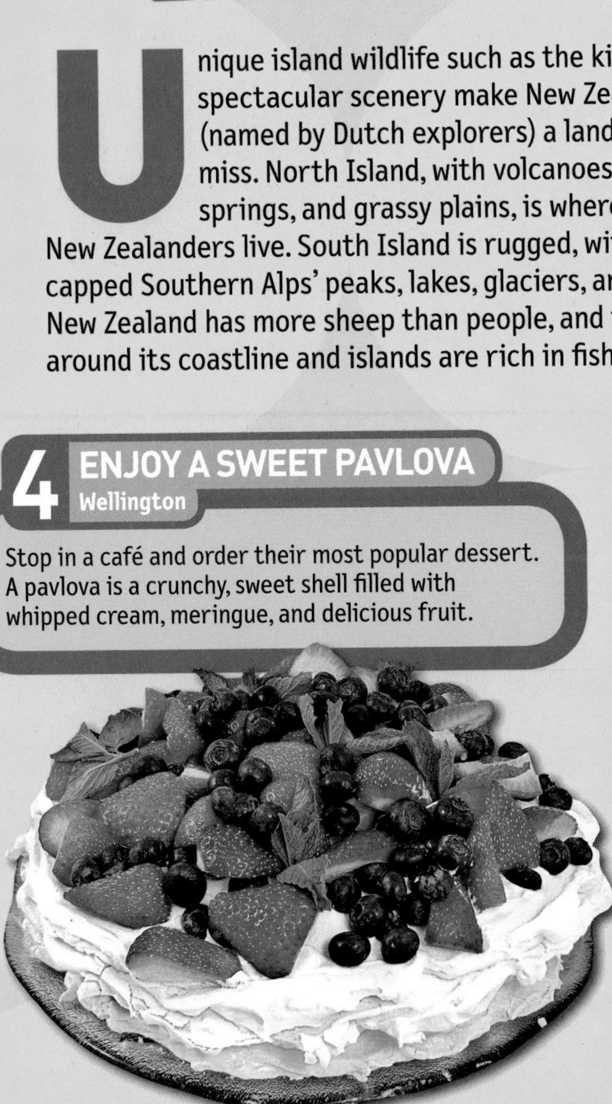

MILFORD TRACK

Hikers love this trail on South Island. To keep the crowd size down and protect the land, officials allow only 90 walkers on the trail each day.

QUEENSTOWN

Here on South Island, a sky-high gondola provides a spectacular view of this lakeside resort town. *The Lord of the Rings* trilogy was filmed here.

WAITOMO CAVES

A boat ride through these caves of North Island will remind you of a starry night. Thousands of glowworms light up the walls of the cave.

DIGITAL TRAVELER!

To a New Zealander, the word "kiwi" is used not only for a type of flightless bird. Use your digital device to find two other popular uses of the word.

NATIONAL BIRD: bird of paradise

NATIONAL TREE: nipa palm

NATIONAL MAMMAL: dugong

PAPUA NEW GUINEA

Rain Forests, Beaches, and Homes on STILTS

Papua New Guinea shares the island of New Guinea with Indonesia, and also covers the islands of the Bismarck Archipelago and Bougainville. New Guinea is mountainous, with dense forests, volcanoes, swampy river valleys, and coastal beaches. Tribal peoples observe traditional cultures in farm-villages, some still making stilt-houses to keep living areas above water.

2 SWIM IN THE BISMARCK SEA
Wewak

Take a swim at a Wewak beach. Then build a sand castle or bury your toes in the soft sand. During World War II, the Japanese built military bases here.

VARIRATA NATIONAL PARK
With grasslands, woodlands, and rain forests, the park is ideal for many kinds of plants and animals. Bird watchers can find kingfishers, cockatoos, birds of paradise, and many others.

KIMBE BAY
The enormous coral reefs are home to about 820 kinds of fish and the world's smallest seahorse, which grows to about ¾ of an inch (19 mm).

NATIONAL PARLIAMENT HOUSE
Local artists have decorated the outside of this government building in Canberra with a mural of mosaic tiles. Enter the lobby by pulling door handles made of *kundu* hand drums.

5 ENJOY A SING SING SHOW
Goroka

Dance to the tribal music as people from different groups and villages share their songs, costumes, and stories.

5 COOL THINGS TO DO HERE

DIGITAL TRAVELER!

There are many annual events in Papua New Guinea that celebrate the culture of native tribes. Search online for colorful photos of events such as the Crocodile Festival and the Canoe and Kundu Drum Festival. Draw your own picture of one of these festivals.

1 OGLE AT ORCHIDS
Lae

Count all the different colors of orchids you see at Rain Forest Habitat. It was built under a cloth canopy on a college campus. Besides gardens with 10,000 plants, you'll see birds, lizards, and flying foxes.

ID CARD COUNTRY FACTS

Size: 178,703 sq mi (462,840 sq km)
Population: 7,179,000
Capital: Port Moresby
Official languages: Tok Pisin, English, and Hiri Motu
Currency: kina
Highest point: Mt. Wilhelm, 14,793 ft (4,509 m)
Life expectancy: 63.0 years

3 VIEW VOLCANOES
Rabaul

Visit the Volcano Observatory to get a glimpse of the most active volcanoes in the country. In 1994, two volcanoes erupted at the same time and devastated the city of Rabaul.

4 SAY HI TO TREE-HUGGERS
Port Moresby

Take a video of this rare animal when you visit Port Moresby Nature Park. Tree kangaroos live in only a few rain forests in the world.

	NATIONAL BIRD:	NATIONAL FLOWER:	NATIONAL MAMMAL:
FIJI	golden fruit dove	tagimoucia	spotted dolphin
SOLOMON ISLANDS	yellow-bibbed lory	temple plant	spinner dolphin
VANUATU	Vanuatu kingfisher	*Veitchia metiti*	Vanuatu flying fox

MELANESIA

Ancient Living CULTURES

The Pacific islands of Melanesia include New Caledonia, Vanuatu, the Solomon Islands, and Fiji. Most islands are hilly and forested, with volcanoes and mountains. They have a tropical climate, with a rainy season from December to March. Traditional Melanesian cultures survive alongside modern life. Most islands are self-governing, but New Caledonia is French.

4 MIX WITH MOUND-BUILDING BIRDS

Savo Island

Stay on the beach at night to watch the megapodes build their nests. They dig down three feet (1 m), lay their eggs, and bury them. If the nests are undisturbed, the eggs will hatch in seven weeks. The babies will dig their way up.

GARDEN OF THE SLEEPING GIANT
More than 2,000 kinds of orchids grow on this Fiji plantation that was once the home of U.S. TV star Raymond Burr. It is one of the largest orchid collections in the world.

GUADALCANAL AMERICAN MEMORIAL
The United States built this to honor Americans and their allies who died in World War II battles.

SRI SIVA SUBRAMANIYA TEMPLE
Painted a rainbow of colors, this is the largest Hindu temple in the Southern Hemisphere. It is in Nadi, Fiji.

5 SEE SPECTACULAR BIRDS

Kennedy Island

Listen to the bird calls all around this small island. It is named for U.S. President John F. Kennedy who swam ashore here after his military boat sank during WWII.

5 COOL THINGS TO DO HERE

1 VISIT A VANUATU VILLAGE
Efate

Learn the traditional ways of the native people at Ekasup Village. They will show you how they fish, cook, weave, make music, and dance.

ID CARD COUNTRY FACTS

FIJI
Population: 860,000
Capital: Suva

SOLOMON ISLANDS
Population: 581,000
Capital: Honiara

VANUATU
Population: 265,000
Capital: Port-Vila

2 TRY FIJI FRUITS
Suva

See mountains of mangos and pyramids of pineapples in the markets where local farmers sell their produce. Try fruits called *wi* and *paw paw*.

3 WATCH SUPER-SIZED SURFING
Tavarua

Hold your breath as you watch a surfer ride on the curl of a giant wave. Professional surfers come to Fiji to surf in wave areas called Cloudbreak and Restaurants.

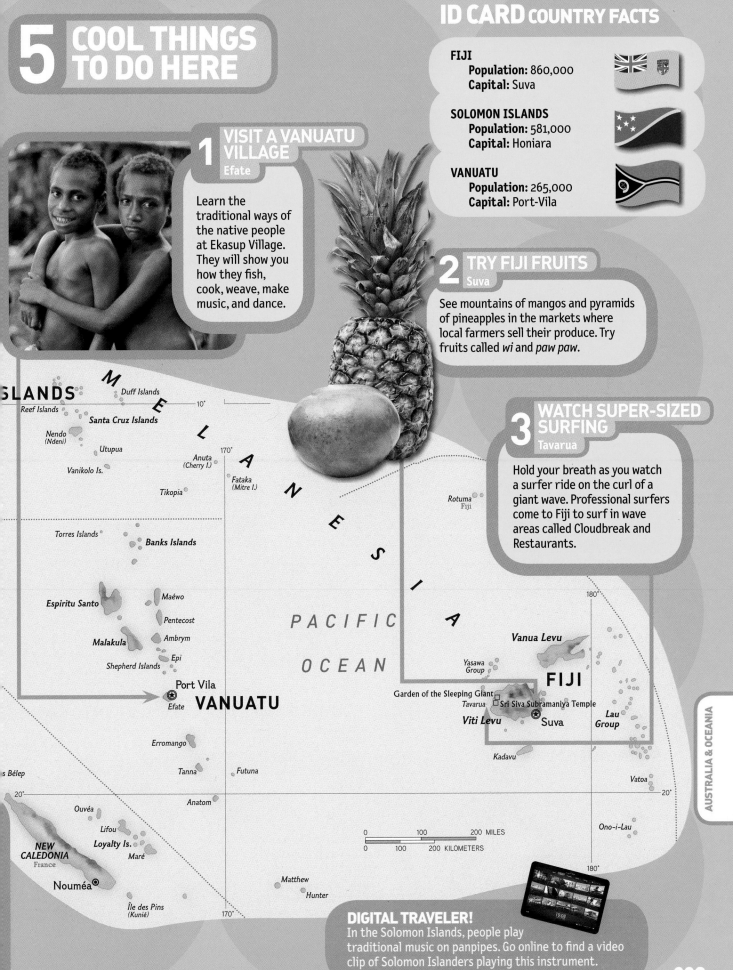

DIGITAL TRAVELER!
In the Solomon Islands, people play traditional music on panpipes. Go online to find a video clip of Solomon Islanders playing this instrument.

AUSTRALIA & OCEANIA

MICRONESIA

Sunny Island PARADISE

Micronesia is a vast island region in the northern Pacific Ocean, and boats are the best way to get around. The larger countries include Palau, Nauru, the Federated States of Micronesia, the Marshall Islands, and Kiribati. "Micro" means small, and many Micronesian islands are tiny coral atolls. Wake Island (U.S.), for instance, has fewer than 200 people on an atoll with a coastline of just 12 miles (19 km).

5 COOL THINGS TO DO HERE

3 WALK A PATH OF STONE MONEY
Yap

Imagine using a stone the size of a car to buy food or a canoe trip. Long ago, stones with holes in the middle served as money. People did not move the largest stones. They just claimed ownership.

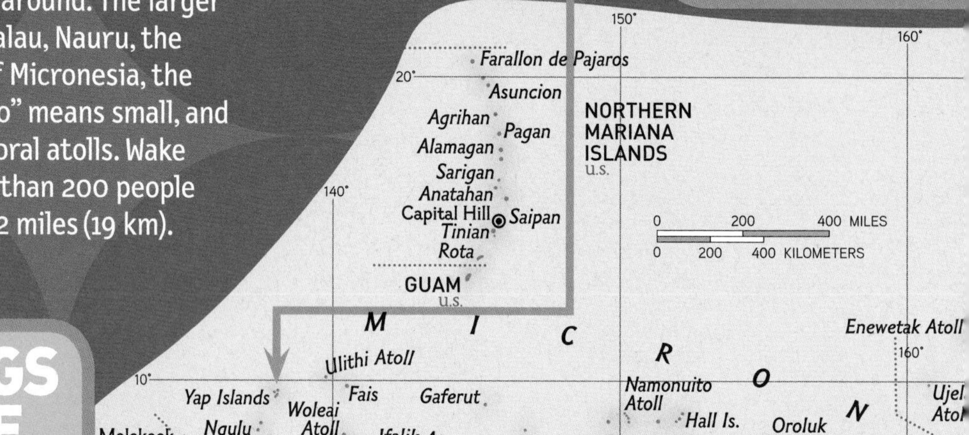

1 READ CARVED STORY BOARDS
Koror

Ask woodcarvers to tell you their stories as they carve pictures in wood. Story boards tell ancient legends about Palau.

2 INSPECT GIANT CLAMS
Malakal Island

Learn how the Mariculture Demonstration Center hatches and grows giant clams. The clams are valuable because people put them in aquariums, use their shells, and serve them for food.

ID CARD COUNTRY FACTS

FEDERATED STATES OF MICRONESIA
Population: 107,000
Capital: Palikir

KIRIBATI
Population: 106,000
Capital: Tarawa

MARSHALL ISLANDS
Population: 56,000
Capital: Majuro

NAURU
Population: 11,000
Capital: Yaren

PALAU
Population: 21,000
Capital: Melekeok

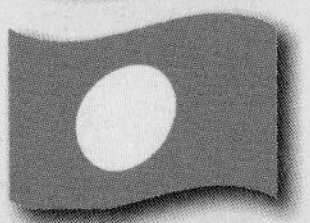

NGARDMAU WATERFALLS
In the Ngardmau district of Palau, hikers reach the tallest and biggest waterfall—the Tiki Falls—by walking a path of old railroad tracks through the jungle.

ALELE MUSEUM AND LIBRARY
Here in the Marshall Islands, a collection of stick charts shows off traditional technology. Made from coconut leaves, these 3-D charts helped islanders memorize wave patterns so they could canoe the ocean safely.

KIRIBATI BATTLE SITES
World War II tanks, ships, and planes are visible on the reef at low tide.

4 REPORT ON A CANOE RACE
South Tarawa Lagoon

Find out why people say that Kiribati canoes are the fastest canoes in the Pacific Ocean. Watch the wind fill their sails as they speed through the water.

5 EXPLORE ANCIENT RUINS
Pohnpei

Ride a touring kayak to the island of Nan Madol, an ancient city now in ruins. Walk among the remains of the home and tombs of the island's kings.

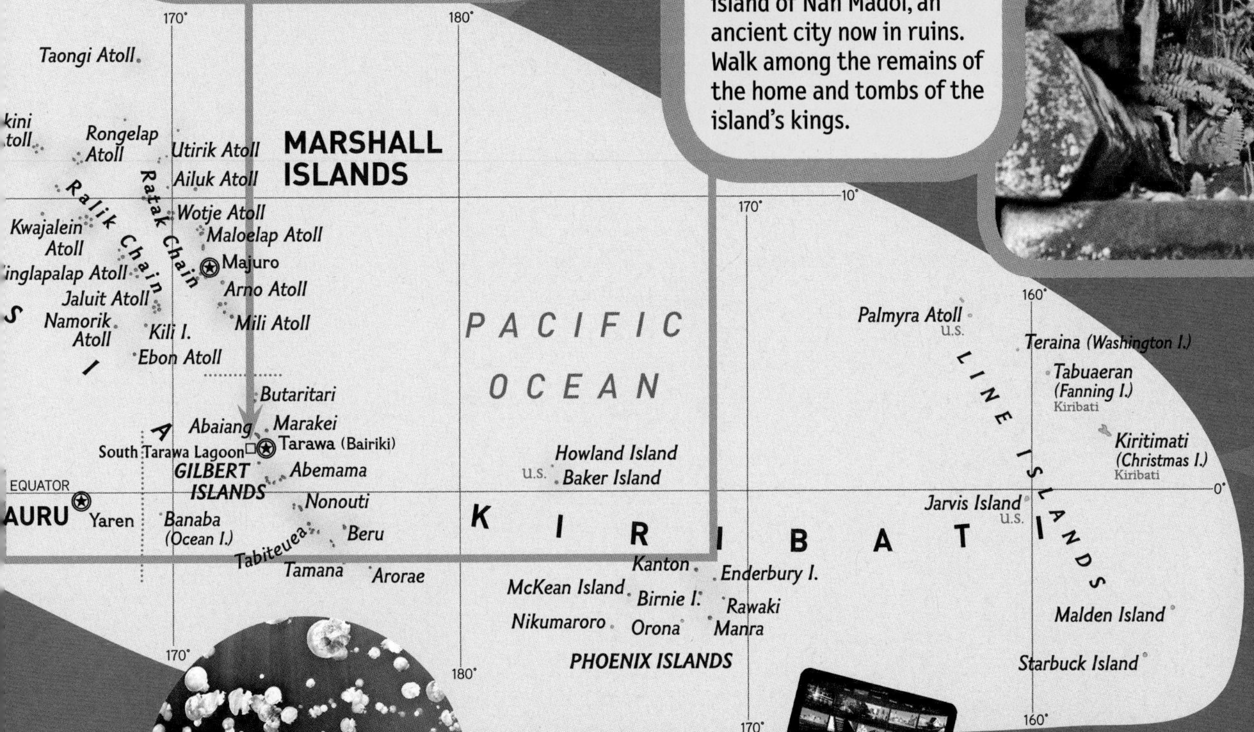

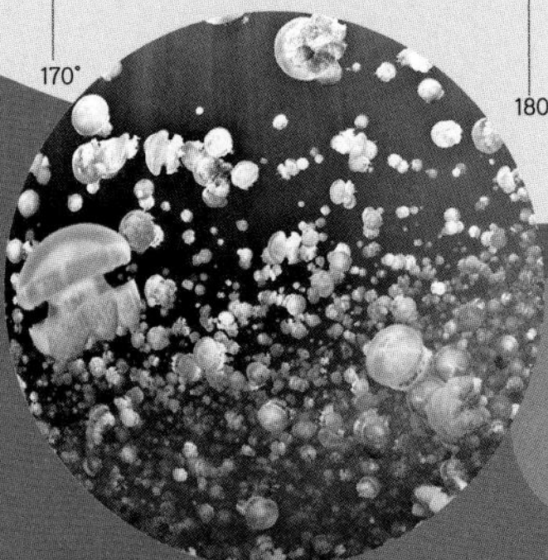

DIGITAL TRAVELER!
People happily swim in Jellyfish Lake in Palau. Do some online research to find out why the jellyfish in this lake do not sting.

5 COOL THINGS TO DO HERE

1 DANCE AT A FATALE
Funafuti

Move to the beat of the drums as you celebrate a *fatale*. Grass skirts, flowers, and joyful music are all part of the festivities.

2 PLUNGE FROM THE SLIDING ROCKS
Papseea

Cool off in a waterfall. Sit on the slippery rocks and glide down into the refreshing natural pool of water. There is one 16-foot (5-m) drop and three smaller ones closer to the pool.

3 DRINK FROM A COCONUT
Tuvalu

Every beach resort and town will have stalls selling coconut milk to drink, necklaces made of seashells, and brightly colored headresses, shirts, and skirts. Buy samples of their goods for a flavor of Polynesian life.

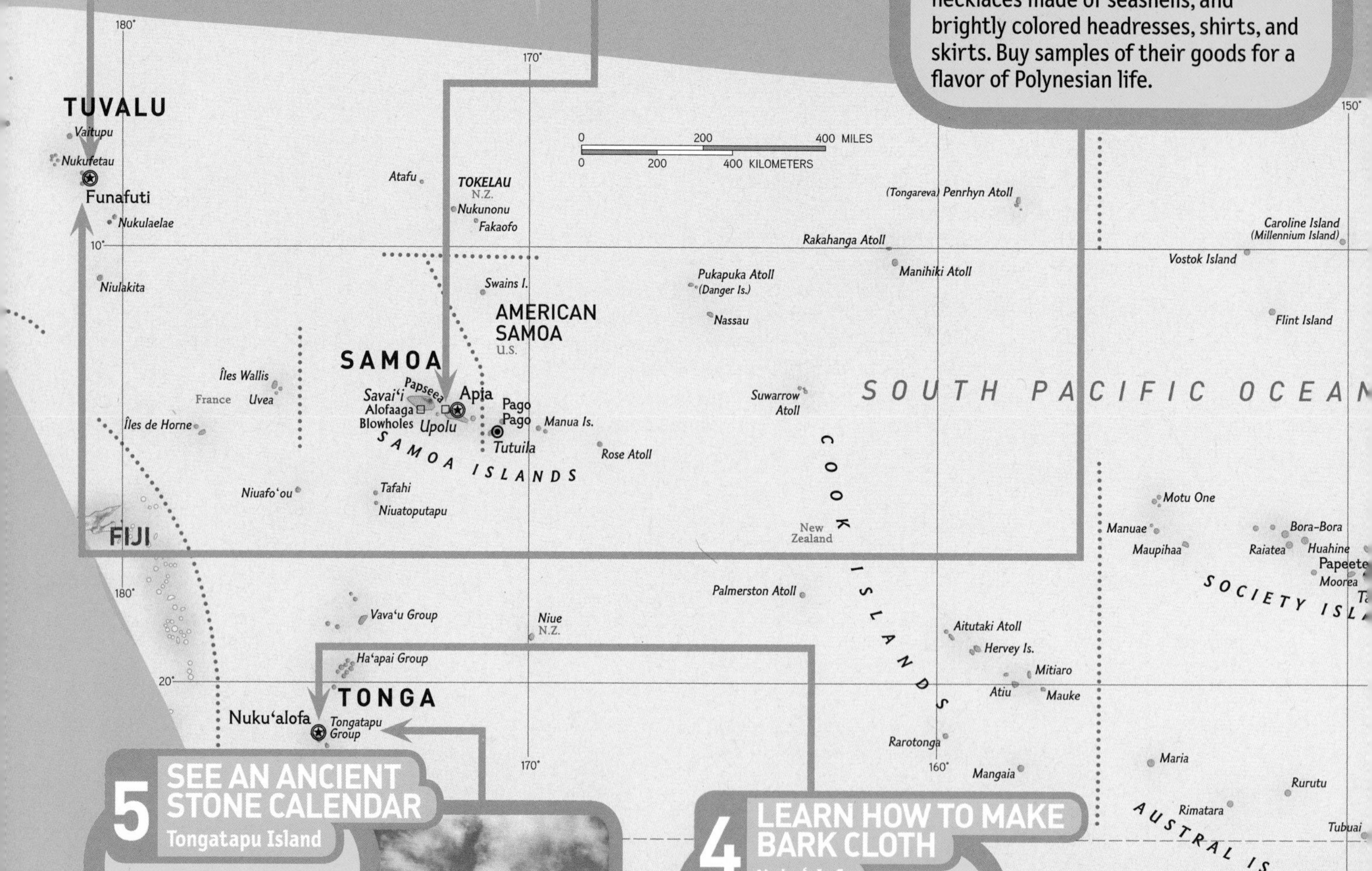

5 SEE AN ANCIENT STONE CALENDAR
Tongatapu Island

In A.D. 1200, the Tu'i Tu'itatui people erected these three huge coral slabs. Recent research tells us that the people used the structure to track the sun and the seasons.

4 LEARN HOW TO MAKE BARK CLOTH
Nuku'alofa

Use a wooden mallet to pound the peeled bark of a mulberry tree. When the bark is thin, several of these tapas are glued together to make a big piece of cloth that is ready for painting.

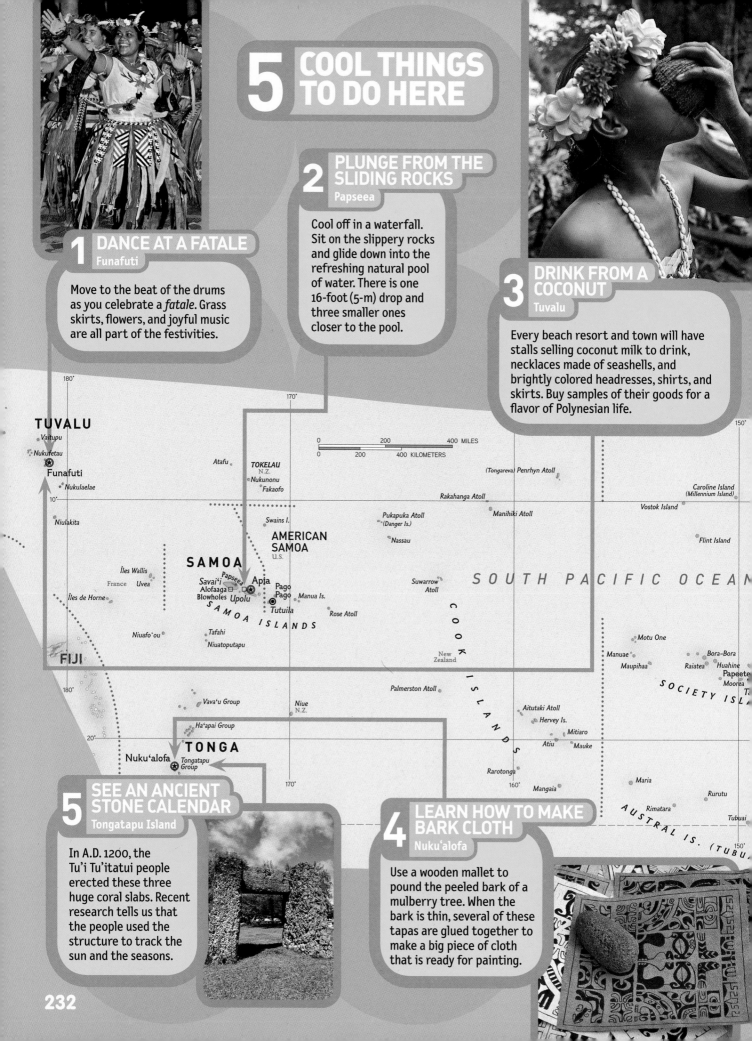

POLYNESIA

Heart of the South PACIFIC

More than 1,000 islands make up Polynesia, in the heart of the Pacific, among them Samoa, Tonga, Tuvalu, French Polynesia (Tahiti), and Hawai'i. Beautiful Hawai'i, a U.S. state, is famous for beaches and surf, and Honolulu is one of the Pacific's largest cities. Many Polynesian islands are small, such as Pitcairn and Tokelau, or remote, for example Easter Island. No wonder Polynesians were traditionally skilled seafarers.

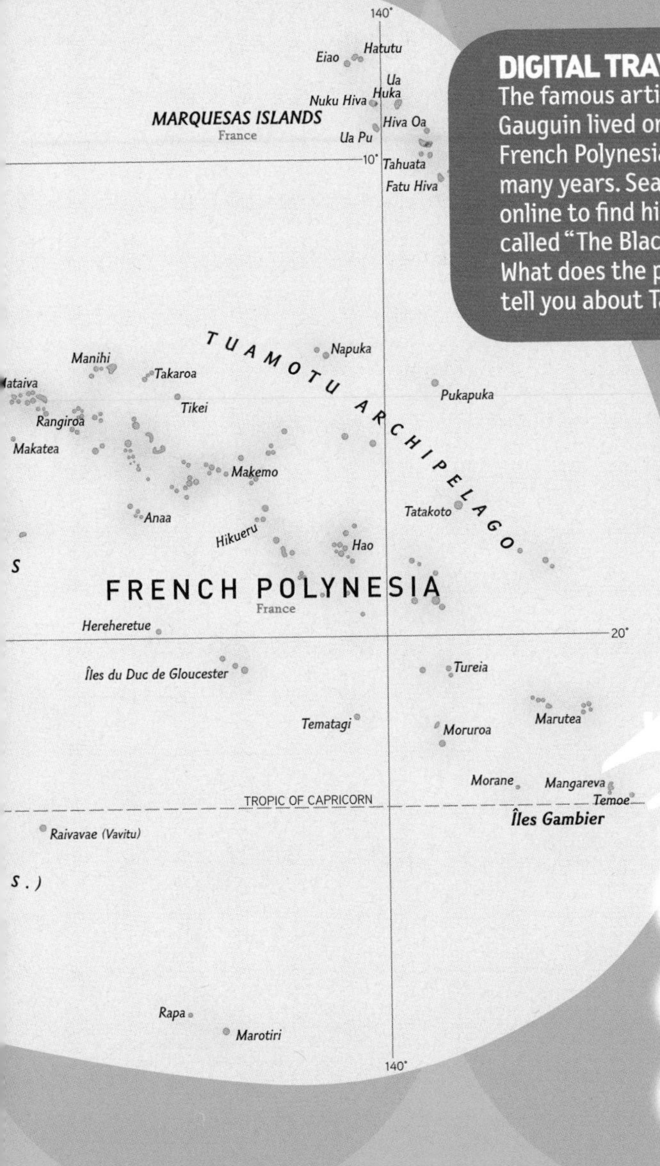

DIGITAL TRAVELER!
The famous artist Paul Gauguin lived on Tahiti in French Polynesia for many years. Search online to find his painting called "The Black Pigs." What does the painting tell you about Tahiti?

ID CARD COUNTRY FACTS

FRENCH POLYNESIA
Population: 278,000
Capital: Papeete

SAMOA
Population: 190,000
Capital: Apia

TONGA
Population: 103,000
Capital: Nuku'alofa

TUVALU
Population: 11,000
Capital: Funafuti

ROBERT LOUIS STEVENSON MUSEUM
In the late 1800s, the author of *Treasure Island* and *Strange Case of Dr. Jekyll and Mr. Hyde* lived here, in Samoa.

STONE MONUMENTS OF MU'A
The tombs, vaults, and mounds were burial sites for Tonga kings between A.D. 1200 and 1600.

ALOFAAGA BLOWHOLES
Ocean waves shoot high into the air through holes in lava rock in Samoa. Locals throw in coconuts and watch them fly out.

AUSTRALIA & OCEANIA

ANTARCTICA

An Immense ICE CAP

Centered on the South Pole, Antarctica is the coldest, windiest, and iciest continent. There are mountains, valleys, and lakes but 98 percent of the land is permanently covered in ice. In many places, the ice is more than 1 mile(1.6 km) thick. In winter (May to July), it is always dark and the surrounding sea freezes to form a belt of ice more than 300 miles (483 km) wide. In summer, the ice belt breaks up to form icebergs, some of which are the size of small U.S. states.

With such a harsh climate. no people live permanently on Antarctica. Tourists regularly visit to see the stunning sights on this vast continent.

ANTARCTICA

A Continent WITHOUT COUNTRIES

The immense ice cap of Antarctica holds 70 percent of the world's fresh water. The icy Antarctic waters are ideal for fish and shellfish, which attract seabirds and marine mammals that feed on them. More than 40 countries, including the U.S.A., Australia, New Zealand, Norway, Chile, Argentina, France, Russia, and the United Kingdom, have signed the Antarctic Treaty, which protects the continent's environment. Conservation groups have urged that limits be placed on fishing in these waters to prevent overexploitation of marine life found there.

ANTARCTIC PENINSULA

This continental arm of the main body of Antarctica is bordered by many islands along the deepwater channels. It lies about 1,000 miles (1,609 km) from the tip of South America.

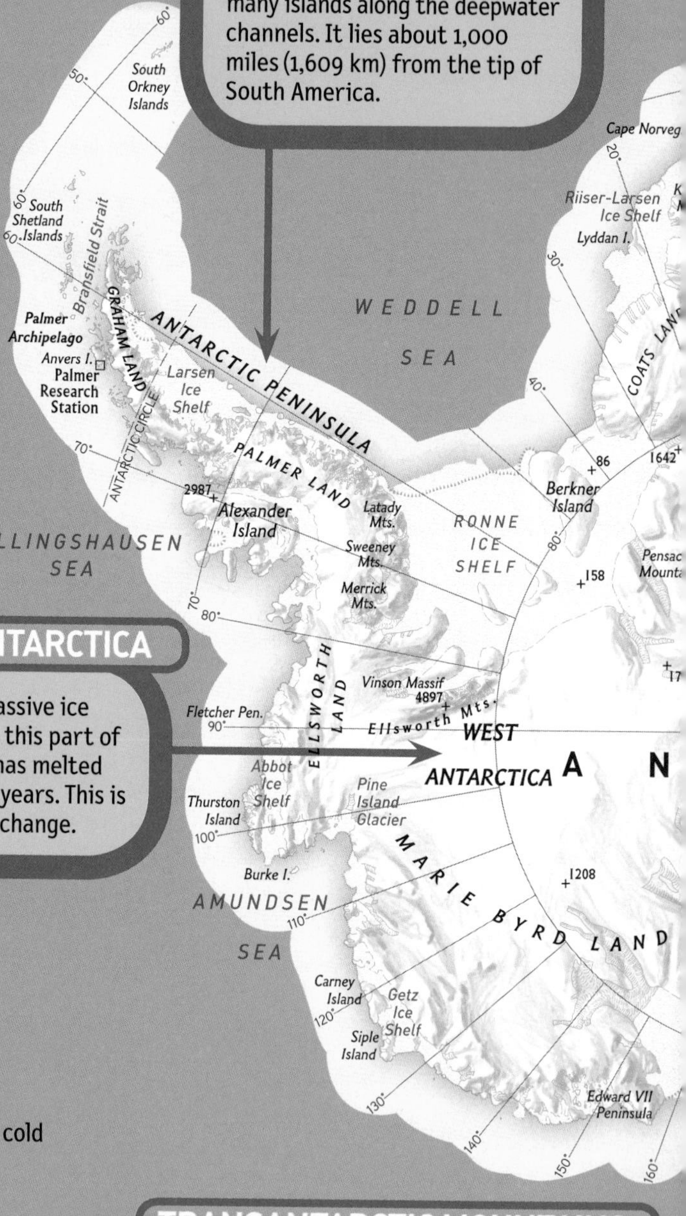

WEST ANTARCTICA

Some of the massive ice sheet covering this part of the continent has melted away in recent years. This is due to climate change.

AUNT BERTHA'S TRAVEL TIPS

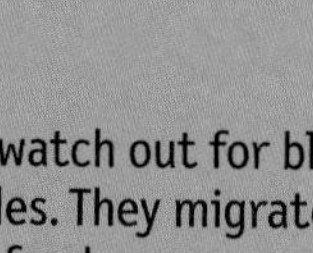

FREEZING COLD

Wear weatherproof clothing here. Near the South Pole, temperatures rarely get above 32°F (0°C). Fierce, bitter cold winds can reach speeds of 180 mph (288 kph).

WHALE WATCHING

If you are sailing the Southern Ocean, watch out for blue, sperm, pygmy, and southern right whales. They migrate to the ocean at various times of the year for food.

COMPASS READINGS

If you are using a standard compass to find your way across the ice, be aware that as you approach the south magnetic pole, the compass needle will try to point downward.

TRANSANTARCTIC MOUNTAINS

A mountain range about 2,200 miles (3,541 km) long runs across the continent. Mount Erebus, the world's southernmost volcano, is part of this range.

QUEEN MAUD LAND

Here, a mountainous coastal area has rocky peaks up to 11,000 feet (3,353 m) high that pierce the ice cap.

RESEARCH STATIONS

Anvers Island

A few thousand scientists spend several months at a time at research stations, studying astronomy, wildlife, climate change, and other areas of science.

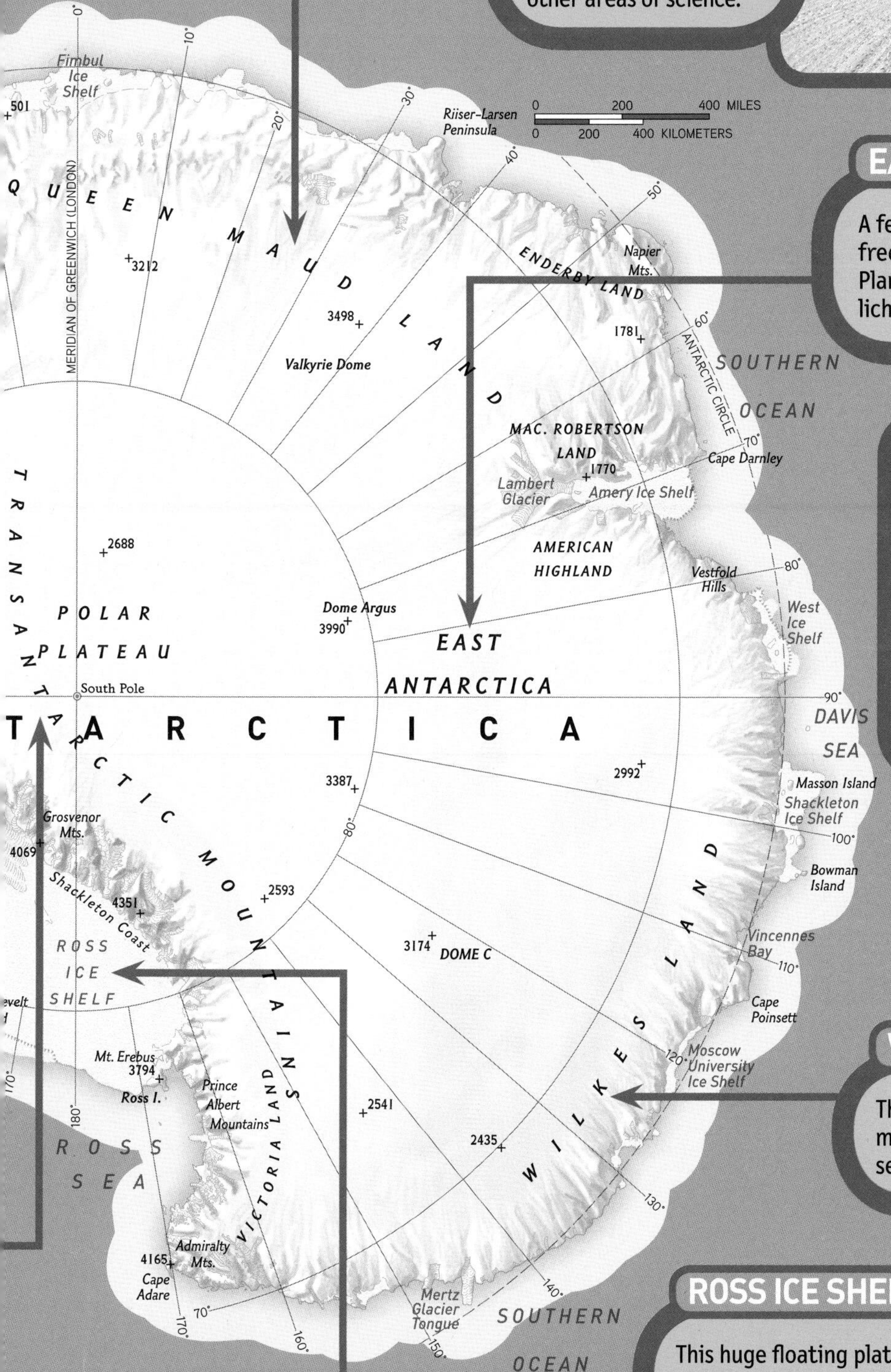

EAST ANTARCTICA

A few areas of this region are free from ice for part of the year. Plant life here includes mosses, lichens, and algae.

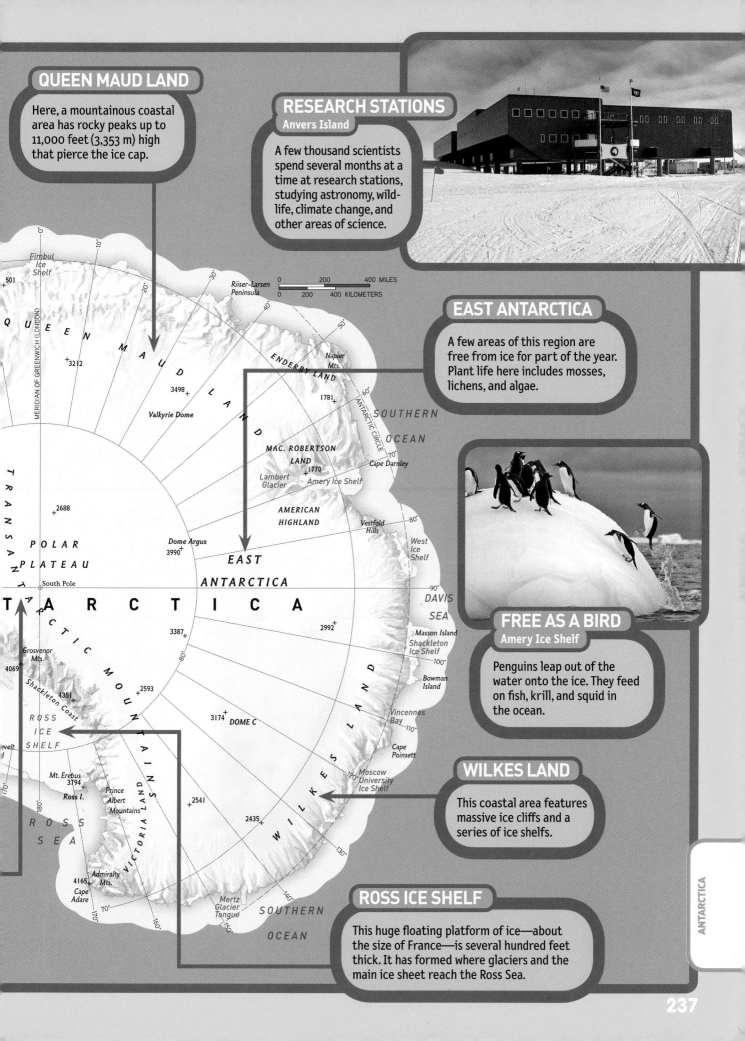

FREE AS A BIRD

Amery Ice Shelf

Penguins leap out of the water onto the ice. They feed on fish, krill, and squid in the ocean.

WILKES LAND

This coastal area features massive ice cliffs and a series of ice shelfs.

ROSS ICE SHELF

This huge floating platform of ice—about the size of France—is several hundred feet thick. It has formed where glaciers and the main ice sheet reach the Ross Sea.

A-maze-ing Paris

Stay on the white paths and help the lost travelers find their way out of a crazy imaginary world underneath Paris, France.

START
PARLEZ-VOUS FRANÇAIS?
Jacques

What in the World?

GOING GLOBAL

These photographs show views of world landmarks. Unscramble the letters to identify what's in each picture.

UATSET FO REIYLBT

TNENEHGESO

DELGON ATEG EIBDRG

ATGER LALW FO AICNH

IGB ENB

LFEEIF WRTOE

ACMUH IPCUCH

JAT AALHM

NIXHPS

LOOK OUT, BELOW!

These photographs show aerial views of Earth's surface. Unscramble the letters to identify each picture.

AMONNITU EGRNA

RFTOSE

LRTAAFLEW

NAONYC

ALCOVON

RSEEDT

DTWSAELN

CGALRIE

PORC LDEISF

What in the World?

DOWN UNDER

These photographs show close-up and faraway views of things in Australia. Unscramble the letters to identify each picture.

NREEBOGAO

OAAKL

RTEGA ARERIBR FREE

ORNGAAKO

LAFG

DRSRBFUOSA

SREAY CKOR

AWSCYSAOR

DENYYS EORAP OESUH

RAIN FOREST ROUNDUP

These photographs show close-up views of animals that live in the rain forest. Unscramble the letters to identify what's in each picture.

GRFO

ABT

OTSHL

RGAAUJ

PREVI

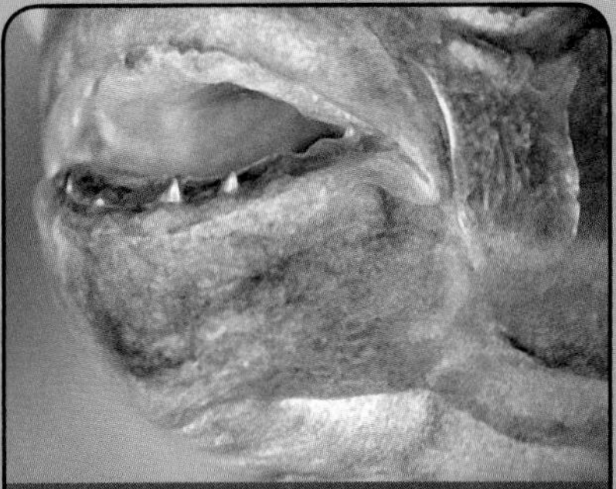

ARPHNIA

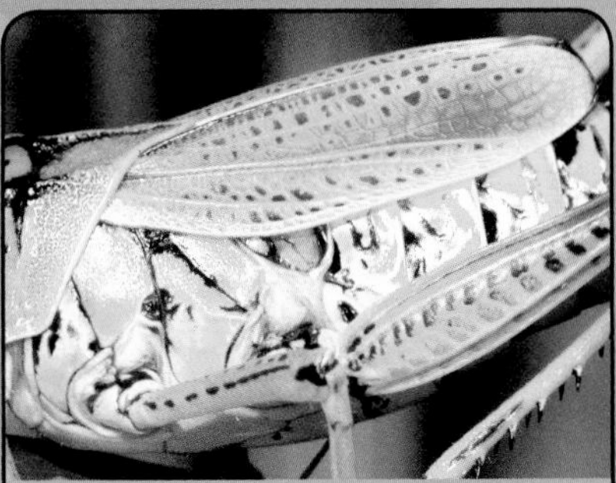

SPAGSREHROP

IRAPT

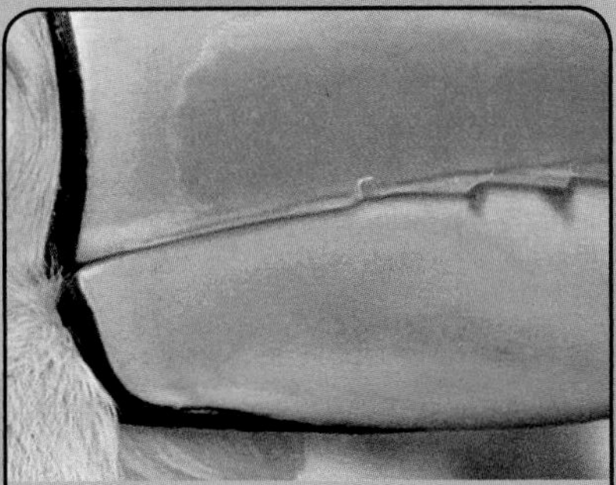

OATNCU

ANSWERS

238-239: Answer A-maze-ing Paris

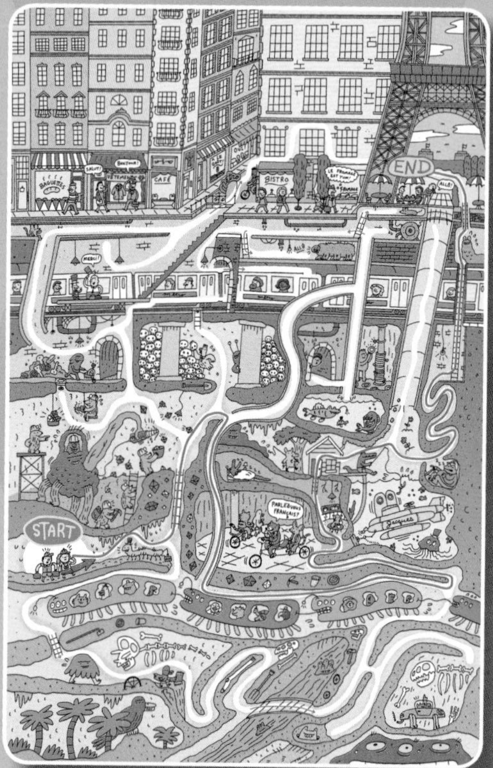

240: Answers

What in the World Places

Statue of Liberty
Stonehenge
Golden Gate Bridge
Great Wall of China
Big Ben
Eiffel Tower
Machu Picchu
Taj Mahal
Sphinx

241: Answers

What in the World Earth

Mountain Range
Forest
Waterfall
Canyon
Volcano
Desert
Wetlands
Glacier
Crop Fields

242: Answers

What in the World Australia

Boomerang
Koala
Great Barrier Reef
Kangaroo
Flag
Surfboards
Ayers Rock
Cassowary
Sydney Opera House

243: Answers

What in the World Rain Forest

Frog
Bat
Sloth
Jaguar
Viper
Piranha
Grasshopper
Tapir
Toucan

GLOSSARY

archipelago a group or chain of islands

bay a body of water, usually smaller than a gulf, that is partially surrounded by land

border the area on either side of a boundary

boundary most commonly, a line that has been established by people to mark the limit of one political unit, such as a country or state, and the beginning of another; geographical features such as mountains sometimes act as boundaries

breakwater a structure, such as a wall, that protects a harbor or beach from pounding waves

bush in Australia, any area with little or no human settlement. It may have very little plant growth or be wooded and forested

canal a human-made waterway that is used by ships or to carry water for irrigation

canyon a deep, narrow valley that has steep sides

cape a point of land that extends into an ocean, a lake, or a river

capital in a country, the city where the government headquarters are. The capital is usually the largest and most important city

cliff a very steep rock face, usually along a coast but also on the side of a mountain

climate the average weather conditions over many years

continent one of the seven main landmasses on Earth's surface

country a territory whose government is the highest legal authority over the land and people within its boundaries

delta lowland formed by silt, sand, and gravel deposited by a river at its mouth

desert a hot or cold region that receives 10 inches (25 cm) or less of rain or other kinds of precipitation a year

divide an elevated area drained by different river systems flowing in different directions

dune a mound or ridge of wind-blown sand

Eastern Hemisphere the half of the globe that lies east of the prime meridian. It includes most of Africa, most of Europe, all of Asia, all of Australia/Oceania, and about half of Antarctica

elevation distance above sea level, usually measured in feet or meters

environment the conditions surrounding and affecting any living thing including the climate and landscape

Equator an imaginary line circling the broadest part of Earth and representing 0° latitude. It divides the globe into the Northern and Southern hemispheres

exports goods or services produced in one country and sold to another country or countries
fault a break in Earth's crust along which movement up, down, or sideways occurs
fiord a narrow sea inlet enclosed by high cliffs. Fiords are found in Norway, New Zealand, and in Scotland in the United Kingdom
fork in a river, the place where two streams come together
geographic pole 90°N, 90°S latitude; location of the ends of Earth's axis
geomagnetic pole point where the axis of Earth's magnetic field intersects Earth's surface; compass needles align with Earth's magnetic field so that one end points to the magnetic north pole, the other to the magnetic south pole
glacier a large, slow-moving mass of ice. As a glacier moves, it scours the land and, near its end, dumps rock debris
globe a scale model of Earth with accurate relative sizes and locations of continents
gulf a portion of the ocean that cuts into the land; usually larger than a bay
harbor a body of water, sheltered by natural or artificial barriers, that is deep enough for ships
hemisphere literally half a sphere; Earth has four hemispheres: Northern, Southern, Eastern, and Western
highlands an elevated area or the more mountainous region of a country
iceberg a large, floating mass of ice
inlet a narrow opening in the land that is filled with water flowing from an ocean, a lake, or a river
island a landmass, smaller than a continent, that is completely surrounded by water
isthmus a narrow strip of land that connects two larger landmasses and has water on two sides
lagoon a shallow body of water that is open to the sea but also protected from it by a reef or sandbar
lake a body of water that is surrounded by land; large lakes are sometimes called seas
landform a physical feature that is shaped by tectonic activity and weathering and erosion; the four major kinds on earth are plains, mountains, plateaus, and hills
landmass a large area of Earth's crust that lies above sea level, such as a continent
large-scale map a map, such as a street map, that shows a small area in great detail
Latin America cultural region generally considered to include Mexico, Central America, South America, and the West Indies; Portuguese and Spanish are the principal languages
latitude distance north and south of the Equator, which is 0° latitude
leeward the side away from or sheltered from the wind
longitude distance east and west of the prime meridian, which is 0° longitude
lowland an area of land lower than the surrounding countryside that is usually flat and without hills and mountains
mangrove swamp a muddy area along tropical coasts thick with mangrove trees that have special breathing roots leading down from branches
Middle East term commonly used for the countries of Southwest Asia but can also include northern Africa from Morocco to Somalia
molten liquefied by heat; melted
mountain a landform, higher than a hill, that rises at least 1,000 feet (302 m) above the surrounding land and is wider at its base than at its top, or peak; a series of mountains is called a range
nation people who share a common culture; often used as another word for "country," although people within a country may be of many cultures
national park an area of a country set aside to protect the landscape or wildlife from human interference
navigable a body of water deep or wide enough to allow boats, ships, barges, and other vessels to pass; any water vessel that can be steered
Northern Hemisphere the half of the globe that lies north of the Equator. It includes all of North America, a small part of South America, all of Europe, about 65 percent of Africa, and almost all of Asia
oasis a part of a desert or other dry region where water is near the surface and plants grow well
ocean the large body of saltwater that surrounds the continents and covers more than two-thirds of Earth's surface
Pampas a flat, treeless part of South America between the Atlantic Coast and the Andes Mountains
peninsula a piece of land that is almost completely surrounded by water
permafrost a permanently frozen sub-surface soil in frigid regions
plain a large area of relatively flat land that is often covered with grasses
plateau a relatively flat area, larger than a mesa, that rises above the surrounding landscape
point a narrow piece of land smaller than a cape that extends into a body of water
population density The number of people living on each square mile or square kilometer of land (calculated by dividing population by land area)
prime meridian an imaginary line that runs through Greenwich, England, and is accepted as the line of 0° longitude
primeval belonging to the first or oldest period of era of living things
projection the process of representing the round Earth on a flat surface, such as a map
rain forest dense forest found on or near the Equator where the climate is hot and wet
reef an offshore ridge made of coral, rocks, or sand
renewable resources resources such as water that are replenished naturally, but can run out by overuse and pollution
Sahel a semiarid grassland in Africa along the Sahara's southern border where rainfall is unreliable
savannah a tropical grassland with scattered trees
scale on a map, a means of explaining the relationship between distances on the map and actual distances on Earth's surface
sea a partially enclosed body of saltwater that is connected to the ocean; completely enclosed bodies of saltwater, such as the Dead Sea, are really lakes
small-scale map a map, such as a country map, that shows a large area without much detail
sound a long, broad inlet of the ocean that lies parallel to the coast and often separates an island and the mainland
Southern Hemisphere the half of the globe that lies south of the Equator. It includes most of South America, a third of Africa, all of Australia/Oceania, all of Antarctica, and a small part of Asia
Soviet Union shortened name for the Union of Soviet Socialist Republics (U.S.S.R.), a former Communist republic (1920–1991) in eastern Europe and northern and central Asia that was made up of 15 republics of which Russia was the largest
spit a long, narrow strip of land, often of sand or silt, extending into a body of water from the land
staple a chief ingredient of a people's diet
steppe a Slavic word referring to relatively flat, mostly treeless temperate grasslands that stretch across much of central Europe and central Asia
strait a narrow passage of water that connects two larger bodies of water
territory land that is under the jurisdiction of a country but that is not a state or a province
tributary a stream that flows into a larger river
tropics region lying within 23 ½° north and south of the Equator that experiences warm temperatures year-round
upwelling process by which nutrient-rich water rises from ocean depths to the surface
valley a long depression, usually created by a river, that is bordered by higher land
volcano an opening in Earth's crust through which molten rock erupts
weather the day-to-day variation in sunshine, rainfall, wind, cloud cover, and other effects of Earth's atmosphere
Western Hemisphere the half of the globe that lies west of the prime meridian. It includes North America, South America, a part of Europe and Africa, and about half of Antarctica
windward the unsheltered side toward which the wind blows

ADDITIONAL COUNTRY DATA

THIS LIST OF COUNTRIES IS IN ALPHABETICAL ORDER.

COUNTRY	SIZE	OFFICIAL LANGUAGE	CURRENCY	HIGHEST POINT	LIFE EXPECTA[NCY]
Albania	11,100 sq mi (28,748 sq km)	Albanian	Albanian lek	Maja e Korabit (Golem Korab), 9068 ft (2764 m)	77
Algeria	919,595 sq mi (2,381,741 sq km)	Arabic	Algerian dinar	Tahat, 9852 ft (3003 m)	76
Andorra	181 sq mi (468 sq km)	Catalan	Euro	Pic de Coma Pedrosa, 9665 ft (2946 m)	N/A
Antigua and Barbuda	171 sq mi (442 sq km)	English	East Caribbean dollar	Boggy Peak, 1319 ft (402 m)	76
Armenia	11,484 sq mi (29,742 sq km)	Armenian	Armenian dram	Aragats Lerrnagagat', 13419 ft (4090 m)	74
Azerbaijan	33,436 sq mi (86,600 sq km)	Azerbaijani (Azeri)	Azerbaijan manat	Bazarduzu Dagi, 14715 ft (4485 m)	74
Bahrain	277 sq mi (717 sq km)	Arabic, English, Farsi	Bahraini dinar	Jabal ad Dukhan, 400 ft (122 m)	76
Bangladesh	56,977 sq mi (147,570 sq km)	Bangla (Bengali)	Bangladeshi taka	Keokradong, 4035 ft (1230 m)	70
Barbados	166 sq mi (430 sq km)	English	Barbadian dollar	Mount Hillaby, 1102 ft (336 m)	75
Belarus	80,153 sq mi (207,595 sq km)	Belarusian, Russian	Belarusian ruble	Dzyarzhynskaya Hara, 1135 ft (346 m)	72
Belgium	11,787 sq mi (30,528 sq km)	Flemish (Dutch), French, German	Euro	Botrange, 2277 ft (694 m)	80
Belize	8,867 sq mi (22,965 sq km)	Spanish, Creole, Mayan dialects, English	Belize dollar	Doyle's Delight, 3806 ft (1160 m)	73
Benin	43,484 sq mi (112,622 sq km)	French	West African CFA franc	Mont Sokbaro, 2159 ft (658 m)	59
Bhutan	17,954 sq mi (46,500 sq km)	Dzongkha	Bhutanese ngultrum/Indian rupee	Gangkar Puensum, 24836 ft (7570 m)	67
Bosnia and Herzegovina	19,741 sq mi (51,129 sq km)	Croatian, Serbian, Bosnian	Bosnia and Herzegovina convertible mark	Maglic, 7828 ft (2386 m)	76
Botswana	224,607 sq mi (581,730 sq km)	English	Botswana pula	Tsodilo Hills, 4885 ft (1489 m)	47
Brunei	2,226 sq mi (5,765 sq km)	Malay	Brunei dollar	Bukit Pagon, 6070 ft (1850 m)	78
Bulgaria	42,855 sq mi (110,994 sq km)	Bulgarian, Turkish, Roma	Bulgarian lev	Musala, 9597 ft (2925 m)	74
Burkina Faso	105,869 sq mi (274,200 sq km)	French	West African CFA franc	Tena Kourou, 2457 ft (749 m)	56
Burundi	10,747 sq mi (27,834 sq km)	Kirundi, French	Burundian franc	Heha, 8760 ft (2670 m)	53
Cambodia	69,898 sq mi (181,035 sq km)	Khmer	Cambodian riel	Phnum Aoral, 5938 ft (1810 m)	62
Cameroon	183,569 sq mi (475,442 sq km)	French, English	Central African CFA franc	Fako, 13435 ft (4095 m)	54
Cape Verde	1,558 sq mi (4,036 sq km)	Portuguese, Crioulo	Cape Verdean escudo	Mt. Fogo, 9282 ft (2829 m)	74
Central African Republic	240,535 sq mi (622,984 sq km)	French	Central African CFA franc	Mont Ngaoui, 4659 ft (1420 m)	49
Colombia	440,831 sq mi (1,141,748 sq km)	Spanish	Colombian peso	Pico Cristobal Colon, 18947 ft (5775 m)	74
Comoros	719 sq mi (1,862 sq km)	Arabic, French	Comorian franc	Karthala, 7743 ft (2360 m)	60
Congo	132,047 sq mi (342,000 sq km)	French	Central African CFA franc	Mount Berongou, 2963 ft (903 m)	58
Cote D'Ivoire	124,503 sq mi (322,462 sq km)	French	West African CFA franc	Monts Nimba, 5748 ft (1752 m)	50
Croatia	21,831 sq mi (56,542 sq km)	Croatian	Croatian kuna	Dinara, 6007 ft (1831 m)	77
Cuba	42,803 sq mi (110,860 sq km)	Spanish	Cuban peso	Pico Turquino, 6578 ft (2005 m)	78
Cyprus	3,572 sq mi (9,251 sq km)	Greek, Turkish, English	Euro	Mount Olympus, 6401 ft (1951 m)	78
Czech Republic	30,450 sq mi (78,866 sq km)	Czech	Czech koruna	Snezka , 5256 ft (1602 m)	78
Democratic Republic of Congo	905,365 sq mi (2,344,885 sq km)	French	Congolese franc	Margherita Peak on Mount Stanley, 16765 ft (5110 m)	49
Djibouti	8,958 sq mi (23,300 sq km)	French, Arabic	Djiboutian franc	Moussa Ali, 6654 ft (2028 m)	61
Dominica	290 sq mi (751 sq km)	English	East Caribbean dollar	Morne Diablotins, 4747 ft (1447 m)	74
Dominican Republic	18,704 sq mi (48,442 sq km)	Spanish	Dominican peso	Pico Duarte, 10417 ft (3175 m)	73
Ecuador	109,483 sq mi (283,560 sq km)	Spanish	U.S. dollar	Chimborazo, 20561 ft (6267 m)	75
El Salvador	8,124 sq mi (21,041 sq km)	Spanish, Nahua	U.S. dollar	Cerro El Pital, 8957 ft (2730 m)	72
Equatorial Guinea	10,831 sq mi (1,002,000 sq km)	Spanish, French	Central African CFA franc	Pico Basile, 9869 ft (3008 m)	52
Eritrea	46,774 sq mi (121,144 sq km)	Afar, Arabic, Tigre	Eritrean nakfa	Soira, 9902 ft (3018 m)	62
Estonia	17,462 sq mi (45,227 sq km)	Estonian	Euro	Suur Munamagi, 1043 ft (318 m)	76
Ethiopia	437,600 sq mi (1,133,380 sw km)	Amharic, Tigrinya	Ethiopian birr	Ras Dejen, 14872 ft (4533 m)	62

COUNTRY	SIZE	OFFICIAL LANGUAGE	CURRENCY	HIGHEST POINT	LIFE EXPECTANCY
Federated States of Micronesia	271 sq mi (702 sq km)	English	U.S. dollar	Dolohmwar (Totolom), 2595 ft (791 m)	68
Fiji	7,095 sq mi (18,376 sq km)	English	Fijian dollar	Tomanivi, 4344 ft (1324 m)	69
France	210,026 sq mi (543,965 sq km)	French	Euro	Mont Blanc, 15771 ft (4807 m)	82
French Polynesia	1,609 sq mi (4,167 sq km)	French	CFP franc	Mont Orohena, 7352 ft (2241 m)	76
Gabon	103,347 sq mi (267,667 sq km)	French	Central African CFA franc	Mont Iboundji, 5167 ft (1575 m)	63
Gambia	4,361 sq mi (11,295 sq km)	English	Gambian dalasi	unnamed elevation, 174 ft (53 m)	58
Georgia	26,911 sq mi (69,700 sq km)	Georgian	Georgian lari	Mt'a Shkhara, 17064 ft (5201 m)	75
Ghana	92,100 sq mi (238,537 sq km)	English	Ghana cedi	Mount Afadjato, 2904 ft (885 m)	61
Greece	50,949 sq mi (131,957 sw km)	Greek, English, french	Euro	Mount Olympus, 9570 ft (2917 m)	81
Grenada	133 sq mi (344 sq km)	English	East Caribbean dollar	Mount Saint Catherine, 2756 ft (840 m)	73
Guatemala	42,042 sq mi (108,889 sq km)	Spanish, 23 Amerindian Languages	Guatemalan quetzal	Volcan Tajumulco, 13,816 ft (4,211 m)	71
Guinea	94,926 sq mi (245,857 sq km)	French	Guinean franc	Monts Nimba, 5748 ft (1752 m)	56
Guinea-Bissau	13,948 sq mi (36,125 sq km)	Portuguese	West African CFA franc	unnamed elevation, 984 ft (300 m)	54
Guyana	83,000 sq mi (214,969 sq km)	English, Amerindian dialects, Creole	Guyanese dollar	Mount Roraima, 9301 ft (2835 m)	66
Haiti	10,714 sq mi (27,750 sq km)	French, Creole	Haitian gourde	Chaine de la Selle, 8793 ft (2680 m)	62
Honduras	43,433 sq mi (112,492 sq km)	Spanish, Amerindian dialects	Honduran Iempira	Cerro Las Minas, 9416 ft (2870 m)	73
Hungary	35,919 sq mi (93,030 sq km)	Hungarian	Hungarian forint	Kekes, 3327 ft (1014 m)	75
India	1,269,222 sq mi (3,287,270 sq km)	Hindi, English	Indian rupee	Kanchenjunga, 28209 ft (8598 m)	66
Indonesia	742,308 sq mi (1,922,570 sq km)	Bahasa Indonesian	Indonesian rupiah	Puncak Jaya, 16024 ft (4884 m)	70
Italy	116,345 sq mi (301,333 sq km)	Italian	Euro	Mont Blanc (Monte Bianco) de Courmayeur, 15577 ft (4748 m)	82
Jamaica	4.244 sq mi (10,991 sq km)	English, Patois English	Jamaican dollar	Blue Mountain Peak, 7402 ft (2256 m)	73
Jordan	34,495 sq mi (89,342 sq km)	Arabic	Jordanian dinar	Jabal Umm ad Dami, 6083 ft (1854 m)	73
Kazakhstan	1,049,155 sq mi (2,717,300 sq km)	Kazakh (Qazaq), Russian	Kazakhstani tenge	Khan Tangiri Shyngy (Pik Khan-Tengri), 22949 ft (6995 m)	69
Kiribati	313 sq mi (811 sq km)	English	Kiribati dollar/Australian dollar	unnamed elevation on Banaba, 266 ft (81 m)	65
Kosovo	4,203 sq mi (10,887 sq km)	Albanian, Serbian, Bosnian	Euro	Gjeravica/Deravica, 8714 ft (2656 m)	69
Kuwait	6,880 sq mi (17,818 sq km)	Arabic	Kuwaiti dinar	unnamed elevation, 1004 ft (306 m)	75
Kyrgyzstan	77,182 sq mi (199,900 sq km)	Kyrgyz, Russian	Kyrgyzstani som	Jengish Chokusu (Pik Pobedy), 24406 ft (7439 m)	70
Laos	91,429 sq mi (236,800 sq km)	Lao	Lao kip	Phu Bia, 9242 ft (2817 m)	67
Latvia	24,938 sq mi (64,589 sq km)	Latvian	Latvian lats	Gaizina Kalns, 1024 ft (312 m)	74
Lebanon	4,036 sq mi (10,452 sq km)	Arabic	Lebanese pound	Qornet es Saouda, 10131 ft (3088 m)	79
Lesotho	11,720 sq mi (30,355 sq km)	Sesotho, English	Lesotho loti	Thabana Ntlenyana, 11424 ft (3482 m)	48
Liberia	43,000 sq mi (111,370 sq km)	English	Liberian dollar	Mount Wuteve, 4528 ft (1380 m)	60
Liechtenstein	62 sq mi (160 sq km)	German	Swiss franc	Vorder-Grauspitz, 8527 ft (2599 m)	82
Lithuania	25,212 sq mi (65,300 sq km)	Lithuanian	Lithuanian litas	Aukstojas, 965 ft (294 m)	74
Luxembourg	998 sq mi (2,586 sq km)	Luxembourgish	Euro	Buurgplaatz, 1834 ft (559 m)	80
Macedonia	9,928 sq mi (25,713 sq km)	Macedonian, Albanian, Turkish	Macedonian denar	Golem Korab (Maja e Korabit), 9068 ft (2764 m)	75
Madagascar	226,658 sq mi (587,041 sq km)	French, Malagasy	Malagasy ariary	Maromokotro, 9436 ft (2876 m)	64
Malawi	45,747 sq mi (118,484 sq km)	Chichewa	Malawian kwacha	Sapitwa (Mount Mlanje), 9849 ft (3002 m)	54
Malaysia	127,355 sq mi (329,847 sq km)	Bahasa Melayu	Malaysian ringgit	Gunung Kinabalu, 13451 ft (4100 m)	75
Maldives	115 sq mi (298 sq km)	Maldivian Dhivehi, English	Maldivian rufiyaa	Addu Atholhu, 8 ft (2 m)	74
Malta	122 sq mi (316 sq km)	Maltese, English	Euro	Ta'Dmejrek, 830 ft (253 m)	81
Marshall Islands	70 sq mi (181 sq km)	Marshallese	U.S. dollar	unnamed location on Likiep, 33 ft (10 m)	72
Mauritania	397,955 sq mi (1,030,700sq km)	Arabic	Mauritanian ouguiya	Kediet Ijill, 3002 ft (915 m)	61
Mauritius	788 sq mi (2,040 sq km)	French, Creole, Bhojpuri	Mauritian rupee	Mont Piton, 2717 ft (828 m)	73
Moldova	13,050 sq mi (33,800 sq km)	Moldovan	Moldovan leu	Dealul Balanesti, 1411 ft (430 m)	71
Monaco	.8 sq mi (2 sq km)	French	Euro	Mont Agel, 459 ft (140 m)	N/A
Montenegro	5,415 sq mi (14,026 sq km)	Serbian	Euro	Bobotov Kuk, 8274 ft (2522 m)	74
Myanmar	261,218 sq mi (676,552 sq km)	Burmese	Burmese kyat	Hkakabo Razi, 19295 ft (5881 m)	65
Namibia	318,261 sq mi (824,292 sq km)	English	Namibian dollar	Konigstein, 8550 ft (2606 m)	63
Nauru	8 sq mi (21 sq km)	Nauruan	Australian dollar	unnamed elevation along plateau rim, 200 ft (61 m)	60
Nepal	56,827 sq mi (147,181 sq km)	Nepali	Nepalese rupee	Mount Everest, 29035 ft (8850 m)	68
Netherlands	16,034 sq mi (41,528 sq km)	Dutch, Frisian	Euro	Mount Scenery, 2828 ft (862 m)	81
North Korea	46,540 sq mi (120,538 sq km)	Korean	North Korean won	Paektu-san, 9003 ft (2744 m)	69

COUNTRY	SIZE	OFFICIAL LANGUAGE	CURRENCY	HIGHEST POINT	LIFE EXPECTA
Oman	119,500 sq mi (309,500 sq km)	Arabic	Omani rial	Jabal Shams, 9778 ft (2980 m)	76
Palau	189 sq mi (489 sq km)	Palauan, Filipino, English, Chinese	U.S. dollar	Mount Ngerchelchuus, 794 ft (242 m)	69
Qatar	4,448 sq mi (11,521 sq km)	Arabic	Qatari riyal	Tuwayyir al Hamir, 338 ft (103 m)	78
Romania	92,043 sq mi (238,391 sq km)	Romanian	Romanian leu	Moldoveanu, 8347 ft (2544 m)	74
Rwanda	10,169 sq mi (26,338 sq km)	Kinyarwanda, French, English	Rwandan franc	Volcan Karisimbi, 14826 ft (4519 m)	63
Samoa	1,093 sq mi (2,831 sq km)	Samoan (Polynesian), English	Samoan tala	Mount Silisili, 6093ft (1857 m)	73
San Marino	24 sq mi (61 sq km)	Itaian	Euro	Monte Titano, 2477 ft (755 m)	84
Sao Tome & Principe	386 sq mi (1,001 sq km)	Portuguese	Sao Tome & Principe dobra	Pico de Sao Tome, 6640 ft (2024 m)	66
Saudi Arabia	756,985 sq mi (1,960,582 sq km)	Arabic	Saudi riyal	Jabal Sawda', 10279 ft (3133 m)	74
Senegal	75,955 sq mi (196,722 sq km)	French	West African CFA franc	unnamed elevation southwest of Kedougou, 1906 ft (581 m)	63
Serbia	29,913 sq mi (77,474 sq km)	Serbian	Euro	Midzor, 7116 ft (2169 m)	74
Seychelles	176 sq mi (455 sq km)	English	Seychellois rupee	Morne Seychellois, 2969 ft (905 m)	73
Sierra Leone	27,699 sq mi (71,740 sq km)	English	Sierra Leone leone	Loma Mansa (Bintimani), 6391 ft (1948 m)	45
Singapore	255 sq mi (660 sq km)	Mandarin, English, Malay	Singapore dollar	Bukit Timah, 545 ft (166 m)	82
Slovakia	18,932 sq mi (49,035 sq km)	Slovak	Euro	Gerlachovsky Stit, 8711 ft (2655 m)	76
Slovenia	7,827 sq mi (20,273 sq km)	Slovene, Serbo-Croatian	Euro	Triglav, 9396 ft (2864 m)	80
Solomon Islands	10,954 sq mi (28,370 sq km)	Melanesian pidgin	Solomon Islands dollar	Mount Popomanaseu, 7579 ft (2310 m)	67
Somalia	246,201 sq mi (637,657 sq km)	Somali	Somali shilling	Shimbiris, 7927ft (2416 m)	54
South Africa	470,693 sq mi (1,219,090 sq km)	Afrikaans, English	South African rand	Njesuthi, 11181 ft (3408 m)	58
South Korea	38,321 sq mi (99,250 sq km)	Korean	South Korean won	Halla-san, 6398 ft (1950 m)	81
South Sudan	248,777 sq mi (644,329 sq km)	English	South Sudanese pound	Kinyeti, 10456 ft (3187 m)	54
Spain	195,363 sq mi (505,988 sq km)	Castilian Spanish	Euro	Pico de Teide (Tenerife) on Canary Islands, 12198 ft (3718 m)	82
Sri Lanka	25,299 sq mi (65,525 sq km)	Sinhala	Sri Lankan rupee	Pidurutalagala, 8281 ft (2524 m)	74
St. Kitts & Nevis	104 sq mi (269 sq km)	English	East Caribbean dollar	Mount Liamuiga, 3793 ft (1156 m)	75
St. Lucia	238 sq mi (616 sq km)	English	East Caribbean dollar	Mount Gimie, 3117 ft (950 m)	75
St. Vincent and the Grenadines	150 sq mi (389 sq km)	English, French Patois	East Caribbean dollar	La Soufriere, 4049 ft (1234 m)	72
Sudan	967,500 sq mi (2,505,813 sq km)	Arabic	Sudanese pound	Jabal Marrah, 10076 ft (3071 m)	62
Suriname	63,037 sq mi (163,265 sq km)	Dutch	Surinamese dollar	Juliana Top, 4035 ft (1230 m)	71
Swaziland	6,704 sq mi (17,363 sq km)	English, siSwati	Swazi lilangeni	Emlembe, 6109 ft (1862 m)	49
Switzerland	15,940 sq mi (41,284 sq km)	German, French, italian	Swiss franc	Dufourspitze, 15203 ft (4634 m)	83
Syria	71,488 sq mi (185,180 sq km)	Arabic	Syrian pound	Mount Hermon, 9232 ft (2814 m)	75
Tajikistan	55,251 sq mi (143,100 sq km)	Tajik	Tajikistani somoni	Qullai Ismoili Somoni, 24590 ft (7495 m)	67
Thailand	198,115 sq mi (513,115 sq km)	Thai, English	Thai baht	Doi Inthanon, 8451 ft (2576 m)	75
Timor-Leste	5,640 sq mi (14,609 sq km)	Tetum, Portuguese	U.S. dollar	Foho Tatamailau, 9721 ft (2963 m)	66
Togo	21,925 sq mi (56,785 sq km)	French	West African CFA franc	Mont Agou, 3235 ft (986 m)	56
Tonga	289 sq mi (748 sq km)	Tongan, English	Tongan pa'anga	unnamed elevation on Kao Island, 3389 ft (1033 m)	72
Trinidad and Tobago	1,980 sq mi (5,128 sq km)	English	Trinidad and Tobago dollar	El Cerro del Aripo, 3084 ft (940 m)	71
Tunisia	63,170 sq mi (163,610 sq km)	Arabic	Tunisian dinar	Jebel ech Chambi, 5066 ft (1544 m)	75
Turkmenistan	188,300 sq mi (488,100 sq km)	Turkmen, Russian, Uzbek	Turkmenistan manat	Gora Ayribaba, 10299 ft (3139 m)	65
Tuvalu	10 sq mi (26 sq km)	Tuvaluan, English	Tuvaluan dollar/Australian dollar	unnamed location, 16 ft (5 m)	65
Uganda	93,104 sq mi (241,139 sq km)	English	Ugandan shilling	Margherita Peak on Mount Stanley, 16765 ft (5110 m)	58
Ukraine	233,090 sq mi (603,700 sq km)	Ukrainian	Ukrainian hryvnia	Hora Hoverla, 6762 ft (2061 m)	71
United Arab Emirates	30,000 sq mi (77,700 sq km)	Arabic	United Arab Emirates dirham	Jabal Yibir, 5010 ft (1527 m)	76
Uzbekistan	172,742 sq mi (447,400 sq km)	Uzbek, Russian	Uzbekistani som	Adelunga Toghi, 14111 ft (4301 m)	68
Vanuatu	4,707 sq mi (12,190 sq km)	pidgin (Bislama or Bichelama)	Vanuatu vatu	Tabwemasana, 6158 ft (1877 m)	71
Vatican City	.2 sq mi (.4 sq km)	Italian, Latin, french	Euro	unnamed elevation, 246 ft (75 m)	N/A
Vietnam	127,844 sq mi (331,114 sq km)	Vietnamese	Vietnamese dong	Fan Si Pan, 10315 ft (3144 m)	73
Yemen	207,286 sq mi (536,286 sq km)	Arabic	Yemeni rial	Jabal an Nabi Shu'ayb, 12336 ft (3760 m)	62
Zambia	290,586 sq mi (752,614 sq km)	English	Zambian kwacha	Mafinga Hills, 7549 ft (2301 m)	56

COUNTRY ABBREVIATIONS

Afghanistan, Afghan.
Albania, Alban.
Algeria, Alg.
Argentina, Arg.
Armenia, Arm.
Austria, Aust.
Australia, Austral.
Azerbaijan, Azerb.
Belgium, Belg.
Bolivia, Bol.
Bosnia and Herzegovina, Bosn. & Herzg.
Brazil, Braz.
Bulgaria, Bulg.
Costa Rica, C.R.
Canada, Can.
Central African Republic, Cen. Af. Rep.
Colombia, Col.
Denmark, Den.
Dominican Republic, Dom. Rep.
Ecuador, Ecua.
El Salvador, El Salv.
Estonia, Est.
Ethiopia, Eth.
Federated States of Micronesia, F.S.M.
Falkland Islands, Falk. Is.
Finland, Fin.
France, French, Fr.
Georgia, Ga.
Germany, Ger.
Greece, Gr.
Honduras, Hond.
Hungary, Hung.
Iceland, Ice.
Ireland, Ire.
Italy, It.
Jamaica, Jam.
Kazakhstan, Kaz.
Kosovo, Kos.
Kyrgyzstan, Kyrg.
Latvia, Latv.
Lebanon, Leb.
Libya, Lib.
Liechtenstein, Liech.
Lithuania, Lith.
Luxembourg, Lux.
Macedonia, Maced.
Mexico, Mex.
Moldova, Mold.
Morocco, Mor.
Northern Ireland, N. Ire.
New Zealand, N.Z.
Netherlands, Neth.
Nicaragua, Nicar.
Norway, Nor.
Papua New Guinea, P.N.G.
Pakistan, Pak.
Panama, Pan.
Paraguay, Parag.
Poland, Pol.
Portugal, Port.
Romania, Rom.
Russia, Russ.
Serbia, Serb.
Slovenia, Slov.
Spain, Spanish, Sp.
Sweden, Sw.
Switzerland, Switz.
Syria, Syr.
Tajikistan, Taj.
Thailand, Thai.
Tunisia, Tun.
Turkey, Turk.
Turkmenistan, Turkm.
United Arab Emirates, U.A.E.
United Kingdom, U.K.
United States, U.S.
Ukraine, Ukr.
Uruguay, Uru.
Uzbekistan, Uzb.
Venezuela, Venez.
Zimbabwe, Zimb.

INDEX

B

C

D

Photo Credits

DT = Dreamstime, GI = Getty Images, RH = Robert Harding, SS = Shutterstock

Cover

Front Cover:(dolphin), tubuceo/SS; (pyramids), Fatih Kocyildir/SS; (Seattle Space Needle), Jeremy Edwards/iStockphoto; (Pamukkale), Stepan Rudyk/SS; (Taj Mahal), Lori Epstein/National Geographic Creative; (penguins), Keith Szafranski/iStockphoto; (lanterns), Flickr RF/Getty Images; (Mt. Kilimanjaro), enote/SS; Back cover: (koala), John Carnemolla/iStockphoto; (bus), Chris Jenner/SS; (rocks), Jim Lopes /SS

Front Matter

2 (hi) Edyta Pawlowska/DT; 2 (L-mid) Eduardo Rivero/SS; 2 (R-mid) Nyvlt-art/SS; 2 (L-lo) Pictac/DT; 2 (R-lo) Alexandre Fagundes De Fagundes/DT; 3 (L-hi) photo25th/SS; 3 (R-hi) Jose Ignacio Soto/SS; 3 (lo) Palette7/DT; 8 (hi) Diego Barbieri/SS

North and South America

10-11 Thomas Barrat/SS; 12 (hi) Joakim Lloyd Raboff/SS; 12 (lo) Daniel Raustadt /DT; 14-1 Oceanfishing/DT; 14-2 Patricia Marroquin/SS; 14-4 Jf123/DT; 15 (hi) Jamie Roach/SS; 15-5 Mark Spowart/DT; 15 (lo) Cris Kelly/SS; 16 (hi) Pictac/DT; 16-1 Dean Riley/DT; 16-3 Jeff Kinsey/DT; 17-2 Vvp/DT; 17 (lo) Mazura/DT; 17-5 Glen Gaffney/DT; 18 (hi) Michael Flippo/DT; 18 (lo) Isselee/DT; 18-2 Melinda Fawver/DT; 18-3 Cenk Unver/DT; 19-1 Lunamarina/DT; 19-4 Alexandre Fagundes De Fagundes/DT; 20 (hi) Okea/DT; 20-3 Feije Riemersma/DT; 20 (lo) Foryouinf/DT; 20-5 Howard Sandler/DT; 21-2 jaana piira/SS; 24 (hi) Eduardo Rivero/SS; 24-5 Pniesen/DT; 25-1 Pniesen/DT; 25-2 Aurora Photos/RH; 25(lo) Michael Lynch/SS; 25-4 Zigzagmtart/DT; 26-1 Gary Hartz/DT; 26-3 Petr Valenta/DT; 26-4 Jan Csernoch/DT; 26-5 Scott Griessel/DT; 27 (hi) Dirk Ercken/SS; 27-2 Nacho Such/SS; 28-1 torsten kuenzlen/DT; 28 (lo) Alexander Lvov/DT; 28-3 Amaiquez/DT; 29-2 Picturemakersllc/DT; 29-4 age fotostock/RH; 29-5 Erez Shor/DT; 30 (hi) Kamira/SS; 30-5 Basphoto/DT; 30 (lo) Aspenphoto/DT; 31-1 Robert Paul Van Beets/DT; 31-2 Robert Harding Productions/RH; 31-3 Elena Zarubina/DT; 31-4 Tommy Beattie/DT; 32-1 eye ubiquitous/RH; 32-2 Inc/SS; 32-5 Guy Thouvenin/RH; 33 (hi) alexsvirid/SS; 33-3 Steven Melanson/DT; 34-1 Monkey Business Images Ltd/DT; 34 (hi) Africa Studio/SS; 34-4 Laszlo Halasi/DT; 35-2 Vilainecrevette/DT; 35-3 Yobro10/DT; 35-5 Richard Cummins/RH; 36-1 Paul Zizka/DT; 36-2 Jason P Ross/DT; 36 (lo) alekleks/SS; 37-1 Stringer/Randy Brooks/GI 37-4 Achim Baqué/DT; 37-5 LOOK/RH; 38-39 Dr. Morley Read/SS; 40 (hi) Celso Pupo/SS; 40 (lo) Odyssey/RH; 42 (hi) Steffen Foerster/SS; 42 (lo) Norman Chan/DT; 42-5 Gary Hartz/DT; 43-1 Max Blain/DT; 43-2 Toniflap/DT; 43-4 Maks Narodenko/SS; 44-2 Jan Csernoch/DT; 44-5 Stephenmeese/DT; 44-4 Rafael Martin-Gaitero/SS; 45 (hi) Fernando Cortes/SS; 45-3 Richard Cummins/RH; 46 (lo) Alexandre Fagundes De Fagundes/DT; 46-3 Worldshots/DT; 47-5 Mick Baines & Maren Reichelt/RH; 47-4 worldswildlifewonders/SS; 47 (hi) Gertan/SS; 48 (lo) Juri Samsonov/DT; 48-2 Alexandre Fagundes De Fagundes/DT; 48-3 Maska82/DT; 49-5 Aguina/DT; 49-4 Steve Allen/DT; 50-2 Dale Mitchell/DT; 50-1 Orionna/DT; 50 (lo) Anibal Trejo/SS; 51-4 Steve Tracy/DT; 51-3 Rafa Cichawa/DT; 51 (hi) taelove7/SS; 52-1 Vladir09/SS; 52-5 Ian Trower/RH; 52-4 Daniel Wiedemann/DT; 52-3 Insights/RH; 53-2 Eduardo Rivero/SS; 53 (lo) Oleksiy Mark/SS; 54 (lo) Leonard Zhukovsky/SS; 54-1 Gavin Hellier/RH 55-5 Ekaterina Pokrovsky/DT; 55 (lo)Oleksiy Mark/SS; 55-4 Nick Stubbs/DT; 55-3 Marco Simoni/RH 56 (lo) Seregam/SS; 56-1 Eduardo Rivero/SS; 57-4 Noamfein/DT; "57-3 Giuliachristin/DT; " 57-2 Michael Zysman/SS; 57 (hi) Olivier Le Queinec/SS; 58-1 Holger Karius/DT; 58-3 Insights/RH; 59 (hi) Lukas Blazek/DT; 59-4 Tomasz Pado/DT; 59 (lo) Vetkit/DT; 60 (lo) lalito/SS; 60-2 Kobby Dagan/DT; 61-5 Alexandre Fagundes De Fagundes/DT; 61-4 Kobby Dagan/DT; 61-3 Angela Ostafichuk/DT

Europe

62-63 Boris Stroujko/SS; 65 (hi) VLADJ55/SS; 65 (lo) nito/SS; 66 (hi) Eric Isselee/SS; 66-1 Luke Smith/DT; 67-2 Tatonka/DT; 67-4 Tupungato/DT; 67-5 Tomas Sereda/DT; 68-1 age fotostock/RH; 68-2 Stuart Black/RH; 68-4 Natalia Rumyantseva/DT; 69 (hi) age fotostock/RH; 69-5 Jens Fiskbaek/DT; 70 (lo) Olesia Bilkei/SS; 70-1 Vojtech Vlk/DT; 71 (lo) mountainpix/SS; 71-2 Image Broker/RH; 71-3 Serjio74/DT; 71-4 Marekpilar/DT; 71-5 Image Broker/RH; 72 (lo) Lorraine Swanson/DT; 72 (hi) jps/SS; 72-1 Aurora Photos/RH; 73-3 Erica Schroeder/DT; 73-4 Still Pictures/RH; 73-5 Lucian Milasan/DT; 74-1 Helen Filatova/SS; 74-2 LOOK/RH; 74-4 Thomas Lindholm/DT; 74-5 Mikhail Markovskiy/DT; 75 (hi) Hgalina/SS; 75 (lo) Madlen/SS; 76 (hi) Peter Schwarz/SS; 76-1 Intst/DT; 76-3 age fotostock/RH; 76 (lo) Oleksiy Mark/SS; 77-4 age fotostock/RH; 77-5 Ints Vikmanis/DT; 78 (hi) Dani Simmonds/SS; 78-3 motorolka/SS; 78-4 Harun/DT; 79 (hi) Jagodka/SS; 79-2 photo360/DT; 79-5 Image Broker/RH; 80 (hi) Sandra van der Steen/SS; 80-1 Image Broker/RH; 80-5 Arco Images/RH; 81-2 Mike Brake/DT; 81 (hi) Aurora Photos/RH; 81-4 Dragang/DT; 82 (hi) Oleksiy Mark/SS; 82 (lo) Dbtale/SS; 82-1 Frenta/DT; 83-3 Ventura69/DT; 83-4 GI; 83-5 Voltan1/DT; 84-1 Patryk Kosmider/SS; 84-2 Slawomir Fajer/SS; 84-5 age fotostock/RH; 84 (lo) Oleksiy Mark/SS; 85 (hi) Africa Studio/SS; 85-3 Ronald Jansen/DT; 85-4 posztos/SS; 86 (lo) iava777/SS; 86-1 Tumar/SS; 86-2 Yjulia/DT; 87-4 Spvvkr/DT; 87-5 Ukrphoto/DT; 87 (lo) taelove7/SS; 88 (hi) D Waljaw/SS; 88 (lo) Carlos Violda/SS; 88-1 Rachell Coe/DT; 89-2 Gvictoria/DT; 89-3 Still Pictures/RH; 89-4 Typhoonski/DT; 90 (hi) anakondasp/SS; 90 (lo) Pablo Utrilla/DT; 90-4 Andrii Deviatov/DT; 91-1 age fotostock/RH; 91-2 Anibal Trejo/DT; 91-5 Zoom-zoom/DT; 92 (hi) Yeko Photo Studio/SS; 92-1 Dennis Dolkens/DT; 93-2 Pixago/DT; 93-3 Lucavanzolini/DT; 93-4 Michael Stokes/SS; 94-1 Gillian Holliday/SS; 94-3 Agnieszka Guzowska/DT; 95 (hi) bonchan/SS; 95-5 Danielc1998/DT; 95-4 Julia Bayne/RH; 95 (lo) Czalewski/DT; 96-5 Vitaly Titov & Maria Sidelnikova/DT; "96 (lo) Studio DMM Photography, Designs & Art/SS; " 97-1 Phillip Gray/DT; 97-2 Neil Wigmore /SS; 97-4 ZRyzner /SS; 98 (lo) Ivonne Wierink/SS; 98-1 Jenifoto406/DT; 98-2 Bengelsdorp/DT; 99-3 Annemario/DT; 99-4 Nyvlt-art/SS; 100 (hi) Katrina Brown/DT; 100-4 mrsnstudio/SS; 100 (lo) Oleksiy Mark/SS; 100-3 Fedor Selivanov/SS; 101-1 Novoselov/SS; 101-2 Rechitan Sorin/DT; 102 (lo) Bjørn Hovdal/DT; 102-1 age fotostock/RH; 103-2 age fotostock/RH; 103-3 Lex Schmidt/DT; 103 (lo) Frenta/DT; 104-2 Eurasia/RH; 104-5 Mesut Do_an/DT; 104-4 Lucvar/DT; 104-3 Sipandra/DT; 105 (hi) Edyta Pawlowska/DT; 106 (hi) Ziablik/SS; 106-1 Paul George Bodea/DT; 106-5 wonderisland/SS; 107-4 Mangroove/DT; 107-2 Nikifor Todorov/SS; 108 (hi) Petros Tsonis/SS; 108-5 age fotostock/RH; 109-1 age fotostock/RH; 109-3 BlueOrange Studio/SS; 109-4 Trykster/DT; 110-2 Kosmos111/DT; 110-3 Onion/DT; 110-4 Anna Martynova/DT; 111 (hi) Palette7/DT; 111-5 Sergey Petrov/SS; 111 (lo) Extezy/DT

Asia

112-113 jarunsak loymee/SS; 114 (lo) Cultura Travel/Mick Ryan/GI; 115 (hi) Hung Chung Chih/SS; 116 (L-hi) diamant24/SS; 116(R-hi) Edward Shtern/DT; 116-5 Aurora Photos/RH; 117 (hi) Sergio Stakhnyk/SS; 117-2 Ailani Graphics/SS; 117-3 age fotostock/RH; 117-4 Michelle Marsan/SS; 118 (hi) Oleksiy Mark/SS; 118-2 Tõnis Valing/DT; 118-3 Still Pictures/RH; 118-4 Hayk Harutyunyan/DT; 119 (hi) Git/SS; 119-5 Anton Starikov/DT; 120 (hi) Alaettin YILDIRIM/SS; 120-5 Sophie Mcaulay/DT; 120-4 Wisconsinart/DT; 121-1 Transnirvana/DT; 121 (lo) Sufi70/DT; 121-2 Huub Keulers /DT; 122 (hi) Aaron Amat/SS; 123-1 Waj111/DT; 123-2 Alexey Stiop/DT; 123-3 Agnieszka Guzowska/DT; 123-4 Jackmalipan/DT; 123 (lo) Edward Karaa/DT; 124-1 Lucidwaters/DT; 124-3 Lucidwaters/DT; 124-5 ChameleonsEye/SS; 125 (hi) Eugene Ivanov/SS; 125 (lo) Aron Brand/DT; 125-4 Vicspacewalker/DT; 126 (hi) mariait/SS; 126-5 urosr/SS; 127-2 Fedor Selivanov/SS; 127-3 Shestakoff/SS; 127-4 slava296/SS; 128 (hi) Irina Fischer/SS; 128-5 Stefano Ember/SS; 128 (lo) Oleksiy Mark/SS; 129-1 age fotostock/RH; 129-2 Ken Gillham/RH; 129-3 Sergei25/SS; 130 (hi) age fotostock/RH; 130-5 age fotostock/RH; 130 (lo) Elena Terletskaya/SS; 131-2 age fotostock/RH; 131-3 Guy Thouvenin/RH; 131-4 Richard Ashworth/RH; 132 (hi) Borna_Mirahmadian/SS; 132-5 Milosk50 /DT; 132 (lo) Goran Bogicevic/DT; 132-4 Valery Shanin/DT; 133-2 Karkas/SS; 133-3 Milonk/DT; 134-1 Franz Gustincich/SS; 134-3 Aurora Photos/RH; 134 (lo) Oleksiy Mark/SS; 135 (hi) panda3800/SS; 135-5 Venelin Petkov/DT; 135-4 Jane Sweeney/RH; 136 (hi) imagedb.com/SS; 136-5 Elena Schweitzer/SS; 136 (lo) Patrick Poendl/DT; 137-1 AFP/GI; 137-2 bluelake/SS; 137-3 Naiyyer/SS; 137-4 Galina Barskaya/DT; 138 (hi) Pikoso.kz/SS; 138-5 Michael Runkel/RH; 139-1 Alexey Filimonov/DT; 139-2 Margouillat/DT; 139-3 David Davis/DT; 140 (hi) KAMONRAT/SS; 140-5 Aurora Photos/RH; 140 (lo) Martijn Mulder/DT; 141-1 Granitepeaker/DT 141-2 Hugoht/DT; 141-3 David Steele/DT; 142 (hi) Richard Peterson/SS; 142-1 Christian Kober/RH; 142 (lo) Oleksiy Mark/SS; 143-2 Koko1687/DT; 143-3 Michael Runkel/RH; 143-5 Still Pictures/RH; 144-1 Tappasan Phurisamrit/SS; 144-2 Jin Peng/DT; 145 (hi) seaskylab/SS; 145-3 Ryszard Stelmachowicz/DT; 145-4 davidelliottphotos/SS; 145 (lo) Hungchungchih/DT; 146 (hi) charles taylor/SS; 146 (lo) Wendy Connett/RH; 146-1 Mrpeak/DT; 147-3 Zaid Saadallah/DT; 147-4 Vacclav/DT; 147-5 Marco Lijoi/DT; 148-1 Pierre-Jean Durieu/SS; 148-2 age fotostock/RH; 148-4 age fotostock/RH; 149 (hi) withGod/SS; 149-3 Bevanward/DT; 150 (hi) Lcc54613/DT; 150-2 Gavin Hellier/RH; 150 (lo) Bikeworldtravel/SS; 151-3 Ximagination/DT; 151-4 Hendrik Halianto/DT; 151-5 Maxim Tupikov/SS 152 (hi) foto76/SS; 152-2 Isselee/DT; 152 (lo) Suchatsi/DT; 153-3 Gavin Hellier/RH; 153-4 Itsmejust/DT; 153-5 Dudarev Mikhail/SS; 154 (hi) vvoe/SS; 154-1 Eurasia/RH; 155-3 Pavalache Stelian/DT; 155-5 Teo Boon Keng Alvin/SS; 156-1 Vitaly Titov & Maria Sidelnikova/DT; 156-3 Ber Lybil/DT; 156-4 Ints Vikmanis/SS; 157 (hi) alslutsky/SS; 157 (lo) Oleksiy Mark/SS; 157-5 Brownm39/DT; 158-2 Dudarev Mikhail/SS; 158-3 Mohamad Ridzuan Abdul Rashid /DT; 158-4 Project1photography/DT; 159 (hi) leungchopan/SS; 159-5 Caroline Weir/RH; 159 (lo) Photovolcanica.com/SS; 160 (hi) Vitaly Maksimchuk/SS; 160-2 LOOK/RH; 161-1 Jonald John Morales/DT; 161-3 Alain Evrard/RH; 161-4 Naypong/SS; 161 (lo) Oleksiy Mark/SS

Africa

162-163 Andrzej Kubik/SS; 164 (lo) Peter Groenendijk/RH; 165 (hi) Hector Conesa/SS; 166 (hi) photo25th/SS; 166-1 Karol Kozlowski/DT; 167-3 Typhoonski/DT; 167-4 Vladimir Melnik/DT; 167-5 Paop/DT; 168 (hi) Lev Kropotov/SS; 168 (lo) Oleksiy Mark/SS; 169-1 Filip Fuxa/DT; 169-2 Dmitry Pichugin/DT; 169-3 AFP/GI 169-4 Infomods/DT; 170 (hi) picturepartners/SS; 170-5 Crobard/DT; 170-4 age fotostock/RH; 171-2 JOAT/SS; 171-3 Coplandj/DT; 172 (hi) Jose Ignacio Soto/SS; 172 (lo) Maxx-Studio/SS; 173-1 Brandpoint/DT; 173-2 Andre Klaassen/DT; 173-3 Mangojuicy/DT; 173-4 Przemyslaw Skibinski/DT; 174-1 Attila Jandi/DT; 174-2 criben/SS; 174-3 Tovkach Oleg/SS; 174-5 Joan Egert/DT; 175 (hi) GoodMood Photo/SS; 175 (lo) Dekanaryas/DT; 176 (hi) Gubin Yury/SS; 176 (lo) Oleksiy Mark/SS; 177-1 David Poole/RH; 177-2 mountainpix/SS; 177-4 eye ubiquitous/RH; 177-5 Brandy Mcknight/DT; 178 (hi) Adisa/SS; 178 (lo) Oleksiy Mark/SS; 179-1 Johan Reineke/DT; 179-2 Lucavanzolini/DT; 179-4 Jean-Pierre De Mann/RH; 179-5 Steve Heap/SS; 180-1 Ferdinand Reus/DT; 180-2 James Michael Dorsey/SS; 180 (lo) Tiziano Casalta/DT; 181-3 Sarahgen/DT; 181-5 Henk Paul/SS; 181 (lo) Trevkitt/DT; 182 (hi) Aaron Amat/SS; 182-1 Paul Kennedy/DT; 182-2 Still Pictures/RH; 182-3 jo Crebbin/SS; 183-4 Trevkitt/DT; 183 (lo) Linda Bucklin/DT; 184-1 eye ubiquitous/RH; 184-2 eye ubiquitous/RH; 184-4 Arco Images/RH; 185 (hi) Eric Isselee/SS; 185-5 Brendan van Son/SS; 185 (lo) Txemanet/DT; 186 (lo) Jacoba Susanna Maria Swanepoel/DT; 187-2 Ferdinand Reus/DT; 187-3 David Lomax/RH; 187-4 age fotostock/RH; 187-5 Xvaldes/DT; 187 (hi) Oleksiy Mark/SS; 188-1 Uros Ravbar/DT; 188 (lo) Zhukov Oleg/SS; 189-2 Jean-Pierre De Mann/RH; 189-3 Bertramz/Wikipedia 189-5 Aurora Photos/RH; 190 (hi) Juniors/RH; 190-5 Gavin Hellier/RH; 191-1 Jackmalipan/DT; 191-2 Zaramira/DT; 191-3 Feije Riemersma/DT; 191 (lo) Oleksiy Mark/SS; 192 (hi) Krzysztof Odziomek/SS; 192-1 Izanbar/DT; 192-2 Andrew McConnell/RH; 192-5 Andrew McConnell/RH; 193-4 Michael Runkel/RH; 193 (hi)/GI 194-1 Mogens Trolle/DT; 194-2 Michal Bednarek/DT; 195 (hi) Eric Isselee/SS; 195-3 Adeliepenguin/DT; 195-4 Rudchenko/DT; 196 (hi) prapass/SS; 196-5 David Youldon/DT; 197-2 Miloslav Doubrava/DT; 197-3 Pierre-yves Babelon/DT; 197-4 Louie Schoeman/DT; 197 (lo) Oleksiy Mark/SS; 198 (lo) Aaron Amat/SS; 198-1 Stu Porter/DT; 199-3 Still Pictures/RH; 199-4 Bezergheanu/204-3 Amo; 199-5 Antonella865/DT; 199 (lo) coxy58/SS; 200 (hi) Mikael Damkier/DT; 200-5 Carla Zagni/DT; 200-4 Greg Amptman/DT; 201-1 Sergey Uryadnikov/SS; 201-2 Aurora Photos/RH; 201 (lo) Kosarev Alexander/SS; 202 (lo) Viscorp/DT; 202-1 Tim Graham/RH; 203-2 David Evison/DT; 203-4 Toxawww/DT; 203-5 Jason Prince/SS; 203 (hi) Joloei/DT; 204-5 Paula Sachar/DT; 204 (lo) wasanajai/SS; 204-3 Lori Waselchuk/South Photos/ AMO 205 (hi) Eric Isselee/SS; 205-1 MP cz/SS; 205 (lo) Sunsetman/DT; 206 (hi) Four Oaks/SS; 206-3 Image Broker/RH; 207-1 Helo80808/DT; 207-2 Ninetteluz/DT; 207-4 Still Pictures/DT; 208-1 Eric Nathan/RH; 208 (lo) Fotana/SS; 209-3 mrHanson/SS; 209-4 Jabiru/DT; 209-5 Maks Narodenko/SS; 210 (hi) Brocreative/SS; 210-5 Stacey Bates/DT; 210 (lo) Oleksiy Mark/SS; 211-1 Simon Greig/DT; 211-2 Faaabi/DT; 211-3 Pancaketom/DT; 212 (hi) Vaclav Volrab/SS; 212-5 Karelgallas/DT; 213-1 Still Pictures/RH; 213-2 Hanlie Fourie/DT; 213-3 Holger Karius/DT; 213 (lo) Oleksiy Mark/SS; 214-1 Luke Schmidt/DT; 214-2 age fotostock/RH; 215 (hi) David Ryznar/SS; 215-3 Thoron/SS; 215-5 Philip Schedler / Africa Media Online 216 (hi) Kkulikov/SS; 216-5 Pehttt/DT; 217-1 Oleg Znamenskiy/DT; 217-2 age fotostock/RH; 217-3 Olivier Goujon/RH

Australia, Oceania and Antarctica

218-219 Stanislav Fosenbauer/SS; 221 (hi) Konstik/DT; 221 (lo) age fotostock/RH; 222 (hi) Smileus/SS; 222-5 age fotostock/RH; 222 (lo) Oleksiy Mark/SS; 223-1 LOOK/RH; 223-2 Jim Agronick/SS; 223-3 Ben Jeayes/SS; 224-2 LOOK/RH; 224-3 Dmitry Pichugin/DT; 224-5 age fotostock/RH; 225 (hi) Eric Isselee/SS; 225-4 Kathie Nichols/SS; 225 (lo) Julia Tsokur/DT; 226 (hi) Videowokart/SS; 226-5 Tuul/RH; 227-1 Lev Kropotov/SS; 227-3 age fotostock/RH; 227-4 National Geographic/RH; 228 (hi) EpicStockMedia/SS; 228-4 Michael Runkel/RH; 228-5 Nazzu/SS; 229-1 Peter Hendrie/GI 229-2 ra3rn/SS; 229 (lo) Oleksiy Mark/SS; 230 (hi) bonchan/SS; 230-1 Michael DeFreitas/RH; 230-2 Aurora Photos/RH; 230-3 Reinhard Dirscherl/RH; 231-5 LOOK/RH; 231 (L-lo) Ethan Daniels/SS; 231 (R-lo) Oleksiy Mark/SS; 232-1 Tim Graham/RH; 232-3 agefotostock/RH; 232-4 Sybil Sassoon/RH; 232-5 Henryk Sadura/SS; 233 (hi) James Steidl/SS; 234-235 age fotostock/RH; 237 (hi) Darryn Schneider/DT: 237 (lo) Stephen Lew/SS

Games: What in the World

240 Top row (left to right): Ron Sumners/dreamstime; Chrisp543/dreamstime; Elf0724/dreamstime; middle row (left to right): Hanhanpeggy/dreamstime; Imaengine/dreamstime; Anthony Baggett/dreamstime; Bottom row (left to right): Alexey Stiop/dreamstime; Saiko3p/dreamstime; Pius Lee/dreamstime; 241 Top Row (Left to right): Dinodia/Superstock; imagebroker.net/Superstock; Alex Maclean/Getty Images; Middle row (left to right): Travel Library Limited/Superstock; Bill Heinsohn/Getty Images; imagebroker.net/Superstock; bottom row (left to right): Vicki Beaver/Alamy; Robert Harding Picture Library/Superstock; All Canada Photos/Superstock; 242 Top Row (Left to right): Kharidehal Abhirama Ashwin/Shutterstock; gary bell/OceanwideImages; Theo Allofs/CORBIS; Middle row (left to right): age fotostock/Superstock; Simon Wilkinson/Getty Images; JTB Photo Communications, Inc./Alamy; bottom row (left to right): Harvey Lloyd/Getty Images; Andy Gehrig/Getty Images; age fotostock/Superstock; 243 Top row (left to right): Brandon Alms/dreamstime; Bidouze Stéphane/dreamstime; Natakuzmina/dreamstime; Middle row (left to right): Ammit/dreamstime; Hotshotsworldwide/dreamstime; Sergey Galushko/dreamstime; bottow row (left to right); Brian Grant/dreamstime; Tamara Kulikova/dreamstime; Ika66/dreamstime.

ISBN 978-0-545-77158-0

Published by Scholastic Inc., 557 Broadway, New York, NY 10012, by arrangement with National Geographic Society. SCHOLASTIC and associated logos are trademarks and/or registered trademarks of Scholastic Inc.

12 11 10 9 8 7 6 5 4 3 2 1 14 15 16 17 18 19/0

Printed in the U.S.A. 08

First Scholastic printing, September 2014

Staff for This Book
Priyanka Lamichhane, *Project Editor*
Kathryn Robbins, *Associate Designer*
Lori Epstein, *Senior Photo Editor*
Bender Richardson White, *Designer*
Martha Sharma, *Geography Consultant*
Ariane Szu-Tu, *Editorial Assistant*
Callie Broaddus, *Design Production Assistant*
Margaret Leist, *Photo Assistant*
Carl Mehler, *Director of Maps*
Sven Dolling, *Map Editor*
Michael McNey, *Map Production Manager*
Mapping Specialists, Martin S. Walz, and XNR Productions, *Map Research and Production*